THE
SECOND
WORLD

THE
SECOND
WORLD

EMPIRES AND INFLUENCE
IN THE NEW GLOBAL ORDER

PARAG KHANNA

RANDOM HOUSE   NEW YORK

Published in the United States by Random House,
an imprint of The Random House Publishing Group,
a division of Random House, Inc., New York.

RANDOM HOUSE and colophon are registered trademarks of Random House, Inc.

ISBN 978-1-4000-6508-0

Printed in the United States of America on acid-free paper

www.atrandom.com

2 4 6 8 9 7 5 3 1

First Edition

Book design by Carol Malcolm Russo

Maps by David Lindroth

To Bhagwan Das Seth:

DIPLOMAT, THINKER, GRANDFATHER

CONTENTS

PREFACE

NO ONE KNEW the world like Arnold Toynbee did. His twelve-volume *A Study of History* is the most cohesive treatment of human civilizations ever written (and the longest work composed in English). But Toynbee waited until he retired from London's Royal Institute of International Affairs before boarding a ship with his wife to "meet people and see places that were already familiar to us from our work, but only at second hand." Over seventeen months, they circumnavigated the globe, traveling from London to South America, the Pacific Rim, South Asia, and the Near East. The dispatches Toynbee penned—containing observations on the remnants of empires long extinct and predictions on an uncertain future—were published in 1958 under the title *East to West: A Journey Round the World*.

A half century later, a leatherbound first edition of Toynbee's narrative was my most insightful guide as I set out around the world to explore the interplay of two world-historical forces he grasped intuitively without ever using the terms: geopolitics and globalization. Geopolitics is the relationship between power and space. Globalization refers to the widening and deepening interconnections among the world's peoples through all forms of exchange. Toynbee had been the first to chronicle the rise and fall, expansion and contraction of history's empires and civilizations, and his life spanned the major waves of global integration that began just before World War I and then exploded with the rise of multinational corporations in the 1970s. Since Toynbee's time, geopolitics and globalization have so intensified as to become two sides of the same coin. I wanted to separate the inseparable.

The regions and countries explored in this book—collectively referred to as the "second world"—are today the central stage on which the future course of global order is being determined. That term, *second world,* once referred to the "socialist sixth" of the earth's surface, and then briefly to the postcommunist transitional states, but mention of the second world gradually disappeared. Yet there are more than twice as many countries in the world today than when Toynbee set sail— and an ever-greater number of them fall into this new second-world space where geopolitics and globalization clash and merge.

Like elements in the periodic table, nations can be grouped— according to size, stability, wealth, and worldview. Stable and prosperous first-world countries largely benefit from the international order as it stands today. By contrast, poor and unstable third-world countries have failed to overcome their disadvantaged position within that order. Second-world countries are caught in between. Most of them embody *both* sets of characteristics: They are divided internally into winners and losers, haves and have-nots. Will second-world countries react by repelling, splitting, or merging into compounds? That is one of the questions this book seeks to answer.

Schizophrenic second-world countries are also the tipping-point states that will determine the twenty-first-century balance of power among the world's three main empires—the United States, the European Union, and China—as each uses the levers of globalization to exert its gravitational pull. How do countries choose the superpower with which to ally? Which model of globalization will prevail? Will the East rival the West? The answers to these questions can be found in the second world—and *only* in the second world.

To comprehend the morphing spheres and vectors of influence across the five regions of the second world, one must begin to *think* like a country, to slip into its skin. World Bank officials joke that they would never purport to be experts about countries they had not at least flown over. Experts of this kind point to statistical indicators and declare "things are getting much better" in this or that country. Usually, this means that a capital city has been cleaned up, provided with sprouting hotels, banks with cash machines, and shopping malls, while crime has been isolated to outer neighborhoods. What about the rest of the country: cities that don't have airports, provinces that have poor roads and dilapidated infrastructure? Are things getting much better out there? Does it even feel like the same country? It is no wonder people are surprised by a coup here, an economic collapse there, in countries that are constantly said to be thriving.

Saint Augustine declared that "the world is a book, and those who have not traveled have read only one page." Only firsthand experience can validate or challenge our intuitions, giving us confidence about risky political decisions in a complex world of instant feedback loops and unintended consequences. During my travels through the second world, I never left a country until I had developed a sense of its meaning on its own terms, until I had assimilated a blend of perspectives from cities, villages, and landscapes, based on conversations with a wide variety of people, including officials, academics, journalists, entrepreneurs, taxi drivers, and students. I stayed until I saw the world through their eyes. This book is devoted purely to exploring how these nations view themselves in this age of globalization and geopolitical flux.

During travel, perception and thought merge; a contradiction can emerge as a truth to be revealed, not some exception to be disproved. Such ambiguity is the corollary of complexity, after all. Reality is famously resistant to theories that measure the world according to what it should be rather than how it really is. Instead, exploring the patterns of the second world aesthetically, honoring the value of purely sensory judgments—this exposes characteristics that are common to the entire second world; differences are revealed to be more relative than absolute. For example, the civility of people's behavior tends to reflect the decency of their governments, which in turn often correlates to the quality of their roads. In the first world, roads are well paved, and the view is clear for miles, whereas clogged third-world roads are obscured by dust and exhaust; second-world roads are a mix of both. First-world countries can accommodate millions of tourists, while visiting third-world states often involves choosing between exclusive hotels or low-cost backpacking; many second-world countries simply lack the infra-structure for mass tourism. Garbage is recycled in the first world and burned in the third; in the second world, it is occasionally collected but is also dumped off hillsides. Corruption is widely invisible in the first world, rampant in the third—and subtle in the second. Diplomat-ically, first-world states are sovereign decision-makers, and passive third-world nations are objects of superpower neomercantilism. Second-world countries are the nervous swing states in between.

A journey around the world reveals an increasingly clear under-lying logic: The imperial norms of the American, European, and Chinese superpowers are advancing. Political borders matter less and less, and economies are integrating. The world map is being redrawn—and the process is not driven by Americans only. Yet even as the world becomes increasingly *non*-American, American attitudes toward the places that suddenly appear in U.S. headlines reflect a deep cartographic and his-torical ignorance. But this book is not written for Americans only, for the task of adapting the United States to a world of multiple super-powers and an amorphous but deepening globalization is too important to be left to Americans alone. War may be God's way of teaching Amer-icans geography, but there is a new geography of power that everyone in the world must understand better. If we do not find common ground in our minds, then nothing can save us.

Parag Khanna
New York
August 2007

INTRODUCTION:
INTER-IMPERIAL RELATIONS

IN THE 1990S, as bombed-out buildings in the Balkans crumbled, who managed the reconstruction of these war-torn nations? When Mexico's currency crashed to the point of debt default, who bailed it out? When the former Soviet republics in Central Asia were flung into independence, who settled their borders and boosted their trade?

In all three cases, the answer is an *empire*: the European Union, the United States, and China, respectively.

These days it is not fashionable to speak of empires. Empires are aggressive, mercantilist relics supposedly consigned to the dustbin of history with Britain, France, and Portugal's post–World War II retrenchment from their African and Asian colonies and the 1990s collapse of the Soviet Union. Many then predicted that ethnic self-determination would drag the world into a new era of political fragmentation, as the number of countries proliferated from fewer than fifty at the end of World War II to, potentially, hundreds in the twenty-first century, with every minority getting its own state, currency, and seat in the United Nations.

But for thousands of years, empires have been the world's most powerful political entities, their imperial yoke restraining subjugated nations from fighting one another and thereby fulfilling people's eternal desire for order—the prerequisite for stability and meaningful democracy.[1] Rome, Istanbul, Venice, and London ruled over thousands of distinct political communities until the advent of the nation-state in the seventeenth century. By World War II, global power had consolidated into just a half dozen empires, almost all of them European. Decolonization ended these artificial empires—small nations ruling by force over overseas colonies—but it did not end empire itself. Empires may not be the most desirable form of governance, given the regular occurrence of hugely destructive wars between them, but mankind's psychological limitations still prevent it from doing better.

Big is back.[2] It is inter-imperial relations—not international or inter-civilizational—that shape the world. Empires—not civilizations—give geography its meaning. Indeed, empires span *across* civilizations; as they spread their norms and customs, they can change who people are—irrespective of their civilization.[3] Because empires care more for power and growth than for the preservation of unique culture, they are, simply put, bigger than civilizations. That Europe and China are ancient civilizations makes them unique, but their status as expansionist powers makes them exceptional.

Today there are *fewer* dominant power centers in the world than was the case during most of history.[4] Since World War II, small feudal entities have fused into modern China, and more than two dozen nation-states have integrated into the supranational European Union. These two and the United States are the world's three natural empires: each geographically unified and militarily, economically, and demographically strong enough to expand. As George Kennan pithily reminded us, the inequities of power among states have always made a mockery of sovereignty. And the more countries in the world there are, the easier it is for empires to divide and conquer.[5]

Yet all empires are susceptible to what Arnold Toynbee called "the mirage of immortality." Americans tend to believe they preside over the world's first global imperium, but in fact Great Britain was the last global empire on which the sun never set. Much of the world belonged to its domain and reported to it.[6] In a decolonized world in which territorial conquest is taboo, America has no such ability to dictate affairs unilaterally on all corners of the planet; America has ambassadors, not viceroys. Nor should America's global military presence be confused with dominance. If power is measured strictly in military terms, then the world is indeed "uni-multipolar"—America at the top, with a strong set of regional powers below. But military power means less today than it did in the past, particularly as the technologies that allow others to resist and defend themselves spread widely. Better measures of power take into account economic productivity, global market share, technological innovation, natural resource endowments, and population size as well as intangible factors such as national willpower and diplomatic skill. In fact, precisely because all great powers now have nuclear weapons, economic power is more important than military power. China's mix of huge population, industrial output, and financial wealth makes it a superpower with unprecedented potential. The European Union is economically wealthier than both the United States and China; its population size fits in between the two, and it has significant military power and technological prowess.

In *The Economic Consequences of the Peace,* John Maynard Keynes wrote, "The great events of history are often due to secular changes in the growth of population and other fundamental economic causes, which, escaping by their gradual character the notice of contemporary observers, are attributed to the follies of statesmen or the fanaticism of atheists."[7] But today it is possible to measure with exactitude the micro-level processes and interactions that add up to large geopolitical shifts, just as scientists measure the symptoms and causes of climate change. The world's superpower map is being rebalanced—but without a single center.* By challenging America's position in the global hierarchy and securing allies and loyalty around the world, the EU and China have engineered a palpable shift toward three relatively equal centers of influence: Washington, Brussels, and Beijing.

---

*Geopolitics has always been driven by the powers of the northern hemisphere, its empires dominating the territories of the south, from Latin America and Africa to Australia and Oceania. Over the past five hundred years, northern empires carved up the planet; by the late nineteenth century, flags were finally planted on every patch of the earth, leaving no more blank spaces on the map. Toynbee succinctly captured this conquest of geography: "Our Western 'know-how' has unified the whole world in the literal sense of the whole habitable and traversable surface of the globe." Toynbee, *Civilization on Trial,* 23. At that moment, external expansion became internal consolidation; geopolitics became world domestic politics—with the West, at that time, on top.

THE GEOPOLITICAL MARKETPLACE

Power abhors a vacuum.[8] The collapse of the Soviet Union left the United States as what the French call *une hyperpuissance*—an entity capable of deploying military power anywhere—but it did not assure America's global hegemony. Instead, America's "unipolar moment" was just that, a brief period of suspended animation during which Europe and China rose from under the shadow of America's regional security umbrellas, shifting gradually from internal consolidation to external power projection. Their rise is now no more preventable than evolution. Everywhere one can feel a planet that is simultaneously being *Americanized, Europeanized,* and *Sinicized.*

Power has migrated from monopoly to marketplace. All three superpowers now use their military, economic, and political power to build spheres of influence around the world, competing to mediate conflicts, shape markets, and spread customs.[9] In the geopolitical marketplace, consumer countries choose which superpower will be their patron; some choose more than one. When one superpower tries to isolate an enemy, another superpower can always swoop in with a lifeline and gain an ally. The world has never before witnessed this sort of truly global competition—a condition that may be the most complicated in all of history, since the superpowers are neither all Western (China) nor even states as conventionally understood (the EU).

America's national security strategy aims to shape "countries at a crossroads" by promoting stability in dangerous regions.[10] But in many such spaces, America is no longer viewed as a provider of security but rather of *in*security, a dynamic that opens the door for China and Europe to bring those countries into their spheres of influence. "Great powers don't just mind their own business," said U.S. Secretary of State Condoleezza Rice, and, indeed, America's declining credibility does not mean that credibility itself cannot be seized by others.

In the geopolitical marketplace, legitimacy is based on effectiveness—and must be *proven* in comparison with other superpowers. In fact, America can learn a lot about legitimacy from Europe and China. After the Cold War, some Americans argued that the diminished U.S. military presence in Europe would lead to a renewal of internal European rivalries, such as between France and Germany.[11] Instead, the European Union has become the one contemporary empire that continues to expand, year after year, by absorbing new countries—with many more in line begging to join. Around the same time, the Pentagon declared its strategy to contain the rise of any great power rival, such as China. Yet China is methodically pursuing its own timeline to become the world's paramount power, restoring its position as the "Middle Kingdom." Like the European Union, it is turning its neighbor states into semi-sovereign provinces, subduing them not militarily but rather through demographic expansion and economic integration. This used to be called imperialism—but the new term for it is globalization.

The United States, the EU, and China represent three distinct diplomatic styles—America's *coalition,* Europe's *consensus,* and China's *consultation*—competing to lead the twenty-first century. During the Cold War, America's anticommunist Truman Doctrine created robust "hub-and-spoke" alliances, as Prussia had in the nineteenth century.[12] By contrast, its current "coalitions of the willing" style of conducting foreign policy negotiates diplomatic alignments on a transactional, issue-by-issue basis. America continues to demonstrate its eagerness to lead: It sets the tone in the UN Security Council and NATO, which commands operations well beyond its original European mandate into the Persian Gulf and Central Asia, and troubleshoots many disputes worldwide. But with individualism as America's creed, its overwhelming emphasis on self-interest results in little diplomatic trust-building. Instead, a short-term focus creates confusion among shifting counterterrorism, democratization, and economic liberalization agendas, while continued reliance on military threats alienates even allies. America today best embodies Charles de Gaulle's quip about (in his case, France) having no friends, only interests.

The European Union is a revolutionary institution with the potential to reverse the westbound rotation of geopolitical centrality.[13] As the most highly evolved form of interstate governance, the EU aggregates countries in a manner more resembling a corporate merger than a political conquest, with net gains in both trade and territory from North Africa to the Caucasus.[14] EU laws supersede the majority of national laws, and most European trade is within the EU. While its members remain sovereign nation-states, they increasingly work together to project their common vision outward. Outside of the military domain, Europe's power potential is greater than that of America, for it is the world's largest market and the de facto standard setter for technology and regulation. European foreign policy reflects all of the virtues and vices of consensus-oriented diplomacy: It is animated by the same inclusive spirit of Europe's welfare policies, even if the process of negotiating and implementing strategies among more than two dozen member-states is immensely time-consuming. Ultimately, however, once EU policies are decided, they consistently pull more and more countries toward the European way.

China has already become a global center of gravity, and it represents a third model of imperial diplomacy. Drawing on ancient Confucian customs, China's consultative pattern of behavior emphasizes areas of greatest agreement while tabling issues lacking accord for more propitious occasions; self-sacrifice evokes admiration and trust. Most of the world's population lies in Asian countries that are acutely familiar with China's uneven past—but also more acclimated to its future potential. They have not only resigned themselves to China's inevitable rise, they have also come to welcome the benefits that it will bring in the form of cheaper goods, more integrated markets, and regional pride. A half century ago, China spent as much as 5 percent of its budget supporting Marxist and Maoist guerrillas; the joke ran that Albania was China's only friend. Now China endeavors to build full-spectrum alliances with all available customers, competing over energy supplies in the Persian Gulf, Central Asia, and South America; engaging in a tug of war with the West for the allegiance of middle-tier powers such as Russia and India; and propping up almost all regimes the United States seeks to suppress, such as Cuba, Venezuela, Sudan, Zimbabwe, Iran, Uzbekistan, Myanmar, and North Korea.

Many believe that the emerging world order is polycentric: China will remain primarily a regional power, Japan will assert itself more nationalistically, the EU will lack influence beyond its immediate region, India will rise to rival China, Russia will resurge, and an Islamic Caliphate will congeal as a geopolitical force.[15] All these views ignore a much deeper reality: The United States, the European Union, and China already possess most of the total power in the world—and will do their best to prevent all others from gaining ground on them. Russia, Japan, and India cannot assert themselves globally, militarily or otherwise; they are not superpowers but rather balancers whose support (or lack thereof) can buttress or retard the dominance of the three superpowers without preventing it outright.[16] In fact, they are being gradually outmaneuvered by the United States, the EU, and China in their own regions. Islam is in the same boat; lacking any diplomatic coherence of its own, it is spread across vast regions that are also bending toward the gravities of the main superpowers rather than coalescing into a meaningful whole. So there are precisely three superpowers in the world, empires that will compete to set the terms until history's other principal vehicle for shaping global order—war—dictates otherwise.

WHAT IS GEOPOLITICS?

"It is a poor sort of memory which only works backwards," wrote Lewis Carroll. Unlike history, geopolitics is a discipline that looks backward explicitly for the purpose of looking forward. If international relations is the meteorology of current events, then geopolitics is the climatology, the deep science of world evolution; geopolitics cannot be updated by clicking "Refresh" on an Internet browser. At the turn of the twentieth century, the German political geographer Friedrich Ratzel argued that empires needed to expand in order to survive. Like rubber bands, empires stretch as people move, altering the facts on the ground and establishing institutions that extend loyalty across territory as far as possible without causing the rubber band to snap.

Ratzel's student, Rudolf Kjellen, coined the term *Geopolitik,* which the Nazi geographer Karl Haushofer appropriated in order to expound his theory of expansive pan-regions requiring racially homogenous lebensraum. Haushofer's deviation from pure geography would be a stain on the discipline of geopolitics for decades.[17] Like his Continental peers, the famous British geographer Sir Halford Mackinder emphasized the life cycle of the "world organism." But ever concentrated on the question of how to defend Britain against Continental powers, he focused on the Eurasian "world island," whose "heartland" was "the greatest natural fortress on earth," for it was inaccessible from the sea—and thus unassailable by British sea power—allowing a land-based power to dominate the world.[18] His strategic counterpoint, the American naval strategist Alfred Thayer Mahan, argued that in fact oceanic power was the key to global dominance, writing, "The empire of the seas is doubtless the empire of the world." Geopolitics has since evolved into a family of holistic power formulae applied across the world and over long time horizons, what Fernand Braudel termed the *longue durée*.[19] But it remains Toynbee's story of challenge and response.

GEOPOLITICS VERSUS GLOBALIZATION?

In the 1990s, a great debate took place between the contrasting visions of Francis Fukuyama (*The End of History*) and Samuel Huntington (*The Clash of Civilizations*), with the former generally caricatured as utopian and the latter as fatalistic. The grand predecessor to this dichotomy was the tension between the worldviews of Oswald Spengler and Arnold Toynbee. Spengler opened *The Decline of the West* (1918) with the bold claim, "This book will for the first time attempt to predict history." He argued that the demise of the classical West was as inevitable as history itself; the symbols of high culture would naturally degenerate into material decadence in a process similar to human aging or the cycle of the seasons. So persuasive was Spengler's conclusion that Toynbee wondered before undertaking his *Study of History* whether the "whole inquiry had been disposed of by Spengler before even the questions, let alone the answers, had fully taken shape in my own mind."[20] But Spengler's tragic revelation proved to be the spark for Toynbee's own explorations, which sought to replace alarmism with foresight and determinism with agency. Toynbee's framework of "challenge and response" (to both natural and geopolitical stresses) set the stage for the West to choose either a compromising adaptation or an inflexible fundamentalism. More than fifty years later, this remains the choice for the West.

The geopolitical landscape is perpetually unfolding across land and sea—and now outer space and cyberspace as well. Yet after all the geopolitical numbers have been crunched, what emerges in world history is a pattern of increasingly cataclysmic global wars, occurring approximately every hundred years, that reconfigure the hierarchy of power, of which the Napoleonic Wars (1803–14) and World Wars I and II (1914–45) are the most recent apotheoses. Almost a century ago, World War I was triggered by false assumptions and misunderstandings among European powers that had much in common: history, culture, geographic space, economic ties, and (for the most part) liberal political tradition. Today, the United States, the EU, and China have very little of this going for them. They do not have culture in common, nor do they share the same geographic space, nor are they all democratic. What, if anything, can prevent World War III in a world of superpowers with such drastically different worldviews, motivations, and forms of power at their disposal? If the twentieth century was what Isaiah Berlin called "the most terrible century in western history," what will make the twenty-first century any different?

Today only one force has emerged that could grind the cyclical wheels of global conflict to a halt: globalization.[21] Like geopolitics, globalization has become the world system itself. No one power controls it; it can only be stopped if everything stops.[22] Yet geopolitics and globalization are considered diametrically opposed concepts and modes of power.* Day and night, cargo ships and oil tankers cross the oceans, airplanes connect thousands of people to new destinations, and financial markets distribute capital—all while civil wars rage, terrorist attacks are planned and executed, and nuclear weapons systems are deployed. Many thinkers overemphasize either the virtues of globalization or the vices of geopolitics, but the very existence of globalization as a rival paradigm is a sign of some evolution over the centuries.

Whether globalization will continue is not the issue—only its extent. Globalization has ebbed and flowed throughout history, but today it is wider and deeper than ever.[23] The so-called antiglobalization movement of the 1990s—comprising protectionist unions, environmental activists, and indigenous groups—has all but fizzled; in its place has arisen a serious global dialogue on how to achieve "globalization with a human face." Globalization is now part of every society's strategy for survival and progress. While protestors were swarming high-level World Trade Organization summits to bring an end to the existing rules of the game, the small producers of sugar and cotton whom they claimed to represent conducted business as usual because they had to do so in order to survive.[24] Even the terrorist attacks of September 11, 2001, did not stop the falling costs of transportation,

---

*To simplify, the antithesis between geopolitics and globalization is manifested in domination versus integration, conflict versus cooperation, hierarchy versus network, politics versus economics, pessimism versus optimism, fatalism versus progressivism. In the language of game theory, geopolitics recalls the defections and betrayals of the past (one hopes) while globalization emphasizes the hope of increasing interaction and interdependence. In Freudian terms, one might cast geopolitics and globalization as the coexisting human desires for dominance (*thanatos,* the death instinct) and peace (*eros,* the love instinct). Only globalization is considered a grand theory of everything on a par with geopolitics, an antidote to counter the world organism's millennia of infection by the virus of geopolitics.

the liberalization of trade, and the explosion of communications technology that drive globalization. Globalization has also created a demographically *blended* world, which means that the "enemy" is located just as much within as without. All three empires are blending ever more deeply with the populations of their peripheries: the United States with Latin America, Europe with the Arab world, and China with Southeast Asia. The expression "We are the world" has never made more sense.

The economic interests favoring interdependence could also forestall simmering geopolitical tensions, forever transmuting them into nonviolent competition. Indeed, the global economy will drive neither far nor fast on only one engine, and the three superpower economies are so deeply intertwined that the costs of conflict have risen considerably.[25] These trading empires are home to global corporations that master worldwide supply chains often located in the domains of the other empires, meaning that their continued prosperity depends on the strength—not the weakness—of the others.[26] Forty percent of America's trade is with East Asia, and most of the rest is with Europe. America depends on cheap Chinese goods and China's appetite for U.S. treasury bonds; China depends on European and American investment and now exports more to Europe than the United States does; Europe and America save costs and boost profits by relocating production to China. The three together have come to resemble conjoined triplets, where severing any artery hurts all sides.[27] Only this sort of globalized integration can possibly prevent the full return of geopolitical rivalry among three such ambitious superpowers on one small planet.

Yet globalization alone will not prevent geopolitical history from repeating itself. Globalization has always advanced and receded on the back of empires that have pushed their systems and rules as far as possible before retrenching.[28] Ancient Greece expanded because commerce brought resources to Athens it would otherwise not have possessed, enabling it to finance a larger military and bribe foreign leaders to protect Athenian stakes within the exclusive trade zone of the Delian League.[29] Globalization's later waves were purely mercantilist, with European powers deepening control over foreign resources—natural and human—in the service of empire. Toynbee wrote in 1950 that "a now ubiquitous Western civilization held the fate of all Mankind in its hands."[30] Even if the world were to become flat—totally integrated, in

Thomas Friedman's parlance—it would not erase this economic and political hierarchy and the sense of injustice that gives rise to conflict, for both geopolitics and globalization are ultimately governed by the same two forces: fear and greed. Today's interdependence is indeed a web—but there are multiple spiders.

The role of empires in driving globalization is thus a double-edged sword. While empires can be a force for peace and prosperity, they rarely resist opportunities for strategic intrusion in one another's realms. Globalization makes this easier than ever. It is precisely because the world is shrinking that the coexistence of multiple superpowers heralds an age of competition more intense than any seen before.[31] Colonies were once conquered; today countries are bought. Globalization was once thought to be synonymous with Americanization; instead it drastically accelerates the demise of Pax Americana.

THINKING LIKE THE SECOND WORLD

"Countries have characters that are as distinctive as those of human beings," wrote Toynbee.[32] The three superpowers are eyeing one another constantly (along with the rest of the world). Everyone knows what everyone else *can* do—but not what they *will* do. States today are like bumper cars: Each driver's psychology is a critical factor in understanding which way and how fast any car will be steered. It was more than cool rationality that motivated Pakistan's Zulfikar Ali Bhutto to declare that "if India develops nuclear weapons, Pakistan will eat grass or leaves, even go hungry" until it did the same. Trust, respect, greed, revenge, and other human emotions all have analogs in world politics, where countries must balance passions and needs, ends and means.* But these irreducible components are rarely in equilibrium, meaning that most states have a schizophrenic character. As Alexander Wendt neatly put it, "States are people too."[33]

---

*Much as Socrates argued in Plato's *Republic* that the human soul has three parts—the desiring *eros*, prideful *thymos*, and rational *nous*—so too does a nation. Thucydides wrote that fear, honor, and interest are a society's motivators; Pericles told Athenians that they were fighting for immortality. Reflecting on the evolution of his own strategic thinking, the great British military historian Basil Liddell Hart mused, "I used to think that the causes of war were predominantly economic. Then I came to think that they were more psychological. I am now coming to think that they are decisively 'personal,' arising from the defects and ambitions of those who have the power to influence the currents of nations."

Human psychology and state psychology have innumerable parallels. An arms race is like a competition among rival gangs for bigger weapons; the historical memory of a country, which forms its national identity, is passed down through generations like family histories and photo albums. And most fundamentally, both people and nations obey Abraham Maslow's "hierarchy of needs," prioritizing deficit needs (the physiological demands of satisfying hunger and thirst), then security needs (shelter and stability), and finally being needs (the sense of belonging, love, respect and recognition).[34] Democratic governance falls into this latter category, for meeting basic survival and economic needs is what gives people the means to participate actively in democratic politics.[35] Pure democracy is like haute couture: One can admire it, but it is not practical for everyday use.

The world's most compelling ideology is neither democracy nor capitalism nor any other ism, but *success*. All societies pursue the one goal Adam Smith identified in his 1759 *Theory of Moral Sentiments*: "bettering our condition." Lacking absolute knowledge, people think relationally: What is the next best thing or status one can achieve? When Iraqis went to the polls in 2005, many of them said that they simply wanted a *normal* country. Today, the definition of success is up for grabs. The three superpowers are increasingly asking what other countries want and what their own vision of success is, because in the geopolitical marketplace, those smaller countries have other ways to get what they want. Like individuals, nations have a head, a heart, and a stomach, and the way to the first two is often through the third. Countries side with the power that gives them what they need through their own "diplomacy of the deed." The superpower that does this best will rise above the rest.

If human relations are about "winning friends and influencing people," then geopolitics is about winning allies and influencing countries. Arrayed along and sandwiched between the world's three main empires, second-world states are the premier arena for comparing the superpowers' strategies to expand their global power base and undermine their rivals. Second-world countries are the tipping-point states of a multipolar world: Their decisions can alter the global balance of power.[36] Some attempt a sophisticated *multi*-alignment, deriving benefits from as many superpowers as possible. Others are too weak to play the superpowers off against one another and fall instead into the sphere of influence of a single one. In particular, second-world oil-producing states such as Venezuela, Libya, Saudi Arabia, and Kazakhstan have become windows through which to observe such hedging strategies. To a large extent, the future of the second world hinges on how it relates to the three superpowers, and the future of the superpowers depends on how they manage the second world.

The second world is a zone of great potential, both actual and unrealized. In a very real sense, every second-world country is in transition. One might be moving from the third world to the second, another might be declining into the second world from the first, and so on. The first world is no larger than the thirty members of the Organisation for Economic Co-operation and Development (OECD)—although Mexico and Turkey are clearly not first-world states. The third world, by contrast, certainly includes, at the very least, the World Bank–designated forty-eight least-developed countries (LDCs)—sometimes even described as "fourth world" or the "global South"—exhibiting the lowest levels of socioeconomic development and state power, mostly located in Latin America, Africa, South Asia, and Pacific Asia.[37] At least one hundred countries—and most of the world's people—fall between these two categories, their future uncertain.

Second-world countries are frequently *both* first- and third-world at the same time. In second-world societies, some percentage of the population lives a modern lifestyle—globally connected with reliable high-wage employment—but coexists with a narrow middle class and the mass of the poor. Second-world countries *would* fall into a global middle class, except no such middle class exists. As in the first world, second-world states have growing public economies and inward investment, but like the third world, they have vast black markets and Potemkin villages.[38] Brazil is a second-world giant that draws funds from the global market, while millions of its citizens have no idea what that is. Second-world countries are often medieval in their geographical distribution of wealth, with the capital city generating a majority of national income—and retaining it. Because such countries grow poorer in concentric circles as one gets away from the capital city, it is no surprise that from Mexico to Turkey to Iran (and even in first-world France), the only job bigger than mayor of the largest city is head of government, explaining why these countries have recently had—or nearly had—former mayors as leaders.

The second world is growing, not shrinking, and it encompasses all of the "emerging markets." But what if, caught between their potential and their liabilities, they never actually emerge? Chile and Malaysia are taking advantage of their late development to rise into the first world, but Egypt and Indonesia may be too large and economically stagnant to rise out of the third world. Second-world countries are ships navigating the turbulent seas of modernity, their political, economic, and social indicators often moving in different directions simultaneously.[39] The difference between a first- or third-world future often comes down to a charismatic, unifying leader; a valuable, exportable commodity; an unpredictable, aggressive enemy; or a magnanimous superpower patron. Almost all first-world countries are liberal democracies—not because democracy brought them there but because entering the first world gave them the means to afford democracy. Because many second-world countries fall in the zone of predicted democratic transition, with per capita incomes ranging from three thousand to six thousand dollars, they are the crucial testing ground to determine if democratization truly is a natural social instinct or if it is rooted in a specific Western culture.[40] Counterintuitively, it is the societies where political, economic, and cultural adaptation is the slowest—Libya, Syria, Uzbekistan—that revolutionary change is the norm, meaning that many such second-world states are perpetually on a knife's edge.

Some view the world as trifurcated among globalized (first-world), partially globalized (second-world), and nonglobalized (third-world) zones, presuming both that all globalization is good and that quantity of wealth correlates directly to quality of life. But second-world countries prove that history is less a seamless continuum than an unpredictable contest pitting material progress against resource scarcity, cosmopolitan globalization against tribalist traditionalism, political union against fissiparous instincts, and autarky against comparative advantage.[41] Whether one is for or against globalization often depends on who is in power. Iran's regime has tried to prevent globalization from empowering opposition to its rule, while globalization has allowed the Baltic nations of Estonia, Latvia, and Lithuania to reassert pre-Soviet or new identities and has kept some second-world societies such as Mexico or Lebanon afloat through cash remittances from their global diasporas.

What second-world countries must master above all else, however, is geography. Countries can choose their friends but not their neighbors. Until technology yields the Matrix, Nicholas Spykman's dictum holds: "Geography is the most important factor in foreign policy because it is the most permanent."[42] Across the second world, borders within major regional constellations are coming down, creating what Toynbee called a "collective sub-conscious psyche."[43] Yet while second-world countries integrate from the bottom up into geopolitical neighborhoods, the tectonic plates of superpower influence are reaching across them. From Eastern Europe to Central Asia, from South America across the Arab world and into Southeast Asia, the race to win the second world is on.

CHAPTER 1

BRUSSELS:

THE NEW ROME

KIEV, TBILISI, AND Baku neither look nor feel like the grand European capitals of London, Paris, and Rome. Littered with the hulking architectural and mental debris of the Soviet Union, these cities—and the countries of which they are the capitals—are in serious need of an overhaul. The trouble is that this requires political stability, economic investment, and most of all a counterweight to Russia, which is still manipulating borders, pipelines, and markets to pull them back into its orbit.

"It's fairly simple: We hate Russia," said an Estonian diplomat in Tallinn, bluntly capturing a problem that is at once emotional and strategic. Of course, this is not a new challenge for Europe's East, where Western Christendom, Slavic Orthodoxy, and Turkic Islam have clashed for more than a thousand years. A century ago, strategists Halford Mackinder and Rudolf Kjellen devoted themselves to containing Russian power; the former argued that an Atlantic alliance was the solution, and the latter pushed for a robust Central European league. What is happening today, however, goes well beyond what either of their imaginations allowed. Instead of Eastern Europe's return to a post–Cold War "crush zone" between Germany and Russia, the European Union is subsuming Germans and Slavs alike, integrating them entirely within the new European empire.[1]

The mental journey of Europe's imperial expansion begins on a map, as one traces a finger along the L-shaped path from the chilly Baltics downward through the Central European Visegrád group of countries (Poland, the Czech and Slovak republics, and Hungary), Ukraine, Romania, the former Yugoslavia and the southern Balkans, then eastward along the Black Sea through Bulgaria, Turkey, and the Caucasus to the oily shores of the Caspian Sea. This contested zone— the original "second world"—was, except for Turkey, once colored red to signify the Warsaw Pact. Today the European Union is painting it blue, indicating that the region is ready to ascend into the first world. Yet as the Anglo-German scholar Ralf Dahrendorf presciently wrote, "The First and Second Worlds are being reunited into something which has no name yet, nor a number."[2] The actual journey through this new European East is extremely bumpy and filled with unpredictable delays, leaps of faith, and all the anxieties of people liberated less than a generation ago from totalitarianism.

For all the postcommunist soul-searching afflicting the region in the 1990s, the EU has already won the easiest fights. Since the Soviet collapse, on average one country per year has been absorbed into the EU, its citizens now traveling far more easily westward within Europe than eastward to their former master Russia. On a single day—May 1, 2004—over a hundred million citizens in ten countries officially became European.* Milan Kundera astutely called these nations the "kidnapped lands of the West," but the West to which they have returned is not the Europe of post–Versailles Treaty fragility and depression. "Our passports tell a lot about the new European mentality: Prior to 1914 no one really needed passports," explained a Czech traveler, proudly waving his new burgundy pamphlet in a train cabin full of young Western Europeans. "Now we have the next best thing: a common EU passport which *also* respects our national languages." In the eighteenth and nineteenth centuries, European elites changed their lingua franca multiple times, but by elevating to official status each new member-

---

*The ten countries were Cyprus, the Czech Republic, Estonia, Hungary, Latvia, Lithuania, Malta, Poland, Slovakia, and Slovenia.

state's language, the EU has preempted one of history's most common sources of jingoism, ensuring a polyglot, heterogeneous empire—a radical turn from Europe's inglorious early- and mid-twentieth-century history.

For over half a century, European nations have been pooling their power, eventually giving small and shattered post–World War II countries a new lease on life. Though EU members remain distinct nations, their greater meaning now comes from being part of the world's only superstate.* War between any two countries within the EU's dense institutional nexus has become impossible, and the promise of greater security and wealth has largely succeeded in aligning the foreign policies of its members.[3] "Our biggest logistical exercise since World War II was not military," an official in one of the EU's shiny, postmodern edifices boasted, "but the circulation of the Euro currency in 2002."

EU expansion is a gamble more expensive than America's war in Iraq—but one that is actually paying off. "We purposely make the EU poorer each time we expand," a sprightly Eurocrat from Lithuania explained in a Brussels pub crowded with multilingual Europhiles. "But the stability we spread can hardly be measured." The EU spends over $10 billion a year just to resurrect the physical infrastructure of its new East, accelerating its recovery from decades of communist negligence.[4] This strategy, which lifted Ireland—the "sick man of Europe" a generation ago—and postauthoritarian Spain and Portugal, is now working its magic in the East.† Though many predicted it would take Hungary decades to catch up to the West, it has already become the regional corporate outsourcing hub, with 80 percent of its production led by European multinationals and 80 percent of its exports going back to the EU. Slovakia has quickly switched from building tanks to

---

*Skeptics view the rise of the EU as hinging on a constitution that determines voting rights, budget contributions, and the roles of a common president and foreign minister. These domestic squabbles do retard European unity, but they do not prevent it, and for an ironic reason: Europe's federative system is already a huge success in dispute resolution through the European Court of Justice and other bodies. The EU hydra has multiple capitals and centers of power; close to eight hundred MPs zip among Brussels, Strasbourg, and Luxembourg, and the EU Commission already unites EU policy in two dozen fields. A simple statement of principles is emerging that lays out the roles of a president and a foreign minister, meaning that a constitution would just be icing on the cake.

†Indeed, the economic logic behind excluding poor eastern countries from the EU—that their labor standards were too low—has now been turned on its head, transformed into an argument for accelerating their integration: Once brought in, they must adhere to the EU's high labor standards, thereby reducing the siphoning off of foreign investment from Western Europe.

building Volkswagens. EU integration has meant that even the government scandals of Poland, Hungary, and the Czech Republic have hardly made a dent in economic growth. "The new members are where European entrepreneurs are flocking for the action," gushed a German management consultant who regularly shuttles to Warsaw and Budapest on one of Lufthansa's growing number of short-haul flights in the region.

EU expansion has also become a virtuous circle of tapping new markets to decrease reliance on exports to the United States—a crucial step in building an independent superpower. The fresh blood of the EU's new members has generated a competitive federalism that boosts the European economy as a whole.[5] The development model of the Baltic countries—entrepreneurial freedom, open competition, and flexible labor laws—has begun to seep back via Central Europe into the laggards of Western Europe. As one Brussels-based EU analyst noted, "Integration is now being led by countries that used to be on the periphery of Europe [but] have learned to meet the challenges, and reap the opportunities, of globalization."[6] The EU's common market is the largest in the world—and will stay that way no matter what America's economy does.

The EU is easily the most popular and successful empire in history, for it does not dominate, it disciplines. The incentives of Europeanization—subsidies from Brussels, unfettered mobility, and the adoption of the Euro currency—are too great not to want. Brussels today rivals Washington with its swarms of lobbyists, including dozens of public relations outfits hired by Balkan and post-Soviet countries actively vying for EU admission. To qualify for accession, however, the still-ruined postcommunist countries from Moldova to Albania to Azerbaijan must do more than just burnish their images: They have to follow concrete steps toward internalizing EU laws and rules as called for in the New Neighborhood Strategy, which locks together military, economic, and governance issues. Eurocrats feed their future subjects the acronym-rich language of the EU in small, digestible doses, turning unruly neighbors into productive members.

But this is not a one-way street: Europe *needs* to expand, or Europe will die. "We don't admit it, but expansion stabilizes our population decline while increasing the labor pool," one EU Commission official confided in his office full of wall-to-wall technocratic studies. Yet the gradual unification of Europe's West and East is not only political and economic but also cultural and psychological. Europe's growing diversity makes Europeanness a gradually attainable ideal rather than a mythical Platonic form, transforming Europe's identities from tribal to cosmopolitan. Even as some Western Europeans fear the dilution of their elite brand, Europe's evolution is giving the term *European* a positive meaning after decades of exclusive (read: Christian) or negative (read: not Russian) ones. Europe in fact already *is* partially Islamic, with growing Muslim populations in England, France, and Germany and almost a hundred million Muslims from Albania, Bosnia, Turkey, and Azerbaijan in the European diplomatic and strategic space via the Council of Europe or NATO. What the EU's strategic guru Robert Cooper calls the "new European commonwealth" has come to embody an ancient imperial truism that the Romans, Mongols, and Ottomans understood but the Soviet Union never did: A successful empire cannot be racist.[7]

"European" has become an identity as strong (or as weak) as "American" or "Chinese." As life imitates art, all countries participating in the European Football Championships and the Eurovision Song Contest consider themselves—and are increasingly considered—European.[8] Most important, an entire post–Cold War generation of students— called the "ERASMUS generation" after the EU's exchange program—is transcending the very national identities their elders fought to establish, all for the sake of European stability. These "postnational" European youth from almost thirty countries now travel virtually visa-free from Belfast to Baku, speak multiple languages, study in continent-wide exchange programs, vote in European parliamentary elections, and are intermarrying into a diverse European society.

As with all empires, the EU rubber band will stretch until it no longer can, growing at least until it has fully replaced the dismantled Soviet Union across Europe's East, creating a borderless and contiguous "Pax Europea" of about thirty-five countries, an imperial blanket covering close to six hundred million people.[9] But the Europeanization of the L-shaped zone is far from complete: Balkan and Caucasus countries are still fragile postconflict regions and have become a convenient crossroads for trafficking in weapons and women; Turkey has a mind of its own and will not be easily subdued; and, of course, no country presents a bigger obstacle to Europe's ambitions than Russia itself.

THE TRANSATLANTIC DIVORCE

Those who see China as an existential Eastern rival to the West argue that the United States and the EU must band together as never before. Richard Rosecrance has called for a corporate-style merger across the Atlantic, forming an economically complementary and politically robust superstructure to balance China's potential.[10] Even absent a China challenge, America and Europe share cultural bonds deepened by the NATO alliance of the Cold War, and it is highly unlikely that the United States and the EU would ever again attempt to undermine each other physically.[11] U.S. State Department veteran Nicholas Burns has described transatlantic relations as a "marriage with no possibility of separation or divorce."[12]

Yet when the transatlantic scholar Robert Kagan described America's strategic worldview as hailing from masculine Mars, with that of Europe descending from more feminine Venus, it was treated not just as a clever analogy but rather as a psychoanalytical comparison of divergent inner beings.[13] Over two centuries America evolved from rejecting Europe to seeing itself as the leader of a united West—with Europe as a junior partner. But as Dominique Moisi suggests, the "Cold War configuration of one West and two Europes" is being replaced by "one Europe but two Wests." Even as the fraternal twins of Western civilization, Europe and America represent two different empires—friendly most of the time, but ultimately competing to advance to the head of the geopolitical class.

Europe has its own vision of what world order should look like, which it increasingly pursues whether America likes it or not. The EU is now the most confident economic power in the world, regularly punishing the United States in trade disputes, while its superior commercial and environmental standards have assumed global leadership.[14] Many Europeans view America's way of life as deeply corrupt, built on borrowed money, risky and heartless in its lack of social protections, and ecologically catastrophic.[15] Meanwhile, Europe has achieved Toynbee's aspiration of a "middle way between free enterprise and socialism."[16] The EU is also a far larger humanitarian aid donor than the United States, while South America, East Asia, and other regions prefer to emulate the "European Dream" rather than the American variant. London's *Financial Times* is the world's most widely circulated newspaper, not *The New York Times*.

The United States and the EU increasingly differ about both the means and ends of power as well. For many Europeans, the U.S.-led war in Iraq validated their view that war is not an instrument of policy but rather a sign of its failure. The backlash against America that inspired al-Qaeda attacks on European soil has heightened their disdain for America's approach to confronting troubled states—while inspiring them to elevate their own strategy of sustainable transformation. It is often said that America and Europe make a strong team because "America breaks and the EU fixes" or that America "lays down the law" while Europe "lays down the rule of law," but this cliché has long grated on Europeans, who would rather spread their version of stability *before* America destabilizes countries on its periphery, particularly in the Arab world.

At a minimum, Europeans now believe the EU should be autonomous from the United States while working with it through NATO in humanitarian operations. But as America downsizes its military forces in Europe, the EU is combining its armies toward common rapid reaction and peacekeeping forces potentially numbering two hundred thousand, and investing in a Eurofighter combat jet and long-range aircraft. EU members increasingly contribute their defense budgets to the European Defense Agency, not Lockheed Martin.[17] Transatlantic relations may be an arranged marriage, but the United States and EU will continue to act as if they are divorced.

CHAPTER 2

THE RUSSIAN DEVOLUTION

FAMOUSLY DESCRIBED BY Churchill as "a riddle, wrapped in a mystery, inside an enigma," Russia remains the world's largest conundrum. As the mismatch between Russia's dwindling population and its continental mass persists, it is useful to think of the massive space Russia occupies not as one unit but four: Slavic, European Russia lying in the Volga basin; Caucasian Russia between the Black and Caspian seas; Ural and Siberian Russia as the gateway to Central Asia; and Pacific Russia bordering Mongolia and China.* Russia must stitch these entities together if it wants to remain Russia at all—and its failure to do so would profoundly affect the map of the entire Eurasian "world-island."

Since Peter the Great moved Russia's capital to St. Petersburg in the early eighteenth century, every Russian contact with the West has exposed it as materially inferior, awakening both its national consciousness and its masochistic soul.[1] The decade of "hot tub and vodka" diplomacy after the dissolution of the Soviet Union numbed

---

*The latter two areas are considered in Part II.

Russia's leaders to their strategic predicament: Because Russia remains so big, neither the United States nor Europe nor China wants it to be strong. In their gilded chambers today, however, the Kremlin's most recent ruling clique is suffering from the resulting imperial hangover, profoundly angry at the once-mighty empire's diminished standing.[2] Russia's diplomatic position is purely residual: If it neglected to show up (or fell out of its chair) at major negotiations on the Arab-Israeli conflict or the North Korean and Iranian nuclear programs, the outcomes would be no different—America, Europe, and China are far more influential arbiters.

"Russia is experiencing a twenty-first-century version of the nineteenth-century debate between Slavophiles and Westernizers—this time between Eurasianists and Atlanticists—with a similar lack of clarity over whether Russia is a part of the West or apart from the West," explained a Berlin-based Russia watcher. Under the steely former KGB official Vladimir Putin, the Eurasianists—who seek to restore Russian glory—appeared to have lifted the country from the 1990s doldrums. Controlling more natural resources—oil, gas, coal, and timber—than the United States, the EU, and China combined, the Kremlin can once again think and act imperially, even at the North Pole.* Just as the sprawling nuclear archipelago was the source of Soviet might, arteries of pipelines pump the lifeblood of today's Russia. As the value of energy titan Gazprom grew from $10 billion in 2000 to close to $300 billion in 2006 (becoming a third of Russia's total economy), Russian diplomacy quickly became synonymous with Gazprom diplomacy. Because Gazprom controls the natural gas distribution network throughout Eastern Europe, the region's states still fall into two categories: those wealthy enough to evade energy extortion by Moscow, and those vulnerable to cabals of shady Russian *biznismen* (partnered with intelligence agents operating in embassies) demanding further buyouts of key assets from Romania to Georgia and threatening obscene price hikes. Putin was particularly keen to undermine the upstart former Soviet Baltic republics, offering to route a new pipeline directly under the Baltic Sea to Germany. "Our pride has suffered," explained a Moscow intellectual over a narrow glass of ice-chilled vodka, "but this only drives our nationalism further." Yet Gazprom's corporate logic has already undermined Russia's

---

*Russia is the world's top natural gas producer and second-largest oil producer.

diplomatic interests by alienating its main ally in the former Soviet Union, Belarus, which resorted to siphoning oil from a pipeline bound for Europe to evade a doubling of Gazprom's fees. In its hostility toward its smaller neighbors, Russia has become a Siberian Saudi Arabia—but with the added fear factor of an insecure nuclear arsenal.

Gazprom not only shapes Russia's foreign policy, it has also become the state itself. In a kleptocratic economy in which public and private ownership are utterly blurred, Gazprom is Russia's largest urban and rural landowner, builds roads and hospitals, and sponsors sports centers—all things the Kremlin never did.[3] The company's recent chairman, Dmitri Medvedev, is also the country's next president. The Gazprom-Kremlin nexus has taken populist measures against the so-called oligarchs (the only other pole of political power in Russia), hoarding renationalized assets in the name of restoring centralized strength.[4] The government shut down all the country's private casinos—and then opened its own outside major cities. No wonder Putin conceded that anyone who successfully registers a business deserves a medal. Each winter the government recesses for weeks of drunken revelry, prompting senior parliamentarian Ivan Grachev to muse, "The less they work, the better it is for the country."[5]

The former KGB headquarters in Moscow is now a high-class disco: Russians today are consumers, not citizens. In the unfolding hypercapitalist coup, the SUV with tinted windows is the vehicle of choice for the perpetually insecure business caste that lives each day like its last, partying with exotic lions and dominatrix dancers, complete with plenty of caviar. One is safe only in the sauna, where everyone is naked and no weapons are allowed. Three-quarters of Russia's economy is centered on Moscow, one of the most expensive cities in the world, with more billionaires than New York. Its Putin-appointed mayor has resurrected the city by way of hulking, obtuse sculptures, a hideous regression from St. Petersburg's baroque palaces. Drivers stuck in traffic might contemplate these eyesores, but the rich buy sirens to blaze through restricted zones at high speeds. Fancy shopping malls charge entrance fees; ordinary people need not apply. In Russian capitalism, the credo "Russia is a free country!" has its corollary: "Because you paid more, you earned it."

The greatest remaining statue of Lenin stands before the Finland

Station in St. Petersburg, commemorating his arrival there in 1917 to launch the October Revolution. His arm confidently outstretched, Lenin appears unshakably, but tragically, bold. A century later, Putin continued the tradition of governing the very thin Russian state apparatus by instinct rather than institution.* Andrei Illarionov was a trusted Putin adviser until he blew the whistle in 2005, riskily declaring that Russia had "ceased to be a politically free country." Independent media, opposition groups, and the judiciary have all been neutered. Think tanks once provided policy research to the Kremlin's apparatchiks, but as a Moscow political analyst lamented in his shabby office, "These days our mundane work couldn't matter less."

Russia has become the archetypal petrocracy, with profligate spending, skewed development, and elite struggles over control of vast natural resources while the nontaxpaying public's demands go unnoticed.[6] Oil revenues have not led Russia to splurge on either guns or butter, however. Its military equipment remains outdated, with disorganized command and control, while it struggles with manpower as the national population collapses at the staggering rate of half a million per year. Two-thirds of Russians across the vast nation still live near the poverty line, dying off in waves during each successive intolerably cold winter. In their crumbling, heatless apartment blocks, they wonder where all the gas has gone. If Russia's energy isn't used to keep Russians alive, there will be no more Russia.

As during the Cold War, the United States and Russia still have nuclear weapons pointed at each other on hair-trigger alert. Yet even as Russia blocks NATO expansion and delays American missile shields, it cannot stop the EU. For over a decade, Europeans considered Russia "too close and too big" to aggravate, and it needed Russia's cooperation to end the Balkan wars. But from Ukraine to Kosovo to Chechnya, Russia proved better at thwarting than assisting European goals like energy security, counterterrorism, and human rights. The tiny Baltic

---

*Many Russians believe that Putin did not want to overcentralize Kremlin control but was driven to do so because of the weakness of Yeltsin-era democracy, which failed to prevent both the 1998 financial crisis and the NATO bombing of its ally Serbia, resulting in demands for stronger leadership and stability. Still, George Kennan's observation from 1947 is equally valid today: "The process of political consolidation has never been completed and the men in the Kremlin have continued to be predominantly absorbed with the struggle to secure and make absolute the power they seized in November 1917." See Kennan, "The Sources of Soviet Conduct," *Foreign Affairs*, July 1947.

statelets then outmaneuvered Russia using diaspora lobbies, slick branding campaigns (think "E-stonia"), and investor-friendly economic policies, seducing the EU into uncommon quick-wittedness. When Russia stalled in settling its borders with the Baltic nations (which by EU regulation should have delayed their membership talks), Europe let these statelets in anyway. With their deep historical ties to liberal Western European culture, Tallinn and Riga today have thoroughly replaced the crumbling architecture of Soviet modernism and revived the European economic linkages of their Hanseatic League heritage. Thirtysomethings dominate both politics and business, with Western European techies clamoring to work for Estonian companies like Skype.

The EU has Eurasianists too, and they want to absorb and Europeanize Russia. Russia is often portrayed as having Europe over a barrel because of its oil and gas reserves, but there are limits to Russia's ability to bite the hand that feeds it.[7] Most of Russia's trade and energy exports go to Europe, but as Europe diversifies its sources (including increased renewable energy and North African natural gas), its leverage over Russia grows. Despite its massive energy windfall, Russia still needs European investment to keep growing. From cars to construction, if something in Russia works, it is probably European. But rather than fuel Russian neo-authoritarianism, the European Bank for Reconstruction and Development (EBRD) invests in upgrading a dilapidated infrastructure and building a noncorrupt private sector—moves that can inspire a future democratic Russia from below. Putin's outbursts demanding respect for the "Russian way" and sponsoring of nationalistic youth cults failed to silence the many Russians who want more such European intrusions. Wealthy Russians prefer to boost the economies of "Londongrad" and Berlin—where exiled tycoon Boris Berezovsky openly called for a coup to depose Putin—depriving the Kremlin even further of talent and resources, while the EU makes a greater Russian stake in its aerospace industry contingent on improved transparency. "We can push Russia into an industrial and political partnership like France and Germany had in the 1950s," a European Council official confidently urged. "Russians constantly plead for visa-free travel to Europe, but selectively admitting Russia's businessmen, politicians, and students is a major diplomatic lever we can use to get the government to play fair."

Russia's superpower days are over. Even as the world's largest petrostate, its economy is still smaller than that of France. And even as it becomes rich on paper, its politics all but confirm that the wealth will not be sustained.[8] Today it is the EU that prevents Russia from ever having a veto over the West, and it is also the EU that can make Russia join the West—and in doing so, save it from itself.

CHAPTER 3

UKRAINE:

FROM BORDER TO BRIDGE

"THIS MAY BE just a corner of Europe, but it's the middle of the struggle with Russia," pleaded a thirty-year-old independent newspaper editor in an Irish pub in Ukraine's capital, Kiev. While grand strategies are plotted in Washington, Brussels, Moscow, and Beijing, victories are won on the ground, using all the weapons of globalization: money, pipelines, diasporas, and the media. Ukraine is a country where this diplomatic game is being played around the clock by politicians, generals, activists, and businesspeople. The stakes are high: subduing Russia and expanding the European empire eastward. The Ukrainian peasantry, divided for centuries between German and Russian masters, was ironically given a national identity by the 1939 Nazi-Soviet pact—but under the Soviet yoke.* To Ukrainians, their country's name means "homeland," but in Russian it means "borderland."[1] Today it remains very much both.

"We are no longer a Soviet republic, but we don't automatically

---

*Roosevelt and Churchill finally ceded areas already under Soviet control to Stalin at the Crimean czarist resort of Yalta in 1945.

trust the other side either. Replacing one form of domination with another is not our idea of progress," scolded a Russia-leaning media tycoon at his vast estate outside Kiev. The West's "Russia first" policy of the 1990s left Ukraine exactly where it had been for centuries: schizophrenically split along the Dnieper River (in Ukrainian, Dnipro) into European- and Russian-oriented halves, unable to achieve its potential as a strategically located country with a population of fifty million. Ukraine still feels like two different countries, with people rarely crossing from its Catholic, agricultural west to its Orthodox, industrial east. L'viv, in the west, is like Poland's Kraków, with people singing and playing chess in public squares, while in eastern, industrial Donetsk, Russian is more widely spoken than Ukrainian. In Donetsk, Lenin still stands proud; in L'viv, his statue is gone, replaced by a giant flowerpot.

Both halves of Ukraine, however, are caught between past and future. Across the country one still senses the turbulence and collateral damage wrought by imperial decay. The post-Soviet orthodoxy of "shock therapy" assumed that yanking away price controls and replacing them with rapid privatization would lead to greater efficiency and welfare, even though there simply was no mechanism for social distribution outside the state, which controlled services, wages—even minds. In Ukraine and throughout the former Soviet Union, entire generations lost their social security as prices skyrocketed, real incomes plummeted, and the cost of basic foods spiraled out of reach. Thousands of elderly perished, either freezing during winter blizzards or wilting without air-conditioning during summer heat waves. Today, Soviet-era buildings are collapsing, and bouts of severe inflation still endanger the livelihood of common Ukrainians. Every taxi driver in Kiev dreads the day his Lada or Volga sputters to a halt in the middle of the city, knowing he can't afford to have it revived and hasn't saved enough for a new one. Lucky, then, that Ukrainians give lifts to total strangers for a token fare. "We suffered enough together, so we still trust each other," explained one such commuter-entrepreneur driving out of downtown Kiev late at night.

As in Russia, capitalism blew its first chance to make a good impression, and Kiev, like Moscow, is a Potemkin village whose urban grandeur masks poverty that grows the farther one moves from the center. Turning Ukraine into the next Poland means elevating it from its strikingly third-world attributes, such as an overwhelming share of foreign investment directed to the capital alone and untaxed barter bazaars around the country. Kiev's underground markets provide shelter from the torrential summer rains, but they are a paradise for pirated DVDs. Travel agents can't penetrate the railway monopoly. "This is the Stone Age," apologized one. Ukraine is also still heavily dependent on remittances from its almost three million people in the Western European diaspora. Like Moscow, Kiev boasts fancy nightclubs such as Decadence, where champagne-soaked, Hummer-driving scions joke: "What's the matter with Kiev? It's surrounded by Ukraine."

As recently as 2003, onlookers predicted that Ukraine would remain a "miserable country surrounded by more miserable countries."[2] President Leonid Kuchma's government resembled Central Asian soft authoritarianism more than Western liberal democracy, running elections transparent only in their fraudulence.[3] But with patience and subtlety, European and American intelligence services stuck their fingers in the narrow crack of breathing space Kuchma gave to parliamentary and civic opposition, uniting poorly coordinated diaspora and student groups with a nascent free media to yank open the window to full-scale popular discontent. Kuchma's preferred successor, Russian-backed Viktor Yanukovych, was set for victory in the country's 2004 election until opposition leader Viktor Yushchenko survived a hefty dose of dioxin poisoning (presumably at the hands of Kuchma's Russian allies) and used his newfound martyr status to force and win a third election round. Just preventing a bloodbath was enough to topple a dictator: At the tensest moment of the showdown, Kuchma's security services, steadily cultivated by Western agents, refused to open fire on the throngs of demonstrators waving orange flags.

There is no connection between Ukraine and the color orange, however. It was thought up by Western consultants seeking an inspiring symbol to lure people out into the dreary, frigid Ukrainian winter. As it turned out, the "Orange Revolution" was more black-and-blue. The aftermath of every such radical transition of the past decade (including Serbia and Georgia) has been marked by the exposure of shamelessly scandalous political practices. Scarcely moments after Yushchenko replaced his former boss Kuchma, opportunistic politicians switched sides, unqualified loyalists were rewarded with high posts, constitutional reforms stalled, and the whole "revolution" seemed more a civic coup replacing one corrupt clique of nomenklatura with another. The joke making the rounds in Kiev went that even a doctor of philology would be trusted to perform heart surgery if he had been standing next to Yushchenko on Kiev's Maidan Nezalezhnosti (Independence Square).

Looking at a map will never reveal whether or not Ukraine is European—only its politics can confirm this. After the Orange Revolution, Yushchenko promptly declared that Ukrainians had—as one nation—"chosen Europe not just geographically, but also its spiritual and moral values." But by European standards of governance, Ukraine is still closer to Pakistan than it is to Poland. The oligarchy and parliament in Ukraine almost completely overlap, with seats sold to the highest bidders. Many members of parliament never literally occupy their seats, however, preferring their corporate offices with fine European furniture to drab government buildings. Ukraine's first post–Orange Revolution prime minister, Yulia Tymoshenko—the "Orange Goddess" with the Princess Leia hairstyle—had the populist charisma of Pakistan's Benazir Bhutto and singularly dominated her parliamentary bloc. Like many leading duos in the second world, Tymoshenko and Yushchenko clashed in 2005, unable to agree on the form of state Ukraine should have: presidential or parliamentary. Yushchenko had promised a transition to parliamentary rule but showed a personal preference for his presidential powers, sacking the prime minister and her cabinet before the year was out. His soft megalomania included repetitively exhorting his own eleventh commandment: "Don't be afraid."

"Trust in the new government was nearly universal after the Revolution," a Kiev pollster with Russian sympathies explained smugly over tea, "but the elites were completely indifferent to our needs." Ballooning inflation put prices for meat and milk out of reach for many citizens. As in Russia, gains from privatization had been so skewed that Yushchenko and Tymoshenko devoted equal time to pursuing re-nationalization policies (euphemistically termed "de-privatization") and to making deals with Yanukovych, based in eastern Ukraine, in the hopes of keeping the country's two halves together. After two years of deadlock and the Orange revolutionary guard's incestuous game of musical chairs, Yanukovych's party fairly captured the 2006 elections. Ironically, it was the pro-Russian Yanukovych whose parliament was then finally able to pass laws capping Yushchenko's power. Because a corrupt, pro-Western government undermines both itself and the West, the West lost the second round of the fight it had picked with

Russia, while interior security and police forces loyal to the rival factions continue to skirmish around political showdowns. A country has to do more than look European to *be* European.

A century ago, the Swedish strategist Rudolf Kjellen saw Ukraine and the Baltics as pivotal defenders of "cultural Europe" against the "Mongol-tainted Muscovite tsarism" of Russia's "Asian unlimited will to power."[4] Without Ukraine, Russia ceases to be a European empire, which makes it so integral to Russia's conception of its "Near Abroad" that Russia has never truly regarded it as a foreign country.[5] Russia's loss in the Orange Revolution thus plunged it into tantrum diplomacy laced with diatribes against Western meddling in the post-Soviet space. It has been said that "Russian liberalism ends where Ukrainian independence begins." Certainly, Ukraine would learn, cheap oil and gas do. Russia's immediate reaction to Yushchenko's victory was to raise gas prices threefold and blockade Kazakh oil shipments to Ukraine. A murky shell company led by Gazprom and Ukrainian oligarchs—also known as the "new Russians"—was set up to control future supply. But such tactics alienated even the millions of Ukrainian Russians who now project a better future for themselves as part of the West. As one Ukrainian foreign ministry official confidently remarked in his airy office, "Russians are so delusional that they don't even learn from their mistakes."

Ukraine's generational shift may naturally end Russia's delusions of grandeur. Noticeable on the horizon from any point in Kiev, the ghastly two-hundred-foot-tall titanium *Rodina Mat* ("Defense of the Motherland") statue remains the centerpiece of the Great Patriotic War Museum. Mothers take their young children there to clamber on the turrets of Soviet tanks, but at school these children are taught that the tanks are symbols not of Soviet heroism but of foreign occupation. For most of Ukraine's population born during or after the perestroika era of the 1980s, there is no trace of Sovietism; they know full well about the famines and political tragedies inflicted on Ukraine by the "foreign" revolution in Russia and two of the most terrible dictators of the twentieth century, Lenin and Stalin. With only the current generation of ex-Soviet apparatchiks separating them from leadership, they are cynically optimistic about their country's European future. As a female university student already fluent in Western European culture claimed, "What we want is a real revolution, not just of elections, but of political consciousness replacing apathy and fear. We don't have that in our history. We need it from Europe."

Inside the hulking, Soviet-era foreign ministry building, Ukrainians have been busy rebranding their country as European—even arguing that its very genetic code is Western. Officials tout the country's technically educated population and literary heroes Gogol and Bulgakov; they even sent maps to Brussels showing Ukraine shaded European blue—*Mitteleuropa,* not *Osteuropa.* "It is like having a much bigger brother looming on one side, but trying to escape to another family," a senior diplomat explained. "Not in the past one thousand years has Ukraine's geography been anything but cursed!"

The EU's better-late-than-never approach may finally change this. Even Kuchma spoke of his hope that Ukraine would eventually join the EU, but the EU balked, fearing Ukraine's massive agricultural dependence, which would cause competition for subsidies with French and Spanish farmers, and its overwhelmingly young population, which would threaten job stability in the West.[6] But for all of its difficulties, the Orange Revolution marked the end of Europe's excuses. Ukraine is still too big and too poor for EU membership—but it is no longer too Soviet.

In the lush forests of Crimea, large tour groups visit intricate churches perched precariously on rocky ledges, indicating Ukraine's recapture of its proud Catholic heritage. Russia has always claimed Crimea, but in 2015 it will lose its lease on naval facilities in the Black Sea port of Sebastopol forever. The Romanovs' Livadia Palace in Yalta, where Stalin redrew the map of Europe on Soviet terms, is now the site of flashy pro-EU branding conferences. "We are now the gateway for IT companies to manufacture microchips and export across the Black Sea to Turkey and the Caucasus," boasted a young entrepreneur in the sturdy Crimean capital of Simferopol. Europeans from all corners also descend on Crimea's beaches for illicit all-night raves. Russian rhetoric has become reminiscent of a conversation in Vasily Aksyonov's dissident novel *Island of Crimea,* in which the protagonist responds to an apparatchik's insistence on Russia's dominance of the peninsula by coolly stating, "Everyone may *know* it, but no one seems to *notice.*"[7]

Not least because Ukrainian oligarchs enjoy basking in the south of France, they now also speak fluently about the Treaty of Nice, which set forth the EU's plan for enlargement and greater financial transfers to the East. But the EU's real favorite game is playing hard to get. It is the lure—not the reality—of higher status with the EU that can nudge Ukrainian leaders to dissolve their shadow cabinets, break monopolies, liberalize the media, clean up the banking system, and create jobs to recruit diaspora talent. Together with massive EU investment, these are the measures necessary to make the Russian legacy just that—ultimately propelling Ukraine out of the second world and toward true Europeanness.

Europe delivers not just grand illusions but also practical solutions. Whereas America's approach to democracy promotion in Ukraine— backing one party relentlessly—led to an entrenched and complacent regime, European parliamentary groups and NGOs support multiple political parties, thus building a stable democratic foundation. Because European governance systems are themselves parliamentary (not presidential, as in the United States), their strategy ultimately serves Western goals better. Furthermore, while American-led NATO used to be the tip of the West's spear, paving the way for EU membership by absorbing not entirely qualified countries into the alliance, the EU's gravitational pull has become far stronger and less controversial. "It's not just Russia which has halted NATO expansion," reminded a presidential adviser keen to assert his country's sovereignty, "but we Ukrainians are also divided about military partnerships which involve subjugation to the United States—the same way we feel about Russia." Yet even the pro-Russian premier Yanukovych is keen on EU membership, since as senior Russian parliamentarian Vladimir Ryzhkov conceded, the EU is "the most successful model in history."

"Ukraine's very existence as an independent country transforms Russia," argues former U.S. national security adviser Zbigniew Brzezinski. Indeed, Russia's eventual acceptance of Ukraine's Europeanization could make Ukraine a model for Russia itself, both geographically and psychologically. It is the transit corridor for Russian oil and gas to its wealthier customers in the West, and Europe's energy diversification efforts, combined with Ukraine's willingness to revive its nuclear power industry (despite the legacy of Chernobyl), boost their combined ability to bring Russia into line when it threatens to hike prices or withhold supply. Now Ukraine has a defter answer to Russian bullying. As one diplomat coyly put it, "We tell Russians we will gladly cooperate more with them—provided the rules conform to those of the EU."

THE EASTERN BLOC PARTY

In 2005, on the sixtieth anniversary of the Nazi defeat, Latvian president Vaira Vike-Freiberga fumed that the Soviet takeover of the Baltics after World War II "meant slavery, it meant occupation, it meant subjugation, and it meant Stalinist terror." The EU anchors of Western Europe have sometimes viewed this pugnacious anti-Russian stance as detrimental to maintaining stable ties with Moscow. But the activism of Europe's new members is the new secret weapon of a more assertive EU *Ostpolitik,* one that lowers competition with Russia to the tactical level. Every few years there is talk of a "new iron curtain," but Europe always knocks it down with its velvet glove.

The most underappreciated aspect of European enlargement is its self-sustaining nature. Over the past decade, countries from Poland to Slovenia clamored to join the EU, all claiming to be the final frontier of the West and downplaying associations with their unruly neighbors to the east. Realizing how easily chaos can spill over borders, however, they quickly adopted an evangelistic zeal for further EU engagement and democratization—especially for their neighbors. It was the presidents of Poland and Lithuania who rushed to Kiev to mediate the 2004 election standoff, dragging a reluctant Javier Solana, the EU's foreign policy chief, behind them.

The recurrent lesson is that second-world countries, acting as a peer group, have more to teach one another than dictates from Washington or Brussels can. And they more readily accept both advice and admonition from one another too. Europe works best when it practices such subsidiarity, delegating responsibility to the actors closest to the mission.[8] Baltic countries know from experience that political breakdown is a certainty if EU-prescribed reforms are pushed off until the final judgment hour, as they were in Bulgaria and Romania. Using the Parliamentary Assembly of the Council of Europe (PACE) and multiweek parliamentary exchange programs, governments throughout the Balkans and the Caucasus have taken on Estonians and

Lithuanians to teach hands-on reform and coach them in handling the EU's strict conditionality clauses. In 2004, young veterans of the Otpor! ("Resistance!") movement (who were instrumental in the 2000 ouster of Serbian strongman Slobodan Milošević) were shuttled in and out of Ukraine to work with the Pora! ("Enough!") movement, which orchestrated the Orange Revolution.

Belarus demonstrates that this peer-group principle is more relevant than ever. It is Belarus where the Soviet effort to eliminate national identity was most successful, where a statue of KGB founder Felix Dzerzhinsky, the fierce Bolshevik head of Lenin's counterrevolutionary Cheka, was resurrected in 2005. Fearing the "virus" of Western-backed revolutions, Belarussian president Alexander Lukashenko has blocked European parliamentarians from entering the country, meaning that the EU and United States must now rely all the more on the savvy of Lithuanians, Poles, and Ukrainians who can smuggle themselves into the country to shelter and train the Belarus opposition. "It is our duty to liberate Belarus from Russian control!" a young Lithuanian activist enthused.

Moldova is an former Soviet republic more resembling an African-style quasi-state, and it is another example of how Europe's second world is leading it toward a more assertive foreign policy. By the time the EU sent a permanent representative to its capital, Chişinău, in 2004, Russia had already enabled the gangster regime of the breakaway province of Transdniester to "accumulate the trappings of statehood while persisting as a time-warped relic of the Soviet past."[9] However, to prove its conflict resolution credentials to the EU, Ukraine took the lead and devised a border-control scheme to wrest the republic from Russia's orbit, beefing up measures against the smuggling of everything from AK-47s to frozen chickens. On Moldova's western border, Romania's entry into the EU creates further opportunities for the Russian client to gravitate toward Europe. Law and order are better established *within* the European empire than outside it.

Defining Europe used to be as simple as the exclamation, "Europe is . . . not Russia!"[10] But whereas the Baltic nations once dreaded NATO's deference to a sensitive Russia, they now apply to Russia itself the principle of not wanting to be Europe's eastern fringe, viewing the formerly great Russian bear more like an alcoholic uncle, with a mix of pity and concern. They know that Russia is capable of infantile paroxysms of rage and that it controls most of their energy supply. And because Russia still holds Kaliningrad, on the Baltic coast, they want to invest in that exclave together *with* Russia, to transform it into a fourth Baltic republic rather than a place that looks as if World War II ended yesterday. Moscow is grudgingly accepting that its former satellites, one by one, now orbit a different capital: Brussels.

CHAPTER 4

THE BALKANS:

EASTERN QUESTIONS

"THE PRESENT EUROPE is unfinished business unless the Balkans are a part of it," declared Lord Paddy Ashdown, the EU's high representative in Bosnia. "It is very simple. Improve stability in the Balkans or you will import instability and crime into Europe."[1] The EU can hardly pretend to be a superpower east of the Balkans until it stabilizes the Balkans themselves, treating the region not as an isolated corner of Europe but rather as the very passageway to the world beyond the West. Yet in the former Yugoslavia—the heart of the Balkans— post–Cold War democracy brought quasi-dictatorships that ripped the region apart in an orgy of ethno-nationalist violence for which the EU was ill-prepared.[2] Outside Bosnian cities, the country still feels gray and abandoned, the air still smoky. On village roads one never knows what obstacle—a checkpoint or a bombed-out truck—lies around the next bend. The same is true of Balkan politics.

Throughout the 1980s, each of the former Yugoslav republics was wealthier than Spain, but while Western Europe integrated in the 1990s, Yugoslavia squandered its unity. Instead, the savage wars of Yugoslav disintegration plunged it into a third-world barbarism in which

half a million people perished in surreal carnage. In the age of globalization, missing out on a decade of the integration process (let alone
five) is both disastrous and cruel. The Balkans became a microcosm of
Western Europe after World War II: shattered, mistrustful, and occupied by foreign powers. "We won't be free until we're rid of each other,"
chafed an elderly Bosnian man in a wooded village near Mostar. "If we
don't get our full independence soon, the Europeans can't stop us from
fighting again."

Yet the eternal failure of the Balkans is no more predetermined than
were its recent civil wars.* Democratic institutions and culture can be
built in the Balkans, and a decade after its initial failures, only the EU
can build them—lifting the region back through the second world.[3]
Greece, Slovenia, Romania, and Bulgaria already prove how the EU elevates Balkan nations. Modern Greece was just another dubious pow-
derkeg until its British diaspora lobbied to hitch it onto the Marshall
Plan gravy train. It remained a dictatorship until 1975, harboring terrorists, engineering a coup in Cyprus, and sniping constantly with Turkey
and Macedonia. In 2006, its GDP calculation was bumped by 25 percent by taking into account revenues from prostitution and cigarette
smuggling. It has clearly taken decades to coax Greece, the cradle of
European civilization, to act like a modern European nation, but that
seems ever more likely now that, with Romania and Bulgaria's EU accession in 2007, it is no longer a geographic exclave of the EU. Drawing
on its Habsburg legacy, Slovenia is already wealthier than half of its fellow EU member-states. For Romania and Bulgaria, the term *second
world* had always been a euphemism to avoid admitting that Europe
had third-world countries, and their incomes still hover at one-third the
EU average. But European agro-technology ensures that Romania,
something of a European Appalachia, can move from a peasant collective to a breadbasket for the region as well as a hub for low-cost industry beyond its trademark AK-47 assault rifles.[4] Similarly, the EU's
threats of admission delays coaxed even perpetually schizophrenic Bulgaria to break up organized crime and human trafficking rings to qualify

---

*Balkan nationalism has not always caused geopolitical headaches. During the more than three decades under
Josip Broz Tito, Yugoslavia was a well-paid, nonaligned, mini–European Union of six multiethnic republics sharing a currency. It was diplomatically sovereign enough to be party to more international treaties than almost any
other country in the world. Even after Tito's death, in 1980, a rotating presidency within the pan-Yugoslavian federation continued for a decade.

for billions in desperately needed subsidies.[5] With the EU stamp of approval, Bulgarians are returning to work in refurbished factories, and Euro-hippies flock by car or on low-cost airlines to its Black Sea beaches. "Bulgaria is the new Costa del Sol!" a British tourist in Burgas chimed.

Given the historical instability of the Balkans, the European empire will remain incomplete and vulnerable until the "Eastern Question" that vexed European statesmen a century ago is settled. Fortunately, the total population of the remaining western and southern Balkan countries—Serbia, Bosnia, Croatia, Macedonia, Albania—does not even add up to that of Romania, with no country larger in population than Manhattan. Their geographic contiguity has added to the case for swallowing the region's infant states in one moderate-sized bite. But Balkan leaders do not always know what is good for them, and they always put up a mean fight. The love-hate relations between the EU and Balkan countries remain tense and volatile even as the EU flag becomes the region's new idée fixe.

SERBIA: THE HOUSE IN THE ROAD

Europe's efforts in the early 1990s to prevent the splintering of the Balkans were hardly promising: Maps drawn up to cantonize Yugoslavia resembled ethnic hopscotch more than political federation. Officials in Paris and Berlin also took a wait-and-see approach toward the demise of Bosnia's Ottoman Muslims, placing them under an arms embargo while Serbia and Croatia inherited Yugoslavia's armaments, their French and German patrons overlooking their clients' atrocities.[6] "All the war criminals could have been captured with a few phone calls," a young Serbian human rights activist vented in a bohemian quarter of Serbia's capital, Belgrade. "But French officials with skeletons in the closet wanted to avoid exposing their complicity." Of course, it was Europe's strategic immaturity that was most exposed at the time.

EU officials are finally proving that European interests in the Balkans overlap. Rather than allow the bloodstained centuries of nation-building to run their course—and drag Europe along—the EU has begun "member-state-building," the procession from quasi-occupation to shared sovereignty akin to "a young adult passing in carefully supervised stages from the family home to a cozy marriage."[7] The paradox of the Balkans, however, is that while they are the part of Europe most dependent on the EU for stability, they are also the most fiercely independent-minded—no country more so than Serbia. After all, almost a century ago it was Serbian resistance to being incorporated into the Austro-Hungarian Empire that led to World War I.[8]

On one side of the prime minister's office in Belgrade lies the army headquarters, a smoldering ruin since its pummeling by U.S. smart bombs in 1999, and on the other side runs the alley in which Zoran Djindjić—the region's first democratically elected leader since World War II, a sort of Serbian John F. Kennedy—was gunned down in 2003 by forces loyal to the homicidal strongman Slobodan Milošević. Milošević was not only tolerated years longer than necessary, he was even called a "man of peace" during the Dayton Accords process in 1995. His countrymen could not have agreed less. For ninety continuous days through the harsh winter of 1996–97, thousands of protestors in downtown Belgrade urged his ouster—even waving French and German flags. "His specialty was making our real problems of unemployment and corruption worse," an Otpor! activist recalled. "We joked that he must have been a Western mole. After all, how could things have possibly turned out any worse for us?" But rather than being provided with overwhelming support for the Serbian opposition, the country was placed under blunt sanctions and bombed by NATO for eighty-eight days, causing immense damage—though one of Milošević's palaces was spared because it housed a Rembrandt painting. "We couldn't believe it," the activist continued. "Whose side were they [NATO] on?" The Serbian political petri dish was left isolated, allowing nefarious criminal elements to continue to fester and multiply inside. No wonder Serbia is the most intransigent holdout to EU accession today.

Small countries like Serbia, which have less economic weight than many large companies, often act as such corporations do, firing a bad CEO first and worrying about who should replace him later.[9] Political strategists, not smart bombs, eventually made the real difference. Serbia's grassroots opposition dislodged Milošević during the country's "October Revolution" in 2000, also known as the "Bulldozer Revolution," since a bulldozer was used to plow into the pro-Milošević television station RTS. The Serbian Radical Party and nationalists who portray Milošević as a martyr (he died during trial at The Hague) still hold the upper hand in the country's parliament, however, harking back to a Serbian golden age that never existed. Student activists are left to push the cause of rehabilitating the country's image, unveiling controversial exhibits documenting Serb atrocities in the Bosnian village of Srebrenica in 1995 that ask, "Do you see? Do you remember? Do you know?" In their quaint university towns such as Niš, they *feel* like Europeans; if only their leaders would let them prove it. "Let's put it this way: There's no way we're *not* European," one student leader argued. "So how long will this limbo continue? If the current leaders were half as creative about providing jobs as they are in manipulating their criminal companies, we'd be in the EU by now."

Belgrade has been destroyed and rebuilt no fewer than forty times over the past two millennia; Serbia's geography is said to be "as lucky as a house in the middle of the road." The EU is the most recent in a long line of empires dismembering Serbia, a process the haughty Serbians find particularly painful. They scornfully referred to the "state union" of Serbia and Montenegro as "Solanium," named for Javier Solana, the EU foreign policy chief who imposed it. "The EU may finally have engaged here, but it's become more like too much of a good thing," a Serbian politician cynically retorted in his ornate office. "With Montenegro now independent, and maybe losing Kosovo, we are just a landlocked rump, economically senseless other than as a passageway for the Danube River."* To accept the inevitable and overcome their national trait of *enat*, a willingness to satisfy their collective ego at any cost, Serbians need both good leaders and good therapists. The conspicuously wealthy of Belgrade, proud of their prewar Parisian artistic connections, might become so jaded at being surrounded by EU members they once dominated—and still condescend to—that they might surrender as well. Serbia cannot last long as a hole in the European donut, as Switzerland has. As one economist in Belgrade pointed out, "We're still a decade away from having a European-class economy. To

---

*The EU is gradually seizing the reins of Kosovo from a panoply of UN agencies, elevating it from a place where Western consultants force-feed the Albanian diaspora's privatization agenda, Christian and Saudi missionaries compete for broken souls, and virtually all employment depends on servicing the UN-military-NGO complex. In Peć, bars and restaurants cater to thousands of UN staff, generating great profits for a desolate city, but no economy has been built to sustain Kosovo once the UN leaves. What the EU—and only the EU—does is devote far greater resources to building the capacity of local ministries, preparing Kosovo for statehood and EU membership, even over Serbian opposition.

enter the Eurozone now would be like installing a world-class kitchen in a dilapidated house."

"No philanthropic pope like George Soros has intervened here," a human rights activist lamented. By necessity, for many Serbians European pragmatism is replacing masochistic nationalism. The Central European second-world peer group of Poles, Czechs, and Hungarians is actively convincing Balkan leaders that European-style governance is good not just for the EU but for its own sake. Serbia is grudgingly emulating Slovenia and Slovakia: Pensions are starting to be paid on time, corrupt police are under pressure, and more students (even those without political connections) are getting university educations.[10] But as one investment promotion official worried, "seventy percent of the young people would still head to the West if they had valid passports." The EU's demanding agreements with Serbia are turning its infrastructure and geography into assets, however, with Fiat and Microsoft coming in to make it their regional hub. While Milošević's verbal tirades continued at The Hague, his party headquarters, once gutted by NATO missiles, was converted into a high-rise business center. A Serbian entrepreneur now tries to lure back diaspora men from Silicon Valley by promising a country full of beautiful, available women. "Since we lost so many brothers in the war, the odds are great!"

BOSNIA: HOMO BALCANICUS AND BRUCE LEE

Driving through parts of the former Yugoslavia still entails much of the maddening hilarity of antiquated nationalistic rituals depicted in the Italian film *Elvjs e Merilijn,* in which two aspiring Romanian actors brave their way through the Balkan war zone to reach a nightclub on the Adriatic. Checkpoints force bus passengers to sit on bridges in no-man's-land in the middle of the night just to stay on the same road. The shameful rhetorical question "This is Europe?" was once used to admonish Europe for its failure to intervene in Bosnia to save it from genocide and dismemberment. Today, "This is Europe" is a pithy statement of the only common denominator among countries that—despite a decade of genocidal conflict—still are not ethnically pure nation-states. As the EU fits the jigsaw pieces of the Balkans together into a meaningful picture, it is accelerating Bosnia's recovery from the bombed-out depths of the 1990s into a central node of Europe's eastward expansion.

The EU didn't break the Balkans, but it still has to buy it. Over the past decade, the EU has applied copious amounts of diplomatic glue to the shattered pot that is the Balkans, finally ending its psychological dependency on America for its internal military stability, which one scholar likened to "a person who uses crutches for an extended time after a serious injury."[11] But with half of Europe's deployable forces stationed in the southern Balkans, the EU's massive neocolonial apparatus—derisively termed the "European Raj"—also arrogated emergency powers, an act that came perilously close to political engineering, as it swiftly dismissed dozens of elected Bosnian Serb officials. To avoid the resentment of its future subjects, Europeans now realize that such bureaucratized trusteeship must henceforth be "avoided like the plague."[12]

But the future hasn't arrived yet, for Bosnia today still embodies a lurking tribalism. The Republika Srpska begins just six miles east of Sarajevo, outside of which a cold fog of fear still hangs in the air. Sarajevo remains the Bogotá of the Balkans, capital of a country divided by three rival factions, each well served by an opaque status quo. With competing criminal syndicates and paramilitaries providing health care and pensions to maintain loyalty, people are still unsure whom to trust; those now driving tractors were driving tanks just before. The furtive Serb war criminal Radovan Karadžić, the "Butcher of Bosnia," remains at large. "We want Europe to give us back control of our country, but not to *those* guys," remarked a Bosnian journalist inside the city's Holiday Inn, newly refurbished in bright yellow paint after years of shelling.

As one enters Sarajevo down winding mountain roads, pockmarked façades still face the hills from which Serbian sniper fire rained into main thoroughfares, part of Ratko Mladić's campaign to drive Bosnians into insanity and submission. The older generation of ex-Yugoslavians still holds a grudge at all levels, right down to pushing to change the language of inscriptions on Bosnia's national theater, currently written in Serbo-Croat Cyrillic. Meanwhile, due to uncertain ownership, the destroyed cinderblock endoskeleton of a shopping mall stands in ruins downtown. All Balkan economies have large deficits, high inflation, and no reliable employment data because so many people work in the nebulous gray market, with scores of Serbians, Croats, and Bosnians driving all the way to Iraq in search of contractor jobs. Modern buses weaving through Sarajevo's narrow streets are gifts of the EU or Japan.

In Sarajevo's old city, however, a generational renaissance is under way. Just steps from the bridge over the Miljacka River where Archduke Franz Ferdinand was assassinated in 1914, Sarajevo's young people party as if they were in Barcelona or Beirut. The thuggish looking *Homo balcanicus* revs up his muscle cars and motorcycles with European (likely stolen) license plates. The most common nonflashy vehicle is the Yugo, the dirt-cheap cult micro-car of the 1980s. Nightclubs blast techno music from basements into the streets, while outdoor café umbrellas advertising Red Bull make it clear what powers the city's youth. All the while, old hotel proprietors stand guard all night, groggily letting European tourists back inside until the early, misty morning. "It began like this not long after the war ended," recounted an engineer in an underground disco. "A lot of us went to Germany and other places to finish school, but we came back as soon as we could. We can't abandon Bosnia now that it's our job to rebuild it."

A statue of Bruce Lee—a symbol of fighting against ethnic divisions—now stands in Mostar near the reconstructed bridge whose destruction was the most powerful symbol of the nation's descent into hell. Mosques and churches are being rebuilt in every neighborhood of Sarajevo as the city attempts to reclaim its mantle as a "New Jerusalem." As a waitress in Mostar claimed, "We young people aren't hung up on Ottoman legacies anymore. We don't care about each other's religion—the way it used to be." The percentage of Serbs and Croats who see their future in Bosnia and Herzegovina has doubled, as has the number of people who believe that war will not break out again once the "European Raj" departs. Ten years after Dayton, Bosnia's government has replaced its tripartite constitution with a unified, nonethnic-based system more appropriate to a multiethnic European nation. Many restored buildings already fly the flag of the EU—which is more visible than Bosnia's own flag. The artificial currency of Bosnia, the "Konvertible Mark," will surely be replaced by the Euro. EU member-states do not need their own currencies.

But EU membership is not itself a cure, rather it is a certificate of health after the invisible hand of the EU's "Copenhagen criteria" of political, economic, and infrastructural reform have taken effect, connecting the various Balkan limbs to their new European heart. This machinery worked for Macedonia: A preventive peacekeeping deployment staved off spillover from the rest of Yugoslavia, and stabilization forces secured its borders to ensure independence. Using the strategy of a tough-minded football coach to rein in an unruly team, the EU is now imposing a stability pact on the *entire* southern Balkans to create another European subregional peer group—making clear that none will enter the EU until all are qualified.[13] "We are doing it the EU way now too," explained an expatriate Bosnian now running a Western NGO office. "We train the future political business leaders from each country *together*, not country by country."

The final components of this Marshall Plan–like program for Southeastern Europe are the repatriation of Bosnian and Kosovar refugees and new transportation networks from Austria to Albania.* The poorest country in Europe, Albania is still unknown to most Europeans except for news accounts of raftbound refugees crossing the Adriatic Sea to Italy, just like Haitians and Cubans to America. But before the architectural symbols of Greek and Venetian colonization could crumble, Europe came back to metamorphose Albania's once sheltered third-world Stalinist bureaucracy into an avatar of European modernity.[14] Following the EU's lead, investment is trickling into the country's marketplaces and vineyards, with tourists making it a hip holiday spot for quiet beaches and cheap beer. In the Balkans, the dubious border politics of *Elvjs e Merilijn* are gradually being replaced by high-speed German ICE trains. "If we can get here by train, it's Europe," quipped an Italian traveler.

But it is still roads that are stretching the frontier of Europe. Driving eastward from Budapest past Belgrade on newly constructed highways, one can fork south toward Skopje (Macedonia) and Thessaloniki (Greece) or east toward Sofia and Istanbul—routes all but mapped onto the Byzantine causeway that once linked Belgrade to Constantinople. This reconnection of roads west and east of the Drina River—which divided the Western Roman and Byzantine empires in the fourth century A.D.—is a major symbolic and historic step toward re-

---

*Infrastructure programs fall under the Community Assistance for Reconstruction, Development, and Stabilization (CARDS) framework.

gional reconciliation and the rise of a European commonwealth.[15] The road to the resolution of the Eastern Question is thus taking a turn none had predicted—quite literally: The final, crucial ingredient to Europeanizing the Balkans involves not only Greece but also Turkey—in cooperation. For centuries Europe has battled the Turks for control over the Balkans, and now they have united to save them.

CHAPTER 5

TURKEY:

MARCHING EAST AND WEST

VENUS WILLIAMS PLAYED tennis on it; David Coulthard drove a Formula One car across it. The Bosphorus Bridge—the seemingly wafer-thin mile-long suspension bridge opened in 1973 on the fiftieth anniversary of the founding of the Turkish republic—is *the* symbol of Istanbul and Turkey's unique position as the gateway connecting Europe and Asia.

Turkey occupies a space so vital that it destroys the idea of distinct continents. Constantinople was the capital of the Byzantine empire for eleven centuries, and then, as Istanbul, was the Ottoman seat of power over territories spanning the Balkans, Asia Minor, and Central Asia—reaching the gates of Vienna in 1687.* Straddling the narrow Dardanelles, it commands the east-west passage between Europe and Asia and the north-south passage between the Black and Mediterranean seas. During the Cold War, Turkey, once the Anatolian nucleus of the Ottoman empire, was NATO's eastern island—a forward base and lis-

---

*In 1071 the Turkic Seljuk armies demolished the Byzantines at the Battle of Manzikert and marched toward Constantinople. Byzantium's only reprieve came, ironically, from another Turkic conqueror, Timur, who countered the Seljuks in the east. So the only reason the Turkic world is not united is that it divided itself.

tening post. Along with Ukraine, on the north shore of the Black Sea, Turkey is one of Europe's two main prongs to the East, and the gateway to the world's principal danger zone of Syria, Iraq, and Iran. Turkey significantly amplifies Europe's strategic weight: If Europe does not find ways to leverage Turkey's strategic strengths, then its prospective eastern role effectively ends in the Balkans.

Turkey's importance begins in Bulgaria. With a population shrinking toward five million, Bulgaria is an EU member more in need of a strong mayor than a president. As a country, it is becoming a suburb of the huge city of Istanbul—an amalgamation that could be referred to as "Istanbulgaria"—which is already the major commercial hub dominating the region from Budapest to Baku. Turkish businessmen have spiced up Sofia's skyline by converting hotels into casinos for their own enjoyment. Beyond the border at Edirne begins Turkey's smooth TEM highway. Built as an emergency landing strip for NATO warplanes, it today boasts a parade of Mercedes and BMW caravans driven by Turks gleefully shuttling back and forth to Western Europe, resting for fresh snacks at "Turk stops" along the way.

Turkey is important not only for *where* it is but also for *what* it is: the most powerful, democratic, and secular state in the Muslim world.[1] As Prime Minister Recep Tayyip Erdoğan admonished in 2005, "Either [the EU] will show political maturity and become a global power, or it will end up a Christian club." That year, Turkey was granted approval to begin membership negotiations with the EU, signaling its readiness to become a true *métissage* of peoples and cultures.[2] It cannot be any other way, for the magnificent Hagia Sophia in Istanbul—first a Byzantine Christian church and then an Ottoman mosque—is still revered by Christians and Muslims alike. Istanbul's exotic boutiques, trendy galleries, and aromatic hammams (saunas) have made it the new Berlin, while the Kreuzberg district of Berlin is called "Little Istanbul." As a slick nightclub promoter in Istanbul boasted above blaring music, "A European DJ who hasn't spun in Istanbul isn't big-time." As Turkey becomes more European, Europe becomes more Turkish.

The key question today is whether there will be an alliance or perpetual tension between the European and neo-Ottoman civilizations. Turkey's relations with the EU have become far more civil since the Ottoman siege of Vienna, although size alone may prevent Turkey—

a country of close to seventy-five million people, significantly poorer than Europeans, on average—from ever becoming a full member of the EU. Yet form is far less important than function. When the European Community began accession dialogues with Turkey more than four decades ago, the focus was almost exclusively on bringing the Turkish economy in line; governance was not much discussed, and there was no common EU foreign policy. (This was NATO's duty anyway, and Turkey has long been a member of NATO.) But as the EU strives to pool its members' sovereignty, it will have to make its case to Turkey, not the other way around.

For a country that has fought wars with nearly all its neighbors, Turkish foreign policy today is a case study in irony. Before World War I, the Sublime Porte, as the Ottoman court was known, cleverly flirted with the German, British, Austro-Hungarian, Russian, and French ambassadors without committing to anyone. With Russian support, the Orthodox peoples of Greece, Serbia, and Bulgaria had ousted their Ottoman rulers by 1913. After World War I, Mustafa Kemal (designated "Atatürk" by the Turkish National Assembly in 1934), the founding father and secular prophet of the Turkish republic, pursued a strategy of "peace at home, peace abroad," the vision that animates Turkey's current "multidirectional" diplomacy, a high-wire act of simultaneously reconciling with Europe, America, Russia, the Caucasus, Iran, Syria, and Israel. Nearly a century after Atatürk led a rearguard war of liberation against the British-led invasion at Gallipoli, Britain is Turkey's leading champion for full EU membership. Even Greece favors Turkey's EU entry, hoping that accession will tame the Turks into abdicating their claims on northern Cyprus.[3]

"These are very tense times on our eastern frontiers, so we use globalization to get friendly with our Arab and Persian neighbors," explained a sophisticated Turkish diplomat in Ankara. Despite Arabs' traditional resentment of Turkey due to the Ottoman colonization, Turkish trade with Morocco, Libya, and Egypt has tripled in recent years. Turkey's recent foreign ministers have been fluent Arabic speakers, and Arabs envy Turkey's market economy status within Europe. "When Syrians and Lebanese want to make serious profits, they not only sell here but partner with us to re-export to Europe. We're much more professional and have the inside advantage over them," a young female entrepreneur in one of Istanbul's newest boutique hotels claimed. By Central Asian and Arab standards, Istanbul is certainly European enough. And another edge Turks have is that they are not the wretched Christian crusaders Arabs so detest. Indeed, Arabs and Turks view American interventionism as the new tyranny, not each other. "Arabs appreciate the Turks' blend of moralism and secularism," an Al-Jazeera correspondent in Istanbul explained. "Turkish and Arabic media are more widely translated than ever before, and we share skepticism of many Western policies. Arabs also know that their democratic deficit is what keeps them from living up to the Turkish model." Turkey also has long-standing diplomatic and military ties to Israel, which it recognized in 1949. In Farsi, the word *Turk* can mean "barbarian" or "vagabond," but billions in trade and energy agreements—in addition to a tacit accord to suppress Kurdish separatism—have boosted ties with Iran as well.

Turkey will look in all directions for friends—because it can. Turkey's maneuvers with Russia best demonstrate how it engages with any partner it wants, no matter what the United States or EU say.[4] For centuries Russia has attempted to control Turkey's Black Sea coast and seize the Dardanelles for access to the Mediterranean Sea. But now, the two countries have found common cause in the Blue Stream pipeline under the Black Sea that leads to Turkey's Samsun port. Russia has become Turkey's second-largest trading partner (behind the EU): Turkish construction companies are rebuilding the crumbling Russia, while Russian gas fuels the Turkish economy. At the rustic Black Sea entrepôt of Trabzon—captured by Russia in World War I— nobody keeps track of what comes on and off Russian yachts and other vessels in its scenic port such as the Slavic "Natashas" ferried in and trafficked as far as Dubai.

"Both America and Europe should know better than to patronize us," an Istanbul intellectual confidently declared while sipping the country's signature coffee. "We can deny both of them what they want, without regrets." The United States and the EU played tug of war for Turkish loyalty in the 1990s, but the Iraq War of 2003 dramatically tipped the scale in Europe's favor. America presumed Turkey's support for the Iraq invasion, but Turkey's parliament rejected America's request for basing rights, fearing Kurdish nationalism in a post-Saddam Iraq, foreign troops on its territory, and the loss of tourism revenues.[5] While America was locked into an outdated habit of relying on the

Turkish military, Turkey's civilian leadership was focused on implementing EU benchmarks of democratic accountability. The Turkish paranoia over the Iraq War suddenly verged on the surreal: In *Metal Storm,* a bestselling Turkish thriller that appeared in 2005, the Turkish secret agent protagonist detonates a nuclear weapon over Washington to avenge America's occupation of Turkey. Since that time, U.S.-Turkish relations have lapsed into banalities about "strategic partnership," while Turkey's total annual trade with the EU is ten times greater than that with the United States.[6] "Americans think their EU lobbying on our behalf has driven our membership prospects, but all it's really done is make the Europeans more stringent," an Ankara-based analyst complained. "We don't want America's backing anymore." The EU ultimately had more influence on Turkey than it did on some of its own members who supported the U.S. invasion of Iraq.*

Europe has surpassed the United States in the Turkish mind—but winning Turkey itself is a far more epic challenge. Though Atatürk claimed that the Turkish republic was forever marching on a "steady course . . . from the East to the West," during the Cold War west was the only direction for Turks to march. But Turkey once again has the region's most formidable military—and knows it. "Since Ottoman times, we have been the ones who define the political geography of the entire region. We dominated Iraq for four hundred years," a Turkish general in Ankara stridently pointed out. "Turkey will never be as pliant as Poland." The new "Young Turks" of the policy elite have also rediscovered their pre-republican past, magnifying their self-awareness. This neo-Ottoman indifference to the West limits how far Turkey is willing to bend socially, politically, and diplomatically. Some Turks are instead seriously and vocally contemplating a "Plan B"—seeking not EU membership but rather only a "privileged partnership" like Britain or Russia, who converge with the EU only when it suits their interests.

Having floated in the limbo of EU accession since 1963, Turkey can teach other EU aspirants the virtue of patience. But even without membership, its economy has already benefited enormously from four decades of trade and migration through Europe's customs union. In the

---

* As one Bulgarian intellectual observed, "Eastern European positions during the Iraq War were a victory of convenience over the consciousness of geographic belonging, but in the long run this geography will be the stronger factor."

early days of the European accession path, Turkish peasants and farmers wore blazers in the fields to proffer their European ethos, and the country has voted strongly in favor of keeping the process on track. The first generation of illiterate *Gastarbeiter* sent their remittances back home to their Anatolian villages, but the second generation of European Turks have become employers themselves, spreading their wealth and their skills back home by building factories and schools. In the central Anatolian province of Kayseri, warehouses churn out large stocks of fine *kilims* (rugs) to augment the region's agriculture.[7] The current, third-generation Turkish diaspora has spread from Berlin to Bishkek, sending back significant funds, which help reduce Turkey's income inequality (which, alongside those of Brazil, China, and the United States, is the highest in the world). "We have so much stability now that even as a migrant people, we look forward to wandering home," a German Turk mused while resting on the drive from Ankara to Kayseri. Indeed, the Turkish economy is now bounding toward self-sustainability.

It took all of Europe to subdue the Turks in the seventeenth century, and with Turkish horizons again spanning all directions, the EU will have to become not only an economic anchor for Turkey but a psychological and political one as well. Turkish pride makes this an extremely delicate challenge. It is said that the first ten times one slaps a Turk, he'll do nothing; the eleventh time, he'll kill you. Indeed, European visitors who claim to come from "Europe" rather than a specific country should beware of getting smacked, for Turkey already *is* a European country—and then some. In Bodrum, Turkish jet-setters condescend to drunken Europeans on their beaches, sealing themselves off in classy enclaves nestled along quaint Aegean inlets. "Turkey's intelligentsia is too busy enjoying the Aegean Sea to worry about influencing European public opinion," a newspaper columnist sarcastically wrote one fine summer day not long ago. Well-to-do Turks in Istanbul already enjoy the accoutrements of European life and education, often owning second homes elsewhere in Europe.

For all the Turks' self-confidence, however, Europe's invisible colonization of Turkey continues apace. As with America's Pentagon, an EU Commission program, once created, is almost impossible to stop. Though President Jacques Chirac of France declared in 2005 that Turkey would require a "cultural revolution" to become European, the commission has unswervingly carried out its mandate to lobotomize the Turkish state. Turkey may have shamed Europe into taking it seriously in the late 1990s, but in response, the EU has insisted that Turkey swallow the full letter—all thirty-five chapters, four more than any other country—of the *acquis communautaire*, without even guaranteeing membership at the end of the road. In the early nineteenth century, the Ottoman vizier Mustafa Reşid Pasha attempted to mimic European administration, but today the EU has imposed a massive restructuring of the (quite literally) Byzantine systems for banking and public services, helping to clean up the country's massive black market and indecisive business culture while backing many of its biggest commercial ventures. Istanbul's glittering skyline was built with European money, and EU regulations have raised Turkish labor standards and product quality. This "tough love" approach to catalyzing Turkish reform is far superior to America's strategy for the transformation of Mexico—a Turkey of its own.

"Geographically we belong to Europe . . . but politically?" fretted the Nobel Prize–winning author Orhan Pamuk while on trial for criticizing Turkey's World War I genocide of Armenians, which falls under the set of crimes labeled "insulting Turkishness."[8] Europe has in fact quietly accelerated a monumental internal debate among Turks over their political history, with regard to both Turkey's treatment of Armenians and the eventual reunification of Cyprus. "It's really impossible to say how long it would have taken for universities to offer more subjects or to offer women more high-status positions if it were not for EU pressure," observed a female social activist in Istanbul. The granting of greater rights for Kurds and non-Muslim groups was undoubtedly the single most controversial demand made by the EU. After two decades of ruthless conflict between Turkish military forces and the separatist Kurdistan Workers Party (PKK), mostly located in southeastern Turkey, which borders on Iraq, the ten to twelve million Kurds spread across Turkey have experienced improved social, economic, and political integration through progressive government programs. High unemployment is still a fact of life in the largely Kurdish peasant–populated Diyarbakir district, where riots flared up around the Kurdish celebration of Nowrūz in 2006. But military roads once used to attack the PKK are being extended to improve trade relations with Syria and Iran, ultimately benefiting Kurdish farmers. Turkey's abolition of the death penalty—even for Kurdish terrorist mastermind Abdullah Öcalan—

would have taken decades if not for the EU incentives that made the Turkish debate as political as it was emotional, whereas before it was entirely emotional.

At the Atatürk mausoleum in Ankara, soldiers perform a grand and lengthy goose-stepping changing of the guard that symbolizes unwavering loyalty to one of the rare world leaders respected as much abroad as at home. As the repository of Kemalism, the military has several times exercised its capacity for divine intervention, most recently staging a "postmodern coup" to oust the anti-Western and pro-Islamic Necmettin Erbakan in 1997.[9] But Turkey's politicians have come to match the military in their professionalism, and with EU backing they have even subdued the military such that the National Security Council is headed by a civilian and has a majority civilian membership. Today both the elite in Turkey, whether civilian or military, considers itself the indispensable modernizers—checking each other and Islamist tendencies in Turkish society. And most important, secular elites, military chiefs, and Islamists *all* view Europeanization as more important than the military's right to intervene in politics.[10] The EU helps Turkey tame itself.

At the same time, Turkey remains the best model of how Islam and modernity can not only coexist but thrive. In Konya, whirling dervishes perform their hypnotic *mevlevi sema* dance honoring the Sufi mystic poet Rumi. Spinning in trances of revelation, they are a reminder that spiritual forces pull *within* Turkey as strongly as geography pulls it in two directions. Turks have tried to define an interpretation of Turkic Islam independent of Sunni-Shi'a divides, pledging to remain Turks first and Muslims second.[11] Turkey's population is widely shaped by Alevi- and Sufi-dominated Islamic variants, each of which cherishes the secularism that Atatürk enforced and has been maintained even by the Sunni Islamist but staunchly pro-European Justice and Development Party (AKP), whose many intellectual members refer to themselves not as "reformed Islamists" but as "conservative democrats," proving their democratic credentials time and again, most recently in the country's soul-searching 2007 parliamentary elections.[12] Wearing a veil is now illegal for women in government offices and universities, a move otherwise taken only by France. Turkey is both one of the world's largest lingerie manufacturers and a leading designer of modest Islamic swimwear. When the mosque's call to prayer sounds during a football match, restaurant patrons simply turn the television volume way up. These three trends in Turkish society—development, democratization, and modern Islam—are precisely the ones America and Europe wish they had the capacity to pursue in the Arab world so coherently.

But the growing Islamist cultural movement in Turkish society is real, with constituencies ranging from the crowded and energized *gecekondu* shantytowns of Istanbul—the support base of former Istanbul mayor and now prime minister Recep Tayyip Erdoğan—to the country's vast and rural east. Eastward from Konya, culture and landscape blend from European to Asian. Wheat fields, melon stands, roadside car repair shacks, stray cattle, and strewn trash are all signs of this other, far larger Turkey. As one drives along endless rows of skinny trees, the tractor replaces the automobile as the mode of intra-village transport, melodic truck horns echo to Central Asia, and street names are both unknown and irrelevant. Many women wear headscarves, several hundred honor killings are reported each year, and the angular Seljuk forts and mosques hark back to a more austere time in westward Turkic migrations.

This massive eastern flank of pine forests and placid lakes is Turkey's strategic protrusion, a geopolitical asset Europe cannot do without. Europe increasingly needs Turkey, both as a Eurasian energy bridge to carry Russian, Caspian, and Iranian oil and gas to the Balkans and as a stabilizer in the Caucasus. But even as the government constructs marvelous bridges and tunnels through walls of rock to unite all corners of the Turkish state, Turkey's geography and culture dictate that it will never belong exclusively to Europe. The European superpower must become a Euro-Turkish superpower.

THE BLACK SEA: EUROPE'S LAKE

For centuries Russian, Ottoman, and Persian imperial aspirations have flowed into the Black Sea, finding their confluence in its dark, serene waters. Crimea's most important archaeological site, the ancient Roman outpost of Chersonesos, now a suburb of Sebastopol, derives its name from the Greek word for "peninsula" and is the site of Prince Vladimir the Great's baptism into Christianity in 988, after which the Byzantine empire faded, only to watch Orthodoxy spread to Kiev and Moscow. Even the Genoese ruled cosmopolitan Crimea briefly in the fourteenth century. In the Middle Ages, the Black Sea was the center of world commerce, linking Venice to the Mongol and Turkic tribes of Central Asia. During its three hundred years under Ottoman control, European merchants referred to the Black Sea as a "Turkish lake." But in the nineteenth century, it was thrust into the geopolitical vortex: European powers initially sought to dismember the Ottoman empire for control of the Bosphorus Strait, but after Russia under Nicholas I devastated the Ottoman fleets, Britain, France, and Austria rushed to prevent the sea from becoming the "Russian lake." The Crimean War thus became the western front of the Anglo-Russian "Great Game" in Central Asia.[13]

The Black Sea today has been described as the Bermuda Triangle of strategic analysis, sitting on the edge of European, Eurasian, and Near Eastern security spaces without being central to any of them.[14] Yet an organic and multifaceted unity among Black Sea nations is being restored—this time within the European commonwealth. Kiev's Maidan Square, for example, where the Orange Revolution was staged, takes its name from the Farsi term for a multifunctional space for festivals and trade. Crimea remains home to almost one million Tatars, descendants of the Mongol horde, the Volga Bulgars, and the Turkic tribes who spread through the Volga and Don river basins—but also related to the many Tatars of the Crimean Khanate who crossed the Black Sea to Turkey after Crimea was annexed by

Russia. Ukraine's other Black Sea port, Odessa, built in the nineteenth century by international architects and aristocracy from France, Austria, and England, is once again a place where contraband flows in from Western Europe and out as far as the Far East, underscoring the restoration of its prime geography.

Indeed, a rising share of Europe's energy imports come from east of the Black Sea. In a thinly veiled effort to undermine Russian influence in the region and resurrect a sense of camaraderie, Georgia, Ukraine, Uzbekistan, Azerbaijan, and Moldova formed a regional diplomatic group in the mid-1990s, one that, with the loss of Uzbekistan, now carries the unfortunate acronym GUAM. A more strategically relevant effort has emerged in the form of the Black Sea Economic Cooperation (BSEC) group, which includes Romania, Bulgaria, Ukraine, Turkey, Georgia, and Azerbaijan. Trade is growing rapidly across the Black Sea's waters, with Turkey investing over $2 billion annually in the Ukrainian economy, helping to revive its faltering shipbuilding industry. With the incremental Europeanization of its littoral nations, the Black Sea is now becoming a "European lake" whose eastern shores lead the West into the Caucasus.

CHAPTER 6

THE CAUCASIAN CORRIDOR

THE CAUCASUS SEEMS an almost negligible extension of Anatolia, a bumpy strip between the Black and Caspian seas forever overshadowed by the looming Turkish, Russian, and Persian empires. But securing the West's new arteries of oil from the Caspian Sea and Central Asia requires all but colonizing the region's otherwise hopeless post-Soviet micro-republics of Georgia, Armenia, and Azerbaijan through which they pass. Europeans have been slow to capitalize on the lack of internal direction in the Caucasus, aware of the scale of change required in countries whose levels of development and corruption put them closer to the third world than the first. Whereas Europe's democratization strategy historically *was* its enlargement strategy, the Copenhagen criteria were also intended to reassure existing EU members that no unqualified countries—such as those from the Caucasus—would be admitted. "We also let the aesthetics of geography dictate our thinking," a European diplomat admitted. "Whatever lies on the other side of Turkey was out of sight and out of mind." The Caucasus is where the un-West begins.

Yet as the need to secure Caspian energy takes precedence over the distant prospect of EU membership, the West is drastically re-vamping its approach to the Caucasus to elevate it from its status as a fractured playground of Russian neo-imperialism. In the early 1990s, European and American diplomats actually trusted Russia to manage the post-Soviet space fairly, as even a residual great power should. That time has passed. With its own empire shattered, Russia has proved far better at dismembering its former republics than rebuilding a genuine Commonwealth of Independent States (CIS). Russia refers to the countries of the Caucasus as its "communal apartment"—code for a region where it can continue to wash the dirty laundry of the grand strategy it knows best: *divide et impera*. Russia provokes conflict and then intervenes, claiming it is the only power capable of separating these squabbling children to keep the peace. To break this cycle, the West's new gamble is to make the Caucasus part of Europe's "Near Abroad" rather than Russia's. If it succeeds, the Caucasus nations will have risen out of the third world, and Western energy security will be that much closer to assured.

GEORGIA: ON EUROPE'S MIND

Imagine a country of abandoned villages, collapsed buildings, battered trucks belching clouds of foul exhaust, women selling corn on the roadside, children bathing in drying riverbeds, and haggard beggars in the capital city. Now imagine that its citizens are white.

For all the rhetoric of reversed fortunes, revolutions reveal far more about how broken a society is than about how ingrained its virtues are. Nowhere is this more apparent than in Georgia, a country whose lead-ership is so convinced it is Western that is does almost nothing to prove it. Georgians may be Christian, but they are not European in any meaningful sense—no matter how relentlessly they fly the EU flag across the capital city, Tbilisi. Their country is at best a Caucasian Cuba of palm trees and bovine slalom driving on tire-puncturing roads. Also, unlike in the comparably sized Baltic countries, the lustration of Georgia's breathtakingly self-serving elders left behind a government of underaged and unprepared neophytes. Like Ukraine and Serbia—and most assuredly any other country that may experience sudden regime change in the coming years—Georgia's electoral democracy

will translate into a liberal state at best slowly, with human rights violations, market manipulation, and crony governance persisting until the
incentives to alter such behavior become overwhelming. The Europeans' well-justified fear for Georgia is that it will experience "revolutionary fatigue" like its third-world counterparts in Latin America,
which do not evolve so much as spin around in a cycle of underdevelopment and instability.

The Soviets were actually the kindest of Georgia's occupiers, particularly when compared to the rampaging Arabs, Mongols, and Persians who came before them. Joseph Stalin, born and raised in the
central Georgian town of Gori, ensured that his republic, which suffered heavily in World War II, paid low taxes and was treated like the
jewel in the Soviet crown. In the 1990s, the regime of Eduard Shevardnadze was both a full-blown welfare case for European aid and an
unlimited sinkhole of corruption. "Because Shevardnadze, as the last
Soviet foreign minister, gifted us the reunification of Germany, we allowed him a very long leash afterwards, supporting him handsomely," a
German diplomat confessed. Georgia was a country where there were
three ways to get by: selling stolen goods on the black market, driving a
taxi, or smuggling—or some combination of the three. In Gori, people
still move around in Asian-style three-wheel scooter-rickshaws.

In the first years after the 2003 "Rose Revolution," things hardly
improved. With no functioning businesses, villages became ghost
towns of shattered glass and jagged concrete blocks. Good roads make
better citizens, and to this day there is not a single decent road in all of
Georgia, a metaphor for the country's governance: bruising and pierc-
ing. The young president—dapper and American-educated Mikheil
Saakashvili—shut down many independent newspapers, TV stations,
and NGOs that opposed his policies. Whereas under Shevardnadze
judges could be bribed to be impartial, under Saakashvili cases were
all but preemptively decided in the government's favor. The previously
nonexistent post of prime minister was created to reward the second of
three Rose Revolution protagonists, Zurab Zhvania. But a rivalry between Saakashvili and Zhvania resulted not only in the government
being split into two halves, with one site controlling Georgia's security
apparatus and the other its economy—but in Zhvania's death under
mysterious circumstances as well. When legislation introduced by the
parliament contradicted the wishes of the president, the latter pre-

vailed without fail. Georgia does not have real political parties, only interest groups with "gov.ge" e-mail addresses. No wonder so many people wax nostalgic about Communism.

Whenever governments champion leaders over institutions, the people lose. Preoccupied with securing its token troop contributions for the Iraq War, America steadfastly retained its bias in favor of Saakashvili's "ready, fire, aim" sham democracy, thus remaining politically blind to the deteriorating reality on the ground. "America was so confident in the Rose Revolution's success," one political activist in Tbilisi vented, "that our human rights groups no longer get funding from American agencies." Saakashvili was actually groomed by the very predecessor he overthrew, and he has even trained cadres of "Young Pioneers," children who go to camps to learn loyalty through firing Kalashnikovs. Ministers still shuffle as if in a game of musical chairs, resembling, as one Georgian analyst angrily remarked, "a zoo where not all the animals have been domesticated."

To be sure, it is not easy to govern a country where only the wine industry survived Soviet management. For fifteen centuries Tbilisi has been the dominant metropolis, but center-periphery relations have always been tense.* Before fleeing to Moscow in 2004, Aslan Abashidze, the warlord of the Turkish border port-region of Ajara, drained all customs revenues and even tried to spark a civil war (with Russian backing). At the same time, Saakashvili siphoned scarce electricity to Tbilisi to keep its residents content and also banned any independent contest for mayor of the capital, appointing a close ally instead. To generate start-up cash for his government, Saakashvili opted to shake down and blackmail rich businessmen, intimidating them into funding public services in exchange for the taxes they never paid. In the center of Tbilisi, one well-connected corporation bribed refugees to vacate a choice property, which it then converted into an office. In Georgia, boutiques and hotels are mere fronts for money laundering, with briefcases of cash picked up like clockwork each morning by mafia henchmen. In Tbilisi one sees firsthand that the world's most coveted status symbol is undoubtedly the black Mercedes with tinted windows—

---

*In the Caucasus, each state is experiencing a phase of "gathering lands"—repeating the efforts of a century earlier at the fall of the Ottoman empire—aimed at defining their borders, shoring up stability, and becoming something akin to coherent states. Revaz Gachechiladze, *The New Georgia: Space, Society, Politics*, Eastern European Studies no. 3 (London: University College London Press, 1995).

often still with its original German plates. Over time, Georgian corruption may decrease and tax collection and police enforcement improve, but this will require a very strong outside hand, not a laissez-faire belief in the virtues of so-called revolutions.

"To hell with the Russians!" fumed Saakashvili, frustrated with Russia's constant support for secessionist movements within Georgia. It was more of a plea to the United States and Europe to repulse Russian meddling and minimize Georgia's own role as a crossroads for weapons trafficking and weapons-grade uranium smuggling. On the Georgia-Azerbaijan border now stands a hulking, U.S.-funded customs post with space-age technology to interdict radioactive material—but it is not enough to overturn Russia's persistent intrusions, including even the littering of undetonated missiles near Tbilisi. With the loss of Ukraine and Georgia, Russia is left with only a narrow Black Sea littoral made even less strategic now that Azerbaijan has ended the flow of oil to the Russian port of Novorossiysk. By dismantling OSCE monitoring missions, giving Russian passports to South Ossetians, and backing a separatist movement in Georgia's northwest coastal province of Abkhazia, Russia is trying to splinter Georgia to maintain military reach to Armenia, which it is backing in its conflict with Azerbaijan over the disputed territory of Nagorno-Karabakh. And through phony front companies, Russia continues to exploit Georgia's gold, copper, and timber resources, drastically retarding the revenues necessary to keep this already tiny country from separating even further. When Georgia called on Russia to vacate its military bases, Russia responded by doubling natural-gas prices—in the middle of winter—the same Gazprom blackmail Ukrainians have also suffered. "For a small country it is exceptionally dangerous to be the neighbor of a large, powerful country," explains Georgian scholar Alexander Rondeli. "If a small country commits a strategic error, that is not a mere luxury but can be suicidal; diplomacy is virtually the only instrument of foreign policy available."[1]

But Russia's dominance of the region could still collapse under its own weight. Despite finally quelling the insurgency in Chechnya, Russia has yet to legitimize its rule in the broader Muslim-populated northern Caucasus region and the republic of Tatarstan, which with Europe's largest mosque in Kazan remains a permissive environment for anti-Russian sentiment.[2] The fierce Chechen character captured in Tolstoy's *Hadji Murat* has sabotaged Russia throughout history—and may yet return. "They have tried to co-opt Chechnya," observed a Georgian diplomat, citing the grand mosque Russia recently built in Grozny, just slightly smaller than that of Kazan. "But Russia never retreats the easy way, always choosing instead to make things more difficult for itself."

A sphere of influence is a sphere of responsibility, meaning that Western energy security and democratization strategies must come together to build another European subregion in the Caucasus—and to accelerate Russia's retreat. Through the 1990s, energy companies were the West's main representatives in the Caucasus, serving as self-interested but strategically backed commercial diplomats. They brokered the "deal of the century," as it was then called: the Baku-Tbilisi-Ceyhan (BTC) pipeline, the second longest in the world, built mostly underground to avoid sensitive areas (including circumventing Armenia altogether) and making Turkey, on whose Mediterranean shore the pipeline ends, a conduit for close to 10 percent of the world's oil.[3] At the inauguration of the BTC pipeline in 2005, Saakashvili declared it a geopolitical victory for Azerbaijan, Georgia, and the West "that will seriously change the balance of power in the region, bringing prosperity and strengthening independence."[4] With a $4 billion price tag, the thousand-mile BTC pipeline is a small price to pay to secure the Caucasus for the West.

Mighty Turkish eighteen-wheelers now clog the Georgian border near Batumi—a city where Georgians have absconded with the manhole covers and sold them as scrap metal to China. The EU is coming to the rescue—through Turkey—with a multibillion-euro transport corridor scheme reaching to Asia. With linked Georgian and Turkish railroads, cargo from Europe can be transported via Istanbul to Baku and across the Caspian Sea on ferries to Kazakhstan and, eventually, to China—and in the reverse direction as well. Georgia condescends to Turkey, hoping that a visa-free alliance with Ukraine will allow it to bypass Turkey in the EU line, but to secure its alliance with the West, Georgia desperately needs Turkey to aid BTC pipeline security and to displace murky Russian firms.

"Now that the West's energy security depends on our strategic position, it will have to help us get control of the country," a Georgian government adviser declared in an office refurbished with EU funds. To remove the shattered debris of Sovietism and build a new Georgia from scratch will continue to cost billions, but now Europe has no choice.

The BTC pipeline makes Georgia's economy an appendage of Azerbaijan's, allowing it to benefit from the spillover effects in the transport, communications, hotel, and catering industries (much like in third-world special economic zones). Georgian banks now operate courtesy of the International Finance Corporation (IFC), while the United States and the World Bank spend close to $100 million annually to buy electricity seasonally from Russia and build roads and gas refineries.

It is common to refer to the long-standing conflicts resulting from Soviet-imposed demographic schizophrenia as "frozen," a very inconvenient fiction that encourages diplomatic apathy. The Caucasus today is like the Balkans a decade earlier: The cessation of hostilities will bring nothing more than the illusion of stability unless the West actively intervenes. The Abkhazia, South Ossetia, and Nagorno-Karabakh disputes will not resolve themselves through divine de-escalation; instead, they will continue to lead to popular alienation, widespread armament, illicit smuggling, and the rising influence of radical Islamism. New nationalisms lie scarcely beneath the surface in the Caucasus, based on the church in Georgia, the Ottoman genocide in Armenia, and, potentially, Islam in Azerbaijan—and all are perversely used to justify inflating military budgets.[5] The still not delimited Caspian Sea is becoming militarized as well, with Russia boosting its shipbuilding industry in the Caspian port of Astrakhan in the delta of its mighty Volga River and proposing a naval patrol force with Iran.

Only by deploying peacekeeping missions to all of these supposedly "frozen" conflict areas can NATO and the EU definitively put an end to Russian and Iranian meddling. NATO has brought Georgia and Azerbaijan together into interoperable military units for pipeline protection, and it has funded the upgrading of Azerbaijan's coast guard for potential interdictions of suspicious Russian or Iranian traffic. The EU is gradually pushing the region toward the Trans-Caucasian federative model that existed briefly a century ago between the Russian Revolution and Bolshevik consolidation. Samuel Huntington suggested the interminability of conflict between Christian Georgia and Armenia and the Muslim states that surround them—but oil is proving to be thicker than blood, as America and the EU offer military assistance, pipelines, and roads to be the ties that can bind all of them. If Georgia's borders are reinforced, then its leadership will have no more excuses to forestall cleaning up its act. As Prime Minister Zurab Noghaideli confessed mat-

ter-of-factly, "Building a better state is 90 percent of the solution."
Georgia can become an anchor of Western energy security rather than a
corrupt liability.

With Russia playing hopscotch among a dwindling number of
bases, the West has a golden opportunity to displace it as Armenia's
protector as well.[6] Perennially unstable and recently even weathering
armed attacks on its parliament, Armenia has survived since independence on investment from Russia, Iran, and its diaspora (especially in
California).[7] But rather than enduring the uncertainty of Russia-Geor-
gia standoffs, normalizing relations with Turkey could open its western
borders to greater EU engagement and gain it symbolic access to its sacred Mount Ararat, which lies in Turkey. Securing Georgia and Armenia could eventually force even Russia and Iran into a broader Black
and Caspian seas energy framework.* Even in the places Europe least
wants to go, expansion serves its interests.

AZERBAIJAN: UNCORKING THE CASPIAN

The Caucasus is the meeting point of Europe's East and Asia's West.†
Latin inscriptions carved by Roman centurions show that Azerbaijan
has been Europe's frontier since the first century A.D.—but the Romans also turned back, declaring that no one could live in the hell of
the Gobustan Desert. After the pleasant descent from the forests of
the southern Caucasus near the Georgian border, reaching the capital,
Baku, whose name aptly means "solar winds," requires crossing one
hundred miles of scorching terrain. But sandwiched between Russia's
Caucasus and Iran's Talysh mountain ranges, Azerbaijan is the final in-

---

* The BTC pipeline has even deepened ties between the Caucasus nations and Israel, for a 20 percent (and rising) share of Israel's oil comes via the circuitous route from the Caspian Sea to Ceyhan and is shipped to Israel—which plans to reexport some of it via the Red Sea to the Far East.

† In the opening passage of the melancholy trans-Caucasian love story *Ali and Nino,* a schoolteacher in Baku
declares, "The eastern border of Europe goes through the Russian Empire, along the Ural mountains, through
the Caspian Sea, and through Transcaucasia. . . . Some scholars look on the area south of the Caucasian Mountains as belonging to Asia, while others, in view of Transcaucasia's cultural evolution, believe that this country
should be considered part of Europe. It can therefore be said, my children, that it is partly your responsibility as
to whether our town should belong to progressive Europe or to reactionary Asia." Kurban Said, *Ali and Nino.*
Though it has become conventional wisdom that Lev Nussenbaum, a Jewish émigré from Baku, was the pseu-
donymous author of *Ali and Nino,* recent historical investigation has yielded an alternate potential author, the
Azeri diplomat Yusuf Vezir Cemenzeminli.

gredient in the strategic recipe to make Europe an alliance of shared interest, not just culture.[8] Europe will fulfill its geographic imperative only if it can accommodate people with Asiatic souls.

Azerbaijan is the new frontier of the West but still feels almost nothing like it. Medieval mosques, hulking Soviet-era apartment blocks, and glass office towers are all symbols of Baku's merger of East and West, of the past and present. Silk and spice caravan routes once flourished, linking the Turkic, Arab, Indian, and Sinic worlds through Baku, Tabriz, Samarkand, and Kabul; the shrines of the Talysh Mountains resemble those of Kashmir. "Our country is in shape and culture like a bird that needs the wings of both East and West to fly properly," mused an Azeri historian. Azerbaijan's national flag incorporates green for Islam, red for freedom, and blue for the Turkic tribes. In 1918, Azerbaijan became the first democratic Muslim state, even granting its cultured, modern women the vote. Though its eight million citizens are mostly Shi'a, what Turkic nationalism imbued—and Soviet atheism imposed—was a strongly secular character. More girls than boys are in school in Azerbaijan, and in downtown Baku, a Soviet-era statue of a woman liberating herself from the veil still stands—directly in front of the Iranian National Bank.

But while women in Baku wear miniskirts, in nearby Nardaran they are often veiled, and Islamic graffiti is emblazoned on many walls. As in Turkey, Islamist revivalism is palpable around Azerbaijan, the result of the removal of the Soviet yoke, the presence of Chechen refugees, and Iran's funding of mosques and media in the poorer southern areas on its border, which are often the only signs of development. "The solution to radical Islam is for us to teach genuine Islam in schools under government supervision like in Turkey," a graduate student in Baku suggested. "Otherwise the first exposure many unemployed and vulnerable youth have to Islam comes at a radical mosque, like in Arab countries."

Zbigniew Brzezinski has called Azerbaijan the "cork in the Caspian bottle."[9] Baku has had oil and gas deposits for millennia: As far back as the fifth century B.C., fire worshippers built shrines near the Caspian shore. By the early twentieth century, Baku was the world's largest producer and exporter of oil, with Russia meddling in the dealings of the Nobels and Rothschilds. Russia later tightly controlled Azeri oil, which constituted as much as 70 percent of Soviet production, and soon after

Azeri independence cooperated with Armenia in an attempt to topple the nationalist leader Abulfez Elchibey.[10] Soviet-era petroleum spas remain the lasting benefit from the decades of Russian subjugation, still providing sweet crude bathing to cure bodily ills.

At the same time, Azerbaijan is one of the only places in the world where pollution is a tourist attraction. Baku's Caspian mini-peninsula is the site of hulking scaffoldings of rusting pipes occupying a space so vast that the government still has little idea what to do with them besides minimize the leakage and sell helicopter rides to similarly abandoned offshore oil rigs in the Caspian. Nonetheless, Azerbaijan is once again praying to the energy gods—literally. Perched above the rusting oil derricks on the Caspian shore is the Bibi Heybat mosque, the only one sponsored by the Azerbaijani government itself. Its special significance is that it was destroyed by Stalin, after which the republic's oil production fell. In Baku, the monument to Marx is now an Azpetrol station.

Some Azeris speak of wanting to build their country into the "Kuwait of the Caucasus." As the source of an increasing share of Europe's oil supply, it is already the richest country in the Caucasus. The customs minister who opened the "six-star" Excelsior hotel might as well have called it the "Burj Baku," after the sail-shaped hotel in Dubai. The same class of European architects and oil barons who built the center of Baku in the late nineteenth century has returned to build mansions on the city's looming but slippery cliffs, and orderly suburban developments have sprouted.

But Azerbaijan was blessed with oil, not wisdom. The question is whether it can accumulate the latter before it runs out of the former sometime in the next two decades. Azerbaijan still functions under a political order that was created by and for one man: Heydar Aliyev. The former head of the KGB and the first and only Muslim in the Politburo, he was an oversized leader for a tiny country and thus naturally came to represent, even eclipse, its national character. Succession provided the only opportunity for a genuine paradigm shift in Azeri governance. Upon Aliyev's death, the hereditary handover to his son Ilham was followed by mock elections to ratify the obvious. "Who won the 2003 election actually depends on whom you ask," an opposition figure protested, perpetually agitating to corral both domestic and foreign supporters. Ubiquitous posters of Aliyev *père et fils*—in which father

Heydar stresses independence, sovereignty, and heroism, while son Ilham emphasizes wealth and development—project a transition toward national stability. But this is mere window dressing. Members of the reactionary old guard are difficult to ease out of positions of authority and possess the knowledge of how to run a government that younger officials lack. The airport code for Baku very much remains "GYD" after father Heydar, a metaphor for how Azerbaijan remains very much his country, even posthumously.

"Corruption is the moral equivalent of war, sucking the lifeblood of Azerbaijan," complained an expatriate Azeri businessman, echoing many other well-meaning members of the diaspora. It is precisely the orderliness of travel agencies and exchange bureaus in Baku that makes them feel corrupt: If everything is so organized, then surely a hidden hand lurks somewhere. Most of the thirty richest Azeris are ministers or members of parliament (as in Iran, they are called the Majlis). The only political competition among them comes in the form of consumerist oneupmanship: how much one paid for an official position, the number of villas one built, the size of one's mansion in London, where money is spirited away into legitimate-sounding companies. Everyone has a story as to how the police force came to drive brand-new BMWs. (Hint: It was not a generous donation from Germany.) The Aliyev dynasty itself makes compromises to suit the moment. The official trade in caviar was banned to protect the dwindling sturgeon stock, but this only made smuggling that much more profitable for Ilham's cronies. Robust deference to nepotistic practices is natural in the Arab-Turkic-Oriental worlds; double standards are the reigning modus operandi. Indeed, the very intensity of cultural corruption remains an excuse to justify it. "Children do not plan for retirement," lamented one Azeri diplomat over dinner in an outdoor garden filled with Baku elites. "Your uncle may be a bad guy, but he is still your mother's brother." In cosmopolitan Baku, families continue to bribe officials to secure slots at the top schools for their children, who in turn pay bribes to graduate without studying.

Yet how the Azeri government manages energy income will determine whether the country follows the Norwegian model of oil-sponsored development or is struck—like Nigeria—by the "resource curse" and remains a Russian-style petrocratic state in which the oil and banking sectors overlap and the government-oligarchy nexus manipulates markets to cash in on high oil prices and currency revaluations.* There has been little effort to develop non-oil sectors—or even the physical regions—outside Baku, with many areas still lacking regular electricity. "An energy shortage in an oil-rich nation is a fairly obvious sign of economic mismanagement," one European diplomat pointed out during a tour of the southern provinces near the Iranian border. One million Azeris have already been internally displaced due to the Nagorno-Karabakh dispute—with many living in teeming apartment blocks in Baku and even occupying a university dormitory—but the government seems not to have noticed them either.

Oil and democracy have not mixed well in Azerbaijan precisely because the oil supply is so limited, enhancing the incentive to cash in as oil production peaks. Ilham has fired a few ministers from the old guard for financing the opposition and allegedly participating in aborted coup plots against him, and he has arrested others on the pretense of "not paying taxes"—both indications that he considers control over the state's burgeoning coffers more important than democratization. Only in paranoid regimes do the riot police outnumber the protestors. That Ilham sometimes allows rallies but at other times violently breaks them up shows that they are, above all, public relations maneuvers.

The Aliyev regime's political and economic corruption makes it a liability for both Azerbaijan and the West. After all, it is the same regime favored by Russia and Iran precisely because it will play all sides. By cheating a Turkish company out of a contract to upgrade the country's electricity grid, it opened the door to Russia to complete a monopoly over the southern Caucasus power supply, and without a diversified economy, the second major source of income for Azerbaijan remains remittances from the two million Azeris in Russia. Drug smuggling is all but encouraged by politically connected gangs on the Russian and Iranian borders. As a result, Russia continues to hold strong leverage over Azerbaijan's foreign policy, and Iran continues its efforts to exert its sway over its Shi'a. NATO has lobbied for a base to monitor both the Caspian and Iran, with Russia offering the United States a

---

* The State Oil Company of the Azerbaijan Republic (SOCAR) has resisted financial inspection, and it has blocked proposals to locate the State Oil Fund (SOFAZ)—which would use a significant percentage of oil revenues for infrastructure and social programs—outside the country, where transparency is required.

lease on its radar station at Gabala, but as one Azeri analyst argued, "We have our own problems, and don't need America to make them worse." Azerbaijan's leanings thus remain as insecure as its alphabet, which bounced between Arabic, Cyrillic, and Latin in the twentieth century alone.

In 1959, American ambassador to the United Nations Henry Cabot Lodge Jr. asked, "The U.S. can win wars, but can we win revolutions?" Ilham dismissed his country's 2005 parliamentary elections, remarking that they "do not affect the course of the government." Though they failed to meet OSCE standards, America ratified the results anyway. But the United States and the EU would be better served by fostering a more credible opposition while also supporting parliamentary reformers already on the inside. The Eastern European second-world peer group is already hard at work in Azerbaijan, hoping that, like a rebellious child, the government will listen more to its friends than to the paternalistic powers. Whether revolution transpires by coup, grassroots revolt, or military invasion, democratic consolidation only happens when locals have the means to pressure entrenched leadership into opening the system.[11] Achieving this could eliminate the need for a "Watermelon" or "Caviar" Revolution, while steadily building a pro-Western political system.

"Any label except 'Former Soviet Union' is good enough for us!" proclaimed a young foreign ministry official. Few in Azerbaijan know precisely what the European Union is, but because they are sure it is preferable to the Russian-dominated CIS still fewer want to be excluded from it. But Azerbaijan already is part of Europe. Though it depends on European investment to develop non-oil sectors such as wine, citrus, and cotton, thousands of European energy-sector employees—from oil-platform riggers to executives—also depend on high-paying jobs in Baku, from which pipelines extend around the Caspian Sea's southern rim, superimposed on ancient trade routes. The Caucasus may be the most distant and troublesome corner of the West's East, but it is also the corner on which Europe's future as a self-sufficient superpower most depends.

CONCLUSION:
STRETCHING EUROPE

The "Common European House" is growing far larger than historian A.J.P. Taylor ever could have expected, turning into a multi-tiered commonwealth of members, partners, and associates with varying degrees of privileges, commitments, and subsidies. Its history of strife is a poor guide for the future, for Europe today is as prosperous and powerful as any single superstate. The EU is also gradually demonstrating its growing willingness to transform every country within its reach—as it does better than any other superpower. Within Europe today, Kurds are protected from Turks, Bosnians and Kosovars from Serbs, and Ukrainians and Georgians from Russians—with the EU at the same time using its institutional alphabet soup to make them work together as well. The EU is right to maintain strict criteria for membership, but it no longer waits for others to learn European-ness passively when its attributes are readily teachable—particularly under the tutelage of its new eastern members.

As European leaders expand their collective empire from the Atlantic Ocean to the Caspian Sea, however, they are hearing the Mephistophelian warning of the itinerant Spanish traveler Mendoza in the closing scene of George Bernard Shaw's *Man and Superman:* "Sir, there are two tragedies in life. One is to lose your heart's desire. The other is to gain it." If intellectual ennui unravels the consensus over the definition and purpose of the European project in its more than two dozen capital cities, replacing ambition with anxiety about the prospect of bordering directly on some of the world's most unstable regions, Europeans could lose their strategic appetite just as they experience their greatest success. With so many cooks in the kitchen of Brussels, it seems unclear which recipe will prevail.

But the costs of nonenlargement are far greater than the burdens of enlargement. Europe's imperial expansion thus follows Newton's law of inertia: An object in motion remains in motion. The corollary is that Europe must avoid rest, for this can lead to insular irrelevance and invite external threats. The logic of "imperial overstretch" has thus been turned on its head, for to avoid enlargement would be to welcome immediate stasis. If the EU were to cease expanding, the west Eurasian zone would essentially feature four autonomous powers governed by London, Brussels, Ankara, and Moscow—four wheels not always driving at the same speed. Yet beyond their collective Western realm, all four powers—plus the United States—face even greater challenges in the region east of Europe's East: Central Asia.

CHAPTER 7

THE SILK ROAD
AND THE GREAT GAME

IN 1891, HIGH in the Pamir Mountains, the intrepid young British scout Francis Younghusband encountered his wily adversary from Russia, Colonel Yanov. Both men were surveying the rugged terrain, which was strategically paramount in part because the other coveted it. Catching a whiff of Yanov's grand designs, Younghusband remarked that the Russians were "opening their mouths pretty wide." Yanov responded, "This is just the beginning."[1] Whoever could survive Central Asia would conquer it.

From the Caspian Sea to the high Mongolian steppe, from Siberia to the Arabian Sea, Central Asia is a massive expanse of near-perpetual gray and brown dryness, sliced by the world's highest mountains, converging at the twenty-five-thousand-foot Mount Garmo (not long ago the "Pik Kommunizma") in Tajikistan's Pamirs. The icy Tien Shan ("Celestial Mountains") curve to the northeast through Kyrgyzstan and Kazakhstan; the glacial Himalayan and Karakoram ranges radiate to the southeast through China, India, and Nepal; and the barren Hindu Kush fans to the southwest across Afghanistan. Across this hostile landscape, both the sunrise and sunset are equally hazy—harsh treatment has come from all compass directions.

"Throughout our history, it has been more important *where* we are than *who* we are," an Uzbek historian in Tashkent elucidated from behind a desk with intricate gold detailing. Central Asia is the historical drain into which all surrounding regions and cultures overflow. Lodged among the Slavic, Arab, Persian, Indic, and Sinic civilizations, Central Asia has seen conquerors from Greece to Mongolia and merchants from Italy to Korea collide in its oases, all leaving an imprint visible today in the ethnically ambiguous faces from Kazakhstan to Afghanistan: Turkic European, Mongol Asiatic, and everything in between. It is said that 10 percent of Asian males are descendants of Genghis Khan, history's most prolific conqueror and rapist.

Today the name of every Central Asian state ends in "-stan," the Farsi suffix meaning "land." The landlocked post-Soviet Stans, particularly Kazakhstan and Turkmenistan, now sit atop massive oil and gas reserves, while the flow of weapons, drugs, Islamic militants, and eventually oil through Afghanistan and Pakistan are crucial to understanding the region as well. Many observers regard the whole area as the crest of a roiling "arc of instability" stretching from West Africa to Southeast Asia—or simply as the "Eurasian Balkans," or, more bluntly, "Trashcanistan." Indeed, none of these primitive states (except Afghanistan) is more than one century old; their ability to master the art of being mastered will prove the difference between a second- or third-world future.

The most fundamental issues shaping global order are unfolding in Central Asia: What is China's credibility as a Eurasian leader? Will Russia remain a Eurasian power at all? Can the United States and Europe cooperate beyond their immediate geographic domain? Will great powers share energy resources as demand outstrips supply? Can poor, resource-rich countries become stable democracies? How can malevolent leaders be targeted without harming and alienating their populations?

Central Asia has been both a Silk Road conduit of East-West globalization and a Great Game laboratory of unambiguous imperial competition, the two metaphors for the region's past as well as its future. Indeed, in the twenty-first century it will be both—for each aspect is inadvertently driving the other. As great powers from all sides seek to secure newly discovered oil and gas resources, they are opening the long-sealed-off region as a gateway for both the West and East to compete over pipelines, roads, and trade networks—the lines on the map that truly matter in our age of globalization.

History's empires have always swept quickly across Central Asia's inhospitable expanses, but most vanished as quickly as they came. By 329 B.C., Alexander the Great had crossed the Hindu Kush and conquered Marakanda (present-day Samarkand), the flourishing satrap of the eastern Achaemenid empire. Though he established the garrison of Alexandria Eschate ("Alexandria the Furthest," modern-day Khujand in Tajikistan), which protected the spread of Hellenist culture from agitating tribes, Buddhist Kushan nomads—based at the junction of present-day Pakistan, Afghanistan, and China—soon gained control of east-west passageways. The Persian Sassanids, Huns, Arabs (who reached as far as Kashgar in 714), and Samanids all followed, establishing ornate caravanserai. Bukhara became the eastern pillar of Islam, with thousands of students streaming into its colorful madrasahs to absorb the Samanid *amirs'* poetic teachings.

The continuous imperial turnover in Central Asia demonstrates that it is not only power that abhors a vacuum but also space itself. "I am God's punishment for your sins," Genghis Khan viciously admonished the Seljuk Turks as his Mongol hordes sacked Bukhara in 1221. The Pax Mongolica "made the empires of Rome and Alexander seem insignificant," wrote B. H. Liddell Hart, and its management of the Silk Road graciously facilitated Marco Polo's fabled voyages.[2] After the plague wiped out much of the region's population in the fourteenth century, Amir Timur (Tamerlane) claimed lands from Kashgar to the Caucasus, and his grandson Babur established the Mughal dynasty in India. But as Czarist forces looked south to compensate for Russia's setback in the Crimean War (and plummeting cotton imports due to America's Civil War), they toppled Tashkent in 1865 and captured as far as Yining in western China. Echoing Genghis Khan, Russia's merciless General Skobelev declared, "The harder you hit them, the longer they will be quiet afterwards." Railways allowed European powers to expand into continental interiors: The French into North Africa, the British into Sudan, and the Russians into Central Asia. Halford Mackinder, who first used the terms "heartland" and "geographical pivot of history" to describe the "grassland zone . . . of high mobility" from which domination of Eurasia was possible, worried that rail and communications networks could allow Russia to "fling power side to side" and challenge Britain's global supremacy based on sea power.* Thus, as Russia pushed south, the British empire pressed north from India. During the ensuing Great Game (or the "Tournament of Shadows," as the Russians called it), Britain and Russia mirrored each other's maneuvers from Kashmir to Tibet to the Pamir Mountains, absorbing khanates and fighting through proxies in the Anglo-Afghan wars.† Younghusband, Yanov, and even the all-in-one Buddhist-Communist painter, mystic, and (perhaps) triple agent Nicholas Roerich were among the occult cast of characters active in high-altitude war plans, deceptive mapmaking schemes, and the many "sycophantic ways of Oriental diplomacy."³ Russian conquest and assimilation led to total requisition of the region's people and cattle for its World War I effort, forcing mass production of clothes and food that was returned to Russia along the Trans-Caspian Railway. After the Russian civil war, the Stans were rewarded with collectivization and its attendant starvation and disease, becoming for the next seven decades a rear base for military hardware production for World War II and virgin terrain for ecologically disastrous cotton production schemes.

With the Soviet Union dismantled, the rapidly morphing geometry of Eurasian alliances is on full display in Central Asia. Former superpower Russia seeks to retain influence in its "near abroad," current superpower America pursues its "global war on terror," and emerging superpowers Europe and China strive to satiate their energy demands while spreading their laws and beliefs.‡ Unlike the region's historical

---

* "A generation ago steam and the Suez Canal appeared to have increased the mobility of sea power, relative to land power. Railways acted chiefly as feeders to ocean-going commerce. But trans-continental railways are now transmuting the conditions of land power, and nowhere can they have such effects as in the closed heart-land of Euro-Asia, in vast areas in which neither timber nor accessible stone was available for road-making. Railways work wonders in the steppe, because they directly replace horse and camel mobility, the road stage of development having been omitted." Mackinder, "The Geographical Pivot of History," *Geographical Journal* 23 (1904): 421–37.

†As George Curzon, then viceroy of India, effused, "Turkestan, Afghanistan, Transcaspia, Persia: To many these names breathe only a sense of utter remoteness. . . . To me, I confess, they are the pieces on a chessboard upon which is being played out a game for the domination of the world." Curzon, *Persia and the Persian Question* (1896).

‡Peripheral powers such as Turkey, Iran, and India form a broader ring of states seeking to shape the region as well. Though Saudi and Iranian missionaries were among the first postindependence visitors to the region, their attempts to export their Sunni and Shi'a ideologies mostly fueled sectarian violence in Pakistan and piqued resistance to any Iranian-style theocracy. Turkey's initial efforts at geopolitical fraternalism were rebuffed by the newly independent Turkic states because they had just been cut loose from one Big Brother and did not seek another. India has notable cultural ties to the region, particularly in Afghanistan, but the geographical barrier represented by its neighbor and adversary Pakistan limits the extent to which it can realize its ambitions for gas pipelines from Turkmenistan or Iran in the near term.

experience of large-scale advance and retreat, however, today's micro-maneuvers more closely resemble fencing, with multiple swordsmen constantly thrusting and parrying, steadily accumulating points and suffering blows. The key powers plot as covertly as possible: Russia continues to sell arms in vast quantities while buying up energy infra-structure; America maintains a network of forward military supply out-posts likened to lily pads in a pond and promotes its heavyweight oil companies; Europe, also a large energy investor, works to modernize economies and institutions; and China floods the markets with low-cost goods and has taken the lead in upgrading infrastructure.

Having crossed the Caspian Sea divide from Europe into Asia, NATO now mingles, overlaps, and rubs against the Shanghai Coopera-tion Organization (SCO). Like NATO's founding treaty, the Washing-ton Charter, the name Shanghai Cooperation Organization gives a very clear indication as to which power is driving this alternative vision for Central Asia. The unfolding dynamic between the American-led NATO and Chinese-led SCO coalitions represents the highest in realpolitik calculations, and it is here that the contrast between American and Chinese diplomacy in much of the second world is most visible. Amer-ica's "Russia first" policy of the 1990s led to neglect of Central Asia, other than the removal of Soviet nuclear warheads from Kazakhstan, and today its limited offers of military support and selective democratic and market-oriented reform programs appear to bring little tangible benefit. By contrast, China practices a seemingly unassailable dip-lomacy of shared development. While the U.S. State Department was still pondering which desk to give Central Asia to—Europe or South Asia—China swiftly settled contested border demarcations with the newly created republics (and its 2,600-mile border with Russia). Its "new security concept" then sought to bind countries close to China by initiating confidence-building measures among the original "Shanghai Five" (China, Russia, Kazakhstan, Kyrgyzstan, and Tajikistan) to con-front their common "three evils": separatism, terrorism, and extrem-ism.[4] Like NATO in the Caucasus, the SCO sets the common rules and procedures for customs and border checkpoints, upgrades high-ways along ancient trade routes, and coordinates joint counternarcotics activities. What began as a forum for anti-American rhetoric is now considered by some to be either the "NATO of the East" or an energy club of oil-rich despots.

"The SCO isn't waiting for NATO to get things done," warned an Uzbek official intimately involved with the SCO process. "Our sherpas are in continuous contact, and our defense officials are cooperating as well." While it still falls quite short of a NATO-style collective security alliance ("All for one and one for all!"), China's massive charm offensive has led to new SCO mandates in energy investment, interbank exchanges, and cultural dialogue—with no discussion of democratization.[5] China not only portrays itself as a consultative leader, it has become the standard bearer for business practices by extending a growing amount of credit (close to a billion dollars) to SCO countries. Such practices represent a modern adaptation of the Ming Dynasty's post-Mongol Silk Road strategy of allowing Central Asian khanates to remain indigenously controlled while participating in a tribute system similar to that then operating in Southeast Asia.[6] With dynastic traditions still the norm, why should diplomacy be any different today?

China's economic, demographic, and diplomatic clout virtually assures that it will replace Russia as the region's organizing principle. But just as Hitler and Stalin each saw America as a hindrance to his cause of Eurasian domination, so too have Russia and China today made common cause within the SCO to limit NATO's Asianization. "Where Russian maneuvers work, they serve Chinese interests as well; and where they fail, Russia takes the heat while China's image as a benevolent power grows," a long-time European diplomat in Kazakhstan observed. The sudden opening of trade has happened not because countries naturally awoke to economic opportunities but because an expanding China provides such incentives through its large investments and SCO leadership. Though most SCO affairs are conducted in Russian, the Soviet-trained generation is fading from the scene; like France in Europe, reliance on language as a symbol of power is hardly a reassuring measure of influence. Russia's latest attempt at regional leadership, the Collective Security Treaty Organization (CSTO), has not fared much better than the failed CIS. "How can we talk about the future of something that does not exist in reality?" a young Kazakh diplomat snorted sarcastically.

CHAPTER 8

THE RUSSIA THAT WAS

RUSSIA'S TWO VAST Asiatic zones—Siberia and the Far East, together five times larger than European Russia—make it the ultimate "swing state" in determining whether NATO or the SCO will have the upper hand in Central Asia. Without Russia, the West has no reliable land access to the fabled heartland seat of Eurasian power, whether because of unstable and fickle allies (Afghanistan and Pakistan), hostile states (Iran), or geographical obstacles (the Caspian Sea).* If the West does not successfully woo Russia, China wins the new Great Game.

Much of the Russian countryside today is "a world turned on its head, inhabited by people abandoned by their government and fending for themselves."[1] Russia's labile borders have stretched and contracted by thousands of miles over the centuries, but even as its vulnerable vastness has all but required an authoritarian structure, the state has

---

*As Henry Kissinger has warned, Europe without the United States is merely a "peninsular extension, even a hostage, of Eurasia, drowned into the vortex of its conflicts and a prime target of radical and revolutionary currents sweeping across so many adjacent regions. . . . The U.S., separated from Europe, is geopolitically an island off the shores of Eurasia like nineteenth-century Britain." Kissinger, *Does America Need a Foreign Policy?*, 52.

never been able to control the lives of large swaths of the Russian population directly.[2] Connecting the peoples of Siberia to the west of the country by road and rail might grant them easier access to markets, but it has also accelerated their voluntary return to undo the calamitous forced movement imposed by Soviet planners.[3] Cities that were closed to the outside world during the Soviet era are now simply closing down, just like failed factories.

Nowhere on earth does a depopulating state so provocatively border on an overpopulated one as do Russia and China. Russians are voting with their feet, migrating west in steady waves. Meanwhile, north of Beijing, the Great Wall is crumbling and roughly six hundred thousand illegal Chinese migrants a year are pouring northward into Russia's depopulated Far East—a number almost identical to Russia's annual population decline. Only seven million Russians remain in the Far East, while China's northeastern provinces alone have a total population of over one hundred million. Such a massive demographic imbalance, combined with the growing resource demands of prospering China, begs fundamental questions: Can Russia continue in its present form? How long can the inertia of existing political boundaries hold? Can national sovereignty be portable, expanding as the citizens who carry it move?

These issues are being resolved in practice faster than in theory, with Russia forestalling China's outright takeover of Siberia and the Far East by essentially leasing partial sovereignty to its far more populous neighbor. But gradually, leasing is slipping into ownership—or at least abuse of privilege. China's enormous financial clout has led to a growing number of joint exploration agreements between Russian oil firms such as Rosneft and China's Sinopec, giving it greater influence in steering oil flows. Russia's virgin Far East also contains massive deposits of zinc, nickel, tin, diamonds, and gold, as well as vast fisheries and timber forests—all of which are attractive to the world's largest importer of raw materials. When the heartland was strongly fortified by Russian garrisons, it lived up to Mackinder's description as a "natural fortress." But today, Russia east of the mighty Lena River is ripe for Chinese plunder, with Chinese companies massively overlogging the Russian taigas, then setting fire to what remains to cover their tracks, and shipping timber roughly a thousand miles to China by sea along the Pacific coastline.[4] A population so large could never leave such a bountiful wilderness untouched.

The Far East has become a Russian dream-nightmare: China is developing the region in ways Russia has not, and it is gradually occupying it as a result.[5] What looks like Russia on a map looks a lot more like China on people's faces. Chinese citizens (and Koreans deported by Stalin) visit Chinese-operated health clinics, and Chinese men even marry Siberian women, whose husbands are either perpetually drunk or already dead as a consequence. Even during the Cold War, Russians laughed that those who wanted to leave the USSR should study English—but those who stay should learn Chinese, noting drily that "there are no disturbances on the Sino-Finnish border." With global warming thawing the Siberian permafrost, China's demographic, economic, and eventually political control over Russia's Far East seems almost cosmically assured. A century ago, Chinese labor built Russia's Vladivostok ("Lord of the East") while Russia seized Chinese Manchuria. But today China is the lord of the East.

China is also using aggressive but quiet mercantilism to recapture its former Qing Dynasty province of Mongolia, now precariously perched between Russia and China. The Mongols once ruled over China, but today the barren country of only three million people is going the way of the integrated Chinese province of Inner Mongolia across the Gobi Desert—with only the trappings of sovereignty to reassure it. Some Mongolians gush that their country is experiencing a modern-day gold rush—earning it the nickname "Mine-Golia"—but it is mostly Chinese firms that have taken ownership of the Gobi Desert's mineral deposits as well as the country's agriculture and northern forests.[6] Chinese laborers work the mines (which provide 70 percent of the country's exports) and have built the skyline of the capital, Ulan Bator. Since most of the profits go to Chinese companies, little poverty alleviation has taken place there. The government has tried to tax gold revenue, which only encourages more smuggling to China. Mongolia calls the United States its "third neighbor" due to the presence of the U.S. military, but a military tripwire can deter China only from invading Mongolia—not from buying it.

Through the SCO and their "special relationship," China and Russia conduct large-scale joint military exercises, while China has become the largest purchaser of Russian weapons—giving the world's largest army increasingly sophisticated technology.[7] Yet this marriage of convenience may be leading to a very ugly divorce. It would not be the first time. On the Sino-Kyrgyz border in 1969, a Chinese soldier mooned Russian troops, who in turn defiled a portrait of Mao—petty events that sparked Sino-Russian ambushes and skirmishes all the way to Vladivostok.[8] The Sino-Soviet split became official, and both the USSR and China flirted with the idea of declaring the other "the Main Adversary," superseding even the United States. Ultimately, the KGB decided to refer to China simply as "a Major Adversary," but China became convinced that Russia was a strategic rival—communist or not.

The West has made little secret of its efforts to displace Russia in Europe's East, but should it want Russia to be dismembered in its own east? China's ultimate regional designs bypass Russia, while Russia fears Chinese encroachment far more than it resents either the United States or Europe. Thus despite Chinese lobbying for a direct Russian pipeline to Daqing in China's Heilonjiang province, Transneft's Eastern Siberia–Pacific Ocean pipeline is being constructed to pass north of Lake Baikal to the Sea of Japan—never entering Chinese territory. By making the pipeline's oil available to Japanese and Korean customers as well, Russia has ensured that China cannot exclusively dictate the flow and price. A century after Japan humiliated Russia in the 1905 war, Russia now keeps itself alert in the Far East by conducting bilateral military exercises with Japan and has invited it to help develop Sakhalin Island's oil reserves.[9] Fearing a second Mongol Asian conquest, some Russians now refer to the Chinese populations in the Far East as a "yellow peril," and the Russian military has devised scenarios in which China seizes eastern Siberia and oil- and gas-rich Sakhalin Island, with Russia using tactical nuclear weapons in response.

Much like the Cold War Sino-Soviet friendship, today's rapprochement may fail as a strategic partnership because it boosts China far more than Russia—indeed, at Russia's expense. And much as President Richard Nixon and Henry Kissinger, his secretary of state, wrested China from its Soviet dalliance in the early 1970s, today the United States and the EU might need to rescue Russia from its potentially suicidal embrace of China in order to remain in the heartland. It is Nixon's interior secretary, Walter Hickel, who now champions constructing the sixty-eight-mile tunnel—an idea as old as Czar Nicholas II—to connect Russia's Far East to Alaska under the Bering Strait. Either way, Russia's dwindling population is spread so thinly across a territory so vast that it no longer even makes demographic sense as a country, making it the state whose map is most likely to change unfavorably in the coming decades, as Europe absorbs its former zone of control from the west while China gobbles it up from the east. Soviet experts now teach in history departments—Russia has no divine right to continue in its present form.

HOUSE OF STANS OR HOUSE OF CARDS?

In 2006, Kazakhstan's Central Bank misspelled the word *bank* on its new currency notes. The cause of this remarkable feat was that as Central Asia's newly independent states recover their identities after Russian domination, their Turkic languages, some of which did not exist in written form until the Soviet era, are being converted from Cyrillic to Latin—with uneven results.

To avoid having their identities repressed and replaced once again will not be easy for the republics of the "Soviet Orient," which were so brutally subjugated during Soviet rule that some of them actually feared their own independence: Unsure how to be republics without a Soviet patron, they even supported the 1991 coup attempt against Gorbachev and voted to remain part of a union that no longer existed.[10] Because they were merely khanates and tribal confederations prior to Sovietization, rejecting the Soviet legacy also entails negating their own current ethno-nationalist projects.[11] All have suffered the brain drain of their German, Jewish, and/or Russified intelligentsias, and all are saddled with the burdens of the decrepit Soviet-era health and education systems—or no systems at all—while they face a mounting HIV/AIDS crisis.

In many ways, the Stans still feel the way Lenin and Stalin wanted them to be: "National in form and socialist in content." Though their legal antecedents include Islamic sharia, Mongol, Timurid, and imperial Russian laws, their political character is driven most by the overlap of Mongol-Turkic tribal hierarchy and Soviet authoritarian diktats.[12] None has evolved beyond self-serving Kafkaesque legal systems. This Asiatic nepotism combines with a Soviet bureaucratic instinct to document—if only to deny—everything, creating a system where permits, approvals, bribes, and signatures are needed even to enter a museum. The residual Soviet architecture of Tashkent or Bishkek is rotten beyond repair, while Asian-style shantytowns are still arranged in Soviet-style grids.

"Central Asians are like Russians—except they're nice!" exclaimed an American academic who frequently visits the Stans. He was not referring to the region's ex-Soviet leaders, however. All the Stans are governed by super-presidential systems that deliberately maintain weak parliaments, while oligarchies control the economy through clan-based patronage. Political and economic powers don't just overlap, they are synonymous. Central Asian leaders have shown a far greater respect for Southeast Asian soft-authoritarianism models than European-style democracy, but in reality they are what Mancur Olson called "stationary bandits," rationalizing theft by temporarily delivering economic growth.[13] They claim to prefer evolution to revolution, but as they age or show weakness, succession crises will escalate and doom their reigns—as they have under all previous dynasties.* Within their arbitrary Soviet-era boundaries, these insecure leaders have undermined one another by harboring neighbors' opposition groups and threatening oil and gas cutoffs. Central Asia specializes in banishing political parties to exile, after which they agitate from abroad. It is a shock that there have been no major conflicts in the region. But can it last?

"Even though we are independent countries now, we still sense that a new Great Game is under way, so the time is ripe for a regionalism that protects our common interests," argued one Kazakh diplomat, keen to avoid any return to subjugation. The Stans' landlocked geography means that they will perpetually depend on foreign goods and investment—particularly as an arid region of desert and grasslands where scarce water has

---

*Evolution, literally understood, refers to random mutations, further underscoring how unpredictable succession will be in Central Asia, even if not by revolution.

long been squandered. Even potentially wealthy, resource-rich countries—Kazakhstan, Uzbekistan, and Turkmenistan—must rely on Russia, China, the United States, and Europe to tap, extract, and bring their hydrocarbons to market.[14] The Stans have now graduated from sniping at one another to negotiating barter agreements between gas-rich Uzbekistan and Turkmenistan and upstream Kyrgyzstan and Tajikistan, which control the watersheds.

What would help the Stans' prescient independence most, however, is for them to become players in the present incarnation of the Great Game, potentially forming a larger bloc that no one superpower can dominate and sparing them the fate of centuries of khanates before them. Kazakhstan and Uzbekistan have manipulated both NATO and the SCO: As members of NATO's Partnership for Peace, they have benefited from military modernization and training, while as SCO members they have received cover against the West's demands for democratization and American basing rights. "We know from experience that outside powers don't have our interests at heart," the Kazakh diplomat concluded. The more the Stans' leaders realize this, the faster they will come together rather than collapsing like a house of cards.

CHAPTER 9

TIBET AND XINJIANG:

THE NEW BAMBOO CURTAIN

IT IS DIFFICULT to find a Westerner who does not intuitively support the idea of a free Tibet. But would Americans ever let go of Texas or California? For China the Great Game was neither inconclusive nor fruitless, something that cannot be said for Russia and Britain. Indeed, China was the big winner. Boundary agreements in 1895 and 1907 gave Russia the Pamir Mountains and established the Wakhan Corridor— the slender eastern tongue of Afghanistan that borders China—as a buffer to Britain. But rather than cede East Turkestan (Uyghurstan) to the Russians, the British financed China's recapture of the territory, which it organized into Xinjiang (which means "New Dominions"). While West Turkestan was splintered into the hermetic Soviet Stans, China steadily reasserted its traditional dominance over both Xinjiang and Tibet (Xizang), today its two largest provinces. Without them, China would be like America without all of the territory west of the Rocky Mountains: denied its continental majesty and status as a Pacific Ocean power.

The new Great Game and the new Silk Road thus began with

China's ongoing subjugation—and elevation—of its western periphery, a process that holds clues for the rest of Central Asia's future. The Great Game was a struggle for land routes, the "instruments of history" that since ancient times have facilitated imperial expansion.[1] Having subdued Xinjiang and Tibet, China is advancing its westward reach through a five-pronged strategy: A "Euro-Asia Transcontinental Bridge," planned to eventually rival Russia's Trans-Siberian Railway; a rail-pipeline corridor across Kazakhstan to the Caspian Sea; refurbished roads over high passes through Kyrgyzstan to Tashkent in Uzbekistan; a sturdy transport highway across Tajikistan and Afghanistan to Iran and Turkey; and an extension of the existing Karakoram Highway through Pakistan all the way to the deepwater Arabian Sea port of Gwadar—all at Chinese expense.

Every backpacker who has visited Tibet and Xinjiang in the past decade knows that the Chinese empire is painfully real: The western region's going concern is undoubtedly Chinese Manifest Destiny. Since the end of the civil war in 1949, China endeavored immediately to overcome the "tyranny of terrain," penetrating and taming the interminably rugged, borderless mountain and desert landscapes with the aim of exploiting vast natural assets, establishing penal colonies and bases for military training and weapons testing, and expanding the lebensraum for its exploding population. Both Tibet and Xinjiang have the misfortune of possessing resources China wants and of being situated on the path to resources China needs: Tibet has huge amounts of timber, uranium, and gold, and Xinjiang boasts the country's largest oil, gas, coal, uranium, and gold deposits, while together they constitute China's geographic gateway for trade flow outward—and energy flow inward—with Kazakhstan, Kyrgyzstan, Tajikistan, Afghanistan, and Pakistan. Decades of raw labor by the army and swarms of workers have paved the way for unchallenged Chinese dominance.* The high-altitude train linking Shanghai to Lhasa that began service in 2006 represents not the beginning of Chinese hegemony but rather its culmination.

---

*Though the Chinese military has a far greater presence in Xinjiang than Tibet, an offshoot of the Southern Military Highway drastically reduced the travel time between the two provinces, allowing the Chinese army to move quickly to crush Tibet's 1959 uprising. See Avedon, *In Exile from the Land of Snows,* 317.

Tibet and Xinjiang today set the stage for the rebirth of a multi-ethnic empire in ways that resemble nothing so much as America's frontier expansion nearly two centuries ago.[2] Chinese think about their *mission civilatrice* today very much the way American settlers did: They are bringing development and modernity. Asiatic, Buddhist Tibetans and Turkic, Muslim Uyghurs are being lifted out of the third world, whether they like it or not. They are getting roads, telephone lines, hospitals, and jobs. School fees are being reduced or abolished to promote basic education and Chineseness. Unlike those Europeans who seek to define the European Union as a Christian club, there are no Chinese inhibitions about incorporating Muslim territories. The new mythology of Chinese nationalism is not based on expunging minorities but rather granting them a common status in the paternalistic Chinese state: Uyghurs and Tibetans are told they are Chinese, even though they are not Han.[3] Mandarin is the only common denominator among China's tapestry of unrelated languages and dialects, including Mongol, (Arabic scripted) Uyghur, Tibetan, and Zhuang. Indeed, although Tibet and Xinjiang border each other, their cultures are mutually unintelligible—and neither Tibetans nor Uyghurs seem to have even heard of the Zhuang, even though they are China's largest minority.

"The Soviet Union collapsed because they experimented with glasnost prematurely, before they achieved unity among the peoples," explained a Chinese intellectual in Shanghai who studies Central Asia. "We will not make the same mistake." Large empires are maintained through a combination of force and law, and China has not wavered in its strategy across Tibet and Xinjiang; it is merely a difference of degree. In even the remotest corners of Tibet, small army bases house platoons of the People's Liberation Army (PLA), with soldiers menacingly practicing martial arts twice daily in public squares, often right next to ancient and fragile Buddhist stupas. Even inaccessible jungle areas designated environmentally protected zones are often actually military encampments. Signs trumpeting "Tibet Power" refer strictly to the Chinese electricity company.

China has pumped billions of dollars into development projects in Tibet, hoping to pacify its peoples and generate goodwill among the scarcely three million Tibetans. In Lhasa, many crumbling stone quarters have been replaced with sturdy single-family homes built along thoroughfares connecting the city to the new railway station. The consequence of Chinese modernity, however, is that a city that once symbolized cultural authenticity has become merely a gateway to the more remote plateaus where wild yak still outnumber people. "Nobody in my family has ever been to China," a young Tibetan guide explained while walking through the village of Gyantse. "But the Chinese people and police are all over. They even wear cowboy hats like us to try and fit in."

An even greater prize than Tibet is the far larger and more populous Xinjiang, with its oil deposits, deserts, and mountains. Its demographic dilution has been dubbed "apartheid with Chinese characteristics." Muslim Xinjiang was always unruly, particularly toward its Qing Dynasty overseers, even briefly securing an independent East Turkestan at the end of the civil war. But beginning with the "Develop the West" campaign of the 1950s, massive Han resettlement has continued unabated under the auspices of the Production and Construction Corps (PCC), the Chinese equivalent of the U.S. Homestead Act, which subsidizes Han farming ventures while marginalizing the tiny plots owned by indigenous Uyghurs. During the Cultural Revolution, Xinjiang was sealed off for a massive pogrom of mosque destruction and Koran burning. Violent clashes in Ürümqi in 1996 proved that no peaceful Islamic culture would prevail in a Chinese-dominated environment. China suspended all mosque reconstruction and launched a "Strike Hard" campaign, executing and imprisoning hundreds of suspected Uyghur separatists. Today one can see the cumulative results of the efforts Mao and Deng began but never completed: a major railway line and highway transporting coal, migrants, and goods straight across the Taklamakan Desert, facilitating the further Hanification of a province in which Uyghurs now make up only half the population.

People riding donkeys all day are usually the last to find out who the latest political master is. The agrarian nomads of Xinjiang survived for centuries on trade with their Turkic-Muslim brethren to the west, and though Xinjiang is now China's fastest-growing province, in its interior China still feels a long way off. Men greet each other with the Muslim handshake of two arms clasping followed by a slight bow and a touch of the heart with the right hand, and many women wear headscarves. The mosques of Yecheng resemble those of Uzbekistan, and its bazaars feature gold-leaf Korans and multicolored *pakul* caps. Women in Afghan-style burqas crouch on street corners and beg, much like in Kabul. The HIV infection rate rose sharply in the 1990s due to growing drug addiction and prostitution. Because China's subjugation of the far west has occurred far away from major Chinese population centers, Han tourists visiting the region in luxury double-decker buses gape at the exotic people and the crumbling Uyghur villages that now constitute a part of their empire.

Even eighteen hundred miles west of Beijing, all clocks are reluctantly set to Beijing time—one empire, one time zone. In Khotan (now Hotan), locals stiffen as Chinese police make their rounds. Once a center for the spread of Buddhism, the cultivation of silk, and Islamic learning in its central pink and blue mosque, Hotan has become like Russia's Kazan, a place where the government intrusively monitors all of the local denizens. America's "war on terror" was a blessing in disguise for Chinese authorities, who quickly labeled Uyghur agitators—mostly frustrated youth and students—Islamic fundamentalists, targeting them in its own "war on terror" that consists of occasional gunfights and crackdowns on cohorts of the East Turkestan Islamic Movement. "If we don't do anything to anger the police, they won't hurt us," said a man selling petrified wood in a bazaar once famous for its rare white jade. "But I cannot imagine that we will have Turkestan again the way we thought was possible when the Soviet Turkic republics were liberated in the 1990s."

Both the former Turkestan capital of Yining and the fabled Silk Road melting pot of Kashgar, near the Kyrgyz border, have also been turned into Chinese metropolises, making the transition from thriving, low-value bazaar towns to major commercial hubs. The Han pioneers who came to Kashgar in the late 1980s symbolically sealed China's Great Game triumph with the conversion of the former British and Russian consulates into the city's two most popular tourist hotels (the British one was renamed Chini Bagh, "Chinese Garden"). A hundred-foot-tall statue of Mao—right arm outstretched toward Beijing—towers over the central People's Square. Kashgar's population is a mix of Uyghur, Tajik, Kyrgyz, and Han—but blue-uniformed children strolling to school all are taught in Mandarin.

The outright annihilation of the local people, history, and architecture and their replacement with shiny skyscrapers paying tribute to modern Chinese capitalism make Ürümqi, Xinjiang's capital, the Shanghai of the northern Silk Road. As in Tibet, remoteness and climate are no obstacle: A six-lane freeway runs through the city, and the new Han majority fuels spiffy new Japanese cars at the large Sinopec and PetroChina gas stations around the city. Ürümqi buzzes with traders from Russia to Pakistan and all the Stans in between who buy cheap Chinese goods to be sold back home at a profit. Uyghurs are now an uncomfortably marginalized minority in the city, afforded neither jobs nor space other than the night markets featuring spicy Uyghur soups and circus tricks. The perpetual flood of Chinese tourists crowds the few accessible natural attractions, making the emerald-colored Heavenly Lake no longer very heavenly.

All that remains of the Shambala dream are Tibetan music and meditation CDs; of Turkestan, the lingering aromatic cloud of grilled kabob that hangs over the Ferghana Valley of Xinjiang. Ironically, China's near absolute sense of security over both provinces is the greatest hope for a Chinese glasnost: China no longer faces any meaningful resistance to its rule and so may someday lighten up. Spiritual Tibetans have long looked south to Nepal and India for their cultural underpinnings, and in the eighteenth century, Tibet was allowed a functional autonomy from China, a model the current Dalai Lama has proposed. Once he passes from the scene, China might be less anxious about opening the province to greater cultural exchange for Buddhists across India, Tibet, and Nepal, further restoring the country's role as the Silk Road passage it was when the Thousand Buddha Caves of Dunhuang were carved over a millennium ago.

Gradually, Tibetans and Uyghurs will become more prosperous than their neighboring third-world Mongols, Kyrgyz, Tajiks, Afghans, Pakistanis, Indians, and Nepalis—and their development may provide a basis for Chinese claims to benevolent hegemony elsewhere in Central Asia. But China will achieve that dominance before it talks about it.

Fearful of any single power capable of uniting Eurasia, Mackinder wrote, "Who rules the World-Island commands the world."[4] The world-island is ever more a single body. Soon it will be possible to travel from Aberdeen to Singapore or Seoul on the Trans-Asian Railway Network, whose various sections have been under construction since the 1960s. Barbarians retreating across the steppe once watched their larger enemies weaken with distance from their core, but today China's growing reach along its infrastructural axes is steadily and confidently compressing the Central Asian space.

CHAPTER 10

KAZAKHSTAN:

"HAPPINESS IS MULTIPLE PIPELINES"

No one comes to Kazakhstan for the weather. But much like dominating trade routes ensured geopolitical advantage centuries ago, today controlling the flow of oil and gas pipelines brings profits and political ties. The combined oil reserves of the Caspian Sea are estimated at over two hundred billion barrels (as compared with the Persian Gulf's proven reserves of over six hundred billion barrels), making the region indispensable as an alternative source of oil for both the West and the East. Kazakhstan has thus become like Saudi Arabia, an energy powerhouse that all superpowers must try to win. Occupying the vast expanse of barren steppe that Genghis Khan so easily conquered, Kazakhstan is the world's largest landlocked country. Through dust storms and blizzards, all of the players of the new Great Game are here building the new oil-slicked Silk Road.

Kazakhs, like Ukrainians, have long considered their geography cursed—and natural resources have only amplified their country's outsize utility to others. Soviets treated Kazakhstan as southern Siberia, referring to the whole region as "Middle Asia *and* Kazakhstan," centrally planning its mines and factories along with those of Siberia.[1] But since independence, Kazakhstan has turned both its geography and geology into a blessing, becoming such a success story that it is hard to even compare it to its failing neighbors to the south. Like Turkey, Kazakhstan is a critical east-west transit state benefiting from strong relations with all sides—which it calls a "multivector" strategy—and holding out as long as possible from choosing any one. Kazakhstan's most influential recent foreign minister, Kassymzhomart Tokaev, is a Sinologist who resists the Americans' domineering diplomatic style, which he contrasts unfavorably with the substantive Europeans and the deferential Chinese.[2] The word *Kazakh* is Turkic for "free," and Kazakhstan today wants neither a return to subservience under Russia, nor subjugation under Chinese hegemony, nor extensive American meddling or bases.[3] But if the country's oil outflow becomes tight, will these competing empires pull it apart?

The new Great Game is less about territorial aggrandizement than access and control of oilfields and the radial pipelines that extend from them. Kazakh officials are perpetually juggling demands for pipeline routes flowing east and west, north and south, all of which fall into three categories: actual, existing pipelines; routes under construction or expansion; and pipe dreams drafted secretly, in various capitals, with little chance of realization. Like fiber-optic cables, pipelines are part of the nearly invisible infrastructure of globalization, new sets of lines on maps that indicate dyads of friendship. As in Azerbaijan, Western commercial companies took the lead in shaping Western interests in Kazakhstan, buying controlling shares of the Tengiz and Kashagan fields, the nation's largest.[4] And much as the Baku-Tbilisi-Ceyhan pipeline in the Caucasus was designed to evade Russia and Iran, the routes that America, Europe, and China prefer for new Kazakh oil pipelines avoid Russia entirely. "Happiness is multiple pipelines," read bumper stickers distributed by Clinton administration officials in Almaty. New tankers now line the east Caspian port of Aqtau, carrying Kazakh oil to Baku, where it joins the Baku-Ceyhan flow to Europe, and Kazakhstan has also proposed a Caspian–Black Sea canal to boost its trade to the West.

Russia has long considered itself Kazakhstan's protector, and it maintains rights to Baikonur, the massive former Soviet space-launch cosmodrome. For Kazakhs, however, Russia is becoming just another player on the Central Asian chessboard. "We've been resisting Russian 'protection' for over a century now," a Kazakh diplomat wearily noted. To guard its tankers sailing to Baku and prevent Russian dominance of the Caspian, Kazakhstan cooperates with NATO through the Partnership for Peace. However, it is wealthy enough that it cannot be bribed into accepting Western military bases whose presence would undermine its relations with Russia and China. Though Kazakhstan and Russia (through Gazprom) have signed fresh agreements to join their natural gas networks, the legacy relationship of existing oil pipelines is plagued by the same irritations as Russia's pipelines passing through Ukraine, namely the efforts of Russia's Transneft to block their expansion unless they are first renationalized under Russian control.

Close energy ties with Russia no longer come at the expense of deals with Kazakhstan's far more significant customer: China. For the Chinese juggernaut, reaching the energy assets of the Caspian is not so much a logistical challenge as a diplomatic one, in a region where sovereignty is very much a tripwire. "The Chinese have told us quietly but clearly that their energy demands are massive and urgent—and that they are willing to pay a steep price to address them," a Kazakh official in the sleek but sleepy capital, Astana, recounted. Unlike American energy companies, China's oil firms have the overt strategic backing of their government without worrying about shareholders; controlling affairs on its borders and importing oil without relying on the Straits of Malacca are incentive enough.

Once a Russian frontier fort at the base of the Tien Shan Mountains, Kazakhstan's largest city, Almaty, is now the region's most cosmopolitan city. On a busy downtown avenue, the Chinese National Petroleum Corporation (CNPC) occupies a guarded building that essentially functions as a second Chinese embassy. Within its high gates, energy deals with Kazakh authorities are cultivated for years before becoming public news. In record time, China funded the construction of a 625-mile-long Atasu-Alashankou pipeline bringing Kazakh oil to China's western energy grid. When the pipeline opened in late 2005, President Nursultan Nazarbayev described it as cementing Kazakhstan's "strategic partnership" with China. Sinopec has also secured several major exploration blocks near the Tengiz oilfield and is negotiating the construction of a cross-border natural gas linkage to China's West-East pipeline, which stretches twenty-five hundred miles from Xinjiang's Tarim Basin to Shanghai.[5]

But Kazakhstan's unwillingness to cede operational control of the pipelines themselves has led to intensified Chinese financial diplomacy aimed at buying more deeply into production-sharing agreements. A century ago, during the Open Door era, China was on the receiving end of such mercantilism, with foreign powers seeking concessionary infrastructure contracts—humiliating arrangements that China viewed as tantamount to occupation. As the mutual dependence among the region's key energy suppliers (Russia, Iran, and the Central Asian states) and consumers (Europe and China) grows, so too does the risk of conflict among them.[6] Kazakhstan's deft balance between Western and Chinese interests can only last as long as its oil supply does—and the friction is already ratcheting up on a monthly basis. For example, when CNPC purchased PetroKazakhstan significantly above market value in 2005, the United States and Russia sided with the Kazakh government's decision to declare the firm a strategic asset, reallocate its refining and production segments, and delay its sale. The nationalization practices that have burned the West for decades in the Arab world could become a weapon against China in the future. The challenge for Chinese diplomacy is thus to remain an attractive partner to Kazakhstan, which is as sophisticated at avoiding domination as China is at exercising it.

Rising empires see insecure spaces on maps the way bears emerging from hibernation see food. As Colonel Yanov boasted of Russia during the Great Game, China is again opening its mouth very wide. Kazakhs have for centuries borne witness to Chinese expansion and contraction, and few are comfortable with China's energetic infrastructural diplomacy even as they benefit from the increased oil revenues. Because China actually lost territory to Russia and Mongolia in the nineteenth and twentieth centuries (through "unequal treaties"), some claim that its expansionism is justified. Murat Auezov, a highly respected former Kazakh ambassador to China, argues that what unites China across three centuries is a "desire to extend its territories." Even without engaging in overt aggression, however, China already impinges on Kazakh resources. To develop Xinjiang's oilfields, China could siphon as much as 2 billion cubic yards of water annually from the Ili and Irtysh rivers; as they terminate in Kazakhstan's already increasingly depleted Lake Balkhash, such a move could potentially turn it into another version of the dried-up Aral Sea.

Though most Kazakhs live in the southeast near the Chinese border, President Nazarbayev moved the capital to Astana in the northern steppe to check Russian ambitions, avoid Chinese ones, and express his own, building a city of glitzy pyramids, towers, and stadiums.[7] But this did not prevent Chinese demographic diplomacy, which has resulted in Chinese and Uyghur shuttle traders forming semipermanent settlements in Kazakhstan, with unofficial estimates reaching three hundred thousand out of a population of fifteen million. More and more signs in Almaty are now in Chinese, reflecting the sharp growth in Chinese restaurants feeding a rapidly growing Chinese population. Near the Caspian, thousands of oil workers live in semi-extraterritorial oil compounds, as are also found in Arab countries.

China's encroachment on Kazakhstan is occurring just as it is becoming a genuine Kazakh nation and surmounting its ethnic and linguistic cleavages. Like Ukraine, Kazakhstan is split along a demographic axis of largely Russian and native populations.

But under Nazarbayev's Kazakhification program, higher Kazakh birth rates have permitted Kazakhs to become a solid majority in their own country. "Speaking Kazakh is now an unwritten prerequisite to entering the higher echelons of power," one opposition parliamentarian observed. In Almaty, many street names now end with the Turkic *koshesi* rather than the Russian *prospekt*. The share of the population that is ethnically Russian has declined considerably to under 20 percent over the past decade, as many returned to Russia—but many Russians have also come back to Kazakhstan. "They actually discriminate against me just because I have a Kazakh passport," a young Russian journalist in Almaty complained after what was intended to be a permanent trip to Moscow. "And so I actually have a better job here." On cool summer evenings, Kazakh and Russian youth mingle in outdoor cafés and restaurants speaking an easy mix of Russian and Kazakh. Kazakhstan has even refurbished the one warmly remembered relic of the Soviet Union: the circus.

Kazakhstan has an opportunity for self-realization that most second-world countries can only dream of, and its social and political stability make the country its own best bet. Its economy is already larger than the rest of Central Asia's states combined, and the value of its energy assets is estimated at $9 trillion. Despite horrendous levels of corruption, diversification is under way even as oil output and profits boom, insulating the economy from future volatility in the global energy market.[8] Matching the ambition of the semi-authoritarian Asian tigers, Kazakhstan has established special economic zones and information-technology parks and has turned biological-weapons plants into food-processing factories. It also plans to utilize its enormous uranium reserves for nuclear energy. New regional airports and wide roads are restoring connections across the continental steppe. Ski resorts are also emerging in the Tien Shan range—to which Europeans may soon flock, if global warming diminishes snowfall in the Alps.

Kazakhstan is becoming a nation of individual consumers rather than cogs in a Soviet-style machine. The private sector now accounts for most of the workforce and economy, and private banks raise funds on the London Stock Exchange. Government assistance to small enterprises, privatized land ownership, agrarian subsidies, and higher government salaries have all contributed to rising living standards—in both cities and rural areas. The poverty rate has declined, unemployment is the region's lowest, and the country is the destination of choice for migrant laborers. New homes and apartment blocks are sprouting around Almaty and Astana, with professionals commuting to jobs with international energy and consulting firms. "We aren't smuggling capital overseas, instead we're taking out mortgages," boasted a young Almaty consultant who works for a Kazakh-multinational joint venture. "Even after studying and training in Europe, many Kazakhs like me have a Western lifestyle right here."

The Kazakh government has become confident enough to practice an increasingly muscular negotiating style, using the threat of expropriation and higher corporate taxes to boost its control over energy assets. But robust partnerships with international companies and institutions have remained part of the secret of Kazakhstan's success. Turkish construction companies employ large numbers of Kazakhs, and foreign experts were instrumental in converting what had been a Soviet academy into KIMEP, a business leadership institute drawing the best students from all neighboring countries. "Often these institutions just serve one politician's political ambitions: When his fortunes change, the school collapses," explained a KIMEP professor specializing in energy markets. "But since we are politically clean and teach mostly in English, we've become the region's center for training the next generation of leaders."

Kazakhstan may even evade "Russian disease," the state capture of oil revenues to fuel a return to Czarist authoritarianism.[9] Kazakhstan is well ahead of Russia in central bank reform, and it has placed over $4 billion in oil profits into a Norway-inspired fund with relatively transparent management. Nazarbayev's pragmatism covers even the most visceral matter of national security. At the time of the Soviet collapse, Kazakhstan had more nuclear weapons than France, Britain, and China combined, but having been the victim of Soviet nuclear testing for decades—radiation caused many grotesque deformities among stillborn children—Kazakhstan worked with the United States to return all nuclear material to Russia and is now pushing for nuclear-free zone status for Central Asia.[10] Russia watches Kazakhstan closely, and even respects it. Perhaps the country could serve as a model for Russia itself.

Kazakhstan has moved from a command to a market economy and from Soviet apparatchiks to Kazakh nationalists, but can it move from authoritarianism to real elections? Kazakhstan is wealthy enough to afford democracy, but as a Soviet-era holdover and Turkic father figure, Nazarbayev would certainly prefer an unquestioningly loyal horde. In recent years, he has shut down the Democratic Choice Party, exiled key rivals, imprisoned opposition figures, and indicated that he will remain president for life. The question in Kazakhstan's 2005 election was not whether Nazarbayev would win but simply by what margin, with advisers fretting in advance about what degree of victory would seem most acceptable to international observers.[11] At the same time, he is not immune to the virtues of gradually instituting some form of democracy among his nomadic peoples. "He is the only leader who will not fall by way of coup, revolution, or assassination, and is more likely to appoint a patriotic technocrat to succeed himself rather than assert one of his daughters as his rightful heir," a Kazakh political analyst in Almaty confidently predicted.

Nazarbayev is powerful enough to take Kazakhstan in virtually any direction he wants, but because he is both ambitious *and* rational, he can still be conditioned from the outside. While America talks about democracy in Central Asia, it is far more interested in gaining Nazarbayev's strategic promises than in supporting his opposition. By contrast, the European Union holds the levers of legitimacy that Nazarbayev covets, but they can be denied. Not only does he seek a Kazakh action plan under the European Neighborhood Policy, he has made no secret of his desire to chair the Organization for Security and Co-operation in Europe (OSCE). In both cases, the EU has persistently played hard to get. The more curious the architectural marvels he builds in Astana—such as a fluorescent tower with a giant golden ball on top—the more Europeans let him know that his version of democracy will not make the cut in Europe. Securing the flow of Kazakh oil out of the country and putting Western values into it are two very distinct issues, but both are progressing according to the "Kazakh way."

KYRGYZSTAN AND TAJIKISTAN:
SOVEREIGN OF EVERYTHING, MASTER OF NOTHING

NEARLY TWO DECADES after their independence, most outsiders still cannot tell the various Stans apart. This may not ultimately
matter in the cases of Kyrgyzstan and Tajikistan, the third-world micro-
states most likely to be swept under the larger imperial carpet steadily
unfurling across Central Asia. In a corner of Central Asia where borders were callously drawn, they are not so much countries as frontier
spaces between empires. Much as occurred a century ago, the Great
Game is playing out on the summits and in the shadows of the Tien
Shan and Pamir mountains.

The Tien Shan range literally bisects Kyrgyzstan's Russified north
from its populous southern cities of Osh and Jalal-Abad, which belong
more to the Islamic culture of the Ferghana Valley in which they lie. It
takes a dozen grueling hours to drive from the capital, Bishkek, to Osh
over treacherous, if spectacular, mountain passes. A coherent, united
Kyrgyzstan could use tourism to put itself on the political map by taking advantage of its world's freshest air and curative Lake Issykul to
boost its health spa industry. Far more likely, however, is that a country
once closed to foreigners by the Soviets will become a scenic passage-

way for a revived east-west Silk Road managed by Kazakhstan, Uzbekistan, and China.

Impoverished Kyrgyzstan is the object of a perpetual tug of war among these far larger neighbors, with whom it attempts to conduct "nonexclusive friendships." When China insisted on settling borders in the early 1990s and cut a deal in which the Kyrgyz government sold off a mountainous patch of several hundred square miles, an angry public uproar ensued. When Uzbekistan cut off gas supplies, Kazakhstan delivered. But while Kazakhstan is the country's most consistent friend, it cut its own road straight to Lake Issykul so that Kazakh tourists could bypass Kyrgyzstan's predatory police. Russian and Chinese companies are buying up the metallurgical industries and food processing sector, leaving most Kyrgyz exactly where they have been for centuries: employed in the archaic horse-drawn agriculture that still constitutes most of the economy. In Bishkek, nice restaurants are more like cafeterias for Western diplomats, while women with nothing better to do incessantly call male hotel guests offering Asian massages.

"President Askar Akayev declared he'd make Kyrgyzstan the 'Switzerland of Central Asia,' but instead he made it Switzerland for his own family," fumed Foreign Minister Rosa Otunbayeva. Yet few historic events labeled as revolutions are as undeserving of the description as Kyrgyzstan's 2005 "Tulip Revolution," which was actually an elite coup after which nothing changed—quite literally. The United States helped fund the small business and media groups that rallied bands of protestors to agitate against Akayev, who fled to Moscow but left the door open for the mafia regime of Kurmanbek Bakiyev. As one political analyst in Bishkek observed, "Anything would have been better than Akayev, so many people gladly backed the opposition. But to have thought that Bakiyev would decrease corruption and create jobs was absurd."

The illegitimacy of every government in Kyrgyzstan since independence has done little to enhance its stability, of course. Rolling the revolutionary ball down mountains as steep as Kyrgyzstan's without steering it can even be counterproductive, for replacing sham democracy with something less predictable opens the door to China and Russia's intensified manipulation of wobbly leaders. For them, the only thing better than an unstable and pliant Kyrgyzstan is a country with no government at all. During the Silk Road era, travelers crossed borders without much noticing it. For China, it doesn't matter who controls Kyrgyzstan, so long as they re-create that state of affairs.

China is bringing about the resurrection of their old Silk Road passages, which thrived until the arrival of Islam, when Arabs forced the Tang Dynasty back across the Tien Shan Mountains at the Battle of Talas in 751. The fabled Torugart Pass on the Sino-Kyrgyz border has now been turned into a sturdy highway suitable for heavy truck traffic stretching across the country into Uzbekistan. Central Asian trade is actually insignificant for China, but for Kyrgyzstan and Tajikistan, China's presence is enormous and grows more so with every passing day. The largest share of Kyrgyz exports now go to China, while the Dordoi bazaar in Bishkek is flooded with Chinese-made clothing and tools. Far more than in Kazakhstan, the cross-border shuttle trade has meant the settlement of more Chinese communities in Kyrgyzstan, with organized Chinatowns now a feature of all but a few cities. In Bishkek itself, Lenin Avenue has been renamed after Deng Xiaoping.

As America's strategic rationale moves beyond Afghanistan to securing pipelines and monitoring China, Kyrgyzstan has returned to its role as a Great Game listening post, and its maneuvering is also reminiscent of the original version: Each power attempts to establish military garrisons, gradually placing themselves cheek by jowl. Russia's army never gave up its sanctuaries in Kyrgyzstan, but it did vacate the former Soviet base at Manas, near Bishkek, which is now occupied by the U.S. military.[1] Along the same border where China and Russia clashed in 1969, they now spy on each other with commercial and camouflaged monitors. When the United States requested basing rights for AWACS reconnaissance planes in Kyrgyzstan, China forced the government to turn it down, revealing that American bases in Kyrgyzstan are less like the nimble "lily pads" to which the Pentagon aspires than islands being flooded in a rising tide of Chinese commercial and infrastructural activity—the real levers of influence in underdeveloped states. The Pentagon's planes can get America there, but then what? America cannot displace China economically, and China can easily lavish with bribes whichever Kyrgyz regime comes next, confining America to its base. If democracy assistance continues to be nothing more than aid to autocrats or salaries for consultants, the very regimes the West hopes to eliminate—those that sell themselves to the highest bidder with little regard for strategic stability—will continue to flourish.

The same micro-politics of roads and access are also unfolding in Tajikistan, turning the country into another Silk Road rest stop. Precariously perched at the roof of the world in the Pamir Mountains, nestled among Uzbekistan, Afghanistan, Kyrgyzstan, and China, Tajikistan is another country that bends in the imperial winds—but with a radical Islamic twist. The country's Islamic Renaissance Party was the only religious party to be recognized in the former Soviet Union, and in the 1980s it was a rallying point for Tajik nationalism as the Communist elite in the capital, Dushanbe, ironically neglected the very anti-Soviet insurgency in Afghanistan that sparked the collapse of the Soviet Union. Almost 150,000 people were killed in Tajikistan's early 1990s civil war, which, like the simultaneous Yugoslav war, demonstrated the frail construction of national identity in the Communist world. Even after prevailing in the country's 1992 election, the Moscow-backed clique of Imamali Rakhmanov had to fight just to get to Dushanbe.

Tajikistan experiences approximately three thousand tremors and earthquakes per year, an apt metaphor for its politics. Rakhmanov's heinously corrupt regime is all but mortgaged to Moscow. Some twenty thousand Russian troops are stationed in the country, and Russian firms operate its most strategic hydroelectric dams, hoarding profits from power sales to neighboring Uzbekistan. In classic third-world fashion, Tajik remittances from Russia actually exceed the country's budget. The country has become a mercy case for the Aga Khan, the World Bank, and the EU, but with over 80 percent of the population still below the poverty line, it is not surprising that Tajiks on both sides of the Afghan border have resorted to the drug trade in order to survive.

But Tajikistan is also a critical bridge for the revival of Sino-Iranian trade routes linking Xinjiang, Osh, Dushanbe, and Herat (in Afghanistan) to Iran, with which Tajikistan shares an ethnic and linguistic kinship. Iran's funding of a tunnel through the Fan Mountains connecting Dushanbe to Khujand allows Tajikistan's two main cities to be connected year-round for the first time, while advancing a new Sino-Iranian energy and trade corridor. "We border China and Afghanistan, not Russia anymore," an astute young Tajik soldier at a dilapidated checkpoint remarked. "Without these roads the Chinese are building, we couldn't even get around our own country."

This new Silk Road passage is less romantic, more industrial, and far faster than its previous incarnations. But once built, highways become pathways not only for trade and oil but also for drugs, infectious diseases, and extremist ideologies. China and Russia thus welcome American and European efforts to stabilize the southern buffer to Afghanistan that Russia no longer holds. Under American and European management, the Tajik-Afghan border trade on the Panj River is efficiently monitored—a stark contrast to when the cash-strapped Soviet army was complicit in drug trafficking through the same junction. But China has already begun to adopt these Western lessons and apply them to SCO border-policing missions—indeed, taking them one step further by devising shared water-management strategies as well. The political, economic, and strategic ties deepening on a daily basis along these restored Silk Road avenues are becoming a filter of influence that could pin the United States south of the post-Soviet Stans in the Soviet graveyard of Afghanistan.

CHAPTER 12

UZBEKISTAN AND TURKMENISTAN:

MEN BEHAVING BADLY

Soon after September 11, 2001, American travelers in Uzbekistan were waved through military checkpoints and cheered as "Friends of Bush!" The country had been recruited as a frontline American ally to support operations in its southern neighbor, Afghanistan, serving as the launching pad for Predator drones used in the attempted assassination of Osama bin Laden, and it later participated actively in the CIA's rendition schemes to interrogate and torture suspected terrorists. The presence of the U.S. military at the southern Karshi-Khanabad ("K2") base also raised Uzbekistan's profile considerably, giving its regime cause to press its status as the region's pivotal central power. Five years later, however, Uzbekistan had failed everyone's expectations: America had all but vacated the country, and political breakdown was a near certainty. What went wrong?

Uzbekistan is the heart of the heartland: Its population is larger than the rest of the Central Asian post-Soviet states combined, and it shares borders with all of them. In the early 1990s, Uzbekistan was considered more likely than Kazakhstan to be the region's leader, with its numerous urban centers and better infrastructure. The country was the world's eighth-largest source of gold, with significant oil, gas, and uranium deposits. Its cotton production and industrial base made it a choice location for large textile factories and automobile plants. President Islom Karimov also seemed a progressive fellow. "Better tennis racquets than military rockets," he once said as host of the highly rated President's Cup tournament in the capital, Tashkent.

But while Kazakhstan's President Nazarbayev nurtured a future-oriented Turkic renaissance, Karimov actually emphasized a backward-looking national identity under the banner of Tamerlane—the great fourteenth-century khan—whose horse-mounted statues replaced Karl Marx all over Tashkent.[1] Unlike Timur, however, who sent caravans in all directions to deepen ties with China, Arabia, and Hindustan, Karimov all but sealed off his country, causing the biggest single blockage in the new Silk Road, and violently turned against his own citizens. The shiny, modern banks in central Tashkent have one client—the government—and the joke runs that they might simply be warehouses for stacks of Uzbek som notes, sacks of which are needed to purchase anything of value. The country has lost most of its talent and competitive business to better-managed Kazakhstan. There is no better symbol of this post-Soviet drift between Kazakhstan and Uzbekistan than the Aral Sea. Once the dried-up, polluted symbol of impractical Soviet-era cotton irrigation schemes, the Kazakh government has built a dam to divide the sea and slowly replenish a "Smaller Aral" from the Syr Darya River flows. Meanwhile, the larger Uzbek portion remains a shrinking, poisonous swamp, with clouds of pesticide hovering above it. As Kazakhstan elevates through the second world, Uzbekistan may well sink into the third.

The palm of Central Asia's hand is the Ferghana Valley, which now contains 20 percent of the region's population in only 5 percent of the territory. But with every ethnic group disproportionately represented within neighbors' borders, it is also the epicenter of Central Asia's version of the still evolving conflict syndrome of the Caucasus, where Stalin similarly drew the lines of fate to create demographic schizophrenia, pitting minorities against one another to prevent them from agitating against the government. In 1990, ugly Uzbek-Kyrgyz ethnic rioting erupted, which Soviet troops did nothing to prevent, Moscow preferred to blame Islam. Demographically, both western Kyrgyzstan and northern Tajikistan remain effectively Uzbek. Given the Ferghana

Valley's dense population and high poverty, a serious escalation could trigger a refugee nightmare. The growth in drug trafficking and the decline in social services under regressive regimes have had a devastating impact on the youth of Ferghana, who, like young Arabs, sit listlessly in street-corner cafés waiting for work.

Today it is still impossible to grasp the vibrancy and architectural grandeur of the Silk Road without visiting the madrasahs and bazaars of Samarkand and Bukhara (both in Uzbekistan), where in narrow, hidden chambers silk is made on wooden looms according to the same techniques smuggled from China to Persia centuries earlier. At Bukhara's fabled Mir-i-Arab madrasah, bald men in *pakuls* with long, wispy beards quietly restore intricate tiles of Islam calligraphy. In a nearby underground shop, musicians collect and assemble centuries-old instruments used in the hypnotic ensembles that produce Silk Road music: high-pitched flutes, tightly strung guitars, Arabic drums—but no one is there to listen to them. Samarkand's mighty Registan madrasah, once the center of all parades, festivals, and bazaars under Tamerlane, is today a looming but eerily empty space. Samarkand could become the symbol of a modern Islamic renaissance, again earning the city the appellation of the "second Mecca." And the Ferghana Valley, the heart of the Silk Road's mélange of currencies and cuisines, could have become a breadbasket for the region, elevating the farmers of all bordering states. Instead, Uzbekistan is a case study in wasted opportunities and warped ambitions.

To boost his country's gravitas in the "war on terror," Karimov forcefully banned Islamist parties and social organizations. The use of such self-serving labels as "extremist" or "fundamentalist" to describe established social and educational institutions such as madrasahs is a deflecting tactic commonly employed by entrenched despots in Central Asia and the Arab world. Ironically, even as a nominal Muslim himself, Karimov repeated the mistakes of the atheist Bolsheviks who fought for over a decade with the Basmachi "bandits" all over Turkestan, driving them into the mountain fringes, after which Stalin destroyed all but perhaps a thousand of the nearly thirty thousand mosques, with the remainder being used as factories or museums. However, the Soviets at least sanctioned an "official" Islam to boost their credibility with Islamic nations, establishing four *muftiyyas* (directorates) with Tashkent as the center.[2] By contrast, Karimov both exaggerated the threat from Islamist groups and overestimated popular patience with autocracy, all the while failing to persuade Uzbeks that he was the proper person to lead a rediscovery of their glorious heritage.

There is nothing inevitable about the spread of a violent Islamist fundamentalism northward from Pakistan and Afghanistan into the Ferghana Valley and beyond. "Islamist groups have largely been a form of political opposition in the region, not a force for radicalization," a former Uzbek official explained after quitting government service out of principle. In Kazakhstan, young men regularly attend mosque without fear of harassment and Islamist discontent is not a factor there. Even in Uzbekistan, radicalism was initially just minor blowback against ethnic Uzbek warlords in northern Afghanistan, but with no intent to overthrow the regime. Most Uzbeks would prefer to remain aloof from the turbulence of political Islam found elsewhere. "We were never affected by religious problems in daily life," he continued. "It is only now that we've taken the wrong route in dealing with Islam."

A balloon that is squeezed will not deflate; it will swell on one side until it explodes. Karimov has created the West's and his own worst nightmare: a state with no functioning opposition other than the organized Islamist groups who have made Uzbekistan and Tajikistan their prime targets.[3] Two major Islamist movements are now dedicated to advancing pan-Islamic nationalism—with overthrowing Karimov as an essential prerequisite. Hizb ut-Tahrir began as a nonviolent Islamic community dedicated to confronting corruption and poverty, but through the use of low-tech pamphlets and high-tech Internet sites, it has become something of a Sunni Islamist vanguard.[4] The Islamic Movement of Uzbekistan (IMU) has active militant cells based in Afghanistan and Tajikistan, receives financing from Saudi Wahhabists and Pakistani madrasahs, and has used sparse camps in the Ferghana Valley to train recruits in combat and assassinations while providing slanted readings of the Koran to justify killing Americans and Jews.[5]

A regime like Karimov's is the best recruiting advertisement these groups could ever have wished for. Thousands of their members are urban youth who were not even practicing Muslims several years earlier, but the failure of Uzbek elites to provide any comprehensive, modern national identity has opened the door to alternatives.[6] Even for secular-minded Uzbeks, there is little that is not preferable to Karimov's oppression, which has ensured that widows join Hizb ut-Tahrir to carry out their murdered husbands' work. In 2004, suicide attacks in Taskhent's public squares—a practice completely unknown to the region—won the sympathy of much of the Uzbek population. "We could wind up like Afghanistan," worried one student in a run-down quarter of the capital. "There is no option but conflict here."

Karimov was always an autocrat, but not an all-powerful one, making him that much more paranoid. His collectivization depressed farmers' incomes by not allowing them to own land, and he imposed high tariffs on imports and tightly controlled foreign exchange. As foreign investment dried up, Karimov even attempted total ownership of the economy and its increasingly worthless som by blocking the shuttle trade at the country's borders in the Ferghana Valley and with southern Kazakhstan. No move could have more quickly undermined loyalty to him among the poor Uzbek traders whose livelihoods depend on the vast outdoor bazaars on either side of the border with Kyrgyzstan at Karasu. There, giant Chinese shipping containers are stacked two by two, forming a labrynthine caravanserai, a dizzying maze of colorful storefronts where Uzbeks shop for cheap Chinese goods blocked for import by the government. The entire setup could be packed up and moved in a matter of days, much like during the Silk Road era. Karimov made sure it did, scrapping the bazaar and demolishing homes on the border. To augment what remained after Karimov's border closure, Soviet-style black markets sprouted throughout the Ferghana region, but profits plummeted, not least because cart-pushing watermelon merchants had to pay larger bribes than car drivers to get across the tightly controlled border, shaking their heads as their day's earnings were lost to baksheesh.

Border closure also meant a longer route back to the nearest large Uzbek city, Andijan, the fifteenth-century birthplace of the Mughal emperor Babur. To intimidate local Ferghana entrepreneurs, Karimov put two dozen successful businessmen on trial, tarring them as Islamist radicals. In May 2005, police brutally gunned down peaceful demonstrators calling for their release, the worst such massacre in Asia since Beijing's 1989 Tiananmen Square uprising. One man arrested on no evidence for alleged extremism was tortured for two years, after which authorities told him, "President Karimov forgives you—but if you tell anyone what has happened here, we'll arrest you again."

Tashkent is now the main police city of a massive police state. Beginning at a 140-mile radius from the capital, military and police checkpoints, often masquerading as redundant internal customs posts, search all vehicles in an effort to prevent any antiregime elements from entering the capital. Any outside agitators reaching Tashkent would be disappointed to find that the main government quadrangle has been ringed off in a manner resembling Beijing's Forbidden City, with "beautification" the official excuse for sealing off any space large enough for demonstrations. Even the Chorsu Bazaar, the city's largest, was cut in half by arbitrarily arranged fences. It is ironic that Karimov fears his own people, given that he commands such a comprehensive security apparatus, which alienates most citizens save the innocent young children selling postcards at Bukhara's shrines. The Interior Ministry and the security services have their own armies and financial interests, augmenting the ranks of an army of sixty thousand troops. Together, they are easily capable of annexing the majority Uzbek-populated Khujand region of Tajikistan.

Karimov painted the Andijan crackdown as in accordance with America's "war on terror," placing the United States in the uncomfortable position of seeing its democratization and counterterrorism agendas set against each other.[7] Before Andijan, Uzbeks were impressed by U.S. CENTCOM chief Anthony Zinni's remark, "I am not Tamerlane; I didn't come here to conquer you."[8] But the West's harsh criticism of Karimov pushed him into Russian and Chinese arms—patrons who gave him the cover of the SCO to demand that the United States withdraw from its Karshi-Khanabad base. Uzbekistan had become yet another venue for realpolitik chess maneuvers, and the outcome remains uncertain.

Karimov also promptly shut down or evicted most American NGOs dealing with with human rights, justice reform, and independent media training. "Every day we either get summoned to court for a hearing or receive notice that we must vacate the country," a Western correspondent lamented. "Our partners want us here to teach them skills, but the government is too nervous." Democracy-promotion NGOs are part of a seemingly contradictory but fundamentally critical U.S. foreign policy approach in which America plays the role of good cop and bad cop simultaneously. They offer to train both sides of society—the rulers and the ruled—an offer usually only taken up by the latter. Even where official U.S. policy supports a regime, its NGOs stand up to bullies, teaching locals how to do the same.

But the gross inconsistencies of this well-intentioned policy also brought about its demise. The paradigm of the "war on terror" led the State Department and the Pentagon to work at cross-purposes: When the former reduced aid due to human rights violations, the latter increased funding for military assistance. Only a tiny fraction of the $500 million spent on Uzbekistan was devoted to democratization. Foreign assistance—which is always both developmental *and* political —ultimately engendered neither economic change nor diplomatic loyalty. And when little or no conditionality on political reform is applied, leaders are emboldened to pursue far more aggressive strategies against their domestic opposition.[9] Karimov, for example, used American funds not to invest in crop diversification to salvage a faltering economy but rather to offer higher salaries to those who would serve loyally in his security services, thickening his armor against regime change. If America continues to focus only on relations with regimes— in contrast to Europe's focus on improving systems—then even Karimov's successors may simply continue the practice of currying favor with China and Russia. As one former Uzbek official accusingly remarked at a quiet restaurant in Tashkent, "Western strategy should change from labeling a leader 'our son of a bitch' to just a plain 'son of a bitch.'"

The trouble with offering military assistance to tinpot regimes in a geopolitical marketplace is that it purchases very little political leverage when other powers can make similar offers.[10] While NATO suspends cooperation with countries that abandon democratic reform, the SCO remains a cozy mutual support group for autocrats who prefer seemingly cost-free Chinese and Russian patronage to heavy-handed Western tutelage. With Karimov's retreat behind layers of advisers, his repressive politics and command-and-control economic style indicate more than just a stylistic shift toward the Chinese or Russian model. Uzbekistan doesn't even border China, but Karimov has willingly thrown his country into China's sphere of influence. Soon after the Andijan massacre, Karimov flew to Beijing and signed energy deals for oil and gas fields in the Ferghana Valley valued at nearly a billion dollars, including a gas pipeline to western China. Comfortable with corruption and opacity in business dealings, Russian and Chinese firms now control most of the area's mineral deposits. Russia and Uzbekistan also signed a mutual defense agreement in late 2005, further diminishing America's position.

But while Kazakhstan has enhanced its security by maintaining good relations with all of the major powers, Karimov has undermined Uzbekistan's stability by cutting off the Western leg of support—leaving his country open to exploitative collusion by China and Russia. At the same time, America and the EU are still popular among the Uzbek population. After Andijan, the United States flew hundreds of Uzbek refugees from Kyrgyzstan to Europe over Karimov's vociferous objections. "We don't get a lot of information, but we know that America and Europe made the right decision, so we still respect them," a young Uzbek academic explained. Europe additionally imposed a travel ban on top Uzbek officials, and fractious Uzbek exiles in Europe are now being trained by Western agencies. Note that in disowning Karimov, the West has not enraged Uzbekistan's Islamist groups. Instead, China and Russia might take the blame for unhinged autocrats like Karimov—and eventually suffer the blowback themselves.

Uzbekistan proves that it is far easier to close a country than to open it. For a leader like Karimov, there is no trade-off among democratization, economic growth, and national security: The stability of one's own rule *is* survival, both for the regime and the state. "There's been no transition or progress here since glasnost," a taxi driver in Bukhara vented. "And there won't be until Karimov is hanging from a lamppost." Karimov's siege mentality utterly precludes any possibility of legitimate succession. Still in power nearly two decades after independence, he will take his tyranny to the grave.

Uzbekistan's largest province, Karakalpakstan, which covers the entire western third of the country, is currently a dried-up desert due to overuse of the Amu Darya River for irrigation; meanwhile, the Aral Sea, which once provided more than a tenth of the Soviet Union's fish, no longer supports life beyond the bacteria that infect local inhabitants. On the other side of this new wasteland lies Turkmenistan, the vast majority of which is covered by the same cracked desert. Its nomadic, horse-breeding tribes are scarcely removed from the days when Merw was the Seljuk Dynasty's second capital after Baghdad, making them the most resistant to Soviet expansion, against which they revolted violently through the 1930s. But with its enormous natural-gas supply, Turkmenistan is essentially one of the world's largest gas stations, albeit with managers who open and close the pumps arbitrarily.

Unlike Islam Karimov, Turkmenistan's leader, Saparmurat Niyazov, who died in 2006, was not too modest to hold himself, rather than Tamerlane or another historical figure, up as the national hero. Niyazov—who dubbed himself the *Turkmenbashi*, Father of all Turkmen—replaced history books throughout the country with his own *Ruhnama* (which was blasphemously accorded the same status as the Koran) and poetry such as "I am the Turkmen spirit and I was reborn,/ To bring you a golden age and happiness." His delusional mix of identifying himself with the state, lobotomizing the opposition, purging the intelligentsia, and plundering the economy was a form of self-glorification on the order of Pol Pot or Kim Jong-Il. He closed hospitals and libraries outside Ashgabat while pouring millions of dollars into flashy apartments, eight-lane highways, and extravagant fountains and statues of himself—one standing 120 feet tall and rotating with the sun. The country has become little more than a sultanate in which power is dispensed through clan-based allies; there is no notion of constitutionalism. To demonstrate his benevolence, he released thousands of prisoners in an annual amnesty ritual. Niyazov crafted policies on a whim and against the advice of his few advisers, earning the country a reputation as an economic statistician's nightmare in which government data represents more "the world the Turkmenbashi would like to exist, not the one in which most Turkmen actually live."[11] In the real world, the masses are unemployed and benumbed by drugs. Upon Niyazov's death, the new nomenklatura sealed the country to prevent citizens from fleeing with gold and then rigged the constitution to maintain their kleptocratic grip on power. "We had hoped for a transition to more reality-based policies, but that's clearly not the new regime's priority," a Western aid-agency official, himself numb from visits to the time-warped country, aridly observed.

In contrast to its Caspian neighbor Kazakhstan, Turkmenistan is evidence that resource wealth need not correlate to sound economic or political management.[12] Niyazov lived in perpetual fear of foreign investment in the energy sector because of the political intrusion it could bring. As a result, oil and gas production actually fell in the 1990s. Ironically, because Niyazov never allowed the volume of his

country's oil and gas reserves to be certified, lacking foreign investment has left Russia's Gazprom still in control of the country's northern pipelines, allowing it to dictate gas prices. A proposed gas pipeline
through Afghanistan and Pakistan to India—one that would avoid
Turkmenistan's gas-producing competitors Iran and Russia—stalled
as much due to the country's lack of transparency as Afghanistan's instability.[13]

Growing demand for new oil and gas resources, however, make
fresh efforts to tap Turkmenistan more a question of when and how
than if. Though Russia still controls the Turkmen gas flow to Europe,
Turkmenistan could evade Russian control and profit from Western energy contracts if, like Kazakhstan, it links its energy supplies across the
Caspian to the Caucasus energy corridor, which extends all the way to
Hungary. The desire to escape Russia has also prompted Turkmenistan
to consider a gas pipeline across Kazakhstan to China.[14] The United
States covets the former Soviet base in Merw, hoping that Turkmenistan might serve its strategic aims vis-à-vis Afghanistan—and also Iran
—just as Uzbekistan once did. It is a sign of the twisted nature of the
new Great Game that Turkmenistan may become the country most cooperative with the West in its efforts to intimidate Iran, rein in Russia,
and boost energy flow to Europe. But it is yet another reminder of how
tenuous outside influence can be on all of Central Asia's khanates.

CHAPTER 13

AFGHANISTAN AND PAKISTAN:
TAMING SOUTH-CENTRAL ASIA

ON THE DIPLOMATIC circuit, President Hamid Karzai of Afghanistan and General Pervez Musharraf of Pakistan are top-billed celebrities, drawing large crowds of curious admirers for their status as leaders of two of the world's most embattled and dangerous countries. Offering two of history's finest examples of trade and invasion routes going hand in hand, both are third-world states with existential legitimacy crises; in each case, the country's very existence is owed to strategic blunders and colonial anomalies. Afghanistan, which to the north blends into the Central Asian steppe historically held by Turkestan's khans, is a microcosm of the entire region, with significant numbers of Pathans, Uzbeks, Turkmen, and Persians (Hazara), yet none of these groups constitutes a majority of the population of thirty million. Pakistan is also a tribal federation with weak institutions (though with a sophisticated postcolonial elite), plagued by illicit flows of weapons, drugs, and Islamist militants. In both countries, suicide bombing has reached the height of futility: Nobody even seems to ask anymore what the message is. Officials are in perpetual survival mode: Neither Karzai nor Musharraf may last much longer. Yet both countries remain crucial east-west and north-south crossroads of the new Silk Road and new Great Game.

The historical accident of America's 2001 invasion of Afghanistan suddenly made it a strategic priority for the West.[1] But five years after the fall of the Taliban, Afghanistan's Karzai was still little more than the mayor of Kabul, his credibility as a national leader expiring until his inevitable ouster (or possibly abdication). Uzbek warlords in the north and Taliban militants in the south continue to struggle against his regime, drawing support from their own militias and drug-smuggling operations through all neighboring countries. "The defense of Germany begins in the Hindu Kush," declared Germany's former defense minister Peter Struck in 2002. Europe, Russia, China, and the United States are all very concerned about Afghanistan's fragility, not to mention the export of drugs through the Ferghana Valley and Russia to Europe, but declarations about NATO's global interests only underscore its failure to ensure Afghan stability.

Afghans have become disillusioned by the West's inability to restore the order that even the Taliban had provided. Afghanistan's budget is made up almost entirely of Western aid, but most such assistance is actually spent on overhead, security, and salaries, with much of the remainder lost to corruption. Under British and Soviet influence, schools, hospitals, and roads were built in Afghanistan, but three decades of grinding internal warfare have reduced the country into an ashen state from which it will take decades to emerge. Not surprisingly, Afghans who once grew vines and raisins have turned to poppy cultivation for their livelihoods, with greater output in 2005 than under the Taliban. It is miraculous that the tens of thousands of Afghans living in huts in the hills above Kabul do not freeze during each harsh winter.

Most observers consider Afghanistan NATO's furthest protectorate, but in fact the country is already—and once again—part of the new Great Game with the SCO. NATO today occupies the same plot of land in Kabul used by the British in the nineteenth century and the Soviet Union in the twentieth. After the United States joined the existing anti-Taliban coalition in 2001, it gradually came to rely more heavily on its fortified bases at Bagram and Kandahar, with the aim of limiting Iranian and Chinese influence in Central Asia. But the abysmal pace of the American-led reconstruction has created an opportunity for these adversaries to turn the tables. The narrow Wakhan Corridor, a sliver of land that connects China and Afghanistan, was demarcated specifically to end the Great Game, but today it merely lets China reopen ancient branches of the Silk Road, with numerous pipeline and road routes—the Salang tunnels of the future—hinging on Afghan stability. As early as 1956 Americans warned the Afghan chief Mohammed Daoud Khan that Soviet assistance "was laying a logistical infrastructure for invasion."[2] China quietly pursued deals with Taliban-controlled Afghanistan in the 1990s, and now takes a free ride on NATO's military presence to underbid on sensitive road projects and large construction contracts along the resurrected routes from Kabul to Herat—a city being resurrected in a gaudy style described as "narcotecture"—with the ultimate aim of safe overland routes across the "Tajik belt" to Iran, which is meeting China halfway through its manipulation of Afghan refugee flows, tactical support for Taliban groups, and investments in infrastructure projects.[3]

Though Afghanistan and Pakistan are considered American allies in the "war on terror," they have already attained observer status in the SCO, with membership a near-term certainty. "China may just be waiting until NATO is exhausted to outmaneuver it through better-coordinated trade, development, and policing programs," a hardheaded analyst of Afghanistan suggested. "It could start as soon as Afghanistan's army becomes fully functional and NATO countries, including the U.S., downsize their presence."

South of the Hindu Kush, the Durand Line, which nominally divides Afghanistan and Pakistan, remains an imaginary boundary, as evidenced by the flow of weapons northward and the flight of Afghan refugees southward during the anti-Soviet insurgency. The two countries have been linked by the Khyber Pass through centuries of conquest dating back to Alexander the Great. Smuggling and trade remain synonymous over the Khyber Pass, where today a constant stream of trucks carrying cement and fruit snakes up and down its narrow passages to Afghanistan—a supply channel that will remain necessary for decades. Pakistan is still home to approximately two million Afghans, who over the past thirty years have turned once-leafy Peshawar into a roiling, overcrowded dump of rubbish-clogged streams. But the guest books of Peshawar *havelis* (guest residences) are full of effusive thank-you notes from the British travelers still welcome there. Despite years of warring with Afridi tribes, the British built a railroad and left as friends. By contrast, America's presence south of the Hindu Kush today is no more secure than north of it.

Situated at the crossroads of Southwest, Central, and South Asia, Pakistan is divided internally by the Indus River, which dictates the regional orientation of its provinces. West of the Indus, Pakistan's vast but sparsely populated North-West Frontier Province (NWFP) and Baluchistan, which today border Iran and Afghanistan, once constituted the outer frontier of British India. In the name of acquiring strategic depth, Pakistan aided Afghan factions in the 1970s, formed the rear base for the mujahideen in the 1980s, and was instrumental in the creation of the Taliban in the 1990s—all of which inadvertently turned the NWFP into the "Taliban spa for rehabilitation and inspiration" it is today.[4] Pashtun tribes have long favored a porous 1,500-mile Pakistan-Afghan frontier as well, seeing it as their own mountainous Pakhtunistan quasi-state. Now they have joined forces with the Taliban, feeding poorly trained fighters from Pakistan's madrasahs into Afghanistan, where they use familiar anti-Soviet tactics to attack NATO forces and recapture key border areas for weapons and drug trafficking. Half-baked "Peace Jirgas" to unite the tribes on either side of the border under the banner of counterterrorism only expose the futility of American, Afghan, and Pakistani government efforts to tame the tribal frontier through schemes that none of them has the competence to implement. Under intense Western pressure, Pakistan is effectively at war with itself.

As far back as the fifth century B.C., Buddhist sanctuaries with marvelous stone stupas such as Taxila thrived in northern Pakistan. Today, halfway between Peshawar, at the base of the Khyber Pass, and the tidy, lattice-grid capital of Islamabad, the tribal areas feature law by *jirga* (tribal elder councils), and blood feuds reign. "By funding the madrasahs, the Saudi government has had more influence here than our own government, which has let the schools and homes crumble," pointed out a chauffeur who has been shuttling between the two cities for twenty years. Even in Islamabad, the Lal Masjid (Red Mosque) had long been the focal point of the city's creeping "Talibanization" until its near-total destruction in a military raid in 2007. But just as Al-Qaeda used Afghanistan even when it had no Afghan members, it can still morph and blend wherever it finds a hospitable environment—at present nowhere more so than Pakistan's Federally Administered Tribal Areas (FATA).

Though Pakistan's conflict with India over Kashmir flares intermittently, its interminable Afghan dilemma and location within both CENTCOM's and China's strategic orbits indicates a Central Asian future.* During the Cold War, the United States "tilted" alternately between India and Pakistan, but when it suspended arms shipments to both countries after their 1965 war, Pakistan found a willing supplier in China, which had gone to war with India in 1962. Ever since, Pakistan has been at the center of China's diplomatic maneuvers, infrastructure routing, and military ambitions. By recognizing Kashmir's northern territories as belonging to Pakistan in the 1960s, China suddenly put India on the psychological defensive and blocked its access to Afghanistan.[5] Pakistan then proudly touted the Karakoram Highway network's extension from Xinjiang over the 15,000-foot Khunjerab Pass (the name means "Valley of Blood")—a "four tank wide" corridor easing the passage of Chinese weapons across the Himalayas.

In the geopolitical marketplace, Pakistan will forge alliances with any available partner—anything to avoid becoming strategically useless, and it has set the standard for manipulating the United States while making few concessions in return. The United States conveniently supplies arms—Pakistan is the third largest recipient of U.S. military assistance—that have little effectiveness against scattered Taliban militants but have high potential for use against India, while Pakistan has forbidden American interrogation of nuclear proliferation mastermind A. Q. Khan and largely resisted American pressure to apprehend al-Qaeda suspects for fear of alienating the tribal population. Instead, it is alleged, Pakistan kidnaps tribal men at random and passes them off to the United States as terrorists. For General Musharraf, counterterrorism has been all about bounty-hunting and booty-collecting.[6]

All the while, Pakistan has become a more reliable client of China, demonstrating far greater loyalty to their "All Weather Friendship" than to America. At China's behest, Pakistan has brutally cracked down on Uyghur activities inside Pakistan, executing militants and ejecting

---

*Pakistan and Afghanistan's widespread classification as South Asian is largely a British imperial, Indo-centric historical construction that does not reflect the present strategic reality by which India is increasingly a part of East Asian power calculations.

Uyghur students from Pakistani madrasahs.[7] The same month that the U.S. Congress reduced aid to Pakistan in 2006 over human rights concerns, Musharraf attended the SCO summit in Shanghai and received promises of financial support. Another example of Chinese interests trumping American ones is Pakistan's southwestern province of Baluchistan—the Kurdistan of Central Asia—whose gas reserves provide over a third of Pakistan's energy needs. China has funded the $350 million extension of the Karakoram Highway along the Indus River all the way to the deepwater port and oil refinery under construction by the Chinese at Gwadar, on the Arabian Sea, bestowing Pakistan the traversal axis it has always coveted, while allowing China to avoid the Straits of Malacca in accessing Persian Gulf oil. "Gwadar was a tiny village of grinding poverty just ten years ago," recalled a Pakistani businessman doing real estate deals there. "All it had were great views. The Chinese are turning it into a world-class energy hub: The *Titanic* would be able to dock there! It also gives the government much more strategic confidence to be a player with Iran and the oil-rich Arabs." Pakistan sees its national unity and long-term interests far better served by diverting troops from the NWFP to quash Baluch separatism—and protect China's port—than by capturing Pashtun militants for the United States. While Pakistan's leaders lambaste America's aggressive policies, a Chinese general recently referred to Pakistan as "China's Israel," all but terming it China's bridgehead into the Arabian Sea. Most tellingly, it was Chinese pressure after the kidnapping of Chinese massage parlour workers that led to Musharraf's swift siege of Islamabad's Lal Masjid.

"While most countries have armies, Pakistan's army has a country," runs the familiar joke. General Musharraf's coup in 1999 was the first ever to occur in a nuclear-armed state. Though his rhetoric of "enlightened moderation" earned him the sobriquet "Shah of Pakistan," Musharraf's unholy alliance with Islamist parties and radical groups has undermined both himself and America's stabilization agenda for Afghanistan, the same thing that happened to his military predecessors. As for modernization, Pakistan's military-controlled economy is actually a fraud of luxury imports and rock-bottom real estate selloffs, including a sleek, Arab-financed "seven-star" property in Islamabad meant to emulate the glitter of Dubai.[8] Karachi is at once the country's richest and poorest city, the center of industry and of radical madrasahs exporting extremists to Afghanistan and Kashmir, and the site of deadly riots between pro- and anti-Musharraf forces. The only thing "booming" in Pakistan are the constant suicide bombings in all corners of the country. Most men are still employed as chauffeurs, security guards, or shopkeepers struggling for a predictable life in an increasingly disorderly country. Income inequality is increasing; carjacking, burglary, and sectarian violence are all on the rise. Over the next twenty years, the population will near two hundred million—unmanageable even for the military. Pakistan is becoming more like faltering, splintering Indonesia than the Islamist democratic powerhouse Turkey.

Musharraf took power in the name of efficiency and anticorruption, not democracy. In Pakistan people talk about elections but never quite know when they might take place or even what form they will take. Under Musharraf, non-Punjabi provincial heads have at times been labeled national security threats, and parliament has been dissolved on a whim. Even after he removed his military uniform to remain civilian president, his misrule has produced a society with three mutually hostile poles of power: the military, civilian opposition, and an array of Islamist groups. Throughout its six decades of existence, Pakistan has alternated between military rule and something resembling democracy. Whether under democracy or dictatorship, however, Pakistan's citizens have become accustomed to corruption and underdevelopment. The cycle is likely to continue once Musharraf's turn is up. Ultimately, despite their celebrity status in the West, Karzai and Musharraf are incapable of stabilizing their countries, both of which have been steadily disintegrating since the British empire withdrew. Western efforts have not been nearly enough. Will China do better?

CONCLUSION:
A CHANGE OF HEART

THROUGHOUT HISTORY, WHENEVER the Silk Road has functioned properly, borders have been opened and prosperity has been shared. Blockage of its manifold passages leads to insecurity, escalation, and conflict every time. Yet as the detritus of a decade of failed initiatives attests, sovereignty still trumps lofty aspirations for a Central Asian confederation of collective resources, which opens the door to imperial interference.[1] China is winning the new Great Game because it is building the new Silk Road, taking the best of the British and Russian strategies from a century ago: preserving buffer states and allies like the former but without the abrasive conquest style of the latter.

The interests of the United States and the EU in Central Asia—counterterrorism, energy security, democratization—still greatly outstrip the two empires' capacity to achieve them. For two decades the West has been both unwilling and incapable of inducing genuine democratic reform in a single post-Soviet state in Central Asia. But as Mackinder wrote in his landmark *Democratic Ideals and Reality,* "In the heartland, where physical contrasts are few, it is only with the aid of a conscious ideal . . . that we shall be able to entrench true freedom."[2]

Without creating more supportive and interdependent institutions within these societies, the West's leverage will continue to diminish—particularly if the next generation of leaders lacks domestic loyalty and legitimacy.

Regional cooperation is the approach that would most quickly achieve the vision of a twenty-first-century Silk Road able to serve the Stans' own needs while advancing the strategy suggested by Zbigniew Brzezinski: to "consolidate and perpetuate the prevailing geopolitical pluralism on the map of Eurasia." The EU and the OSCE are viewed as honest, if intrusive, brokers, the only patrons not perceived as attacking Islam. The EU can make greater aid to Central Asian governments conditional on adherence to the norms of the Council of Europe of which the post-Soviet Stans are members, and it can teach them to maximize their participation in the SCO to bind China and Russia to commitments rather than becoming helpless quasi-colonies. The promotion of liberalism and regional cooperation remains the West's best weapon.[3]

Europe may still benefit as much as China from a revived east-west transport corridor lined with fiber-optic cables stretching from Frankfurt to Shanghai. It is worth recalling that it was the Roman appetite for Eastern treasures that inspired the first Silk Road and that the term was coined in the nineteenth century by the German geographer Baron Ferdinand von Richtofen. The Silk Road may have an Eastern connotation, but it is very much a Western construct. Europe once again covets all sorts of Chinese merchandise, making Central Asia—through its deepening economic ties with both East and West—part of a greater Eurasian economy of growing trade among and between European and Asian blocs.[4] After Ladas, the most common cars in the Stans are old Mercedes, Volkswagens, and Audis. Rather than allow its cars to be stolen and smuggled east, Europe could simply build them in Kyrgyzstan, saving on costs and creating jobs while boosting sales in China and Kazakhstan. Upgrading Turkmenistan and Uzbekistan into manufacturing hubs will allow those states to compete with China rather than being flooded by Chinese goods made with native cotton. But China's remarkable ability to shape both infrastructure and markets through shrewd diplomacy is not limited to Central Asia. It is also evident far across the Pacific Ocean, in South America.

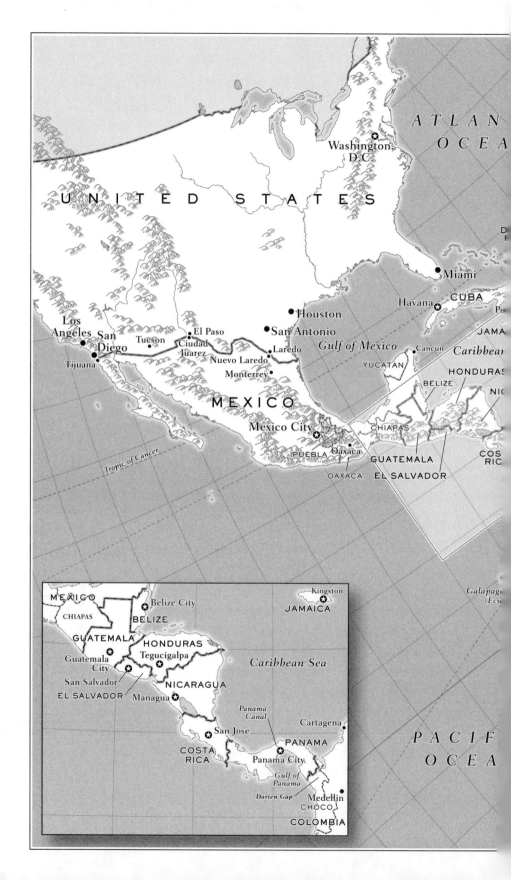

PART III
THE END OF THE MONROE DOCTRINE

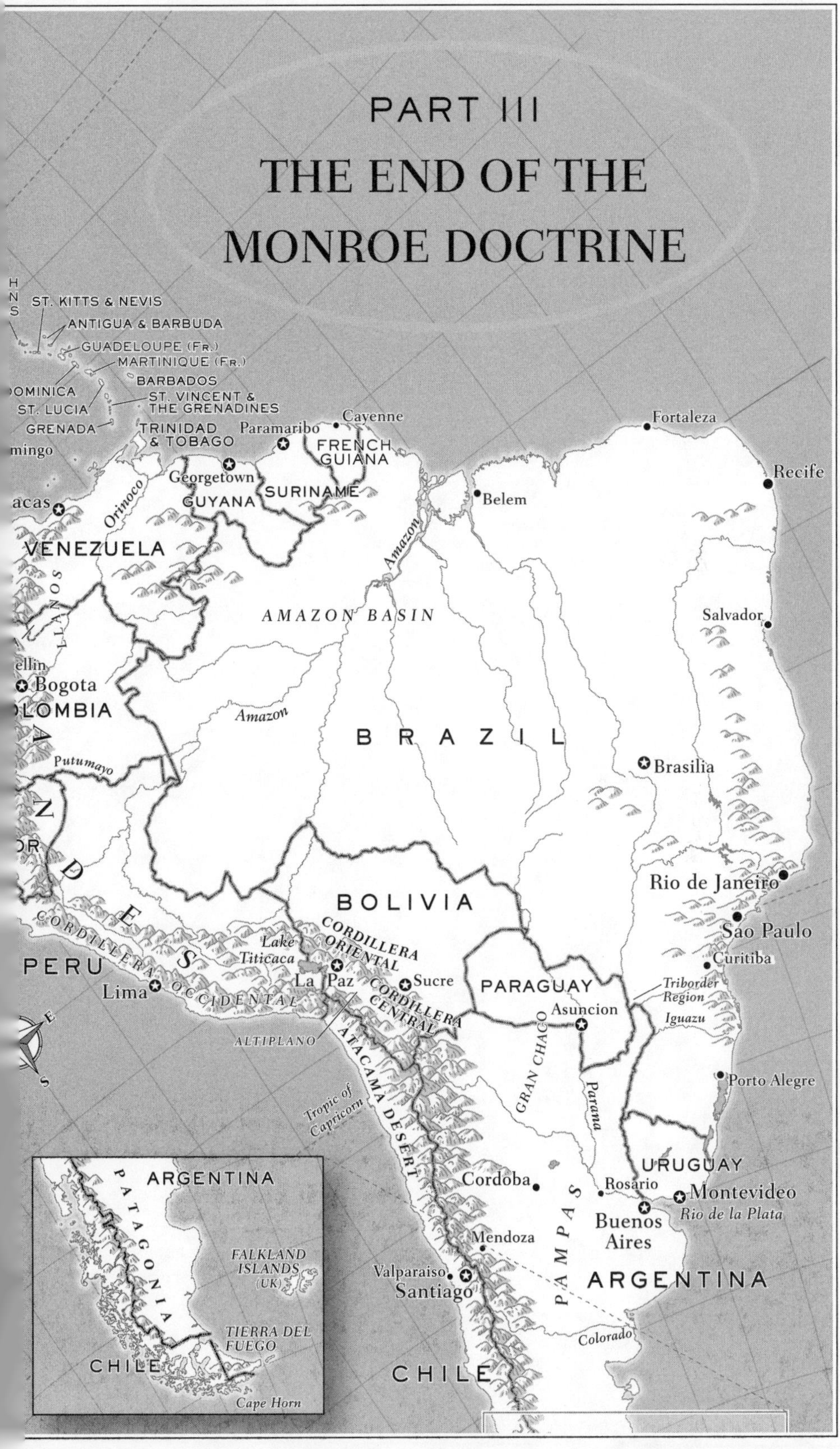

CHAPTER 14

THE NEW RULES
OF THE GAME

EFFECTIVE HEGEMONY CAN be like oxygen: ubiquitous as the air we breathe, permeating our physical environment, and dictating the limits of human life—yet completely invisible. But hegemony can also suffocate like a sealed room in which the oxygen is slowly being sucked out. America's twentieth-century global ascendancy was preceded by a century of building hegemony throughout the Western Hemisphere. In the twenty-first century, however, this hegemony is eroding in America's traditional backyard of Latin America, where gravities of influence are at play that a complacent geographic determinism could not have predicted. South America's plentiful natural resources can now reach global markets—particularly Asia—faster than ever. If globalization means the death of distance, then a pillar of U.S. power—dominance by proximity—has ended. But if America does not speak for the Americas, then who does?

Latin America has long seemed a geopolitical non sequitur, oceans away from the world's principal strategic theaters. But today it is casting its eyes east and west to avoid the north. The stakes are existential: Solid American relations with Latin America could mean substantial energy self-sufficiency in the Western Hemispheric pan-region and independence from the turbulence of Eurasia. Oil from areas stretching from the Arctic to Canada's Alberta to the Gulf of Mexico to Venezuela, combined with new sources of power, such as Brazilian ethanol, could unite North and South America in a trade bloc unsurpassed in the rest of the world. But America has taken its southern neighbors for granted—a mistake that is potentially disastrous in any relationship. "This is not America's continent; it belongs to a dozen countries and we define it," flatly stated a Brazilian diplomat. Mexico, Brazil, and Argentina together account for two-thirds of Latin America's population, with Venezuela and Colombia making up much of the rest. If these core states can overcome their inner demons, they would form the spine of a coherent Latin America capable of rising from the margins to shape global order. Globalization and America's geopolitical rivals are giving them—individually and together—that chance.

Imperial systems can be compared to bubbles blowing up in size, expanding and rising, then bursting and falling. Latin America has always been caught in others' imperial bubbles, and never been able to form its own. Indeed, because Latin America's resources have always served the developed world, its own *under*development was integral to the rise of world capitalism. "The division of labor among nations is that some specialize in winning and the others in losing," wrote the Uruguayan dissident Eduardo Galeano. "Latin America was precocious: it has specialized in losing ever since those remote times when Renaissance Europeans ventured across the ocean."[1] Beginning with the arrival of Christopher Columbus, competition to subjugate the hemisphere's vast expanses was ruthless. United only by a commitment to spread Catholicism, the Spanish and Portuguese monarchies divided all the colonies of the New World. Spanish conqueror Hernán Cortés destroyed Mexico's Aztec empire in the 1520s, and during Spain's direct domination of Portugal from 1580 to 1640, Spain alone essentially controlled the entire Western Hemisphere. Native populations were subjugated by the sword and exotic disease, while Christian charity justified the bleeding of the New World for its silver and gold. In 1551 Spanish priest Bartolomé de las Casas wrote *The Devastation of the Indies,* a damning critique of slavery by agents of the Spanish Crown, sometimes described as the first human rights report in history—even if the imperial mentality was impervious to such appeals to conscience. After the Protestant Reformation, the New World reentered calculations of the global balance of power, with France and the Netherlands undermining Catholic Spain by seizing territories from Canada to the northern coast of South America. No matter which power prevailed, however, hegemony meant mercantilism, client regimes, and cultural domination.[2]

America's psychology—and thus its diplomacy—toward Latin America reflects a striking continuity over the centuries. Even as it supported independence movements from Mexico to Colombia, American statesman Rufus King in 1799 wrote passionately to Alexander Hamilton, "I am entirely convinced if [South America] and its resources are not for us then they will speedily be against us." Similarly, Thomas Jefferson saw South America as a "continent unto itself"—by which he meant a continent to be fully controlled by the United States. America's gradual assertion of hemispheric hegemony from the 1790s through the War of 1812 and onward was not a classic imperialist quest for land and labor, but it succeeded in supplanting European powers through a mix of pocketbook diplomacy and military conquest.[3] The Monroe Doctrine, articulated by the U.S. president in 1823, promised to complete the ejection of European powers and ensure unfettered American dominance in perpetuity.

America's "Manifest Destiny" was not merely a westward expansion to the Pacific Ocean, as is often supposed; it was also a vision of northern and southern hemispheric control. President James K. Polk took advantage of Mexico's weakness from its long war of independence to annex Texas in 1845. By 1867, when Secretary of State William Seward purchased Alaska from Russia, he imagined an American imperial domain stretching from Greenland to Guyana—with Mexico City as a second capital. Adopting the theories of naval strategist Alfred Thayer Mahan, President William McKinley's advisers argued that expanding markets for export would prevent economic depression and promote social harmony at home. But their technique—the Open Door policy of the early twentieth century—aimed to extend America's power "without the embarrassment and inefficiency of traditional colonialism."[4]

But America has always carried a big stick even if, contrary to Theodore Roosevelt's dictum, it has not always spoken so softly. The most vivid example was Cuba. The United States declared war on Spain on April 21, 1898, ostensibly to liberate Cuba and initiate its democratic evolution. Roosevelt, then assistant secretary of the navy, sought not only to vanquish Spain but also to control the Philippines, which the United States simultaneously seized. Almost a century after America instituted the Monroe Doctrine, the Roosevelt Corollary was an imperial anticolonialism that justified American interference. Roosevelt's guiding premise was clear: "Peace cannot be had until the civilized nations have expanded in some shape over the barbarous nations." The case of Panama seemed an almost natural case for U.S. hegemony due to its dependence on agricultural export to America and an oligarchic political system that facilitated American control over the Canal Zone. The perceived shift in worldview from Roosevelt to Woodrow Wilson had more to do with style than substance. Masked in the rhetoric of selfless moralism, Wilson also felt it was his responsibility to "teach the South Americans to elect good men" while pursuing America's economic advantage.[5] Yet none of the forty governments America has overthrown in Latin America since 1898 became democratic—quite simply because the plan was to implant democracy in form only.[6] In the tension between opening markets and spreading democracy, imperialism always won.

In contrast to his distant cousin Teddy, Franklin D. Roosevelt realized that direct interventions were not only ineffective but counterproductive, instead charting a "Good Neighbor" policy that diplomatically compelled most Latin American nations to sever ties with the Axis powers after the Pearl Harbor attack. But after World War II, America, now a full-blown superpower, wasted an opportunity to create a collective hemispheric security system. Instead, the Cold War ushered the old psychology of suspicious imperialism back in. "We are willing to help people who believe the way we do, to continue to live the way they want to live," declared Secretary of State Dean Acheson.* Washington's policy swung from opposing authoritarian regimes to supporting them wholeheartedly. Curiously, in a *Foreign Affairs* article published under the pseudonym "Y" in 1950, State Department veteran Louis Halle condescendingly blamed the persistence of autocracy on the region's political immaturity, but John Foster Dulles was more

---

*As William Appleman Williams explains, American diplomacy contains within itself three contradictory principles: a generous humanitarian impulse, the pursuit of self-determination overseas, and a third principle irreconcilable with the first two—that others' problems must be solved the American way. Williams, *Tragedy of American Diplomacy*, 13.

candid when he advised: "Do nothing to offend the dictators. They are the only people we can depend on."

The Cold War in Latin America was a thirty-year "dirty war" between the Latin American left and the usually more powerful right, which generally enjoyed American support. The vigorous counterforce strategy of containing Soviet-leaning communism required the United States to urge Latin America's regimes to outlaw Communist parties and repress the non-Communist left, crush all but the most docile worker movements, and cut ties with the Soviet Union.[7] So scant was the commitment to self-determination that by April 21, 1961, the United States undertook and then aborted the ill-fated Bay of Pigs invasion to depose Fidel Castro, violating neutrality laws as well as the treaty system it had created. But President Kennedy also made economic ties a pillar of American strategy, initiating an "Alliance for Progress" to unite the agendas of democracy, economic growth, and anticommunism.[8] A huge industrial expansion ensued from Mexico to Argentina. Yet after over half a century of the Open Door and Good Neighbor policies, the stability/democracy/capitalism nexus America pursued remained a distant reality. In the words of former Brazilian president Fernando Henrique Cardoso, democracy was an "exotic plant" compared to the region's swings between right-wing militarism and leftist *caudillismo*.[9] Most leaders of the era campaigned on the left and governed on the right, and modernization was a paradoxical code word for dependency on America.

Latin American leaders finally began to coalesce in the 1970s under the banner of the New International Economic Order (NIEO), a movement that demanded greater gains from raw material exports as well as increased foreign aid. But in reality, Mexico, Venezuela, Brazil, and Argentina had to borrow ever greater sums of money just to service their debts, like drunken sailors being served drinks by a drunken bartender. The result was the "lost decade" of the 1980s, in which Latin America became, in the words of former Venezuelan trade minister Moisés Naím, "Atlantis—the lost continent."[10] Crisis followed crisis. To make matters worse, the IMF responded to the United States "like thunder to lightning," forcing Latin American regimes to tighten their belts as prescribed by the "Washington Consensus" orthodoxy of rapid liberalization, an international variant of trickle-down economics.[11] Over a century after the Pan-American Union effort, the heated de-

bate over how to meet Latin Americans' rising expectations despite un-
equal American trade continues in the form of a proposed Free Trade
Area of the Americas (FTAA) stretching from Alaska to Tierra del
Fuego.

But China's commercial presence in the Western Hemisphere is also
deepening; thus, so is its strategic presence. China has entered Latin
America through McKinley's Open Door, but its appeal to the region lies
in its being a superpower without colonial designs. Chinese trade with
the region has climbed from $200 million in 1975 to nearly $50 billion in
2004.[12] No developing country can refuse the high prices China pays for
commodities such as soybeans and iron ore, revenues that account for
much of Argentina and Brazil's recent growth. When the United States
relinquished control of the Panama Canal in 1997, the government
quickly sold rights to operate ports on both ends to a Chinese firm that
now essentially controls the canal's operation. In 2006, Panamanians
voted to expand the canal, making it capable of accommodating China's
huge tankers. China has also renovated other Central American ports and
factories to expedite the delivery of its goods to the United States. And
just as China has expanded its influence to its north across Russian
Siberia, it is also reaching east toward another Arctic country—Canada—
quietly becoming its second-largest trading partner and jointly building a
$2 billion pipeline to transport oil extracted from Alberta's oil-rich tar
sands to the Pacific coast of British Columbia.

America always seeks an external enemy. Ronald Reagan's myth-
making about the Soviet Union included claims that it planned to organize Asia's hordes and even the people of Latin America—after which
America's fall would be all but automatic.[13] Some now see China as this
nefarious force, exploiting Latin America's mineral resources and promoting high-level ties among defense officials.[14] They further worry
that just as the United States has ceased to support Latin military dictatorships, China's presence could undermine America's human rights
and democratization agenda, while contributing to another round of
volatile natural-resource dependency.[15]

For Latin Americans, China represents a new way of doing business outside of America's thicket of codes and regulations, one that imposes no political conditionality whatsoever other than lobbying Latin
American countries to rescind their recognition of Taiwan, which for
years had purchased diplomatic loyalty across the region, particularly

in Central America, and received market economy status in their trade relations. On the whole, China is not yet putting its mouth where its money is. It's not China's fault if Latin American leaders stand up to the United States. High oil prices and corrupt governance are the prime causes of natural resource dependency, not China's surging demand (which still accounts for less than 10 percent of Latin American trade).[16] And ultimately, China's economic interest in Latin America is both a blessing and a curse, bringing current account surpluses for the first time in decades, along with fierce competition, as China rivals inefficient producers *both* in their own markets and in exports to the first world.

To invoke a romantic metaphor, China is only dating Latin America, not marrying it. But its focus on the basic needs of states—such as infrastructure—means that it can purchase their neutrality in the discourse about democracy and human rights.[17] If the United States is sincere about democratization in Latin America, it should see China's presence as an opportunity: Greater export revenues could allow governments to improve their social safety nets, empower popular participation in political institutions, and increase imports from America. But the United States must then convince Latin American leaders that China is not an alternative to American leadership but rather its complement. To date, however, America's hot-and-cold style of diplomacy, careening between the extremes of absent and overbearing, has contributed to the rise of leftist leaders since the 1990s who respond to American encroachment with the rhetoric of cultural resistance, loudly bucking the Washington Consensus and the pleas to democratize. Even in so perfunctory a body as the Organization of American States (OAS), whose charter vainly emphasizes "respect for individual personalities," America has been unable to introduce a peer-review mechanism anywhere near as sophisticated as Eastern Europe's intra–second world levers. And though past OAS secretaries-general have been virtual spokesmen for American interests, the group pointedly rebuffed all of America's top candidates to take over the organization in 2005. It is a sure sign that American imperialism has failed in Latin America when even democracy promotion—its preferred unobjectionable imperial cover—fails.

The deep ambivalence over how to deal with "El Norte" is more than ever a defining condition among Latin Americans, who now confidently view Columbus's arrival as more conquest than discovery, the beginning of a continuous chain of exploitation that culminated in multinational monopolies of key industries like sugar. Despite more than a billion dollars in annual development aid and its overwhelming role in Latin American trade, the United States no longer rules the hemisphere "by fiat," the term used by Richard Olney in 1895. If America's imperial psychology does not change, Seward's vision of an inter-American pan-region will never be achieved—particularly when other partners are so eagerly waiting in the wings.

Yet unlike other regions that are rife with anti-American hatred and fear of U.S. military invasion, Latin Americans actually want nothing more than for the United States to live up to its universalist rhetoric of free trade and democracy, without exceptions. When democratization and globalization are successfully linked, America has been the prime beneficiary: Mexico, Brazil, and Chile are the region's most globally integrated economies and also have the most pragmatic approach to dealing with the United States. American soft power has also had an impact in these countries, not least through the dozens of Ivy League–trained technocrats spread across key ministries who, by the late 1990s, were themselves the most forceful advocates of free trade.[18] Linking Canada's vast Arctic energy reserves to the beefy pampas of Argentina would create a free trade area of thirty-four countries with exchange valued at over $13 trillion dollars—by far the largest of any region. And as wages rise in East Asia and Eastern Europe, the United States is also coming to realize that Latin America is a strategic economic opportunity, and is increasing its investment with the aim of generating a strong, low-cost manufacturing base to compete with Asia, potentially generating a race to the top that elevates the region from backyard to neighbor. But America still focuses too much on regulating markets and too little on building them. Economically integrating the Americas should have been much easier than integrating Europe, but Latin America's subregions have yet to create deep economic ties even among themselves.[19] It is precisely the institutional changes in Eastern Europe, diligently pursued, country by country, that have enabled the proper match of political form with economic function, preventing the social and political disturbances that continue to plague Latin America. America is not immune: Mass unskilled-labor migration, drugs, and gang violence are all spilling northward through Mexico.

BETWEEN AFRICA AND EAST ASIA

There has been no serious conflict between any two South American countries for decades; it is a continent where the concept of interstate war has become obsolete. At the same time, almost every Latin American country is constantly at war with itself over its raison d'être, leadership, resources, and social stability. The gruesome violence in Latin America's streets, from small towns on the U.S.-Mexico border to the slums of São Paulo, contrasts starkly with the region's lush habitats and splendid colonial architecture.

Situating Latin America between third-world Africa and a potentially first-world East Asia best captures this precarious state of affairs. With only two major languages, territorial contiguity, and no overt military tensions, Latin America should have been able to achieve greater integration than East Asia has to date. Yet after centuries of rule by mercantilist powers, Latin America and Africa remain largely neglected by their powerful northern neighbors while doing little more than posturing for fraternal brotherhood with their actual neighbors. Both regions are plagued by a vast illegal commodities trade that threatens to undermine any long-term economic progress and suffer from severe brain drain and capital flight to Europe and the United States. Somewhat as Nigeria and South Africa are to the continent of Africa, Latin America would barely exist on the diplomatic map if not for Mexico, Venezuela, and Brazil. Neither region is economically competitive, suffering from high debt, excessive spending, low tax collection, falling productivity, low innovation, low education standards, high business costs, and stalling poverty reduction in both cities and rural areas.[20] Latin America and Africa have the highest income inequality in the world, but Latin America's is, but worse because it has more wealthy people. The region's indigenous peasants are a high-altitude version of Africa's destitute farmers tilling tiny plots, while super-wealthy African and Latin elites live in mansion villas with abundant first-world amenities.

Latin America's dances—salsa, samba, rumba, tango—all involve swift, jerking maneuvers, even unpredictable lurches. The same is true of Latin politics. It is the inability to carry out economic reforms—more than the reforms themselves—that is largely to blame for Latin America's slow growth and poor social performance.[21] Latin Americans have a high degree of self-respect and pride, but as rampant crime and squalor attest, they do not show much respect for one another. Latin culture radically favors the masking of power in the language of esteem and purpose, but truth in Latin politics is about reading between the lines, even inverting what one is told. With notable exceptions, exaggeration is integral to communication for Latin politicians, more important than reality as it actually occurs. The result is a culture that implicitly asks, "Why tell the truth when you can lie instead?" The legacy of subverting colonial rule is a prime justification for habits that now only subvert themselves. The social contract of laws and institutions in Asian countries—whether guided by Confucian or Islamic values—is all but absent in Latin America. Trust and commitment to leaders—these things do not exist: Few governments ever complete a first term. Latin culture is far too tolerant of "good corruption"—the kind that eases contract negotiations to make things move along—not recognizing that it actually derives from and perpetuates "bad corruption," the prevalent system of big family rule and crony capitalism that operates in even Latin America's best democracies. These gatekeepers and power brokers dominate all aspects of life, and democracy exacerbates the incentives for leaders to steal what they can and then flee.

But Latin America could still become a solidly second-world region due to weighty economies like those of Brazil and Mexico, vast oil and gas resources, and proximity to the importing behemoth that is the United States.[22] In inaugurating South America's visa-free zone, Brazilian foreign minister Celso Amorim declared, "Integration is an imperative because in a world of large blocs, we will be stronger if we are united." If the proposed South American Community of Nations (SACN) evolves coherently, the continent will soon negotiate on far better terms with the first world.

CHAPTER 15

MEXICO:

THE UMBILICAL CORD

THE NORTH AMERICAN Free Trade Agreement (NAFTA) was supposed to propel Mexico into the first world, but on the day it went into effect, January 1, 1994, the Zapatista National Liberation Army (EZLN) began an all-out insurgency to draw attention to the plight of marginalized farmers, seizing four southern municipalities and assassinating two top leaders of the governing PRI Party. President Carlos Salinas responded by unleashing a brutal crackdown against the Zapatistas and thousands of their peasant supporters. "Mexico was revealed as more third-world than first," remarked one journalist. Both Mexico *and* America will continue to suffer until they find better ways to pull Mexico out of the second world.

Joining NAFTA has inevitably meant Mexico's abdication of any pretension to lead an independent Latin America. Mexico now lies forever under America's strategic umbrella—even as fences go up to separate them. "Our problem is not security—nobody is going to invade Mexico," explained a Mexican diplomat-turned-academic. "Globalization is our real existential crisis: harsh adjustments to international competition, wider income gaps, and more drug and people trafficking through our territory to the U.S." Since NAFTA's inauspicious 1994 launch, foreign investment in Mexico has nearly quadrupled. Like Kazakhstan, Mexico is diversifying away from perpetual dependency on a single commodity. It was once mainly an oil exporter, but manufactured goods now account for 80 percent of its exports.[1] But Mexico's modernization is limited to *maquiladora* assembly plants in islands of clean business like Monterrey. By contrast, China's rapid and widespread upgrading of worker training has meant that since joining the World Trade Organization (WTO) in 2001, it has rapidly outpaced Mexico in manufacturing and textile exports to the United States. Despite Mexico's geographic advantage, more than three hundred *maquiladores* have shut down and moved to China, resulting in three hundred thousand Mexican jobs lost, almost directly correlating to a massive spike in illegal immigration into the United States.[2] With or without a border fence, Mexico's problems may become America's even faster than they already are.

Inequality and instability go hand in hand. Outside Mexico City— and certainly within it—is a country of colonial monuments juxtaposed at every turn with ramshackle slums, with public investment in hospitals and schools an afterthought. The former mayor of Mexico City, Andrés Manuel López Obrador, picked up the slack and built his reputation by creating social and food support programs for the elderly across the sprawling metropolis of twenty million people, almost propelling him into the Mexican presidency in 2006—which he lost by a narrow margin and only after the contest was pushed to the electoral court. As elsewhere in the second world, power in the capital city is tantamount to national power. Obrador took his campaign back to the streets, sponsoring waves of demonstrations in *his* city to cripple his elected rival, Felipe Calderón. With or without Obrador, Mexicans have been regularly protesting by the tens of thousands against jacked-up prices for tortillas and other basic foods.

The rural-urban split in Mexico's politics reveals that there are in fact four Mexicos: a northern region on the American border where dollars and pesos are interchangeable; central Mexico, the country's capital and breadbasket; the indigenous, beautiful, economically destitute isthmus region; and the "New Maya" region of the Yucatan, unevenly modernizing and overwhelmingly poor.[3] Once a colonial jewel, the Mexican state of Oaxaca in 2006 witnessed months of brutal clashes involving armed gangs, police squads, and indigenous activists, destroying its tourism industry. It is from areas like Oaxaca that Mexicans overcome militarized fences and armed troopers along the two thousand miles of border seeking a stable life in Los Angeles. Profit-hungry *polleros* (the "coyotes" who traffic in illegal aliens) continue to smuggle far more immigrants into the United States than are recorded, and although most illegal drugs consumed in the United States are produced in Colombia, they are largely trafficked through Mexico via local organized crime groups. This turns border towns like Nuevo Laredo into frightening spectacles of robbery, kidnapping, and gang warfare.[4] Mexican immigrants are a double-edged sword for the United States, taking jobs in construction and restaurants Americans don't want, working harder and for longer hours, but also straining underfunded education and health systems.[5] The $16 billion in annual remittances they provide from all fifty American states are a primary source of Mexico's national income, helping raise its per capita GDP to $9,000, almost double the level at which emigration should begin to decrease. But because the country is so unequal—with up to half the population living in poverty —illegal immigration continues whether America likes it or not.

It will require more than laissez-faire NAFTA-nomics to make one country out of Mexico. America's most magnanimous gesture toward Mexico was bailing out the peso during the 1994 financial crisis, but since then NAFTA has fallen far short of what the EU has done for Turkey. It would be unspeakable in the United States to offer Mexico what it demands the EU grant Turkey: membership, citizenship, members of parliament, open migration, massive subsidies, and language rights within a borderless union. And yet while Europe has long been absorbing Turkey on these concrete economic and political levels, the United States has scarcely invested in the micro-entrepreneurship and mass education programs necessary to encourage Mexican talent to remain in the country. But keeping migrants and crime from spilling into the United States—and cleaning up the toxic waste already dumped by *maquiladores* into the Rio Grande—will require nothing less than a "North American Community" disbursing massive, EU-like development funds.[6] Make no mistake: America must buy Mexico, not just rent part of its border region.

With or without NAFTA, a far deeper demographic and cultural *blending* is already taking place across the entire Western Hemisphere.

The bridges of culture and migration promise not only to keep Latin America on the U.S. radar screen but also to change the screen's color entirely. Because Mexicans are the only immigrant group with a historical claim to U.S. territory, the waves of Hispanic migration to the United States have been dubbed the "Reconquista" by Mexican writers. Whereas the familial spirit of Latin America was once exclusive of North Americans, it is spreading north a lot faster than "American values" are spreading south. Not only are regions of the southwestern United States economically integrated with Mexico, but in states with large Hispanic populations, such as California, Texas, Arizona, and New Mexico, dual loyalties are the norm.[7] Spanish is rapidly growing as America's second language, and the two dozen Latino members of Congress are but one sign of the recent spike in the immigrant influence in national politics. While elderly Americans have begun to move to Mexico for affordable health care, millions of illegal Mexican immigrants take advantage of American social services at taxpayer expense. American conservatives fear that their country will become like the Roman empire, a conglomerate of races held together by a regime.[8] With Miami as the base of Latin America's elite and drug-money launderers, it is not surprising that many Latinos joke that "we love Miami because it's so close to the U.S.!"

And yet it is only through schemes like Mexico's "Puebla to Panama" plan that Central America can take advantage of its geographical position between two large continents and become a significant corridor of intercontinental globalization. The region is approximately the size of California and has a similar population of about thirty-five million, but it is splintered into seven separate countries, the familiar "banana republics" of the early twentieth century. Each was once heavily militarized, but today their fragile social security system is their greatest weakness. With such high poverty and unemployment, these third-world states mainly specialize in flowers, drugs, and guns. Though the Reagan administration fought potential avatars of the "evil empire" in Grenada, El Salvador, and Nicaragua, the United States is learning the hard way that even without powerful guerrilla armies, Central America may embody the true security threat in the hemisphere. After the United States expelled convicts back to their countries, gang formation proliferated drastically, with over one hundred thousand estimated gang members across the region (including Mexico) today. With 70 percent of Guatemala's economy based on the informal sector, its only real competition with Mexico is between their gangs to smuggle drugs and laborers into the United States. Cells of the MS-13 gang increasingly coordinate their criminal enterprises across the United States from San Salvador. Central America was once America's battlefield, but now America's streets are theirs.

But Central America is also becoming a laboratory for the potential triumph of hemispheric integration. The Central American Free Trade Agreement (CAFTA) has lowered U.S. tariffs, which should create jobs and raise exports as NAFTA did for Mexico. As the *New York Times* editorialized, CAFTA is "hardly likely to lift [the region's] economies into the 21st century, but it may be enough to lift them into the 20th century."[9] At the same time, America's general neglect of the tiny markets of Central America and the Caribbean has allowed others to pick up the slack. Indeed, because American investors mostly seek large payoffs in countries like China, China itself has moved into Central America, building factories closer to the ex-port market of the United States. America's embargo against its mini-nemesis Cuba has left the door open to China to become one of its largest investors (behind Venezuela but ahead of Canada), even as it occupies ex-Soviet spy posts and develops oil deposits, with Chinese flags flying over its rigs. The case of Haiti is particularly embarrassing: The United States has occupied Haiti numerous times over the past century with the intent of stabilizing the island but has been unable to elevate it above its dubious distinction as the most destitute country in the hemisphere, located just several hundred miles from America's shore. Under UN auspices, it is Chinese, Chilean, and Brazilian peacekeepers who have kept Haiti from a relapse into anarchy.[10] One of the underemphasized benefits of globalization is that any small country feeling underserved by its large, wealthy neighbors can seek attention in the geopolitical marketplace. If America cannot demonstrate its hemispheric benevolence in its backyard, such leadership could rise northward from South America itself.

CHAPTER 16

VENEZUELA:

BOLÍVAR'S REVENGE

FIGHTING TO LIBERATE South America from Spanish rule in the early nineteenth century, the daring anticolonial revolutionary Simon Bolívar dreamed incessantly of continental unity. But his Gran Colombia soon splintered into numerous revolutionary republics, leaving Latin America without a single pole of power around which to rally—greatly facilitating the longevity of the hemispheric hegemony of the United States. But today the main avenue of Caracas is named for its native son *El Libertador*, and it is Venezuela—not China or Europe—that most powerfully embodies the death of the Monroe Doctrine. Venezuela without oil would be just another third-world agricultural backwater with populist leaders and the occasional coup, but Venezuela *with* oil is something altogether different: It could become a major energy provider, a regional success story of balanced governance and development, and a diplomatic catalyst to finally achieve Bolívar's dream. But the odds are against it.

The naturalist explorer Alexander von Humboldt praised Venezuela's "eternal Spring," but the country actually suffers from an acute case of "bad latitude."[1] After World War II, middle-class Spanish, Ital-

ian, and Portuguese merchants and workers considered Venezuela a
land of opportunity, and their children rose to be the country's doctors
and lawyers. In the 1950s, oil development by local oligarchs and foreign corporations combined to propel Venezuela into the first world.
Caracas was one of the world's safest and most cultured cities. But in
South America, it has always been political uncertainty—not a lack of
resources—that has stymied progress. The elected autocrats of the
1960s left a legacy of "superhighways in shambles and devastated
ecosystems, ruinous debt and workers no more punctual than they ever
were."[2] In the early 1970s, Venezuela and other founding members of
OPEC raked in the single largest transfer of wealth without war in history, reigniting aspirations for greatness.[3] But Venezuela was spoiled by
oil, abandoning its agricultural economy and tumbling into "Dutch Disease." Deluged by petrodollars, the public-private oligarchy doubled
spending while corporations replaced society as the main constituency.
But the 1980s drop in oil prices compounded deficits; debt spiraled,
production faltered, capital fled, inflation accelerated, and foreign bor-
rowing increased.[4] In the words of OPEC's founder, Juan Pablo Perez
Alfonzo, Venezuela was "drowning in the devil's excrement."

The same cycle could be repeating itself in Venezuela today. In the
personality politics of Latin America, strong leaders always come at the
expense of strong institutions. The region suffers not only from bad latitude, but also bad attitude—none worse than that of Hugo Chávez,
whose numerous self-reinventions have culminated in a character best
described as "narcissist-Leninist." After a failed coup attempt and im-
prisonment in 1992, the left-wing nationalist Chávez swept to presidential power in 1998 on a platform aimed at the disenfranchised, his
escalating savage discourse of resentment and suspicion exploiting the
elite's indifference to the underclass.

The barrios of Caracas rise above the multistory hovels of shabby
office buildings down in the valley, waves of shantytowns blanketing
the hills like a swarm ready to descend. The question for their inhabitants is not whether or not there will be corruption, theft, or graft, but
simply if they will get enough of it to keep them happy.

"The government could be across town or on the moon," a poor
man in the Petare barrio district of Caracas groused. "All we want is a
paycheck." Charming and irresponsible, Chávez manipulated these
poor masses who don't demand accountability in either governance or

oil-revenue spending because they don't realize that the state and its resources ultimately belong to them.[5] "The people are loyal to Chávez no matter what he does, for he has given them hope," a Caracas political analyst explained. "Chavistas will throw down their bodies for him."

Gas is cheaper than water in Venezuela. Given the models of successful oil funds from Alaska to Norway to Kazakhstan, Chávez could easily have developed a permanent fund to redistribute oil profits, with the least getting the most, and everyone getting something. In less than a decade, the fraction of Venezuela's population that lives on less than two dollars a day, currently a majority, could have been reduced to virtually nil.[6] But whereas in Kazakhstan property rights have been spread widely and oil wealth has been used to spur private enterprise, Chávez's notion of "Bolívarian socialism" retains an ironclad emphasis on state control. Peasant cooperatives violently seized from wealthy landholders cannot be privately owned; labor unions have been eliminated.[7] Chávez appeared to be doing everything right with his *misiones*: subsidized loans, agricultural credits, food distribution networks, and preventive medicine programs using Cuban doctors.[8] But within these collectives, people produce for a single consumer—the government—whose payroll has inflated to over three million people. Chávez uses oil *fondos* the same way every other Latin country has, to serve political ends more than to actually mitigate inequality.[9]

Chávez's heart may be in the right place, but his spending of oil wealth resembles a crack addiction: He needs more and more to maintain his high. The government has simultaneously quadrupled the internal and external debt, while hospitals have crumbled, their managers fired for voting against him in a 2004 referendum. Price controls have made meat scarce. Chávez scored points when the Caracas mayor seized an exclusive golf course to build housing for the poor, but urban squalor persists as ever. Despite over $20 billion in annual oil revenue, per capita GDP is at best half the level of 1954.

Venezuela remains what economist Hernando de Soto calls a "society of accomplices." Chávez went after the state oil company, PDVSA, dismantling its technocracy, which had so skillfully created the nation's entire system of public utilities a generation ago. His surrogate, military-managed apparatus now produces over one million barrels less than peak capacity. PDVSA also operated independently of the government, while Chávez has created his own treasury ministry

(Banco de Tesoros) from which he fattens his European bank accounts. The country's manufacturing sector has collapsed as Chávez's commissars take over corporate boards and seize profits. "Now that he's destroyed the professional class, it doesn't matter that we're the largest oil producer besides the Arabs," an ex-PDVSA employee defiantly claimed from his self-imposed exile in America. "There is no one left who can competently manage the money." Long lines of professionals at the Spanish embassy seeking to reclaim citizenship are a visible proof of the third-world brain drain.

With all other voices drowned out, Chávez has made himself synonymous with Venezuela. Chávez has repeatedly been elected democratically, but his democracy is more like mobocracy.[10] Chávez's "Bolívarian Republic" functions like Musharraf's Pakistan; Chávez appoints all governors and mayors and bestows estates onto ex-officers, the new entrenched, conservative power brokers who jealously guard their newfound status.[11] With both the National Assembly and Election Council in his pocket, there is no "veto party" left.[12] Chávez did not have to change the constitution (again) to continue ruling until 2013. Eduardo Galeano once termed this style of leadership "democratoship," an apt description for Chávez: "Democracy might be a transvestite: she strips, and a *colonel* is revealed."[13]

At least six different militias loyal to Chávez menacingly roam the streets of Caracas on foot, on motorcycles, and in jeeps, wearing camouflage and body armor. With machine guns casually dangling from their shoulders, they are jovial with red-shirted Chavistas, but intimidating to all others. Rampant crime keeps opposition off the streets, and while they're stuck at home, citizens watch Chávez's marathon monologues on the television stations he has seized. A state of perpetual crisis is the wrong atmosphere for real democracy, but it's a great one for sowing disarray to one's own advantage. Other than isolated pockets of comfort such as five-star hotels and flamenco lounges, Caracas has palpably descended into a self-segregated, third-world capital with a former defense ministry official as the urban overlord. The rate of gun death is the world's highest, and kidnappings are on the rise—including "express kidnappings" involving a blitz of ATM machines for a speedy ransom. Caracas also has some of the worst road congestion imaginable: Drivers at the central Chacao intersection ignore traffic signals to create a multidirectional gridlock stretching for miles. In

2006, a bridge on the main access road out of the city simply collapsed after fifteen years of disrepair, forcing a circuitous, four-hour route to the airport, just ten miles away.

A revolution not under threat ceases to have justification, and Chávez has inherited Fidel Castro's antihegemonic mantle and spread its dogma around the hemisphere. Like Bolívar, Chávez conveys the sentiment that America will forever plague the region in the name of liberty. It is sad that this acrimony should develop between America and the country with which so many strong ties evolved through the oil industry, car manufacturing, and a shared love of baseball. Like ordinary Iranians or Uzbeks, Venezuelans are not anti-American, but anti-Americanism remains a crucial crutch for their leaders. Capitalizing on America's endorsement of the 2002 coup attempt, Chávez began to demonize both the United States and the opposition parties it supported as a threat to the Bolívarian revolution.[14] He has antagonized the United States by all possible means: declaring a desire to develop nuclear power and weapons; threatening to suspend oil exports to the United States; buying a hundred thousand AK-47s from Russia to build a pan-continental fighting force; blocking efforts to curb drug trafficking, promote free trade, and isolate Castro's Cuba; signing oil and gas co-production agreements with Iran; allegedly providing safe haven and training grounds for Islamic fundamentalist groups; and even delivering low-cost heating oil to poor communities in the United States itself. "Whatever Chávez is doing is justified," one Chavista intellectual pronounced while walking through Caracas on an unbearably humid day. "He had been democratically elected. America had no right to try and topple him. We don't pretend we're ever going to be as powerful as America, which is precisely why we expect it to treat us fairly."

If U.S. hegemony in Latin America is a myth, then Hugo Chávez is calling America's bluff. Whereas Bolívar liberated the Andes provinces but could not prevent their fragmentation, Chávez's neo-Bolívarian vision seeks to render these mistaken borders ideologically and economically meaningless.[15] "Leaders who toss up ideas without the resources to pursue them are laughed at, but when they are backed with a five-billion-dollar checkbook, they are taken very seriously," a Brazilian analyst explained, worried as many Brazilians are about the radical image Chávez has given the continent. With little use for Venezuela's

formal diplomatic intelligentsia, Chávez travels the continent and beyond to buy off leaders and to buy elections for them, rousing audiences
with speeches demanding that Great Britain return the Falkland Islands to Argentina. His roadmap for the unity of South America's resources includes a state-to-state barter system of oil, cement, cattle,
doctors, and engineers stretching from Cuba to Argentina. To inspire a
self-bootstrapping continent, Chávez outspends the United States fivefold in terms of bonds, debt purchasing, aid, and oil subsidies. In the
Caribbean, he has paid to modernize oil refineries in Cuba and Jamaica
and distributed $3 billion worth of oil at giveaway terms. Most impor-
tant, he has begun dredging the ground for what will be the world's
longest pipeline, from Venezuela through the Brazilian Amazon to Argentina, enabling a continental energy grid and, potentially, South
America's energy autarky. Taken together, Chávez proclaims, these projects herald "a great bloc of political, economic and social power to seek
world equilibrium."[16]

Taking on the United States is like picking a fight with a bully, but
Chávez realizes that bargaining between the United States and any
Latin American country will never be on equal terms unless the latter
has a strong outside patron. He thus loudly plays his "China card,"
threatening to cut off the flow of oil to the United States (while indeed
slowly redirecting it to China) and selling ownership of refineries in the
United States in order to invest in Asian ones. China provides tacit en-
couragement of Chávez's zero-sum petro-politics: It now provides half
of Venezuela's total foreign investment, has sold him tankers to ship
Venezuelan oil fifteen thousand miles across the Pacific, and drilled rigs
to boost his exploration capacity. China could not actually replace the
United States as a principal destination for Venezuelan oil (given that it
is about sixty days away versus a week for the United States), but its
share of Venezuelan oil purchases has boomed. China has also offered
to send workers to Venezuela to help build thousands of homes, a fiber-
optic communications network, and an irrigation system.

By sowing transatlantic disarray, Chávez also has a "Europe card"
to play. Europe is still Venezuela's largest investor in both energy and
services, and though EU monitors issued a scathing critique of the
2005 election, European countries, particularly Spain, have generally
sympathized with Chávez's agenda of greater autonomy from the
United States and are predisposed toward his rhetoric of poverty re-

demption. The United States has tried to block Spain's deal to sell
Chávez more than thirty high-speed patrol boats. The potentially three
hundred million barrels of super-heavy crude in the central Orinoco oil
belt would make Venezuela a larger oil producer than Saudi Arabia, but
despite the superior technology possessed by American oil companies,
Chávez has frozen them out, inviting only state oil companies from
China, Russia, Iran, Indonesia, and Brazil to participate in exploration—
a new second-world energy axis. Such companies are happy to sign joint
production agreements through "mixed companies" with murky standards, even if they have to pay a higher windfall tax—which Chávez uses
to ratchet up pressure on European oil companies already operating in
Venezuela. Since America has already thrown in its hand, will Europe
play its cards to rein in Chávez?

Between China and Chávez, Venezuela might still achieve a lasting
contribution to both the spirit and practice of Latin American cooperation, one based on a post–Washington Consensus model of mutual aid
and indigenous institutions. But history may also ultimately repeat itself
in Venezuela, with surging oil prices and Chinese demand allowing
Chávez to rely on energy exports and ignore other industries, leaving the
economy vulnerable to price fluctuations. The country now resembles
Iran prior to the overthrow of the Shah: oil wealth, inequality, and disenfranchisement, a classic prerevolutionary situation. But even if Chávez's Bolívarian revolution fails, he has awakened a sense among all
South American leaders—even those who think him a clown—that
they must work much more closely together to become a prosperous
and sovereign second-world continent rather than a third-world Atlantis. The Bolívarian dream will live on well beyond Chávez—and he
will stick around as long as possible to make sure it does.

CHAPTER 17

COLOMBIA:

THE ANDEAN BALKANS?

When Arnold Toynbee sailed to Cartagena de Indias he wrote evocatively about the massive walls of cannons atop the fortress of La Tenaza aimed at the open sea, "fortifications of immense perimeter built of the finest hewn stone, compacted with cement that is the envy and despair of modern engineers. . . . Cartagena was designed to be the shield for a whole continent."[1] Chávez's vision of continental unity cannot be realized without Colombia, the only South American country with both Pacific and Caribbean coasts. With a population of forty-four million and larger in area than France and the Iberian Peninsula combined, Colombia borders all of the Andean Mountain nations and will be the central hinge of any effort to undo the splintering of Bolívar's "Gran Colombia." Colombia represents the possibility that South America might profit handsomely from both the north as well as the Far East: The Pan-American Highway could be completed as a land and energy artery to Central and North America, and an oil pipeline may cross from Venezuela to the Pacific coast. If South America is going to connect to the world, it will happen in Colombia.

Even as the future prosperity of the fractured Andes hinges on it, Colombia is itself a deeply divided society. The country is split by three Andean mountain ranges, creating distinct cultural patterns recognizable in the colorful ponchos worn like flags by indigenous tribes. The Pacific coast and the Amazonian Llanos region are the most deprived economically, making up the bulk of the 60 percent of the population that remains in poverty. Most of the land is under the control of feudal oligarchs, patrons who oversee their constituents like quasi-governmental overlords. Superimposed on these natural and historical divisions are the urban power centers—eight cities of over a million residents, each with its own web of interests and loyalties commanding the 80 percent of the population that is now urban (a complete reversal from the 1930s, when 80 percent of the population was rural). To make matters even more complicated, there are three political poles of power vying for control in the various cities and rural spaces: the government and its army, drug-trafficking rebels, and paramilitary groups. Decades of civil war among these groups has created an internally displaced population of 3.5 million people (the third largest in the world), many living in the slums of Bogotá.

"Our reputation as the center of the drug trade at least acknowledges our geographic significance," joked a Bogotá intellectual in his posh, high-rise apartment. Historically, the United States has been content to have one strong ally in South America, and after the resignation of Argentina's Carlos Menem, that sole ally is now Colombia under Alvaro Uribe, the only leader in the Andes who supports neoliberal economic policies and America's "war on drugs." Yet having just one ally is not enough, for the war on drugs is a battle in the ungoverned spaces between all the Andean economies. In the early 1990s, counterdrug policies in Bolivia and Peru pushed Colombia's coca leaf and cocaine production to world-leading levels. Similarly, the U.S.-sponsored Plan Colombia has today pushed the militant-Communist Revolutionary Armed Forces of Colombia (FARC) guerrillas toward the borders of Bolivia, Ecuador, Peru, and Venezuela—a balloon effect whereby drug production diminishes in the country where it is squeezed, but expands in the surrounding areas. Drug cartels make partnerships far more quickly across these borders than governments do, as evidenced by the growing drug transit through the vast Arauca province along the twelve hundred miles of Venezuelan border, and by Brazil's growing cocaine consumption and shipments to Europe.[2] In 2005, a low-cost airline flying from Brazil to European destinations was shut down once the tons of drugs that subsidized the cheap fares were seized.

America's militarized approach to the drug problem is hardly helping it win the war, something it clearly has not realized yet. The Pentagon's Southern Command (SOUTHCOM) limits itself to naval assistance, border monitoring, and humanitarian relief in the hemisphere—except in Colombia, where several hundred military advisers operate commando bases from which they work side by side with the Colombian army on interdiction, disruption of trafficking networks, and counterinsurgency activity. Uribe has massively boosted the country's defense budget and even created peasant militias to patrol mountains and rivers.[3] Most of the nearly $5 billion spent through 2005 on Plan Colombia has gone toward military training and expensive, polluting fumigation programs—with little left over for providing alternative subsistence. Not surprisingly, Andean coca production remains near peak levels, and Colombia remains the source of almost all of the cocaine and half the heroin sold in the United States.[4] As in Afghanistan, drugs are not only more lucrative than all other agriculture exports, they are also a source of political power. Only a few years ago, as Uribe's anti-FARC offensive was bearing fruit, FARC accelerated a virtual buyout of major paramilitary groups such that the line between the AUC (the umbrella paramilitary organization) and the FARC became virtually indistinguishable. Not only do the paramilitaries have their own infrastructure for coca and poppy production, but their international trafficking contacts are even stronger than the FARC's. While some paramilitaries have demobilized in staged public ceremonies, they use drug proceeds to buy up prime real estate and direct gangs in bucolic Medellín. Merely catching drug czars is about as effective as catching terrorists: Unless root causes are addressed, the problem only multiplies. No wonder being a guerrilla is said to be a way of life in Colombia, the only country where rebels seem to die of old age.

The cosmopolitan mannerisms of Colombia's elite cloak the reality that the country is so permeated by strife that it fits the medical definition of chronic: not deadly, but continuous and corrosive. It is a society not only splintered, but also privatized, embodying a much broader Latin American trend. Toll roads are owned, maintained, and operated by powerful feudal companies. In Bogotá, private guards stand on most residential corners, high brick walls imbedded with jagged glass turn homes into fortresses, drivers run red lights at night for fear of carjacking, and businessmen are regularly kidnapped for large ransoms. The lack of total territorial control by the government, the many armed groups, elite factionalism, and privatized security—all are symbols of a country facing internal, not external, threats.

By what magic has Colombia clung to the second world rather than fragmenting, as third-world Afghanistan has? The comparison with Venezuela provides part of the answer. Colombia was the Spanish viceroy's home, Venezuela his barracks. Rather than Bolívar, it was Bolívar's trusted commander Francisco Santander who imparted the strong institutions of the presidency, the courts, and the central bank in Colombia. "Arms have given you independence, but the law will give you liberty," he declared. Whereas Venezuela has experienced decades of fluctuating stability, Colombia has steadily evolved from its state of total poverty in the 1930s to legal and economic modernity. Except for the mid-1950s, Colombia boasts a century of entirely legitimate democratic transfers of power. Uribe's reelection in 2006 made him the only Andean leader to win a second term since the days of Bolívar.

"We are far more humble than our bigger neighbors," an official promoting foreign investment reflected at a hotel in Bogotá's splendid colonial La Candelaria district. "We hire real experts to create a viable profile for the country." Colombia has capitalized on an Ireland-like diaspora that has traveled far and wide but has also given back financially and intellectually, and it has suffered less capital flight and brain drain than Venezuela or Argentina. It has never experienced hyperinflation or massive debt defaults, and it has the best-performing stock exchange in the region. Bogotá today is a bustling metropolis experiencing an architectural renaissance, both of its well-preserved colonial architecture and of its internationally designed modern offices. Even its slums have a certain order and dignity, rather like those of Istanbul— and they are safer than any part of Caracas.

Whereas Venezuela is failing to recapture its glory from its last oil boom, Colombia appears to be succeeding in reversing the damage of its recent drug boom. The 1990s approach to dealing with the drug trade was characterized by melancholy resignation. President Ernesto

Samper acknowledged that there was a tolerance for living alongside drug traffickers in Colombia, much as there is a tolerance in the United States for drug use itself.[5] Not surprisingly, perhaps, his campaigns were funded by the Cali drug cartel. After previous president Andrés Pastrana's "deal with the devil"—which ceded giant swaths of territory to the FARC—Uribe now enjoys substantial domestic support for his effort to reassert state authority and finally end the long civil war in Latin America's oldest democracy.

In Colombia, building the state and winning the war on drugs go hand in hand, an enterprise that Toynbee shrewdly characterized as "an audacious one of taming Nature in a continent where she still has the upper hand over man."[6] The improvement of mountain roads and tunnels has increased the government and military's ability to reclaim authority, with police and courts strengthening the enforcement of the rule of law. At the beginning of Uribe's tenure, approximately half of all towns had police forces; now all do. "The military now has major narco-trafficking groups and paramilitaries either plea-bargaining or on the run," an American military observer of Colombia noted. Uribe is lucky that the FARC, though resilient and creative, is more concerned with drug and kidnapping profits than in actually seceding from the state. The drug trade has seriously undermined the FARC's ideological credibility among the people, and it no longer even lives up to its well-worn description as "Karl Marx on top and Adam Smith all the way down the supply chain." Instead, the FARC has become a parastatal business and appears content to operate on the geographical margins. Its largest mobilization failed to hold the city of Miraflores for longer than a week; kidnapping operations have been reduced mostly to the interior cultivating and coastal trafficking zones; and the increasingly urban population has frequently collaborated with authorities to turn in FARC members rather than enter into business with them. "We are educated and decent people. Unless you are in on the drug business, there's no reason to support the FARC," a professor in Bogotá elaborated, adding that Colombian antidrug police have begun training their Afghan counterparts in picking off drug-smuggling "mules."

As Colombia is united internally, its poorest department, the indigenously populated and rain forest–covered Chocó, could develop into the Pan-American Highway's gateway—rather than bottleneck—

along the Pacific coast. Greater export of coffee to Asia and the United States could provide a sustainable livelihood for the many internally displaced people and poor farmers who once took up coca production or joined paramilitaries. The EU has increased not only its financial backing of demobilization and reintegration programs but also its aid for the country's poorest regions.[7] If this strategy is applied to the sealed-off jungle area of the Darién Gap on the Panamanian border, the Western Hemisphere's economic artery would be unblocked.

The United States could do a lot more to look after its sole ally in South America—and prevent it from falling into Venezuela's sphere of influence. By dragging its feet on a free trade agreement and not lifting its heavy farm subsidies, America still imposes unfair competition on Colombian exports while hindering diversification away from such basic commodities as oil, coffee, bananas, and flowers. "Why does the U.S. outsource textile production only to Asia?" an economic ministry official wondered. "It should set up Mexican-style *maquiladores* here for manufacturing reexport to the East Coast—which is as close to our Caribbean coast as the Mexican border." America's heavy-handed antidrug certification process has also slowed the very regional integration necessary to clean up money laundering and counterfeiting operations in Colombia and its dollarized neighbor, Ecuador. And by not complementing its antidrug strategy with an economic and social one, America unwittingly fuels the disenchantment with the United States that will inevitably undermine its support. But it is no surprise that the United States has focused little on life in Colombia beyond the drug trade, since its diplomats are warned not to explore even the timeless charms of Bogotá's La Candelaria district. To the blind all things are sudden.

The Andean war on drugs and the Bolívarian integrationist quest now exist side by side in a microlevel contest of roads, tunnels, and pipelines similar to that occurring in Central Asia. In Bolivia, coca cultivation is the only means of livelihood for the destitute farmers who in 2005 elected one of their own, Evo Morales, to lead the country, which has long been one of the third world's principal battlefields over the relationship between liberalization, globalization, and democracy. But Morales is no self-serving populist; indeed, his agnosticism over globalization represents a reality check against the corrosive nexus of abusive foreign companies and corrupt leaders whose radical privatization led to the malfunction of even the most basic public utilities, such as water.[8] Bolivia's fabled mining town of Potosí was once the wealthiest city in the hemisphere due to its rich silver deposits, and today the country boasts natural gas reserves second only to Venezuela. But because Bolivia lacks anything like Brazil's Petrobras or Malaysia's Petronas, modern state-owned oil companies with sound management and technology, Morales's soft extortion of foreign energy companies—by threatening nationalization or raising corporate taxes—and the creation of an indigenous enterprise fund are the only ways for Bolivians to become masters of their natural endowments. No tears need be shed for foreign energy companies, whose profits remain massive.*

As in Central Asia, cross-border cooperation in counternarcotics operations, energy, and trade may be the only way to break the Andean pattern of fractured geography, underdevelopment, and weak democracy.[9] In a region where millions are trapped by mountains and deserts, access to the coast is an economic lifeline. While landlocked African countries continue to invade their neighbors, Bolivia leases access to Peruvian ports, and trade between Venezuela and Colombia has accelerated as Chávez seeks a pipeline to the Pacific that won't get blown up by the very drug traffickers he quietly supports. Andean nations are also planning highway and port expansions as well as an energy grid to channel electricity and gas across the continent. The EU's greater support for small farmers and entrepreneurs in the Andes is encouraging a gradual shift away from raw material exports alone, while Spain's armada of corporations, which virtually runs South America's banking and telecom sectors, educates local competitors.[10] China too has shown up in the Andes, searching aggressively for oil contracts in Ecuador while dumping everything from textiles to cell phones onto Andean markets. Beijing is deeply interested in a transoceanic highway that will link the mineral-rich Amazon to Peru's Pacific coast, a cross-continental vein that would make the Andes ever more a strategic crossroads.

---

*By contrast, the same week Morales was elected, the president of Chad backed out of a World Bank–sponsored arrangement where profits from his country's pipeline to Cameroon would be spent on education and health, diverting profits instead toward "security," which usually means private jets, heavy weapons, and armored Mercedes. Chad may remain a third-world state forever; Bolivia under Morales has a much better chance.

Colombia may remain America's "aircraft carrier," China may make the Andes its continental foothold, European-style regionalism may develop—the outcome remains unclear. But it can safely be said that no Andean leader will ever slavishly privatize his (or her) country's economy in the excessive fashion touted under the Washington Consensus, and their countries will be the better for it.

CHAPTER 18

BRAZIL:

THE SOUTHERN POLE

STARTLED BY A map during his 2005 visit to Brasilia, President George W. Bush blurted, "Wow! Brazil is big!" Confusing Brazil for just another South American country rather than the continent's over-whelming geographic fact is a common American error.

Brazil is the United States of South America. Its size alone makes it—not Venezuela—the continent's natural leader. Taking up about half the continent, it borders every country except Chile and Ecuador. "Our self-perception involves nothing less than being the organizing principle of the continent—not displacing the United States, as Venezuela would like, but alongside it," a former diplomat living in São Paulo explained. Brazil is South America's magnet, attracting labor and investment from all sides. With no pretensions to being a competitive military power, Brazil's global role is based purely on its environmental resources and its massive economy, and Latin America's geopolitical ambitions in turn depend almost entirely on Brazil. But those aspirations will only become reality if Brazil can bridge divides as deep as its landscape and population is variegated.

The blessed climate of Brazil's lush central and southern regions makes it the world's largest exporter of beef, oranges, sugar, coffee, poultry, pork, and soy. Yet with exports nearing $100 billion per year, agriculture actually accounts for only 10 percent of Brazil's economy, which is one of the world's ten largest. Over 80 percent of the continent's top five hundred companies are Brazilian. Excepting Toulouse (home to Airbus) and Seattle (headquarters of Boeing), São Paulo is the world's most important center of airplane design and production— as well as Latin America's second global city (along with Miami). The discovery of massive oil and gas fields along the Atlantic coast has also elevated Brazil's status in the global energy trade.

It has taken three revolutions for Brazil to become Latin America's great power.[1] The end of the Old Republic monarchy in the late nineteenth century yielded to provincial clan rule over key commodities such as sugar and coffee, but plummeting prices prompted greater centralization in 1930. Next came the 1950s boom in foreign investment and the development of the steel and automobile sectors. The rivalries that emerged between industrial aristocrats and entrenched landowners culminated in the 1964 coup, which ushered in twenty years of bureaucratic authoritarianism. As in Southeast Asia, a "miracle" growth rate of 10 percent was achieved for almost a decade using import substitution policies to overcome submissiveness to foreign producers, but income inequality rose to world-record levels. By the 1980s, both the economic boom and the military regime had collapsed.

Fernando Henrique Cardoso, a left-leaning sociologist who had fled the dictatorship to Chile and France, rose to the presidency on the argument that even as globalization erodes state power, it nonetheless demands an expansion of the state's mandate beyond law enforcement and foreign policy to include human rights, social equity, and environmental protection.[2] And since globalization weakens bourgeois dominance, stronger democracy is necessary to mediate among increasingly powerful interest groups representing capitalists, unions, and the poor. But Cardoso inherited a country with no fiscal discipline, lacking even a budgetary ministry.[3] While he oversaw Brazil's economic deregulation and nurtured regional trade, mounting deficits and currency devaluation saddled the country with massive debt. In every second-world country that has defaulted on unsustainable debt the social consequences have been traumatic, and Brazil was no different. In the late

1990s the peripheral slums of São Paulo grew while the center froze, paralyzed by rising crime, especially murder and kidnapping.

The election of Luiz Inácio Lula da Silva in 2002 was supposed to mark a turnaround toward a focus on social equality, but Brazil's governance system was still stuck in the overly decentralized early-twentieth-century era of uneven municipal authority.[4] Because key cities are driven by a narrow band of industry captains and multinational firms, state authority remained too weak to exercise redistributive powers. The lack of a navigable tax code perpetuated tax evasion and other tricks that boosted the estimated size of the informal economy to equal that of the official economy: over $800 billion. Numerous corruption scandals involving Lula's Workers' Party led to jokes that he was so corrupt that "Chávez learned it all from Lula." In 2006, it was none other than the mayor of São Paulo who closely challenged Lula for the presidency.

Guided by its national mythology of coequal status with the United States, Brazil has always looked multidirectionally, persevering in its quest to become the anchor of Latin diplomacy (despite its Portuguese language).[5] Its highly professional foreign service, Itamaraty, is the continent's premier bureaucracy. During the Cold War, Brazil was solidly on the side of the "Giant of the North," and since the decolonization of the 1960s, it has been a key player in development and environmental debates, hosting the famous 1992 Earth Summit in Rio de Janeiro. However, much as it failed to attain a seat in the Council of the League of Nations in the 1920s, its recent bid to gain a permanent seat on the United Nations Security Council won little support even from its own Latin neighbors, who believed that Brazil, despite its rhetoric of a "diplomacy of generosity," was trying to leave them behind rather than bring them along. Yet with its booming economy building South-South bridges across the developing world, Brazil's diplomatic maturation has proved itself in the most crucial arena of global trade.

Brazil has elevated *fútbol* to an art, and thus not surprisingly has excelled in negotiations sometimes likened to multiple games of soccer being played on the same field where nobody knows the score and players continuously switch teams, yet all keep playing despite the exhaustion. A half century after Brazil's steel industry helped power America's World War II effort, America opportunistically blocks imports of Brazilian steel. At the WTO's 2003 ministerial meeting in Cancun, Brazil took the lead in forming a G-20 coalition alongside China, South Africa, and India. Despite America's efforts to lure developing countries away from the G-20 bloc, most continue to rally around its prescriptions for global trade reform (particularly in denouncing first-world agricultural subsidies), finally enabling a coherent counterposition to the United States and EU to emerge.[6] Brazil's demands in free trade negotiations for compensation due to the asymmetries caused by subsidies are a powerful example of second-world states standing up to the first world in ways the third world cannot. Brazil has even imposed reciprocal visa requirements on Americans (the only Latin American country to do so) while Europeans enter at will.

Brazil's domestic and diplomatic evolution parallels that of China: In advancing out of the third world, both are seen as its natural leaders. Almost half of Brazil's exports now go to developing countries, and it hosts large summits to boost trade with China and Arab nations. Brazil and China's evolving "strategic alliance" is an illustration that America no longer has any automatic allies in the geopolitical marketplace and that second-world countries can cooperate to keep one another balanced even as they compete. Since China's massive importing binge began in the 1990s, the economies of the "Giant of Asia" and "Giant of South America" have proven remarkably complementary, with Brazil exporting iron ore, timber, zinc, beef, milk, grain, and soybeans, and China investing in hydroelectric dams, steel mills, and refineries. Bilateral trade has boomed, with a significant surplus in Brazil's favor.[7] But Brazil's links to the Chinese juggernaut has wiped out its own toy and shoe industries, and like Mexico, its clothing industry is suffering due to the Chinese "textile tsunami." As a savvy Chinese businessman in São Paulo explained while juggling calls in Portuguese, "The terms of trade may soon be reversed, but Brazil is backing down from imposing import safeguards since if China retaliates, Brazil would suffer more." Each country has actively sought ways to add value to the other's products, for example smoothing Brazilian companies' purchase of textile factories in China in order to share profits. Among such key second-world players, technical exchange is also flourishing outside of Western corporate ownership demands and political concerns over dual-use technologies, with Brazil, for example, sourcing equipment for natural gas extraction from Russia. If Venezuela is forging a second-world energy axis, then Brazil is captain of a second-world trade axis.

Brazilian culture is what happens when both mind and body are in a good mood. Unlike in third-world countries where waterfront real estate is often privately owned, there is a sacred equality to beach access along the entire coast, where Brazilians indulge in natural sports of the body such as soccer and volleyball—in contrast to the U.S. preference for sports of body armor like football and NASCAR. Freedom needs to be enjoyed, not protected.

Within its population of close to two hundred million, Brazil maintains the Southern Hemisphere's melting pot. It is at once the largest African country after Nigeria (with African descendants centered in coastal Bahia), the largest Lebanese country after Lebanon, the largest Italian country after Italy, and the largest Japanese country after Japan. No matter what the occasion—from Boa Morte to Carnival to Oktoberfest—Brazil has the right ethnic or religious blend to celebrate it. Whereas America's ethnic groups are hyphenated—Irish-Americans, African-Americans, Indian-Americans, Arab-Americans—Brazilians identify themselves as just that, sharing a belief in the unrealized potential of their country. On the surface, Brazil appears to be as racially unintegrated as America was forty years ago. But though there are vast economic disparities dividing European descendants, African descendants, and indigenous peoples, these have more to do with geographical distribution and the concentration of capital in cities than with structural racism. Seventy percent of the population is some mix of African, European, or indigenous; thus, segregation is more class- than race-based.

Globalization has amplified these class divides, making Brazil the country where the first and third worlds most visibly coexist. Brazil's society is like an hourglass, with a large indigenous and African population at the bottom (both in the cities and the vast interior), and a narrow bottleneck all but blocking mobility to the elite caste at the top. The slender middle class struggles just to stay where it is on incomes hovering at 1993 levels. The average lifespan in Brazil's north is a full seventeen years less than in the south. Human trafficking flourishes amid such economic disparity, with rural women serving as sex slaves in cities and urban men working as bonded laborers in Amazonian gold mines. Most schools do not have phone lines, let alone Internet connections.

In a country that is three-quarters urban, São Paulo has grown into something beyond mega-city sprawl: it is a well-nigh infinite city, with a population that can neither be contained nor measured. Its countless steel-gated apartment complexes are, in effect, high-rise favelas for those who can afford housing. São Paulo's Rua Oscar Freire has been rated one of the world's top luxury shopping streets, and wealthy Paulistanos boast the highest rate of private helicopter usage in the world—but at chic restaurants, women make sure to have their purses bound with wire to their chairs. By contrast, marvelous and desperate Rio—stretching so many miles on the coast that a marathon there would require no loops—is a beachfront metropolis noted as much for its favela shantytowns as its trend-setting restaurants. But like Istanbul, there is an underlying rhythm, even coziness, to the inevitable chaos of a city so large it is sometimes difficult to tell whether Rio is claiming nature or nature is claiming Rio as they expand and encroach on each other.

But it is the psychological fear of itself that is most worrying in Brazil. In societies so divided in their ability to meet basic needs, values are at best tenuously shared.[8] Many Brazilians consider the country's favelas too dangerous to enter—and thus do their best to ignore their existence altogether while warning tourists against visiting them. In 2003, Brazil had the highest rate of gun deaths in the world, topping forty thousand, as Brazilian pistols sold to Colombia's FARC found their way back onto the country's streets. As former Brazilian president Itamar Franco stated, "The only thing distributed with equity is fear." Despite the use of crime-mapping technologies imported from Colombia, Brazil is still a country where armed gangs can battle the police at will and stage massive prison riots.

The sand is falling through Brazil's hourglass. Will it run out, or can Brazil turn the hourglass over? In other words, can Brazil elevate its masses? Brazil is undertaking a transformation of its vast third-world zones in ways other Latin countries are not. By spending more on poverty reduction than all the rest combined, Brazil, through its "Bolsa Familia," "Zero Hunger," and "Light for Everyone" programs, provides food, cash transfers, education credits, and power generators to over forty million people. In Rio, favela tourism has even emerged, trading insights into alternative culture and social structures for income. Lula's government has even launched an armada of riverboats up the Amazon River and its tributaries to serve as mobile offices providing medical and social services to the indigenous people living in even the most remote corners of the Amazon.

As a country nearly synonymous with the word *environment*, Brazil's innovative energy strategy complements its development strategy—and both are working. Brazil's investments in modern extraction technology are elevating Petrobras's oil output almost to heavyweight Venezuela's level. Despite its energy self-sufficiency, it is also enriching uranium to power nuclear plants. Most impressively, Brazil has planted and converted enough sugarcane into clean-burning ethanol to become its largest producer and exporter. The flex-fuel cars that run on it are appearing everywhere. But ethanol production is owned by wealthy families and conglomerates, while poor farmers still hack the sugarcane with machetes. Cities such as Curitiba and Porto Alegre have become models for the world—whether first, second, or third—in environmental management with their bold and efficient mass transit and recycling projects, earning comparisons to such paragons of civic planning as Norway.

Such innovation is crucial to preserve the earth's greatest ecosystem, which is located (mostly) within one country: the Amazon rain forest. If the world is an organism, the Amazon is its lungs. But deforestation has cost the Amazon close to the 20 percent of its size; the earth is losing its capacity to breathe. Public awareness and certification projects and massive protected zones are under way to slow the rampant logging that topped ten thousand square miles in 2004, a scale of destruction that makes Brazil the largest carbon-dioxide emitter of the developing world behind China and India. Relief operations during the 2005 Amazon drought were the largest ever undertaken by the Brazilian army and civil defense forces, underscoring that it is ecological and social—not military—security that most threatens the continent.[9] Brazil's experiments in all these spheres are both the most revealing and the most consequential; for as Brazil goes, so goes South America.

CHAPTER 19

ARGENTINA AND CHILE:
VERY FRATERNAL TWINS

THE STORY OF Argentina is a sobering reminder that neither first-nor second-world status is a permanent condition. Despite being spared geopolitical hazards, the country has been rendered all the more fragile by the forces of globalization. Today only continental goodwill can save the country that was once the continent's leader. In 1776, Buenos Aires became the capital of the Spanish Bourbon dynasty's viceroyalty, covering all of central South America from Chile through Brazil. After the decimation of the native population and the establishment of colonial *estancias* populated by Italian and Spanish immigrants, Argentina prospered for many decades under the mid–nineteenth century progressive liberalism of President Juan Bautista Alberdi. Given its advantageous climate and resources, Argentine geographers and intellectuals viewed their country as a hemispheric rival to United States: A famous map by Uruguayan artist Joachim Torres-Garcia showed South America and North America's positions inverted—with the South on top of the world. By the 1920s, Argentina was the seventh-richest nation in the world, thanks to its thriving production of beef and wheat, boasting higher real incomes than those earned by Swiss or German workers. Unharmed by World War II, Argentina welcomed the capital and talent of European émigrés, further propelling it toward the first world. Buenos Aires ever more resembled Paris, with Spanish spoken in Italian lilts.

Argentina's exceptional beauty and style, however, have unfortunately been matched by an arrogance bordering on masochism. V. S. Naipaul saw Argentina as an "artificial society imposed on a flat, desolate land," succeeding at colonial mimicry but itself sterile. Only mediocrity could replace the demolished myth of aristocratic colonialism.[1] The imperious leadership of Juan Domingo Perón, who ruled Argentina on three different occasions, improved labor conditions but also fractured the country to such an extent that in the 1970s the military junta unleashed a "dirty war" against the left. An estimated fifteen thousand *desaparecidos* (arbitrarily disappeared persons) perished in what constituted a "sharp regression towards barbarism."[2] The military's brave but ill-advised seizure of the Falkland Islands in 1982 resulted not in preemptive decolonization but rather a swift beat-down by British forces. Since that time, the macho boldness of the prevailing political and economic programs has been matched only by the corruption scandals engulfing them. The obsession with avoiding mediocrity remains palpable in the country with the world's highest proportion of psychologists. Image is everything.

But globalization has created new metrics for judging where a nation stands in the international hierarchy, and these have revealed Argentina to be not a first-world exporter of capital but an emerging market prone to the same vicious cycles that have afflicted many such second-world states in the 1990s: liberalization of enterprise, booming investment, rapid growth, expanding vulnerabilities, failed rescue packages, and, finally, economic and political unraveling. Argentina was a poster child for the Washington Consensus dogma in the 1990s, but it could neither continuously attract massive levels of foreign investment nor sustain the freewheeling spending that went with it. It simultaneously experienced both a recession and a bubble, while debt exploded. It takes two to tango, and after numerous IMF rescue packages meant to prop up the economy and prevent default and contagion, the international financial community stopped dancing with Argentina in 2001. To pay its debts, the government seized billions from pension funds and then imposed martial law to quell massive riots. For several weeks the presidency changed hands several times, sapping public confidence in any of them. Per capita income fell from $8,500 in the late 1990s (double Mexico's at the time) to $2,800 in 2002. Over half the population was below the poverty line.[3] Often compared to Paris, an entire class of residents of Buenos Aires became so-called *cartoneros:* poor, usually homeless citizens scrounging through trash for food and goods to resell.

Argentine leaders blame the U.S. Treasury, the IMF, and Wall Street for failing to support their earnest efforts to reverse the deepening crisis. Though less corrupt than Indonesia or Russia, other states that experienced financial crises in the 1990s, Argentina's fall from grace has been devastating—not least to its ego. Its entire economy is no larger than São Paulo's, and its dependency on foreign investment puts its economy on a permanent knife's edge. The tension between affordably priced basic social goods and meeting international monetary obligations so pervades Argentine politics that Perónist leader Néstor Kirchner feared social backlash from the prospect of raising utility prices before elections in 2005, so instead he rolled over and rescheduled IMF debt payments—and rolled over leadership to his wife in 2007.

Former economics minister Ricardo López Murphy complained that Argentina has an African ability to deliver services, and indeed it suffers from many of the third-world maladies associated with far poorer countries, such as abysmally low tax collection and an overly decentralized federal structure that holds little sway over the free-spending provinces. The utility company in charge of water and sewage has perennially underdelivered while raising prices due to currency devaluation—and this for only the half of Buenos Aires households that are connected to the sewage system. "Even the rich don't find this country respectable anymore," a Buenos Aires intellectual confessed at an outdoor café in the city's Bohemian quarter. "They now identify themselves more as Italians or French, stressing their European origins, rather than as Argentines."

Argentina has become something of a geopolitical welfare case as well, barely standing on its own feet, let alone recovering its past leadership status. Since its financial meltdown, few investors are willing to take big risks there, making it increasingly dependent on agricultural exports to China, which now account for most of its growth. Without a regional credit facility like Southeast Asia's, Argentina owed a significant share of total IMF debt, binding it in payment traps with little room to maneuver or set terms. With its own natural gas supplies dwindling over the next decade, it is desperately eager for Bolivian gas and the arrival of the ambitious oil pipeline across the Amazon planned by Hugo Chávez—hence welcoming his buyout of its debt as well.

Brazil and Argentina are geographically as close to Europe as to America, thus neither is intrinsically loyal to the United States. Rivals for most of the past two centuries, both had active nuclear weapons programs into the 1990s, but together they constructed the Mercosur trade block as the Southern Cone's answer to American-dominated trade. Paradoxically, the major Pacific-facing countries—Colombia, Peru, and Chile—all have free trade agreements with the United States, while the major Atlantic-facing countries—Brazil and Argentina—are most resistant to America's current high-tariff and heavy-subsidy policies and also have the most to gain from greater trade with resource-hungry China, across the Pacific.[4] Brazil and Argentina now coproduce most of the automobiles they export, and they cooperate in monitoring the Amazon and the Triple Frontier region, where groups ranging from the FARC to Hezbollah have been involved in drug trafficking, weapons smuggling, and money laundering.*

Though they will never admit it, the country Argentines most wish to emulate is Chile. With a Pacific coastline of over three thousand miles, Chile is as long as America is wide. Almost impossibly narrow, Henry Kissinger referred to the Andean sliver as a "dagger pointed at the heart of Antarctica." Protected from the excesses of colonialism by its mountain shield, Chile has a clear topographical identity. Proof that Chile is the region's most vibrant economy is everywhere: a four-lane freeway linking the northern Andes to the southern lowlands, profitable vineyards in the fields around the major port of Valparaiso, re-

---

*Integration across the Southern Cone could even change the fortunes of landlocked, third-world Paraguay, a country that has long been a testing ground for social experiments from Jesuits to Mennonites yet is ironically still desperately in need of redemption. Since independence, the country has been ruled by absurd dictators who most recently sold huge tracts of land to South Korea's Moonies for quick cash, allowing shenanigans that perpetuate the feudal, subaltern conditions of indigenous peoples. In the vast western Chaco plains, Lebanese, Taiwanese, and Amish communities are semisovereign. Paraguay was created as a buffer between South America's traditional powers after the War of the Triple Alliance (1864–70) but such a buffer is no longer needed. South America should strive to unify like Europe rather than splinter like Africa. Already almost all of Paraguay's electricity comes from the world's largest power station at Itaipú in Brazil, and most of its foreign trade consists of tax-free sales and electronics smuggling in Ciudad del Este near the majestic Iguazu Falls. In other words, Paraguay is being absorbed by its neighbors, who could cultivate its lands away from their use as a playground for cults.

search centers on engineering innovation, and glass skyscrapers in the capital, Santiago, the continent's second business hub behind São Paulo. Chile has as many Internet users as Mexico—with one-sixth the population. Chile increasingly acts like the England of South America, keeping its distance from unruly continental affairs while seeking pragmatic alliances far and wide. In all of Latin America, Chile is the only country that stands a reasonable chance of joining the first world in the coming decade.[5]

It is the subject of considerable debate how Chile became the region's role model. In the Cold War game, the Nixon administration attempted schemes from strikes to sanctions to undermine socialist leader Salvador Allende, whose election Henry Kissinger attributed to the "irresponsibility" of the people. Though Allende posed no threat to the United States other than what the CIA assessed as "psychological costs," the violent, U.S.-backed coup (*golpe de estado*) that brought General Augusto Pinochet to power in 1973 ushered in an era of domestic crackdowns and thousands of *desaparecidos*. Three decades later, Pinochet is often held up as an icon of how authoritarian rule can lead to greater growth and stability, paving the way for the needed transitions to market economics and democracy—in contrast with Venezuela, where decades of democracy have left the country with the quasi-socialist autocrat Hugo Chávez.

There are many false assumptions and logical leaps surrounding this conventional wisdom, and the sooner they are dispelled, the more likely it is that U.S. policy toward Latin America will manage to connect economic, social, and security issues. First, owing somewhat to the work ethic of the thousands of German farmers and mechanics who arrived in Chile in the nineteenth century, the country was relatively developed, by Latin American standards, even before Allende, so Pinochet cannot be entirely credited with Chile's modernization. Furthermore, Allende's early years were characterized by economic growth despite his nationalization program; it was plunging copper prices that played the decisive role in his unraveling. For his part, Pinochet plundered the pension system and slashed social benefits to return the country to surpluses—much like a CEO who lays off thousands of employees and gives himself a golden parachute. Most importantly, in the post-Pinochet era (he lost a plebiscite in 1990), Chile has achieved consistent 5 percent growth under a succession of center-left coalitions, with ex-president Ricardo Lagos, now Latin America's elder statesman, leading the country through high growth and declining unemployment under a moderate socialist platform. The last thing the second world needs is more Pinochets.

The Milton Friedman–inspired "Chicago boys" who helped General Pinochet deregulate Chile's economy in the early 1980s provided only half of Chile's model. Beyond the Washington Consensus—which wrongly assumed that economic growth would in itself reduce poverty rather than exacerbate inequality—Chile's recent governments have emphasized education and technology.[6] Incomes have doubled since 1990 and poverty is below 15 percent. It is Chile—not Chávez—that best shows how to reduce poverty even in the face of its uniquely challenging geography. Chile alone is too small to lift the continent out of poverty, but it can serve as its gateway to overseas markets. It is the only Latin American country with free trade agreements with the United States, the EU, and China, the latter creating many jobs for Chileans and boosting trade to over $6 billion in 2004, with a sizeable surplus for Chile thanks to booming copper exports. Japan and Korea have also signed free trade agreements with Chile, resulting in surging agricultural exports across the Pacific. With top honors in openness to trade and low corruption, Chile's commercial integration with the rest of South America can help spread predictable business practices. And its flexible pension system, combining public and private accounts, is a worthy experiment for Andean countries with small budgets.

Chile faces numerous bumps in the global marketplace, but so far it has managed them with confidence. Chile and Bolivia no longer fight over territory as in the War of the Pacific, which made Bolivia landlocked. Instead, Chile gives Bolivia access to its ports in exchange for almost all of the oil and gas Chile needs. (An outstanding Andean argument remains which country created the Pisco Sour cocktail, Chile or Peru.) Even as it builds dams on its southern rivers to generate hydroelectric power, it is protecting its environmental preservation areas and grazing plains for cattle.[7] Chilean miners went on strike against their international bosses, bringing a halt to extraction at the Escondida mine in the Atacama Desert (which produces 8 percent of the world's copper) in 2006, ironically because workers were being pushed too hard in order to boost output to capitalize on rising prices without any increase in wages. Chile's strategy showed mining companies that if they don't cooperate with local needs, the only thing that would become *escondida* (hidden) would be their profits.

Chile's governance style also represents the best that Latin America has to offer. As in Europe's East, the countries that have most steadfastly reckoned with their blood-stained authoritarian pasts are the furthest ahead in the path to stability and prosperity.[8] General Pinochet was stripped of his senatorial immunity, and Chile's current president, Michelle Bachelet, is a former revolutionary, torture victim, divorced single mother, pediatrician, and ex–defense minister—all in all, breaking quite a few national taboos. The stability of Chile's politics since Pinochet has meant that it no longer matters who governs, for pragmatism is the order of the day for both left and right. The lesson for the rest of the region—and America—is that natural resources and left-leaning democracy are never in themselves the causes of institutional decay in comparison to gamesmanship and corruption. Chile should be the continent's best teacher, if for no other reason than that in Latin America, jealousy is the greatest cultural motivator.

CONCLUSION:
BEYOND MONROE

IN A CONTINUATION of Cold War–era thinking, America for over a decade has reactively sought simply to avoid losing ground in Latin America, but the elements of the Monroe Doctrine—that America would prevent any foreign power from influencing Latin America, intervene at will to protect its interests, and manipulate each nation's economic affairs—are all candles being slowly extinguished. In the early twenty-first century, three models emerged from within the region for relating to the United States: Venezuela's belligerent rejection of American regional dominance and a vision of an alternative, self-bootstrapping continent of socialist greatness; Colombia's friendly relations with the United States, built on common economic and security interests; and Brazil's pragmatic and selective cooperation with America, complemented by greater diplomatic assertiveness. As the region increasingly shapes itself, American influence will not persist by inertia alone.

A true Western Hemispheric pan-region of shared energy and trade self-sufficiency remains dazzlingly potential, but it cannot come about until the pride that overruns Latin American politics is satiated through a balanced mutual recognition with the United States. A new "Alliance for Progress" is needed to elevate the region into a productive partner in hemispheric integration—but this time, the new American doctrine shouldn't be named after an American president, or Latin American leaders might make good on the pledge to take their business elsewhere. Even if America's de facto role as the organizing principle in the Western Hemisphere continues for a century or more, far less certain is how the superpowers will interact in the region that lies at the intersection of all their interests: the so-called Middle East.

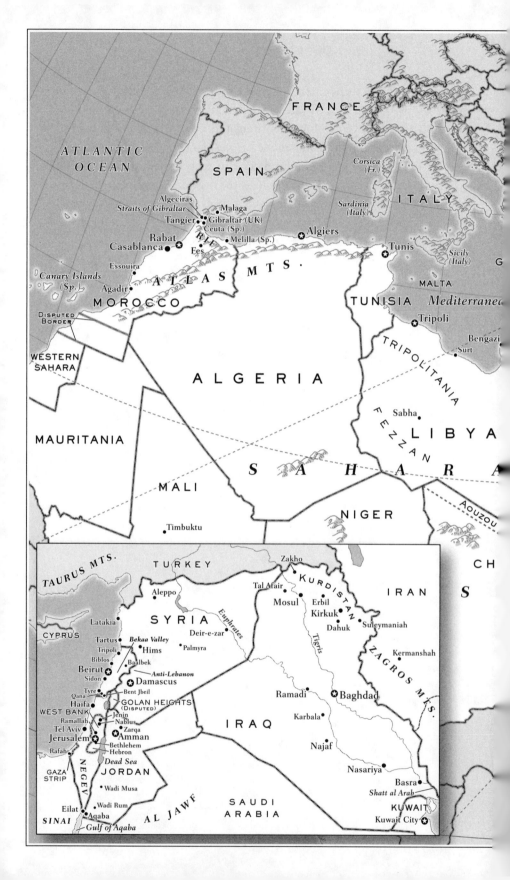

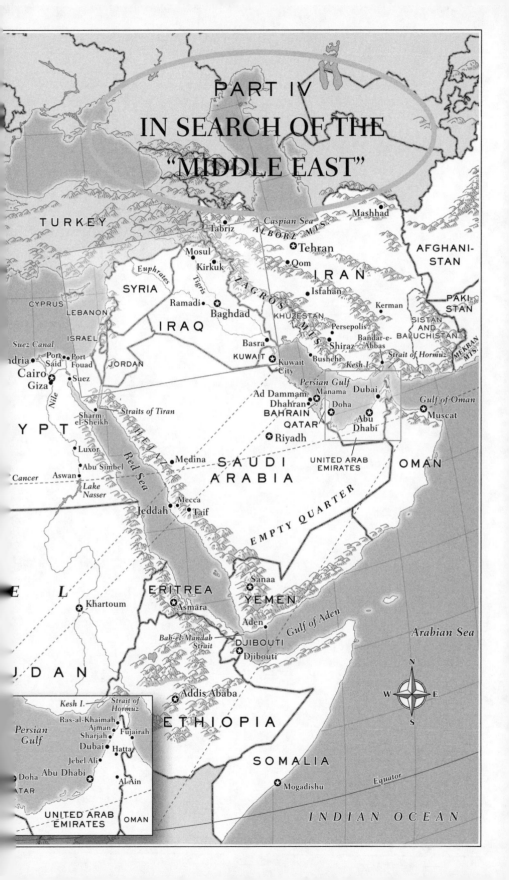

PART IV
IN SEARCH OF THE "MIDDLE EAST"

CHAPTER 20

THE SHATTERED BELT

OUTDATED BRITISH SLANG is no way to define the vast and multifaceted Arab civilization, whose geography, supplemented by non-Arab Israel and Iran, stretches from the Atlantic Ocean across North Africa, the Arabian Peninsula, and the Mesopotamian Valley. It is bounded by the Anatolian Zagros, Taurus, and Caucasus mountain ranges and the Caspian Sea to the north, the Indian Ocean to the south, and Pakistan's Indus River to the east (where South Asia begins). Yet British naval vocabulary grafted onto Greek geographical orientations still shapes Western discourse. "Near East" implied early refueling in Cyprus, "Middle East" signified Yemen's port of Aden, and "Far East" referred to the Indian Ocean and beyond. The only immutable fact inherent in the term *Middle East,* however, is that it refers to a central world region. That there is still no better term for the region only underscores how conflicted and complicated it remains for all within and around it.*

---

*Terminological debates as to what to actually call this region continue into present-day policy (and politics), with transatlantic countries now favoring the "broader Middle East," the World Bank loyal to "Middle East and North Africa" (MENA), in which they include Afghanistan and Pakistan, the UN using "West Asia," and China preferring the geographically neutral nomenclature of "Southwest Asia."

Even as Western lexical confusion continues, Arabs are fundamentally redefining their region in ways not seen in close to a thousand years. From the seventh through the thirteenth centuries, Damascus under the Umayyad dynasties and Baghdad under the Abbasid Caliphate ruled from the Atlantic to the Indian oceans. But for centuries afterward, Arabs were fractured and dominated by Turks, Persians, and Europeans. During the Cold War, the political geographer Saul Cohen declared the region a "shatterbelt . . . incapable of attaining political or economic unity of action" due to "marked internal differences" and because the region was "crushed between outside interests."[1] Today the Arab world has its first chance in a millennium to determine its "natural" order.

Globalization is allowing this shattered belt to recover its organic wholeness. The world from the Sahara across Arabia is largely barren desert divided into jigsaw pieces, but the more appropriate metaphor is of a vast sea of choppy waves constantly folding into one another, with ships of Arab and Bedouin tribes sailing in all directions. "Language and religion are reawakening our deepest connections to each other," gushed a journalist in Dubai, the Arab world's unofficial capital. Each symbolizes one of the only two forces that have ever captured Arab hearts and minds: Arabism and Islamism—the two faces of globalization in the region today.

Struggling with self-definition within suspiciously straight colonial borders, few Arab states command national loyalty; their people are more residents than citizens. Political form is flexible among these "tribes with flags," making it that much easier for Arabs to think of themselves as a single block of three hundred million people.[2] "Every broadcast we do lets Arabs see the world through their own eyes rather than America's CNN," explained an Al-Jazeera correspondent emphatically. "Now that we have the technology, we have the power." This sentiment has been elevated by the American—usurping the role of the British—war in Iraq, the inescapable sense of imperial déjà vu further uniting Arabs.

While the Arab realm still features odious regimes and widespread social and economic malaise, it is undeniably a second-world zone because unlike Africa and South Asia, it possesses all the natural resources, money, labor, and talent to develop *itself*—and, after centuries of stasis, is finally in the process of doing so. The post-9/11 oil windfall is largely being invested *within* the Arab world, as oil-rich states invest in their oil-poor cousins' economies and laborers flow in the reverse direction. Many of the 150 million young Arabs are on the move as investors, construction workers, drivers, and entertainers.

Arabs will not be left out of globalization; they are shaping it. The West holds the Arab world to be backward by such measures as Internet penetration, foreign travel, and book translation.[3] As scholar Edward Luttwak sarcastically notes, the region's "biggest industries are extravagant consumption and the venting of resentment."[4] But the far more important reality is that from the days of the Silk Road through the Crusades and World War II, the Arab world has been the physical passage connecting Europe, Africa, and Asia. Much of the world's oil and gas supplies are found in Arab countries, making them irreducibly central to the global economy.[5] The Arabs' archipelago of commercial hubs—Cairo, Riyadh, Beirut, Amman, and Dubai—are among the most revealing testing grounds of globalization's impact on common livelihoods, both for good and for ill. While Western culture is individualistic, for Arabs the Internet is a profoundly social activity. From Morocco to Muscat, Internet cafés are packed around the clock, particularly at night, when the air is cooler. Young men and women send instant messages across town or across the world, engage in chat rooms on politics and pop culture, or use video links to seduce Westerners to marry them and help them emigrate. "None of us has a computer at home, so here we are with each other and young people around the world at the same time," a teenager in Fes grinned, blushing as he revealed the countless hours he spends there.

Can Islamism subsume this new global Arabism? "All members of the Arab League are also members of the larger Organization of the Islamic Conference, are they not?" challenged an Islamist activist in Cairo, citing the Vatican as a model of how religion can have diplomatic clout. It is not least because Arabism is constrained by arbitrary colonial borders that Islam provides a natural alternative identity.[6] Ideology spreads best when divorced from a specific cultural context, which explains why Islam and Christianity have become the world's widest-reaching religions.* Islam's appeal converted the rampaging Mongols, and by 1700, four Muslim empires—the Sharifan in Morocco, the Anatolian Ottomans, Persia's Safavids, and India's Mughals—ruled most of North Africa and Eurasia. Islamism today again attempts to subsume the Arab ethnoscape into a united Islamic belt.[7] A seamless *Umma Islamiyya* would stretch far beyond the Caliphate of a millennium ago, including not only the Muslim populations of Europe, Turkey, and Central Asia but also those as far off as the Indonesian archipelago, in Southeast Asia. What President George W. Bush fearfully described as a "radical Islamic empire from Spain to Indonesia" has positive connotations among some Muslims, for the Islamic age was one of commercial, territorial, and intellectual expansion. Furthermore, a world divided into a *Dar al-Islam* (House of Islam) and a *Dar al-Harb* (House of War) restores Muslim honor in the clash with America's "war on terror." Westerners pity the Muslims' material degradation, but they equally fear the zeal of Islam's wounded pride, seeing Islamists as a new Bolshevist vanguard capable of ousting apostate regimes while jihadist networks—such as Al-Qaeda's Maghreb and Mesopotamian franchises—eject foreign armies and push back against the powers north of the Islamic belt.[†] Much like the anti-Soviet mujahideen in Afghanistan, the anti-American insurgency in Iraq has drawn Muslims from around the world. "Islamist violence," the activist argued, "is both self-defense and revenge." While America's denigration of "jihadists" only elevates these opponents for whom jihad is a noble struggle in the path of God, the *Dar al-Islam* more naturally inclines toward peoples of the Far East who are more "just, balanced, and clement than the West."[8]

"Islam is not a geopolitical force," a Tehran Shi'ite said dismissively. "It's just a menace. Islam's inner enemies are greater than its

---

*As Toynbee wrote, "The rise of Islam is perhaps the most amazing event in human history. Springing from a previously negligible land and people, Islam spread within a century over half the earth, shattering great empires, overthrowing long-established religions, remoulding the souls of races, and building up a whole new world. . . . Islam sallied forth on its great adventure with the slenderest human backing and against the heaviest material odds. Yet Islam triumphed with seemingly miraculous ease, and a couple of generations saw the Fiery Crescent borne victorious from the Pyrenees to the Himalayas and from the desert of Central Asia to the deserts of Central Africa." Toynbee, *Civilization on Trial*, 205.

†At the Paris peace conference in 1919, Woodrow Wilson reportedly observed, "There was certainly a latent force behind Bolshevism which attracted as much sympathy as its more brutal aspects caused general disgust. There was throughout the world a feeling of revolt against the large vested interests which influenced the world both in the economic and in the political sphere. The way to cure this domination was constant discussion and a slow process of reform, but the world at large had grown impatient of delay."

external ones." Despite the furor, a coherent global Islamism is not materializing. There has indeed been an Islamic awakening, as measured by mosque attendance and the proliferation of Islamist media, political parties, and financial institutions. But this consciousness lacks cohesion. Four decades ago, Henry Kissinger mused about the difficulty of negotiating with the *idea* of pan-Arabism—a problem that applies in spades to the "Islamic world." In reality it is as useful to speak of "the Muslims" as to refer to "the Christians." The rhetoric of a united "Islamic world" is both premature and counterproductive, highlighting the very identity-driven politics Western leaders seek to avoid.[9] Islam today has even less bureaucratic coherence than the Ottoman empire, with no agreement among the core states driving the *Umma* and thus no Soviet-style alliance-building to put flesh on the Islamic ideological skeleton. Islamist groups are highly divided along ideological and sectarian lines, with Sunnis and Shi'a slaughtering each other far more than non-Muslims. Also, Islamist parties are predominantly domestic because even as they rally anti-Western sentiment, they are keenly aware that Muslims are nowhere more subjugated than in their own countries. Islam, which gives all believers equality in faith, is accorded little liberty in its own domain.

Arab Muslims, like most people, ultimately ascribe greater importance to economic than spiritual ends, making it more likely that Arabism will return as a regional political-cultural movement than that Islam will congeal as a superpower. At the same time, the gravities of the *real* superpowers—the United States, the EU, and China—are bending the Maghreb (North Africa), Mashreq (Southwest Asia), and Khaleej (Persian Gulf) subregions, challenging both Arabism and Islamism for supremacy from Tangier to Tehran.

CHAPTER 21

THE MAGHREB:

EUROPE'S SOUTHERN SHORE

"CALL US 'NORTH African,'" demanded a Tangier native during a walking tour through the city's hilly alleys. "We are not like those Arabs to the east." If any part of the Arab world thinks vertically rather than horizontally, it is the Maghreb. The great historian Fernand Braudel wrote that despite continual and dramatic change, Mediterranean civilizations were united "by the movements of men, the relationships they imply, and the routes they follow," and thus share a common destiny.[1] Until the Punic Wars, Phoenician Carthage (in present-day Tunisia) controlled the North African coast and southern Iberia, as well as Corsica, Sardinia, and part of Sicily—islands that for centuries have been both fortresses and land bridges for mutual conquest across the Mediterranean.[2] Subsequent Roman and then Byzantine domination of North Africa was eventually overcome by Arab invaders from the east at the end of the seventh century. A millennium later, in the nineteenth and twentieth centuries, Spain, France, and Italy returned to establish massive colonies across North Africa, firmly linking it to Europe. When Western policy makers today speak of the "broader Middle East," they inadvertently appropriate Braudel's "Greater Mediterranean," lands of poverty and want, nomads and caravans, and Islam. And when French president Nicolas Sarkozy declared his desire to build a "great Mediterranean Union," he echoed Albert Camus, who, growing up as a Frenchman in Algeria, envisioned an inevitable Euro-Arab federation—for Mediterranean civilization's southern border has always been the Sahara Desert.*

Never in history has the Maghreb been so deeply integrated in the "Eurosphere."† Each year, North Africa and southern Europe become physically joined by new natural-gas pipelines, providing Europe with alternatives to its energy dependence on Russia while boosting Maghreb budgets. Europe is also by far the largest aid donor and importer of food in Africa while consuming most of the other merchandise that crosses the Maghreb and Mediterranean. Migration from the Maghreb is altering Europe's demographic profile as dramatically as the blending taking place in the Western Hemisphere, prompting some to speak of "Eurabia." If Latin America is the United States' backyard, then Africa is certainly Europe's. But is the Maghreb an example of imperial backlash or imperial opportunity?

For Maghrebis, Europe is the land of opportunity. Sensing their own relative depravation, thousands of Moroccans drift to Gibraltar in leaky vessels that often sink days before landfall. Yet in Brussels, Morocco has already arrived, with petty criminal immigrants stealing handbags right on the ornate Grand-Place. In Paris, the elderly live in fear of thuggish Arab immigrants from the former colonies. And in London and Madrid, terrorist attacks have been perpetrated by jihadist cells based in Morocco. Europe has to date been guilty of giving out too many car-

---

*Because the Maghreb countries lie between Europe and third-world Africa, it is swelling migration not only from the Arab world that Europeans fear, but also from West and sub-Saharan Africa as well. Timbuktu, once a great center of Islamic learning and the starting point for Saharan caravans, today represents much of Africa's inability to achieve even the level of material progress and social organization that existed a century ago under colonial rule. Hordes of young West African men traverse and hide in Mauritania, Morocco, Algeria, and Tunisia before storming the Spanish exclaves of Ceuta and Melilla to gain entry into Europe. Mauritanians have desperately sailed in overwhelming numbers to the Canary Islands, which are viewed as a weak link in "fortress Europe," arriving dehydrated, sick, and without identity papers. The tiny EU island of Malta has been overwhelmed with African migrants washing ashore and has built detention camps for their processing. The many Africans who don't make it beyond the Maghreb's shore exacerbate the existing economic and social stresses in their new homes.

†The emerging "Eurosphere" of influence includes not only the EU's own 450 million citizens but also the 385 million residents of the countries that share land and sea borders with the EU, from North Africa to the Balkans to Turkey and the former Soviet Union. The EU provides $2 billion in development assistance annually to the "Middle East and North Africa" region and $6 billion to sub-Saharan Africa, far more than any other power. Mark Leonard, *Why Europe Will Run the Twenty-first Century* (London: Fourth Estate, 2005).

rots to Maghreb leaders while rarely employing its stick. The EU's "Barcelona Process" of the 1990s was more inclination than policy, with France and Spain focused more on cultivating postcolonial networks to push arms deals and airplane sales than on promoting political reform.[3]

From the pirates of the sea to Islamist desert pirates, Europe and America have always mixed bribery and assault in taming North Africa's Mediterranean surges. In the early nineteenth century, a series of small wars ("To the shores of Tripoli," as the U.S. Marine Corps hymn memorializes) ended the Barbary pirates' raids on British and American merchant ships. Today, the governments of Morocco, Tunisia, Libya, Chad, and Niger—as well as Djibouti and Eritrea, in the Horn of Africa, and Yemen, across the narrow Bab-el-Mandeb Strait—all share Western fears of radical Salafist cells (now calling themselves "Al-Qaeda in the Maghreb") operating in the Sahara Desert. With the stability of oil-producing West African states and North African gas suppliers at stake, the United States has established a distinct AFRICOM military theater that coordinates initiatives to curb terrorism, illegal weapons shipments, and trafficking in humans. At the same time, the EU funds border patrol operations, microenterprise development, regional trade promotion, and human rights monitoring and has opened employment centers around the region to create jobs and eventually stem the brain drain to Europe. Amid the rusty rigs and hulking cargo containers at the port of Tangier today, there is tight security screening of the ships constantly loading goods and passengers to and from Spain and France.

Though the Maghreb states lie closer to Madrid than Mecca, the EU membership carrot, so effective in the Balkans and the Caucasus, is not yet plausible, meaning that the European Neighborhood Policy has to create a new system of incentives and rewards linking energy, trade, development, migration, and political reform. The Maghreb suffers from the great irony of labor shortages despite high unemployment, indicating a massive disconnect between what Arab youth are educated (or not educated) to do and the jobs that are available (and not available).[4] But because Europe can fill its labor shortages from Ukraine and Turkey, it can be far stricter with Maghreb governments that spend little on reducing poverty while their citizens depend on remittances from Europe, forcing them to support entrepreneurs and do away with opaque investment laws. Even if the EU brings Maghreb migrants already in Europe on board, it is imperative that these nine million mostly poor Arabs become a progressive diaspora to modernize the region—as the Turkish diaspora has done—rather than a disenfranchised bridgehead of Islamic discontent.

Crossing the narrow Gibraltar Strait from Algeciras to Tangier, the regression from Spain's modern agroindustrial irrigation to the age of rain-fed agriculture is visible beyond Morocco's steep Mediterranean cliffs into the unruly, mountainous Rif region. Europe remains stubborn about cutting its agricultural subsidies, which undermine the Maghreb's crucial farm exports (most of which go to Europe), while at the same time forcing tariff cuts to comply with EU rules. But for the Maghreb to get ahead in trade first requires making something worth selling. A half century ago, Toynbee observed that Maghreb farmers "dream not of pacts and treaties, but of pumps and tractors."[5] The same is true today.

Though the kingdom of Morocco bounced for centuries between Spanish and Portuguese control, today it is the EU's principal experiment in Europeanization without colonization.[6] Yet Morocco is not one country but two: More than half of the population is not Arab but Berber, and throughout history its dynasties have alternated between them.* Berber markets sprawl out in sandy villages in the Atlas Mountains and medieval centers such as Fes, which has the oldest still functioning medina in the world, its narrow alleys jammed with carts carrying bales of mint and stalls offering intricately engraved brass pots. The previous Arab inhabitants of the Fes medina have migrated to Casablanca, which juxtaposes a downtown of modern, stylish architecture with a traditional old city filled with disenfranchised masses. After laboring all day, street children loiter around streetlights at night hoping to avoid trouble—while coveting glue tubes to sniff. Just one wall or avenue in any Moroccan city separates the exotic from the pitiful.

It is such *pre*-Islamic cultural attributes that constrain Arab development, preventing political evolution beyond the noble families who actually run each country.[7] Arab leaders deify themselves through ubiquitous portraits hanging in every bazaar stall from Rabat to Damas-

---

*The great historian Ibn Khaldun classified this pattern over six hundred years ago, writing of a permanent tension between Bedouin (*bedu*) and sedentary (*hadar*) peoples—the former attacking the latter's cities in waves and weakening the central state. Over three generations, Khaldun explained, the Bedouin became complacently urbanized, exposing themselves to fresh attacks by a new wave of rural tribesmen.

cus. In such patriarchies, regime survival, not democracy, is the primary concern for leaders who are unsure whether they will wake up the next morning. Most Arab autocrats have yet to sponsor the modernization that Southeast Asian military regimes did, gradually empowering the same forces that ultimately undermined their power. Instead of this "development paradox," Arab regimes practiced defensive modernization, bestowing no more social and economic freedom on their people than absolutely necessary.[8] Even though Ibn Khaldun's native Tunisia, home of the ruins of Carthage, is considered an exemplary experiment in modernization—featuring women's rights, literacy, widespread home ownership, and impressive social equality—its development has taken place under undisputed authoritarian rule.[9] President Ben Ali calls his country the "land of enlightened thinking," but as a young Tunisian hitchhiking east to Dubai complained, "I will never be able to do what I want at home." Rome and Carthage had similar political structures, but only Europe has evolved beyond them.

Morocco's deepening ties to Europe are reminiscent of Turkey: Many Moroccans actually *want* them, and Europe's younger generation intuitively considers Morocco a prospective EU member—the first from across the Mediterranean.[10] It is a hopeful trend that promising democracy has become important for self-legitimization, but this requires accepting that it is monarchs—not presidents—who because of their Islamic credentials and popular support are most likely to initiate liberalization at all. Morocco's King Mohammed VI (and Jordan's King Abdullah) are both more subtle and more just than tribal autocrats. "This is not a simple matter of rewriting constitutions," an academic in Casablanca explained. "Traditional, Bedouin societies care less for mimicking European politics than maintaining personal, tribal, and religious honor."

Morocco will not become England anytime soon, but young Mohammed VI sees himself more as a manager than as an arbiter. He not only sacked his father Hassan II's heavy-handed interior minister but also initiated a Truth Commission, which in 2005 released a report reckoning with forty years of human rights violations. What sustains autocratic behavior is fear of revenge over past injustices against Islamists—a vicious circle that only ends when leaders launch such commissions and then accept their conclusions. Inspired by Turkey's governing AKP, the Islamist Justice and Development Party steadily gained parliamentary influence after moderating its original positions, and one Islamist party does not even recognize the monarchy. Whereas civil society in Algeria and Tunisia continues in an uneasy pact with the sovereign, Moroccan NGOs are easy to form, make pointed demands, and have achieve improved treatment of political prisoners and a relatively free press. "No doubt there are still abuses, and we are very careful what we say," a Marrakech journalist explained, "but the government is listening to us." What Morocco seems to have accomplished is a progressive tradeoff between human rights and counterterrorism such that a greater role for Islamism in politics doesn't entail an Algeria-style bloodbath.

Oil-rich Arab states such as Algeria are sometimes dubbed "supertankers" due to their energy reserves, but the analogy also explains how long it takes to rotate their political compass. Like driving on Arab roads, wrong turns are punished with arduous, frustrating loops that drain time, energy, and patience. Algerian politics took one such wrong turn in 1991, when the military annulled the Islamic Salvation Front's victory in the national elections, unleashing a vicious civil war in which more than one hundred thousand people were massacred. It took fifteen years for any national reconciliation to begin, and even this process has not been of the Chilean or Moroccan variety, with amnesty and restitution combining to restore legal order. As a result, the Arab world continues to suffer from "Algeria-phobia," by which Algeria serves as a warning *not* to include Islamic parties in elections. But could the result of Islamist participation conceivably have been any worse than the calamitous civil war excluding Islamists? It has not made driving any easier either: Insurgents shot out the traffic lights in Algiers, making urban congestion unbearable.

Responsibilities come very early to Arab youth, who take on family and professional duties based on their physical abilities, often to the detriment of their intellectual maturation; many youth seem to speak neither Arabic nor French well. The quality of public schools has fallen all over the Arab region, while Islamic social networks provide food, shelter, and spiritual fulfillment to restless youth seeking a sense of belonging and importance—but similarly neglect to teach marketable skills. Idle hands do the devil's work, and the social tinderbox created by undereducation and unemployment can be mobilized either to build a modern society or to destroy it. As the epic film *The Battle of Algiers* demonstrates, even 150 years of European colonialism failed to transform Arab society. What else can be done?

For years Tunisians, Lebanese, Egyptians, and other Arabs have wandered in search of work in the oil industries of Libya, Iraq, and Saudi Arabia, and cross-border supply chains are finally emerging that can take advantage of this fluidity of Arab labor.[11] Europe has invested in special investment and export havens—a status the freewheeling port of Tangier has always enjoyed—which are emerging along the Mediterranean to create jobs, ease exports, and increase profits. Morocco now has a free trade agreement with the United States as well, and it benefits from additional assistance for education and women's rights. Indeed, it is French and American advisers who, as early as the French colonial administration in the 1920s, have urged the Moroccan government to preserve the charming mystique of its medinas rather than allowing them to degenerate like other unregulated shantytowns— ultimately ensuring that tourist interest and revenue grows.[12] Even as oil and gas constitute 97 percent of Algeria's exports (increasingly via undersea pipelines to Europe), the EU is pressuring it to spend its energy revenues on infrastructure and agriculture. In Tunisia, French call centers employ thousands of otherwise listless university graduates. As per capita income gradually rises, Maghreb emigration could slow substantially, simultaneously addressing Europe's migration issue and the region's development problems. Greater European investment in the Maghreb means economic transition before political transformation— but in the Arab context, the former must come before the latter.

Along Morocco's breezy Atlantic coast, the surprising sight of French pensioners in quaint villas reveals the organic economic and social space reemerging across the Mediterranean. What for them is a low-cost retirement, however, for Arab states is a huge investment in houses and hotels. Even Islamist parties cannot reject this reverse influx of Europeans into Morocco, instead making tax breaks designed to attract them a plank of their political agendas. Like Azerbaijan, Morocco is becoming European even if it never becomes part of Europe.

LIBYA: SEEING GREEN

"Libya has always had an identity crisis," a Tripoli bookseller confessed in his neat but dusty shop. "We absorb everything around us, but mean nothing to ourselves." Beginning in the sixth century B.C., Phoenicians from Tyre (in present-day Lebanon) and Greeks colonized North Africa, creating trading outposts that began as rest stops en route to Spain, where they would purchase precious metals. Libya's two coastal provinces—Tripolitania and Cyrenaica—were gradually subsumed into the Roman empire. The massive granite columns and marble baths of Leptis Magna were largely imported from Aswan in ancient Egypt, from which roads terminated in its majestic port. All settlements clustered along the Mediterranean coast then passed under a procession of imperial hands: Byzantine, Arab, and Ottoman.

The millennium of Arab rule before Ottoman subjugation is evidence of how little Libya can be understood through an Arab lens alone. In the seventh century, Amr Ibn el Asi's Arab conquerors required over a month to capture Tripoli from the Byzantines, who like the Ottomans and Italians after them fortified the Roman foundations of the city's Assaray citadel to defend against land and sea invasions. Because the Arab expansion aimed to spread Islam and Arabic—not to leave an architectural legacy—only the simplest of mosques, reflecting the functional Bedouin vernacular, remain. The only living testaments to their traditions are the Tuareg nomads, whose deeply colored gowns and shields continue to guide caravans across the oceanic Sahara. Leptis Magna's decline actually began with the Arab expansion, and it remained buried in the sand for centuries until Italian excavations began in 1923. New artifacts are constantly being unearthed at Leptis today, while Libyan musicians fill its amphitheater with Bedouin music to the delight of tourists from Tripoli. Though Italian colonizers merged the transit oases of the western province of Fezzan with the two coastal provinces in 1934 to create modern Libya, the country remains more a magnificent desert vacuum buffering the region's western Berber kingdoms, southern African tribes, and Arabic Egypt than a coherent Arab state. Passengers flying to Libya today ask each other, "Are you going for the ruins or the oil?"

The concept of shifting sands is taken quite literally in Libya. Tripoli is occasionally hit by blinding sandstorms known as *ghibli* that turn day into night, seemingly burying the city. Libyan politics has been one *ghibli* after another. Inspired by Gamal Abdel Nasser's *Philosophy of the Revolution,* Colonel Muammar Gaddafi seized power at the age of twenty-eight in 1969, exiling King Idris I to Egypt after a decade during which the extraordinary wealth generated from the discovery of oil

(Libya was the world's fourth-largest oil producer in the 1950s) remained concentrated in royal and elite hands. Having driven across all
of Libya in an old Volkswagen Beetle to rally clandestine support for his
revolution, Gaddafi came to know Libya better than anyone else ever
had or ever will. That car, parked inside Tripoli's national museum, is a
shrine surrounded by tablets laced with anticolonial epithets.

There are reportedly eighty-seven official ways to spell Gaddafi's
name, and probably just as many interpretations of his eccentric philosophy of communal socialism known as the Jamahiriyya system
("state of the masses").* Having moved over half a century from Ottoman backwater to Italian colony, from conservative monarchy to revolutionary regime, and from rags to riches, Libya was a blank slate for
Gaddafi's clever but extreme experimentations contained within his
"Third Universal Theory," which espoused a blend of humanism, socialism, and Islam.[13] Some of the vision of his multivolume *Green
Book* did make the leap from theory to practice, such as universal
health care and education (including for women), and Libya has the
region's highest per capita income at about $7,000. But his distrust of
entrepreneurship drove at least a hundred thousand educated Libyans
out of the country within the first decade of his rule. His unpredictable
diplomatic antics have also earned him a reputation he may never live
down. In the name of pan-Arabism, he attempted a merger with
Tunisia in 1974, and he once drove a bulldozer through a fence marking the Egyptian border. In the name of pan-Africanism, he invited
millions of African workers to come to Libya but then treated them like
animals. Then he fought a fruitless decadelong war with Chad over the
Aouzou Strip, along the border between the two countries, only to be
humiliated in defeat. More recently he forged a friendship with South
Africa's Nelson Mandela to posture as a mediator of African conflicts
(including Darfur) while demanding European reparations for coloni-

---

*Gaddafi's Jamahiriyya system actually channels the country's past, beginning with the Greek agoras dating to
the first century B.C. embodied in the ruins at Cyrene (present-day Shahhat), where statues of Apollo once
stood near temples honoring Dionysus. Gaddafi aimed to create such a pure participatory democracy, admon-
ishing party-political systems with the claim that "representation is a falsehood" and insisting on his *Green
Book's* tautology that "the authority is for the people alone, who should have authority." At the same time, since
Libya's inheritance includes Islam, he declared that the "Holy Quran is the Law of Society," and indeed, there
are similarities between the Jamahiriyya system and Islamic Shura councils. Finally, Libya's governance fuses
Gaddafi's own experience as a military strongman; hence, despite the *Green Book's* pretense to democracy, it
pithily notes the inevitable reality that "those who are strongest in society hold the reins of government."

alism to all African nations. Most significantly, Gaddafi's sponsorship of the PLO and IRA, his complicity in the bombing of Pan Am Flight 103 over Lockerbie in Scotland, and his blatant attempts to acquire nuclear weapons technology have all contributed to making Libya a founding member of America's "state sponsors of terrorism" watchlist. President Ronald Reagan labeled him a "mad dog" and launched a missile attack on Tripoli in 1986 (as payback for the Berlin disco bombing that killed three American servicemen) that ended up killing Gaddafi's adopted infant daughter.

Libya could long ago have become an Arab version of Norway, but Gaddafi's delusions of grandeur invited sanctions that took advantage of the country's isolated geography, making the movement of goods other than via the arduous land and sea routes virtually impossible. By 2003, Gaddafi had abandoned both his nuclear quest and his terrorism pursuits, instead denouncing nuclear weapons and issuing a bounty for the capture of Osama bin Laden. He also formally reopened diplomatic relations with the United States. Libyan crude is well-suited to the American market—with the added virtue of being deliverable without passing through the Suez Canal. After being banned in the 1980s, English is once again being taught in Libyan schools, and students are clamoring for U.S. scholarships. In 2006, just a week before Gaddafi organized a conference to commemorate and denounce America's bombing of Libya twenty years earlier, throngs of Libyan youth cheered an American rock band performing at a Tripoli trade fair, wildly waving U.S. flags.

Tripoli has become a pearl in the southern Mediterranean necklace of Arab nations once again selling most of their resources to Europe, while Europeans flock in, offering the classic combination of aid, trade, and arms. Libya's hefty new role in the global energy market may accelerate the Maghreb's centrifugal spin toward Europe.[14] Tripoli's only five-star hotel is a hive of deal making and future planning—under the approving gaze of multiple enormous Gaddafi portraits. The up-front payments from just two international energy consortia were enough to cover Libya's $3 billion payout to the victims of the Pan Am bombing. Italy inaugurated an undersea gas pipeline from Libya in 2005, while Chinese and Malaysian oil companies have also bid aggressively to ensure a global balance in Libya's oil exports, and were willing to swallow less favorable terms including high revenue-sharing costs. The influx of migrants into Libya from Algeria, Tunisia, Chad, Niger, and Egypt is a testament to Libya's stability. One million Egyptians make up nearly a fifth of Libya's population, their accents noticeable as they congregate on Tripoli's rustic corniche. But many African migrants, having been tortured in government detention centers, choose to lie low, clinging to their preferred cafés and back neighborhoods.

Yet Tripoli still resembles a sleepy southern Italian port more than bustling Tangier or Beirut. As when Gaddafi swept into power, Libya once again has grand plans and plenty of money, but a great deal has to be knocked down physically and psychologically before Libya comes of age. True to its history, Tripoli is in perpetual creation, with sturdy apartments emerging in some districts while others crumble and splendid colonial façades falling into irreparable decay, as in Havana—faster even than the Roman ruins, two thousand years older, which have better withstood the test of time. In 2006, $7 billion was budgeted for infrastructure alone, but there are few cranes in Tripoli, for the most fundamental repair is to replace the city's veins: pipes, sewage systems, and roads. Anxious tourism marketers describe Libya as "booming," potentially entering the league of Morocco or Egypt, but the reality is far more prosaic. Though it boasts twelve hundred miles of Mediterranean beach, Libya's coastline mostly features sheep, horse, and camel farms and occasional heaps of scrapped automobiles. Heavy, unmanaged tourism in third-world hotspots such as Nepal or Cambodia has transformed them from virgin to wrecked within a generation—without ever becoming developed. Conservative, placid Libyans are serious about not becoming an overcrowded Costa del Sol of nude and drunk Europeans, cautiously designating only a few, peripheral island plots to Italian resort developers (so far). "We Libyan Bedouins find the very idea of hotels embarrassing. We insist on offering the hospitality of our own homes," a tourism official insisted in his humble office near Tripoli's port, where only occasional cruise ships carrying Italians or Russians dock.

Gaddafi's *Green Book* bemoans the "influences of property and possession," but coffers swelling to over $40 billion sharply test his classless aspirations. Though his own revolt was launched specifically due to the mismanagement and theft of the country's newfound oil wealth, his lofty rhetoric of "partners, not wage earners" has been little consolation for those receiving Libyans' archaic salaries. Both skilled and unskilled laborers need new opportunities—the former to prevent a brain drain

and the latter to provide the burgeoning youth population with something to do other than listening to mobile phone ring-tones on street
corners. If Libya spends its wealth wisely, it is not impossible that the
only five million Libyans—90 percent of whom are concentrated in the
northwest Jafara plain, within a few miles of the Mediterranean—could
experience a meteoric rise in their living standards. If it completes the
Great Man-Made River project to channel fresh water from southern
aquifers to the northern coast and a reforestation program to increase
arable land, Libya could finally produce more food than it imports.
Like Kazakhstan, Libya has created a Norwegian-style Generation
Fund to invest in schools and hospitals, which under the international
sanctions declined in the 1980s and 1990s. And like Colombia, it
spends lavishly on top-tier international consultants to steer the privatization of agriculture and industries, restructure the banking sector,
develop strategies for petrochemical plants and tourism, and retrain
scientists from weapons programs to water desalination and petroleum
geology—the topics of books that have been gathering dust for decades
in Tripoli's archival bookshops.

"I studied on scholarship in the U.S. in the 1970s," a Libyan oil
executive recalled. "And now I want to do more than just make this
country rich. I want to build solid bridges with America. But it's not
easy when things move so slowly." Though the *Green Book* lacks a section on bureaucracy, Libyan governance robustly overcompensates, its
culture stuck in a time-warp where one cannot be fired for doing nothing, only for doing something that a superior may not like. "It's hard
even to get tourists in the country, let alone take them where they want
to go," a desert tour operator lamented about possibly the world's most
arbitrary visa procedures, by which even distinguished visitors have
been invited to the country only to be left standing on the airport runway and then sent back. There is plenty of talk about updating investment laws, but no one seems to know what the laws are. A bunker
buster was not required to unravel Libya's clandestine nuclear weapons
program, but a similarly seismic shakeup may be necessary to induce
the profound psychological countertraining needed to adjust Libyans to
modern international business or diplomacy. A country governed by a
doctrine that could vanish upon the death of a single man must do more
than offer promises of safe investment to lower its political risk rating.

"Politics is just trouble," sneer many Libyans. It is hard to consider any Libyans citizens of their own country.[15] Thus when Gaddafi's revolution does come to an end, the question will not only be *who* replaces him but also *what*. The one-man regime is effectively a nonsystem grafted onto a dysfunctional milieu of tribes and amorphous assemblies. "People's Committees" were meant to be democratic agora but instead afforded people apathy from politics, in addition to the general fear of being liquidated for dissent. The title Gaddafi carries is the humble "Brother Leader and Guide of the Revolution," which gives no indication as to which of his children, if any, would formally succeed him. The Western-educated Saif al-Islam al-Gaddafi has become something of a roving informal foreign minister, and he believes that "a country's political system should not be based on loyalty or lineage." Whoever replaces Gaddafi when the next *ghibli* sweeps him into history will have the same chance as his father did to reinvent Libyan identity.

CHINA MOVES IN

As its ever-larger embassies across Africa attest, China exploits geopolitical openness—but globalization is its principal weapon. China now ranks right behind the EU and the United States as Africa's third-largest investor, with $50 billion in trade in 2005. Particularly with regimes that have souring ties with the United States, China builds strategic alliances by deepening commercial relations.[16] With its voracious appetite for natural resources, it has taken a lead in oil and gas production from Angola to Algeria to Sudan, importing more oil from Africa than from Saudi Arabia.[17] As with the other superpowers, China's engagement can mean the difference between peace and genocide: In Sudan, China has sent UN peacekeepers but also covert military personnel to protect its oil facilities and a (nearly) thousand-mile pipeline to the Red Sea, all the while sandbagging UN resolutions aimed at halting the civil war in the country's south and the ethnic cleansing pogroms in the Darfur region, where Chinese machine guns are plentiful. Countries from Libya to China are fueling Khartoum's real estate bonanza despite American sanctions.

China portrays African states as its partners, not as mercy cases, and many Arab and African governments enthusiastically speak of a "China model" of closed regimes with open economies. To revive the mid–twentieth century Sino-African kinship, China's comprehensive packages of assistance, investment, professional training, and doctors dispatched throughout Africa demonstrate a fraternal spirit of "doing what it can," as opposed to the Western-style economic "shock therapy." China has canceled most African nations' debts, provided soft loans, and increased imports from Africa by a factor of ten, moves that compete with and undermine Western aid policies that are increasingly perceived as ineffective. Billions of dollars in Western aid have failed to build a railway network in Nigeria or power grids in the Horn of Africa as quickly as China did. When Western agencies pulled out of the Horn of Africa during the Eritrea-Ethiopia war in the 1990s, China built Ethiopia's Takazee Dam on the headwaters of the Blue Nile; it now generates hydropower for the region.[18] Addis Ababa, the location of the African Union's headquarters, is also China's regional hub for amassing commercial contacts to sell military hardware.

But America, Europe, and China are *all* far more interested in securing energy supplies than urging political reform in Africa.[19] While China backs the despotic regime of Robert Mugabe in Zimbabwe, which has turned the continent's breadbasket into a basket case of starvation and strife, America has chosen to bankroll the kleptocratic and inhumane regime of Equatorial Guinea, which ships over half a million barrels of oil to the United States each a day. Ultimately, China's resource grab in Africa literally erodes the economic base of many countries. Over forty trade agreements with Africa have led to a Chinese "textile tsunami" that has eviscerated countless African jobs, while WTO loopholes allow Chinese textiles access from

Tangier factories to Europe, easily outmaneuvering African exporters. Chinese oil and gas workers, often taken from China's vast prison population, sleep on work sites and contribute virtually nothing to local economies. China may ultimately do as much to keep African countries in the third world as it does to lift them from it.

CHAPTER 22

EGYPT:

BETWEEN BUREAUCRATS AND THEOCRATS

IN THE THIRD century B.C., Egyptian king Ptolemy II presided over the Great Library of Alexandria, the largest in the world with over seven hundred thousand scrolls. Its destruction nearly seven hundred years later in a fire caused by Roman barbarism marked the end of Egypt's place as the center of global learning. Today, gracefully elevating from the Mediterranean seaside stands the resurrected Bibliotheca Alexandrina. Though it contains no more volumes than it did over two millennia ago, the Norwegian-designed Bibliotheca is the grandest symbol of Arab civilization's potential to overturn centuries of inversion during which Europe's golden age coincided with the Arabs' dark ages and vice versa. On its walls, hieroglyphic, Greek, and Arabic scripts decoratively narrate Mediterranean encounters, and postmodern sculptures dot its courtyards. The Bibliotheca houses the Anna Lindh Institute, named for the slain Swedish foreign minister who devoted herself to intercivilizational dialogue, boasts cutting-edge facilities for three-dimensional molecular imaging, one of only four mirror sites for the entire World Wide Web, and research centers partnered with European universities.

Napoleon's invasion of Egypt in 1798 marked the beginning of the modern subjugation of the Arab world. But no matter who its rulers are, Egypt has always seen itself as central to the Mediterranean, African, and Arab worlds. Four thousand years ago, Egypt's pharaohs represented the height of human civilization, but their way of life depended on the Nile, the world's second-longest river, which originates deep in the headwaters of Burundi and Ethiopia. Moving upstream (the Nile flows south to north) through Luxor (the ancient Thebes) and Aswan reveals that Sudan, once Egypt's Nubian kingdom, is today the buffer between the Arab and African worlds. Today even the poorest Nile basin countries are building hydroelectric dams that threaten the water levels of the Aswan High Dam and Lake Nasser, Egypt's strategic water reserve against droughts.[1] Almost all of Egypt's population and arable land still lie along the Nile, so for Egypt any reduction in its water supply constitutes an act of war—but war will not create more water. From Cairo to Aswan, the Nile already resembles a fetid lake, with diminished mineral flows, petrochemical pollution, and planned nuclear reactors potentially turning the already clogged Mediterranean delta into a swamp as well. Aswan is now as much a strategic liability, for its potential destruction in any attack (a tactical card threatened by Israel) would cause flooding amounting to ecological genocide.*

The Maghreb and Mashreq regions take their names from their positions west and east of the Egyptian Nile, underscoring how long Egypt has been the Arab pillar, forming one corner of a triangle with Turkey and Iran, with all three continuously maneuvering to assert influence in the space they define. Egypt's Sinai Peninsula is also the junction of Saudi Arabia, Jordan, and Israel, which occupied it from 1956 to 1973. At the northern end of the 120-mile-long Suez Canal lies Port Said, from which one can easily jump from Africa to Port Fouad in Asia by ferry or by crossing the Mubarak Peace Bridge. About 10 percent of the world's sea trade still passes through the Suez Canal, earning Egypt $5 billion in annual fees, which are transforming Port

---

*Though the Horn of Africa historically has greater ties to Yemen and the Gulf states—with identical mountainous topography on either side of the narrow Bab-el-Mandeb Strait separating Africa from Asia—Egypt and the West seek to stabilize the region to protect naval passage from the Suez Canal through the Red Sea and the Straits of Tiran into the Gulf of Aden and the Indian Ocean. Horn countries such as Somalia, Ethiopia, Eritrea, and Djibouti are essentially failed states beset by famine, civil war, small-arms proliferation, and disease. American and European bases have been established in tiny Djibouti to counter threats from radical Islamist groups such as Al-Qaeda, which have established active cells in the Horn.

Said from a decaying beach collecting Mediterranean litter into a quaint city with European chalets—much as when it was the British East India Company's land base. Along the canal, the dredging is under way to accommodate the passage of giant ships to and from its new main user: China.

Much of Egypt's diplomatic clout has rested on its position as the Arabs' main interlocutor with Israel, against whom it has also sacrificed the most blood. Anwar Sadat's 1979 peace treaty with Israel, however, earned it expulsion from the Arab League for over a decade. The subsequent "cold peace" with Israel led to a flourishing of the southern Sinai tourist paradise of Sharm el-Sheikh, on the Red Sea, to which throngs of unemployed young Egyptians flock in search of work. Even at slave wages, the pristine resorts seem like a dream to them.[2] Bedouin in the Sinai have complained that they were treated better under Israel's occupation than under the crass Mubarak regime, which has failed to use tourism revenues to turn the peninsula into a crossing for pilgrims rather than drugs and weapons. Israel's further withdrawal in 2005 from the narrow coastal strip of Gaza makes it essentially an unstable province of Egypt. At the lawless border at Rafah, Palestinians surge unchecked into Egypt for family visits and medical care. "Egypt is many Palestinians' savior from Palestine," a strategic analyst in Cairo remarked, shaking his head at the failure of efforts to bring peace and stability to Palestine.

"We are still the largest Arab state, so still the natural bellwether for the Arabs' geopolitical leanings," claimed a Cairo historian in his overflowing library. Modern Egypt's founding father, Mohammed Ali, rose through the ranks of the Ottoman governorate in the early nineteenth century and achieved quasi-independence for Egypt by pushing for autonomous industry and agriculture. European powers sought to undermine Egypt's pro-Arab maneuvers, but Gamal Abdel Nasser's takeover in 1954 (at the age of thirty-six) and nationalization of the Suez Canal two years later inspired a generation of anticolonialists, even giving hope to the Soviet Union, which sought a deeper foothold in the Arab world after France and Britain's mercantilist ambitions were nakedly exposed in their ruthless effort to retake the canal. But Soviet advisers never properly integrated with Egypt's political class, opening a strategic gap, which America then exploited.[3]

But Nasser had little interest in being America's anticommunist bulwark a half century ago, and Egypt's proud establishment will hardly pass up opportunities to play all sides today. "Between supporting the 'war on terror' and tolerating our pro-Israel stance, Egypt actually does far more for the U.S. than vice-versa," an American diplomat conceded. American military and economic assistance (totaling just under $2 billion) artificially inflates America's influence in Egypt, though it buys far less than it did thirty years ago. "This relationship with the U.S. isn't worth the price of their meddling in our politics. We don't need their leftover weapons, and we can build our own sewers," one official remarked. Egypt increasingly spends its military budget on Chinese weapons, and it has offered itself as a bridgehead for China's growing ties to Africa. China is projected to replace the United States as Egypt's top trading partner through its investments in the Suez Canal, cement factories, electronics companies, and convention centers.[4] Chinese cultural traits such as an emphasis on honor play well in the Arab world, where its diplomats show deference to local culture by learning Arabic and even taking Arabic names.

Europe's influence in Egypt may eventually supersede that of the United States as well. Europe does far more to build Egypt's markets, and it can guide Arab democratization toward decentralized parliamentary systems over the current presidential ones. While Americans recoil at navigating the labyrinthine bureaucracy, European companies have spent over $500 million to upgrade Egypt's tourism, construction, and agriculture. Factories producing Mercedes and Peugeots could increase automotive employment from the sixty thousand workers of today by a factor of ten. With Europe and China making strategic inroads, Egypt has put itself in the geopolitical marketplace like never before.

Egypt's central geography has not made it any easier for the nation to find its *inner* direction, making it a country ripe for revolution. Egyptian scholar Gamal Hamdan has argued that Egypt's place in the Arab world is analogous to that of Cairo in Egypt: It is the cultural, economic, and political hub.[5] A millennium ago, Cairo controlled transcontinental markets like no place since Rome, subsuming Maghreb, African, and Gulf peoples within its textured Pharaoic, colonial, and cosmopolitan urbanscape, and today it is still a city of countless mosques, churches, estates, and markets, with grand Victorian architecture juxtaposed with bland revolutionary edifices. But it would be futile to attempt to count the population of a megalopolis of perhaps twenty million people. It is, like so many such cities in Africa and Asia, a virtual country unto itself, particularly for the millions of poor—including over a million street children—who are born in the city and never leave. "Foreigners, other Arabs, and even we Egyptians all get lost here in Cairo," a tea vendor in the Old Cairo neighborhood aphorized. No wonder Cairenes believe Cairo and Egypt are synonymous.

Cairo today is very much a microcosm of how Arabs are scraping their way out of the third world despite lacking the sophisticated discipline of their Pharaonic and Islamic forebears. Once one stops blaming colonialism for modern ills and assesses what has replaced it, the failures of Arab governance stand out in bold relief. Many of Cairo's poorest residents live in a shanty district beneath the towering citadel of Mohammed Ali in the city's heart, while the elite live in luxury with private schools and hospitals. But even Cairo's chic buildings are crumbling, with shards of tile and piles of broken concrete strewn everywhere. The fact of Egypt's two economies is visible on many corners, where most people judiciously select vegetables in street markets while the privileged few pay Western prices for a single cappuccino in European cafés. Donkey-pulled vegetable carts and cross-legged shoe shiners work on the same streets that contain high-rise hotels and grand museums. Along Cairo's outer ring road, makeshift brick tenements claim thousands of acres of arable land, their resident squatters hitchhiking into the city each day. Will the government raze these shelters while private citizens build higher gates and walls around their estates, or will it compassionately invest in the practical adobe housing that Egypt itself invented millennia ago?

"We have plans—*real* plans—to recapture our historical glory," an official from the ruling party declared with an air of hectic frenzy. A national highway from Alexandria to Aswan will accelerate access to less populated areas, a high-tech financial center will host Egypt's growing stock market and government offices, and a new taxi service has been deployed to clean up the underground transport sector. Billions of dollars in inefficient subsidies are being cut to reverse decades of failed stopgap reforms. Tax-free zones are cropping up from the Mediterranean coast near Libya to across the Suez Canal. "All investment is good investment," is the new mantra of Egypt's business class, which pushes for free trade agreements with the United States and the EU in order to force the government to upgrade its regulations. Where five years ago there was just desert, "New Cairo" has emerged as a hazy horizon of low-rise suburban developments, its population growing at close to one million people per year. Egypt also luckily discovered significant natural-gas reserves just as its modest oil deposits are expiring, resulting in lucrative exports to Israel, Jordan, and Europe.

But as several hundred thousand young people enter the workforce each year, Egypt faces a relentless unemployment crisis. "This is our biggest problem by far," worried one businessman while driving through New Cairo. "We have more young people than we know what to do with." As in the Maghreb, the race is on to give restless youth something to do before they rise up against the government through street violence or religious radicalism. Sigmund Freud wrote of the "cultural frustration" of life in a large, impersonal metropolis such as Cairo, which makes the bored hordes susceptible to any stimulus, whether good or ill. Fretting to defuse this socioeconomic time bomb, entrepreneurs fund vocational schools and lobby to turn thousands of empty government plots into soccer fields.

Their task is not made any easier by the emerging development that Egypt must also compete with one of its new benefactors: China. In the Ataba market district of Cairo, Egyptians buy Chinese products they should be making themselves, such as their own national flag, knockoffs of the popular Fulla Arab Barbie doll, and even Ramadan lanterns that can chant in Arabic. China's demand for construction-grade steel also pinches Egypt and other countries chafing to clamor out of the third world by forcing them to spend far more on infrastructure than they can afford. As with Mexico, the end of the Multi-Fiber Agreement exposed Egypt's lack of preparation for stiffer competition in the $500 billion annual global textile market. China now harvests high-grade cotton to rival Egypt's most delicate export, which accounts for one-third of Egypt's industry. But if it designed better garments than the Chinese—hardly a tall order—it could vastly enhance their value.

Egyptian officials keenly point out that their country has been "a tourist destination since the beginning of tourism," pinning their hopes on boosting the already 60 percent of the economy that revolves around catering to foreigners. But it is precisely Egypt's most touristy areas that exhibit all of the third-world mistakes that will continue to hinder development instead of advancing it. In Aswan and Luxor, home of fabled temples and tombs, a handful of key agencies controls all hotels, limiting the growth of private services that would absorb more of the massive employable youth population. Children living around these ancient attractions sell postcards and offer felucca rides on the Nile; their schools are no better than those in poorer areas. Unless speaking gibberish in five languages counts as education, greater tourism and wealth are not likely to improve literacy. At Sharm el-Sheikh, Egypt's jet-set aquatic sanctuary, waste and sewage from hotels is dumped into the Red Sea rather than in the open desert, polluting the water and eroding the coral that attracts so many scuba divers and snorkelers. And as five-star hotels outside Cairo encroach on the once-remote Giza, the Great Pyramids seem commensurately less exotic. Will the millions of annual first-time visitors to Egypt bother to return?

"We may look like the pharaohs, but we are a thoroughly uncivilized nation," fumed a Cairo entrepreneur in his enormous villa overlooking a golf course. Egypt's leaders are hardly convincing in channeling any pride from ancient Egypt's glorious age. Can Islam restore Egypt's dignity? Egypt is the central sieve through which Arabism and Islamism have for centuries flowed and blended, never more so than today. Hassan al-Banna, who in 1928 founded Egypt's Muslim Brotherhood, sought to revive Arab civilization after the collapse of the Ottoman empire through a nonviolent pan-Sunni movement. After his assassination in 1949 by Egyptian authorities, his disciple Sayyed Qutb carried forward his teachings with the added urgency of seeing the world at an intolerable crisis point of Western-backed oppression of the Arabs' pious Islamic bedrock.[6] Though the Brotherhood spread its reach to Jordan and Syria, its biggest comeback has been at home. Egypt—not Iraq—is the Arab tipping point for both Islamism and democracy.

For over a thousand years Cairo's Al-Azhar mosque and university, so old they intricately blend the entire history of Islamic architecture, have been cornerstones of conservative Islamic thinking. Arab rulers have often touted their Muslim credentials to gain the support of this Islamic establishment, but Islamists would never voluntarily endorse the current Arab political stasis. For the millions of frustrated Egyptians left out of the country's new economic possibilities—or who are stuck in traffic trying to get to them—the call to prayer is an emotional stabilizer that inspires not radicalization but its opposite: a reminder of core values in a materialist environment that appears to be losing them. After a day of loitering, young boys suddenly skip to a mosque on Cairo's Zamalek Island at sunset because prayer and discussion focus the mind and give meaning. Just across the pathway is the resplendent Opera House, but who can afford to go there?

All the conditions for Islamist revolution are present in Egypt today: wealth disparities, elite conflict, religious oppression, and political alienation. Hosni Mubarak has ruled since Anwar Sadat's assassination all the way back in 1981; his previous position was vice president, a post he somehow never got around to filling. His Mukhbarat keeps constant surveillance on teeming, restive towns, while his government does little to address their needs. For a quarter century, the systematic elimination of competition in Egyptian politics has resembled Orwell's *Animal Farm*, with Mubarak so unwilling to share power that he imprisons even secular liberals so as to leave only Islamist parties as an unpalatable alternative to himself—a ruse to which America still naively falls prey. The specter of Islamist parties in power is only the latest in a long line of excuses given for the Arab world's lack of political evolution: The Gulf oil sheikhdoms' rentier model provides for the people in exchange for total political control, while other Arabs blame colonialism, America, Israel, or poverty.[7] The special irony of the Islam excuse is that it comes from within.

"Our choices are not easy," a newspaper editor pondered while smoking a *nargeela* (water pipe). "Most Egyptians have a conservative reflex: We choose to feed our children over fighting for democracy. We prefer modest adjustments to radical change." Sitting in open-air cafés to smoke a *nargeela* and play dominoes has long been more popular than political activism in Egypt. But a renaissance in Arab civil society and media has inspired a democratic culture that promises a third way between the apathy of mint tea and the militancy of the machine gun. Nonviolent protests are now a regular occurrence, and in 2006 two dozen Egyptian publications ceased printing to protest a draconian media law.

A government that provides neither moral leadership nor public services is a perfect target for Islamist groups well equipped to provide both. Islam is not a doctrine of resistance against an oppressive state, but given its spiritual and increasingly social foundation, it is no surprise how well it has functioned as one.[8] Islamist groups in Egypt and other Arab states have become crucial providers of health care and education, which incompetent autocrats have neglected even as their populations swell. Because Islamists don't actually need traditional political outlets to send their message, outlawing them only gives them an excuse to manipulate the masses in the mosques or to take violent revenge. The Mukhbarat actually fired on pro-Brotherhood voters during the 2005 election—hardly the pageant of democracy Mubarak claimed.

The busiest and cleanest hamburger chain in Egypt, Mu'meneen ("Faithful"), aptly captures who is revitalizing Egyptian politics. For decades autocracy was the bulwark against communism and Islamism; now democracy is Islamism's weapon against autocracy. The logic of Islamic democracy is that Islam is about liberation, not submission, and democracy is a means to exercise it.[9] Through social activism and slick televangelism, the Brotherhood appeals to Egypt's struggling middle and lower classes, compelling voters through slogans such as "Islam is the solution" or "If Islam were applied, no one would be hungry!" But even as the Brotherhood debates whether Islam is "a" or "the" source of law, its platform actually has little to do with religion, focusing simply on countering corruption, creating jobs, and improving social services. The Brotherhood's presence has awoken the parliament from decades of dormancy through its persistent calls for Mubarak to repeal his arbitrary emergency laws. Islam and democracy are certainly more compatible than authoritarianism and democracy.*

From Morocco to Iraq, sporadic, anonymous bombings during elections are the growing pains of democracy. But the only way to diminish the credibility of Islamist radicals who act like nineteenth-century Russian anarchists is to give greater opportunity to those who act like twenty-first-century democrats.[10] Democracy has moderated Islamist parties across the Muslim world, and in Egypt they now condemn terrorism perpetrated in their name because Egyptians are

---

*It is unclear whether the Muslim Brotherhood would be a wolf in sheep's clothing, achieving power democratically only to cancel elections, seize the apparatus of power, assault minorities such as the Christian Copts (10 percent of Egypt's population), and implement sharia law. It is equally likely that the Brotherhood's leadership would keep mosque and state separate to avoid ceding any of its hard-earned power to clerics and that it would remain committed to democracy and its popular anticorruption platform. If the Mubarak regime would recognize it as a political party, it would go a long way toward distinguishing it from an Islamic association. See Samer Shehata and Joshua Stacher, "The Brotherhood Goes to Parliament," *Middle East Report*, no. 240 (Fall 2006).

themselves appalled by the rising extremism. Tourism workers decry bombings at the Valley of the Kings or Red Sea resort villages such as Dahab that damage the industry on which their livelihoods depend. "We expect our leaders—whether secular or Islamist—to stop such violence, not accelerate it," insisted a democracy activist in Cairo, adding, "Islamists have more credibility to dissuade fanatics than anyone in the Mubarak regime."

"Imposed democracy is an oxymoron," complained an Egyptian Islamist outside the Al-Azhar mosque. "Islamism does not define itself with respect to Western ideals." Since America's personal alliance is with the greatly resented Mubarak—not with the Egyptian people—its reform efforts are truly slow, shallow, and narrow, highlighting the hypocrisy of sheltering the all-powerful executive.[11] The United States has been reluctant to offer pacts to entrenched leaders, protecting them in secondary roles in exchange for allowing their countries to move on—rather than be dragged down with them.[12] As a result, argues Tunisian human rights activist Moncef Marzouki, American foreign policy "greatly facilitates the growth of extremist Islamist forces."[13] Indeed, America is most disliked in countries with U.S.-allied regimes; after all, almost all of the September 11, 2001, hijackers came from Egypt and Saudi Arabia. If the West wants democracy in Egypt, it must accept Islamists as part of that democracy. As one analyst wrote, "The U.S. can force a shuffling of the deck, but cannot determine where the cards fall."[14]

"We like the Europeans because they are less committed to Mubarak, and have the kind of parliaments to which we aspire," a reformist politician explained. Mubarak treats the Egyptian constitution like a chessboard on which the pieces—the articles and clauses—are moved or removed to shape power relations among branches and factions, and his National Democratic Party (NDP), now led by his son Gamal, continues the tinkering to secure dominance through the 2010 parliamentary elections.[15] But while Mubarak has resisted American pressure to sign even the Alexandria Declaration—described as an "Arab Magna Carta"—Europeans continue to train judges and activists who can lobby for an independent judiciary. The majority of Egyptians are too young ever to have known a leader other than Mubarak. The greatest gift the West could give them would be to let them fairly choose whether Mubarak's successor will share his last name or not. "We want a leader who has used public transportation," proclaimed an engineering student while devouring a plate of kebabs in Cairo's Mohandessein district.

The Western policy of prizing stability over democracy has become a pathetic cliché, for such stability never lasts more than a generation and culminates in *in*stability. "We need to just have it out like Iran did, purging this regime," a female university student in Cairo vented in a smoky coffeehouse. Egypt may not be heading for an Algerian-style civil war, but an Iranian-style revolution is not unthinkable—something Ayman al-Zawahiri hoped the assassination of Sadat in 1980 would inspire. Democracy is the better alternative, even if it means an Egypt that is less friendly toward the United States in the short term and forces the government to cultivate ties with the Brotherhood. This is not a matter of religious preference or personal loyalty but simple strategic necessity— playing all sides *within* Egypt, much as Egypt has begun to play all of the superpowers. Ultimately, a democratic Egypt is likelier to focus on internal problems than denounce the United States.[16] And if it still veers off course, it would have only itself to blame.

THE RETURN OF ARABISM

Arabs are lucky. Unlike Latin Americans, the combination of dense familial and social networks and religious prohibitions makes the Arab world quite safe: There isn't a single Arab city free of American or Israeli occupation that is dangerous when compared with a comparable city in the Western Hemisphere. The honor-based *hawala* (trust) method of money transfer ensures the rapid exchange of enormous sums both across the region and internationally. Remittances transmitted in this fashion helped reduce poverty in Egypt and other Arab states despite the economic stagnation of the 1990s. Arabs are both hospitable and ingenious, and in the absence of disposable income they show a remarkable ability to improvise in the repair of broken-down cars. Impossibly old Fiats and Peugeots still sputter along in Cairo today that would be the envy of Ukrainian taxi drivers.

In the great informality of Arab encounters, the culture of *wasta*—personal connections—is preferred to modern institutions.[17] Beyond the narrow elite, which seems lost without the use of English, bloated public sectors from Libya to Saudi Arabia and also Iran remain bastions of stultifying inefficiency. The workday begins late and ends early. Bureaucrats have no incentive to perform even the most mundane functions, let alone take the occasional risk. All chains of command lead to one authority, thus all accountability lies with a single supremely unaccountable leader—one for each Arab nation.

Arabic, *wasta*, *hawala*, and Islam have integrated Arab peoples for centuries, but politics has divided them. While nationalism bloomed in nineteenth-century Europe, Arabs were still subservient to the Ottomans. Early pan-Arab intellectuals believed in an overarching democratic, secular, and egalitarian Arab nation, a promise that simultaneously threatened to liberate individual Arab states from their recently acquired and thus cherished sovereignty.[18] While this greater Arab realm was meant to unite in the face of confrontations with the West and Zionism, pan-Arabism lost its magic with the stunning defeat to Israel in the 1967 Six-Day War.[19] The ultimate irony came in 1990, when Iraqi president Saddam Hussein prattled on about his pan-Arab leadership even as Saudi Arabia was inviting the U.S. military to repulse his invasion of Kuwait.

Today, the Arab psychological pendulum is swinging back in the direction of committed Arabism. Arabs have learned that the West will never run out of excuses—oil, democracy, terrorism—to intervene in their affairs, making Arabism a movement both *against* American encroachment and *for* Arab unity. The ease with which Egypt and Syria merged to form the United Arab Republic in 1958, the countermerger between Jordan and Iraq, the rapid failure of both, the nascent Arab Maghreb Union—all demonstrate the fluidity of Arab civilization and the alien nature of state systems imposed upon it. More than ever, the Arab world has all the elements—land, labor, capital, language, access to technology, common interests, and shared enemies—to form a natural geopolitical bloc, globalizing itself such that Arabs' mutual occupations become a legacy of the past.

The Arab League, not long ago considered defunct, is in a process of self-reinvention—not as a threat to individual state sovereignty but as an Arab United Nations, fostering technical cooperation through specialized trade, education, and agriculture agencies. In the buzzing corridors of its Cairo headquarters, Arab League officials speak of the European Coal and Steel Union as an appropriate parallel to their effort to transcend the mutual condescension between Egypt and Saudi Arabia (Egyptians view Saudis as uncultured Bedouins; Saudis see Egyptians as scheming beggars) to unite the most populous and wealthy Arab states as the natural locomotives of revived Arabism. Arab League projects now include an electricity and gas grid to link the Maghreb via Egypt to Jordan and Syria, water desalination from the Gulf to water-deprived Egypt and Jordan, and cultivation of the fertile lands of Sudan. An Arab Parliament began to take shape in 2005 with standing committees to monitor Arab executive institutions and strengthen parliamentary powers. Arab politics may eventually catch up to Arab economics. "Maybe an Arab peacekeeping force will put lives on the line for Muslims the way the U.S. and Europe already do," pondered one Arab cynic.

CHAPTER 23

THE MASHREQ:
ROAD MAPS

IT IS THE Mashreq region that is most frequently implied by the terms *Middle East* or *Mesopotamia*, or the equally vague French *Levant*. Though it was considered the Soviet Union's backyard in the Cold War, that the region is still sorting out its post–World War I formation reveals how deeply lodged its dislocations truly are. Mashreq history has all the elements of a protracted family feud overseen by horse-trading imperial referees. The British hoped to inspire an Arab-wide, anti-Ottoman revolt during World War I, but Arab resistance was more separatist than nationalist: Instead of unifying for independence, Arabs manipulated the Allies to regain individual fiefdoms.[1] At the Paris peace conference, Woodrow Wilson sought to end the manner in which peoples and provinces were "bartered about . . . as if they were chattels or pawns in a game." But France and Britain had already partitioned Syria between them in the 1916 Sykes-Picot Agreement, nonchalantly using maps dating from the mid–eighteenth century that depicted the Ottoman empire's Catholic diocese. The French marched on Damascus in the early 1920s and ousted the British-installed puppet, Emir Faisal, who was given Iraq as a consolation. Europeans took for granted that Arabs and Zionists could share Palestine, but by 1924, the young monarch ibn Saud's conquest of the Hejaz unified Saudi Arabia, leading Faisal's older brother Abdullah to move his forces into Syria, where the British broke off three-quarters of Palestine and made him king of Transjordan.

Just when it seemed the region could no longer meaningfully blame the British for its disarray, along came the Americans. Despite President Wilson's noble intentions a century ago, is America destined to meet the same fate as its European predecessors? Like the British, America launched a war (on Iraq) that was partially justified in the name of Arab liberation, but the move made it the region's most resented power instead. The British also meddled in Muslim affairs, treating Islam as a single entity that could be co-opted and separated into spiritual and temporal units or even replaced through other forms of loyalty to the nation or a ruling dynasty—yet they missed the spectacular rise of the region's most potent religious force: the Wahhabist *Ikhwan* ("Brethren") in Arabia. Ultimately, the lofty goal of shaping distant fortunes withered into a concern for sparing soldiers and cutting expenses.[2] It is these colonial legacies—plus the resurgence of Islamism, political repression, foreign military intervention, and terrorism—with which the Mashreq today is grappling.

Though it is certain that the Mashreq countries are perennially being woven into a single carpet, the correct pattern of the threads remains to be designed. Arabs do not naturally tend toward national chauvinism; it is the nation-state system that foments rivalry where coexistence is far more the historical experience. Ottoman maps had flowing, curvy patches to denote tribes and the oases they tended, while today's hastily drawn borders depart from any sensible logic for dividing nations: Egypt has the largest Arab population but minimal arable land; Kuwait and Qatar have tiny populations but are blessed with nearly bottomless reserves of oil and gas; the burgeoning Palestinian population is nearly equal parts dispersed refugees and residents of a cramped quasi-state. The multiethnic mosaics of Jordan, Lebanon, Syria, Iraq, Palestine, and Israel are more usefully understood as a network of urban centers mapped onto ancient trade routes than the sparsely populated, structurally weak countries they represent today. In all of them, democracy can mobilize people but not necessarily unite them or make them liberal-minded. Without strong minority rights, democracy means majoritarian rule and the potential annihila-tion of ancestral traditions and even the state form itself. If Mashreq leaders would adopt the territorial indifference of the Ottomans, trade and toleration could win out over local tyrannies and opportunistic ex-tremism, and Palestine could sit at the heart of a lattice linking Tel Aviv, Jerusalem, Beirut, Damascus, Amman, and Baghdad.[3] As in Central Asia's Fergana Valley, the choice is between the suppression of peoples within states to which they may not intrinsically belong and shared spaces and resources. Nowhere in the world is state splintering—but also state opening—more necessary or more dangerous than the strate-gic crossroads of the Mashreq.

ISRAEL AND PALESTINE: TORN TOGETHER

Since the call for a Jewish homeland in the 1917 Balfour Declaration, Israel has been the chief example of migration as a vehicle of state for-mation. But Israel's existence does not guarantee its security, for the mi-gratory force of Palestine's Arabs has yet to achieve sufficient resolution. Since its victory in the Six-Day War, Israel's occupation of Gaza, the West Bank, and East Jerusalem has created demographic bridgeheads of almost 250,000 settlers. Yet though these settlements are often called "the facts on the ground," it is still an open question who will oc-cupy them in the future. The growing presence of Palestinians—either as refugees, guest workers, or citizens—in Israel, Jordan, and Lebanon has given striking impetus to Palestinian statehood, for their own im-posed lack of national identity challenges that of each of their neigh-bors. Because there are far more Arabs than Jews today between the Mediterranean Sea and the Jordan River, it has become one of the supreme ironies of the Arab-Israeli conflict that only the creation of a Palestinian state will ensure the survival of Israel as a Jewish state.

Like Lebanon and the United Arab Emirates, Israel is a string of oases built out of coastal desert with immigrant labor. While Tel Aviv resembles a modern European city whose residents speak of "NASDAQ, not Nablus," they cannot escape the twin troubles of ter-rorism and flagging tourism, especially when highly educated popula-tion centers such as Haifa are all but evacuated during conflict, such as during the 2006 war with Lebanon. Yet some economic integration between Israel and the Arab states already exists: Even as a high-tech manufacturer for American companies, Israel's products—such as Motorola chips—are relabeled in Cyprus and sold to the mobile phone addicts in Arab countries. Qualified Industrial Zones (QIZs) promoting joint production plus cooperation across three neighborhing Red Sea ports—Egypt's Taba, Israel's Eilat, and Jordan's Aqaba—could turn them from mutual hostages into a collective transport mega-hub.

Toynbee described Jerusalem in the 1950s as "split like an atom into two mutually hostile cities which stand and grow side by side without meeting."[4] But Israel's military checkpoints, self-serving umbilical highways, and diaspora money cannot unmake the shared foundation of the Western Wall, the Dome of the Rock, and the Church of the Holy Sepulcher. Jerusalem is the ultimate polytheistic city: Jews, Christians, and Muslims have all fought for an exclusive control that has always eluded them. In the Old City, the overlap of church bells and the mosque's muezzins makes for a constant cacophony, while the same shops simultaneously sell iconography of Orthodox Christianity, Judaism, and Islam, a constant reminder of Semitic similarities. However, so severe is the psychological instability of the faithful in historic Palestine that Christians, put off by the hulking "security barrier" now dividing Jerusalem from their holy city of Bethlehem, are leaving Israel in significant numbers.

Israel's security barrier is evidence that it thinks of itself as the eastern frontier of Western civilization, yet it exists in a permanent state of psychological (or actual) warfare with all of its neighbors. Indeed, Israel is blending and bleeding with its Arab neighbors more and more. Palestinian suicide bombers and armed Israeli soldiers, both of the generation that represents the region's future, have battled to a stalemate. The righteous and the wicked are one. As the Mashreq's rejected organ, Israel is more likely to die than the body if it does not integrate itself peacefully. As elsewhere in the second world, foreign policy and domestic policy overlap in Israel more than ever. As in so many second-world countries, Prime Minister Ehud Olmert was previously the mayor of the capital city. "There is a lot of poverty here," a Tel Aviv taxi driver pointed out amid the modern downtown edifices. "For most of us jobs and hospitals are more important than always making the military the priority." Despite the enormous subsidy it receives from the U.S. government and the Jewish diaspora, Israel realistically has to spend less on the military and more on welfare.[5] From tourism to trade to terrorism, Israel and Palestine can separate in theory but never in practice.

Many Americans have come to see Israel like they do Pakistan, an "ally" that contributes more to America's problems than its solutions.[6] By 2005, Israel had quietly become China's second-largest provider of weapons behind Russia, including antiradar drones and air-to-air missiles—even though China in turn sells missiles to Iran, ironically boosting their target range to include Israel. China, in return, is investing in expanding Israel's ports to become its hub for export across the Mediterranean into Europe. There may come a time when China supports Israel as much as America does—but even that will not solve Israel's existential problem, the Palestinians.

The various iterations of the Israeli-Palestinian peace process always saw small, peripheral measures as major victories, leaving aside the big issues of refugee resettlement and the status of Jerusalem, which spoilers on both sides have used to derail the process at the final moments of truth. Zionists used terrorism as a principal tactic to oust the British during the decade prior to Israel's founding, much as Palestinians do today.[7] "We live in a purgatory, always subservient to international bureaucratic masters," a Palestinian official in East Jerusalem protested, frustrated at the lack of genuine Palestinian self-rule and freedom of movement. After the Hamas victory in the 2006 elections, Israeli security closures forced the parliament to convene by videoconference, a reminder that Israel's current bantustan model for the Palestinians is unsustainable both economically and politically.[8] As in the third world, development is lost when the politics of aid take priority over building indigenous governance. International aid agencies take care of urgent needs but create a bubble economy that disappears once they do (as in Kosovo). The majority of the Palestinian budget comes from funds donated from European and Arab governments, and the United Nations remains Palestine's largest employer (with Israel's Shin Bet security service said to be second largest through its informal network of blackmailed informants). Palestinians feel humiliated by the international assistance that serves as a subsidy for Israel's occupation—which Israel is legally obligated to pay for under international law. "We have been reduced to building others' nations rather than our own," the official continued, referring to Palestinian immigrants in Jordan, Iraq, and Kuwait. The presents ituation is more Pali-stan than Palestine.

But Palestinians may finally be empowered to build their own state. Their crises of high unemployment, weak infrastructure, and rampant population growth (projected to reach 6.5 million by 2020) could be addressed by building a corridor of rail, telecom, electricity, and gas lines linking Jenin, Nablus, Ramallah, East Jerusalem, and Hebron with Gaza City and Rafah on the Egyptian border. Such an arc would connect the national airport and seaport in Gaza to the West Bank, enable urban and suburban communities to cluster around the key corridor nodes, and potentially employ as many as 150,000 Palestinians.[9] If the European Union and other international donors devote the estimated $6 billion needed to construct this backbone arc of Palestine, debates over tactical aid cutoffs to Palestinian agencies would go by the wayside, and Europe could take credit for funding the resolution of one of the world's most intractable conflicts. Transatlantic cooperation in resolving the Arab-Israeli conflict must mean more than multiple phone calls urging restraint.

For decades Arab and Muslim nations have slighted the Palestinians out of selfish self-interest, but now they are taking the Palestinian question into their own hands. Though Palestine has long had its own flag, government, and Olympic team, the United States and Israel have stymied Arab support to Palestinians by freezing assets and blocking money transfers—leaving few options beyond smuggling cash in suitcases from Jordan and Egypt. But the American dogma that Hamas cannot "have one foot in politics and the other in terror" carries little weight among Arabs, especially since American weapons supplied to Fatah have fueled Palestinian factional strife, which culminated in Hamas evicting Fatah authorities from Gaza in 2007. When the United States withdrew its support for the Palestinian Authority in 2006, Saudi Arabia, Egypt, and Iran stepped in to cover its operating budget, demonstrating that the democratically elected government could no longer be blackmailed by America. "Thanks to our diaspora, Arab brothers, and Islamic charities, Hebron is being rebuilt," explained a Palestinian adviser in Ramallah, where sprawling neighborhoods of cream-colored villas have sprouted in just a few years. Until Palestinians are granted statehood, pressure on Hamas to recognize Israel is premature and ironic precisely because Palestine is an entity, not a state, and thus is in no position to offer such legal recognition. Henry Kissinger stated in 1975 that "no solution is possible" without the creation of a sovereign Palestinian state. Three decades later, this remains the precondition to peaceful regional integration.

JORDAN: BETWEEN IRAQ AND A HARD PLACE

For a country as geographically trapped as Jordan, failure perpetually looms. Its very existence is always at stake. No neighbor will pick up the pieces if Jordan falls apart; Israel, the Palestinians, Saudi Arabia, Syria, and Iraqi Sunnis would simply take what they can get for themselves. Jordan embodies the complexities of Arab geopolitics on every possible level. Its very birth was the result of colonial promises mixed with Arab dynastic rivalries, marking the division of the royal houses of desert Arabs into the kingdom of Saudi Arabia and the Hashemite kingdom of Jordan (both carrying the names of their familial rulers). To this day, it continues to use intermarriage with Gulf royal families both to protect its independence and to attract investment from them. Jordan has also been a Cold War buffer state, used by the West to block Soviet expansionism. Though the British officers were all sent home a half century ago, it now takes its talking points from the United States. American pressure made it one of the first Arab countries to establish relations with Israel even without gaining resettlement rights for Palestinians or water rights for itself. Whenever Palestine has destabilized, its rich and poor refugees have flowed into Jordan, bringing both money and social grievances. "We aren't a country," an Amman intellectual complained during a drive through both white-stucco and trash-strewn neighborhoods. "We just get rented out by everyone else."

But Jordan's specialty has become taking advantage of its victimized geography. A Jordanian businessman put it best: "We always profit from wars—so long as it's our neighbors and not us!" West Amman was built on a mix of Gulf money after the Gulf War as well as successful Palestinians holding real estate assets just in case they would have to flee the West Bank less than sixty miles away. Hundreds of Jordanian and Syrian companies were implicated in the UN oil for food scandal by which kickbacks were paid to arrange the evasion of the sanctions on Iraq under Saddam Hussein. Foreign contractors use Amman as a staging point to service Iraqi reconstruction, utilizing Jordanian sub-contractors for everything from transport to medical services. At the same time, much of Iraq's middle class fled to Jordan to escape their own civil war. Even those on the lowest rungs of Jordanian society are implicated in Jordan's inadvertent war economy. Outside the Iraqi embassy in Amman, hundreds of middle-aged Jordanian men line up on a daily basis to apply for "free job" visa waivers, allowing them to cross into Iraq in search of high-risk, high-wage work. All over the country, poor farmers can be seen loading trucks with produce to sell in Iraq, from which they no longer receive free oil, as they did under Saddam. "Smuggling household goods from Saudi Arabia and Jordan to Iraq is still standard operating procedure," the businessman admitted. Despite the uncertainties of Iraq, wealthy Lebanese investors are developing the sandy port of Aqaba for shipping and snorkeling, and tourism around the mineral-rich Dead Sea thrives. When Iraq's civil war ends, longstanding plans for an oil pipeline to Aqaba could become a reality, while in the opposite direction, truck traffic from Aqaba to Baghdad could generate a stable Mashreq trade corridor.

Jordan may be an island of stability, but the rising temperatures in its surrounding waters are threatening to cook it alive. Not only a million Iraqi refugees but also hardened fighters from Iraq's civil war have spilled into Jordan, expanding their struggle onto neighboring turf. It has tallied the second highest number of terrorist attacks and casualties behind Iraq, with perpetrators including Iraqis, Saudis, Libyans, and Jordanians themselves. Every major hotel in Amman has dense security screening, from chassis and trunk checks to metal detectors and body searches. If Iraq splits into three parts, it is the rump, volatile, and resource-deprived Sunni region that will become Jordan's backyard. "Iraq may prove to be a disaster for us, but there is nothing we can do about it," a foreign ministry official admitted while nervously greeting fellow elites in an upscale hotel lobby.

Jordan has very little oil or gas, and even less of the other resource that increasingly drives Mashreq power relations: fresh water. The Jordan River valley, shared by Israelis, Palestinians, and Jordanians, and the Tigris-Euphrates fertile crescent—which has given life to Mesopotamian civilization from the Sumerians to present-day Iraq, Syria, and eastern Turkey—are the Mashreq's natural corridors. The ancient

Nabataens relied on sophisticated irrigation still visible in the smooth grooves along the Siq passage in Petra. Can the region's nations manage their precious water supply so well today? Dam projects in southeastern Anatolia have markedly improved the quality of life for the area's Turks and Kurds, but the water tables downstream are dropping at the alarming rate of six feet a year. Water-sharing agreements and technology could alleviate the mismatch: Power generated from Turkey's hydroelectric dams could be sold cheaply to Syria and Iraq, and desalinated water from the Gulf could be channeled northwards to Jordan to boost irrigation and agricultural output. A Red Sea–Dead Sea canal is already being dredged, evidence that "water wars" are by no means inevitable.

America's search for Arab allies has elevated Jordan from a buffer state to a geopolitical bridgehead. A free trade agreement quickly made America Jordan's largest trading partner, and Jordan has been made an example of positive economic collaboration with Israel through Qualified Industrial Zones (QIZs). The reality, however, is that few Jordanian companies have the manufacturing wherewithal to exploit the QIZs, and the Jordanians who work for them hold low-skill jobs that provide for sustenance, not wealth. The real beneficiaries have been Israeli and Chinese companies, which register their textile firms in Jordan and buy up the largest QIZ shares (the same globalization loophole China exploits in North Africa to gain advantageous export access to the EU). Chinese engineering firms based in Jordan have also built four of its five new dams with remarkable efficiency.

Because so much of Jordan's economy is centered on Amman, other areas have been neglected, such as the second-largest city of Zarqa, which is heavily polluted from manufacturing waste and poor water sanitation. Its conservative underclass produced Abu Musab al-Zarqawi, Iraq's most ruthless Al-Qaeda operative until his death in 2006. On the whole, however, no radical ideologies have emerged from Jordan's modest Bedouin population, reflecting a sedate nature visible in the country's humble mosques. As survival-conscious people, Jordanians had little spare energy to ransack the Danish embassy after the Prophet Muhammed cartoon scandal in early 2006. "We just stopped serving Danish beer," a waiter in a Western restaurant in Amman pithily explained. But that could change. From any of its major hilltops, Amman seems a modern horizon of white rooftops. But like other large Arab cities from Marrakesh to Riyadh, the divide between the new and the old sections exposes the cultural rift between liberal and conservative populations. Outside of Amman, many young women say they choose to wear a veil as a symbol of responsibility to Islam and as a reaction against the perceived over-Westernization of the elite. Modernization and conservatism are two simultaneous trends coevolving across the Arab world—each constantly feeding off the other.

King Abdullah is the man who has to pursue the former without ignoring the latter. Abdullah is frequently bestowed by Western leaders with the somewhat patronizing moniker "moderate," a term practically synonymous with eunuch in Arab power politics. In fact he is not as liberal as Westerners think, still deploying the Mukhbarat, his secret police, to infiltrate most clans and other social groups to protect himself from coups. But he also does not use the secret police as a criminal death squad. Abdullah's father, King Hussein, was a master politician during his half century of rule, co-opting the Muslim Brotherhood while keeping an unnatural society of Palestinians and Arab Bedouins unified. For decades he ensured pliant elites by handing pro-government groups the private sector, allocating ministries on the basis of tribal loyalty, and shaping election laws to give the king a very expedient parliament.

In a region where leaders still prefer to be feared than loved, however, Abdullah is balancing hereditary power with demands for development and democracy. Like Morocco, Jordan is making a gradual transition from tribal oligarchy to technocratic governance. Its vaunted education policy, for example, was spearheaded by a group of "digital ministers" who designed new school curricula and built science parks to inspire a nascent IT industry.[10] With most of Jordan's population centered around Amman, an increase in investment could quickly raise exports and dramatically boost its per capita income. The talented diaspora is returning, bringing both professional know-how and cash for high-tech investments. "We'll export knowledge, not people," an Amman computer programmer boasted while strolling through the campus of the city's main technology park. Other entrepreneurs have brought in $200 million in recent years from Hollywood alone, which uses Jordan as its desert film set.

Abdullah's attempt to modernize Jordanian society is far more complicated. He was himself the architect of the Tunis Declaration, which laid out the counters of electoral charge, women's rights, and judicial reform within conservative Arab parameters and adopted the Arab Human Development Report as an impartial set of indicators for Jordan rather than labeling it a conspiracy. He has tried to unite Islamic schools of jurisprudence against extremist hijacking in matters such as fatwa declaration and laws governing honor crimes, while gradually opening elections to Islamist parties—a strategy that has diminished radical violence from Morocco to Saudi Arabia. Abdullah's high-profile, supermodel–cum–social worker wife, Queen Rania, boosts his popularity and loosens his image, leading one Jordanian indifferent to the monarchy to proclaim, "If you have to have a king, he's your guy!" But ultimately, his success—and Jordan's—depends on how well he navigates these domestic pressures and the Mashreq's turbulent vortex.

LEBANON AND SYRIA:
THE LEVANT'S UNBEARABLE LIGHTNESS

The Lebanese embody all of the contradictions of modern Arab society: They are passionate but shallow, egotistical but fatalistic, cultured but materialistic, decadent but restless. Trilingual and flamboyant, theirs is the only Arab country where one can ski on fresh powder and surf in the sea on the same day.

In theory, Lebanon is the Arab world's first and only democracy, but in reality, the chronology of its car bombings has more to say about its political evolution than its electoral history does. In 1989, President René Moawad was assassinated by one, sparking a series of military offensives that ended the country's fifteen years of civil war in 1991. Fifteen years later, Prime Minister Rafiq al-Hariri and a dozen of his aides where blown into the sky in downtown Beirut, setting in motion the March 14 movement to demand removal of Syria's military occupation. Because Lebanon has no stability, it has freedom and democracy by default. Syria, by contrast, is stabilized by leaders who allow neither freedom nor democracy. Both are linked by three major forces: the legacy of Phoenicians and Greek rule over the Levant (Tyre, Byblos, and Sidon were wealthy trade centers), European colonialism, and now a cross-border fraternal rivalry in which frequent assassinations are fair game and the sons of the now-deceased leaders Rafiq Hariri and Hafez Assad—Saad Hariri and Bashar Assad—struggle to defend their fathers' honor.

No one actually controls Lebanon, least of all the Lebanese. Lebanon's politics are reminiscent of its archaeology in two ways: It is multilayered after millennia of being conquered while demonstrating an ability to rebuild time and again. Despite its tiny size, Lebanese politics are as complex as anywhere in the world, governed by a highly tenuous power-sharing agreement known as "consociational democracy," which brings together Christian Maronites (who hold the presidency), Sunnis (prime minister), and Shi'ites (speaker of parliament). Democracy is not an enlightened choice but rather the result of this sectarian polyarchy in which each group has distinct political goals with little consistent overlap. During the civil war, Christian sects welcomed the Israeli invasion to weaken the Sunnis, and other Maronite communities have been anti-Syrian strongholds while their leaders cut deals with Syria to retain government positions. Sunnis chafe against the disproportionate weight held by Christians, who have prevented a national census from being conducted since 1932. And the depressed Shi'ite majority sees little glory in the cosmopolitan prewar Lebanon over which Sunnis wax so nostalgic. None want to give a voice to the Palestinians, who constitute 10 percent of the population and occupy appallingly overcrowded refugee camps outside Beirut and elsewhere in the country, such as the Nahr al-Bared camp near Tripoli in the country's north, which was the battleground for the Lebanese army's monthlong skirmish with the Sunni radical group Fatah al-Islam in 2007. Though the consociational structure makes dictatorship impossible, its self-administering regions also make effective federal rule a nonstarter. There are nineteen independent religious communities (such as the Druze) in Lebanon and a dispersal of judicial power along sectarian lines that makes a mockery of its secular pretensions.[11] Lebanon's army is riddled with sectarian divides, and Beirut neighborhoods are still segregated along the sectarian lines that formed as militias swept through the city during the civil war, coercing and bribing families to relocate or become refugees.

Lebanese are not democratic by nature but capitalist, even profiting by funneling European women into Saudi harems during the 1970s oil boom. Soon after the civil war, during which fully a tenth of

Lebanon's population was killed, Rafiq Hariri, a sort of political Donald Trump of Lebanon, began funneling the country's fortunes through his Solidere Corporation to raise the country from its charred ashes.* In Beirut at least, he superimposed a glamorous façade over a landscape of total ruin, an approach befitting both Lebanese society and much of the second world: targeted political philanthropy grafted onto sectarian divides with status and influence for sale. Beirut today has no rival as the Arab world's most edgy city, combining the elegance of Istanbul with the seediness of Tangier, and still promises to live up to the original meaning of the Levant ("rising") as a place where people of all religions come together and thrive in prosperous coexistence.[12]

But street politics are as important as real politics in Lebanon. Protest size is the true representation of willpower. Sectarian youth gangs tag their neighborhoods with graffiti and skirmish with others. A facetious advertising campaign in 2006 declared "Parking only for Shi'ites," with other billboards touting similarly exclusive services for various sects, implying that sectarianism is as much a threat as ever. Because no side can agree on how to update the constitution to reflect demographic and power realities, fears of a renewed full-scale civil war linger. In no country does one so often hear the refrain, "No one knows what will happen tomorrow."

"No side is actually for us; they all just use us," scowled a Beirut journalist, his teetering bookcases a metaphor for the country's stability. Lebanon is where the sponsors of terrorism, terrorists themselves, and their battlefield all overlap, and the low psychological threshold of tolerance among Mashreq neighbors is ignited by even the smallest spark. Israel's 2006 invasion of Lebanon in response to Hezbollah's capture of two Israeli soldiers came just as the country was preparing for another record-breaking tourist season, marking another year of progress toward national rehabilitation after the Hariri assassination. By bombing Beirut's airport, blockading its port, and pulverizing entire neighborhoods and southern villages, Israel demonstrated that it, like the United States, treats opponent groups and their host nations as equally culpable. The re-destruction of Lebanon was reminiscent of the 1980s invasion, in which Israel sought to exterminate the PLO,

---

*Before becoming prime minister, Hariri's wealth was estimated at $2 to $3 billion. After his death it was estimated by *Fortune* magazine to be $16 billion.

but it was magnified by the power of advanced weaponry that killed ten times more civilians than military personnel (even though Hezbollah was the stated enemy), even repeating the 1996 massacre near the refugee camp at Qana in southern Lebanon. Oil spills resulting from the bombing of Lebanese power plants led to the worst environmental crisis in the history of the Mediterranean. "Our music finally went quiet," the journalist sighed nostalgically.

Hezbollah has been likened to a state within a state, a shadowy army capable of declaring war on behalf of the government—and also of toppling it. Despite its deep roots in Lebanese society, Hezbollah is also undeniably part of Iran (its "unofficial treasury") as well as Syria's grander plans to bleed Israel dry. (If anything, an independent Palestine is a hindrance to their achieving this goal.) Rather than Hezbollah withering after Israel's withdrawal from southern Lebanon in 2000, arms and finances only increased. By 2006, Hezbollah's militias had scattered thousands of short-range rockets into hidden positions around southern Lebanon and used Iranian decryption and targeting technology to pinpoint and destroy Israeli tanks while raining missiles on northern Israel, forcing the evacuation of Haifa. With no more than ten thousand fighters—one-eighth the size of Lebanon's national army—Hezbollah outperformed any existing Arab army, elevating it to mythical status across the region.[13] Hassan Nasrallah, Hezbollah's clerical leader, became the most popular leader in the Arab world (even though he is a Shi'ite) based on his incorruptible devotion to resisting Western tyrannies. (George Bush, by contrast, appears to be less popular than Ariel Sharon—quite a feat.) For Arabs there is a moral equivalency between Israel and Hezbollah—one is armed by the United States and the other by Iran and Syria. And Hezbollah's credibility in fulfilling the twin functions of statehood—defense and welfare—has been magnified by its construction company, aptly named Jihad Construction, not merely rebuilding schools and hospitals in Shi'ite slums and southern villages but also paying for individuals' tuition and treatments in them.

Lebanon remains a tinderbox, moving quickly in opposite directions, which threaten to tear it apart again. At the same time that international donors in Paris in 2007 pledged $8 billion for reconstruction and Lebanon's wealthy, globe-spanning diaspora (estimated at nearly triple the national population of four million people) from Brazil to Indonesia once again poured money into the country, Saudi and Iranian elements backed competing parties while sectarian militias rearmed and trained in neighboring countries. Lebanon now rebuilds even as it braces for re-destruction.

Syria's trampling of Lebanon during the civil war was sealed with a "Treaty of Brotherhood and Cooperation" that made Lebanon a "wholly owned subsidiary" of Syria, which didn't even bother to have an embassy in Beirut.[14] During the 2006 conflict with Israel, thousands of Lebanese fled to Syria, another reminder that nominally independent Lebanon remains Finlandized. While they exchange $500 million a year in official trade, in reality Syrians have plundered Lebanon for $5 billion per year of smuggling and remittances, a greater amount than its own exports.

T. E. Lawrence wanted to give the Arabs a "dream palace" of national chambers after the post-Ottoman "procession of Arab freedom from Mecca to Damascus."[15] Today, however, Syria is more like Uzbekistan than a chamber of freedom. Lying right at the Mashreq's heart, Syria is a historical crossroads between the Egyptian and Mesopotamian civilizations, its wondrous ruins at Aleppo revealing the first steps of organized human settlement, agriculture, and language. Yet decades of failed Baathist socialism have turned a potential industrial powerhouse of twenty million people into the chief obstacle to a regional Silk Road. Like Heydar Aliyev of Azerbaijan, Hafez al-Assad ("protector of the lions") built a political order to serve only himself, providing his son Bashar little wisdom in how to run a nation that isn't one. Lacking much of the loyalty commanded by his father, Bashar and his minority Alawite coterie purged both the Baath party and the security services, expanding their clan outward by marrying into powerful Sunni families. In the bazaars around the grand Umayyad mosque in Damascus, citizens have been reduced to dejected conspiracy theorists surrounded by ubiquitous portraits of Assad *père et fils*, less intimidating than they are numbing.

"Syria's stature comes from being talked to. The appearance of influence is enough for them," explained a Lebanese political consultant. "And most of all, they want to talk to the Americans . . . but just to screw them. Whatever the Americans say, they will do the opposite." America's emphasis on toppling Assad has entrenched him further, inspiring an external survival strategy that has included stronger ties with Turkey and Iran while returning to its days as a Soviet client by allow-

ing Russia to relocate its Black Sea fleet to naval bases near the sleepy
Mediterranean ports of Tartus and Latakia. The largest investor in
Syria's oil and gas exploration projects is China. While Europe has hes-
itated to engage with Syria's business elite, opposition parties, the
Muslim Brotherhood, labor unions, NGOs, media, and Beirut-based
exiles, Turkey at least stepped into the void to teach Syria how to reform its central bank.

The best symbol of the debilitating durability of the Mashreq's
postcolonial demarcations (and another living irony of pan-Arabism) is
the Hejaz railway. Built to transport hajj pilgrims from Istanbul to
Mecca, it has fallen into a state of near-total disrepair, functioning only
in Jordan but at a laughably slow pace. Western country-by-country
strategies (if they can be so called) will never smooth out the Mashreq's
knots of Iranian interference, Syrian intransigence, Lebanese weakness, Israeli aggression, and Palestinian desperation. Only the EU,
which now leads the peacekeeping mission on the Lebanon-Israel border, can offer the region a grand bargain to support its trade, tourism,
and transport potential along the lines it pursues in the Maghreb. Indeed, Europe's integration with Turkey places it once again geographically in close contact with Syria, Iraq, and Iran, countries it abandoned
a half century ago. The EU's transportation network currently extending
into the Caucasus could be replicated as a road system from Turkey
through Syria, Lebanon, Israel, and Jordan, with the EU providing guarantees for pipelines and other cross-border projects and threatening
credit cuts to noncooperating states. The Hejaz railway could finally extend to Cairo, Baghdad, and beyond. Ultimately, Mashreq countries
may weave themselves more deeply together out of enlightened self-
interest—or due to the aftershocks emanating from the geopolitical
earthquake occurring in neighboring Iraq.

CHAPTER 24

THE FORMER IRAQ:

BUFFER, BLACK HOLE, AND BROKEN BOUNDARY

Wars are a geopolitical reset button: They recalibrate the hierarchy of power as countries either triumph, battle to stalemate, or disappear altogether. Both are happening in Iraq since the American invasion in 2003 failed to create a unified and democratic state. Every faction within Iraq and in each surrounding country is fighting for its own vision, meaning that Iraq itself will cease to exist, since no one is fighting in its name. Iraq has become a cartographical fiction.

When Baghdad ruled the Abbasid caliphate from the eighth to the tenth centuries A.D., it was the mightiest of Muslim empires, stretching from North Africa to Central Asia, its bustling Mesopotamian society revolving around transcendent religious institutions.[1] After World War I, Britain lumped together three Ottoman zones that had been independent for centuries: a Kurdish north ruled from Mosul, a Sunni center governed by Baghdad, and a Shi'a south tied to Basra. But Iraq was never a modern state. It was a feudal capsule in which land-owning clans magnified their power through a central regime. Even when it was considered a secular and cosmopolitan society (as Afghanistan and Iran once were), dictatorship under Saddam Hussein, the Iran-Iraq War of the 1980s, and the punishing retribution for Saddam's 1990 invasion of Kuwait drove its people toward various forms of isolated conservatism.

Centralized, Western-created Iraq has been disappearing in form and content ever since. Even the Soviet Union condemned Saddam, with Gorbachev remarking that the weapons it had sold to Iraq were intended for its defense, not to invade its neighbors.[2] Saddam remained afloat for over a decade by manipulating the UN oil for food program while sanctions degraded the public health system and prevented an opposition from incubating. Western containment was more like "infanticide masquerading as politics."[3] The U.S.-imposed northern and southern no-fly zones effectively cut Saddam off from those resource-rich regions, whose current struggle to return to a pre-Iraq past through a sovereign future is playing itself out in a repeat of what Sir Arnold Wilson described as Mesopotamia's "anarchy plus fanaticism . . . with little or no nationalism."[4] Since individual Iraqis pledge their loyalty to clan, ethnicity, or sect over state, the promises of federalism failed to stem the civil war that has accelerated the country's re-Balkanization—including ethnic cleansing, mass emigration, and population exchange—through which a Kurdistan, Shi'astan, and Sunnistan are gradually coming to life.

The Iraq War exposed the United States as a superpower whose intelligence does not match its aspirations. Unable to differentiate meaningfully among Arab tribes and Islamic sects, the United States rashly abdicated its ethical responsibility to understand the country it was occupying, both for its own sake and for the sake of those it occupied.[5] Hulking American military structures (as well as the gargantuan new American embassy) became the symbol of America's treating Iraq as if it were for sale (to above-the-law private contractors whom Iraqis, with some justification, view as rampaging looters) rather than a liberated country. Even strategies that had worked in the Balkans—such as providing security, access to basic goods, and a banking system—were ignored in Iraq, which became a twenty-first-century Afghanistan for thousands of foreign fighters: an opportunity to receive training for global missions against a mighty imperial occupier, training that paved the way for anti-Western terrorist attacks in places like London and Bali, and, even more important, the locus of a clash between Sunnis and Shi'a Muslims.[6] Numbed by the grotesque violence of the civil war, ordinary Iraqis have been too proud to show that they are past the breaking point; they just bury their dead and move on. Yet as the combination of the death toll and exodus mounts, one must wonder how many Iraqis will be left to rebuild their country when the war ends.[7] Most Iraqis continue to feel that they are worse off today than under Saddam's rule—with some outsiders ironically remarking that only another dictator could save Iraq. "The Americans have been so busy trying to kiss their own asses that their heads are stuck," snapped one Iraqi translator.

It is said that if Arabs had been drawing the maps after World War I, Iraq would never have existed anyway, and today the race is on among the United States, Iran, and the Sunni powers of Egypt, Saudi Arabia, and Syria to reshape the region where Iraq once sat at the center. Three times larger than Iraq with four times the population, Iran uses Iraq as a vessel to expand its edge over Sunni rival and Gulf energy giant Saudi Arabia. Despite decades of animosity and a lengthy war that cost over a million lives, Iran's influence now easily crosses over the Shatt al Arab waterway, formed by the confluence of the Tigris and Euphrates rivers, the border between them dating to a 1639 treaty between the Ottomans and Safavids. A hundred and thirty thousand American troops could do nothing to diminish Iran's ability to easily permeate Iraqi politics and security services at all levels; it currently provides the most effective explosive devices to insurgents. The Iraqi government even turned to Iran for security assistance and recognized Iran's right to a nuclear program. Evidence of Iran's economic colonization is everywhere, from trade with Kurdistan to mosque reconstruction in Najaf to the airport, railroad, and electricity provision to Basra, where Farsi is widely spoken.[8] While Sunnis, particularly in Saudi Arabia, chafe at the prospect of Persian regional hegemony, they too have no interest in an Iraq restored to its former strength, particularly since they no longer receive cheap oil from the martyred Saddam. They will, however, not hesitate to provide weapons and funding to the rump Sunnistan, further fueling the civil war until Iraq is no more.

Despite it all, Iraq still cannot be considered part of the third world. Even Iraq's poorest districts have adequate housing, and some neighborhoods have been spared violence simply because they are poor. Sufficient money has been pledged to rebuild the country's infrastructure once the violence abates. Furthermore, enough revenues from Shi'astan and Kurdistan's oil supplies will be diverted to a feeble Sunnistan center that it will not become a barren wasteland. Iraqi refugees will return—whether from serving as workers in Jordan or prostitutes in Syria—to restore their lives, while Lebanese, Syrians, Jordanians, and Saudis will flood the markets with telecommunications, construction equipment, and agricultural exports, integrating it by road and rail with the rest of the Mashreq.

America may feel it has made the region better off by ousting Saddam, but that is not something it ever had the power to judge. Europe's colonial experience in the region effectively ended with the Suez Crisis in 1956, and America's neocolonial experience will also wind down in the same country in which it began, leaving the Mashreq a zone of shifting alliances and competing regional postures.[9] While many American hawks snidely noted that the debate over the Iraq War brought out a disunity between "old" and "new" Europe, it has proved far more vividly that the EU's denial of cooperation hurts America, even as Europe's economic, political, and peacekeeping presence in the region is growing. Through its road construction, China already reaches Iran and can thus also access Iraq for commercial and strategic purposes as well, and it has already signed a $100 million arms deal with the Iraqi government—against American opposition—to provide light weapons that America has not. Centuries before China illegally sold air defense systems to Saddam Hussein, Genghis Khan's grandson Hulagu Khan made it all the way to Baghdad, which he sacked in 1258, thus ending the Abbasid caliphate. Iraq has been terminated before, and history will do so again. In the long term, the region could be the better for it.

The final settlement of the eastern Ottoman question will not be complete until the death of Iraq, which also solves the question of the Kurds. Trapped among Turkish, Arab, and Persian civilizations, Kurds have been abused by their neighbors for centuries. In the Iraqi Kurdistan's capital, Erbil, little remains of the three-thousand-year-old citadel where Alexander the Great clashed with the Persians. Kurds are an Indo-European people speaking an Indo-Iranian language. Despite their short-lived independence as the Mahabad Republic in the late 1940s, neighbors refused to recognize Kurds as a people—in Turkey they were considered "mountain Turks"—but they constitute the region's largest minority, spanning Turkey, Syria, Iran, and Iraq. With no state granting them a home of their own, their saying rings true: "Kurds have no friends but the mountains."

Arnold Wilson warned in 1920 that the "war-like Kurds would never accept an Arab ruler," and today the Kurdish nation, labeled only vaguely on Ottoman maps, is slowly and methodically hardening into a full-fledged Kurdistan.[10] After having their villages razed and their people gassed with chemical weapons, the Kurds' present schadenfreude toward the plight of Saddam's Iraq seems natural. "We have had autonomy from Iraq since 1991, and our young generation has never been to Iraq, speaks no Arabic, and has never seen an Iraqi flag planted on Kurdish soil," explained a Kurdish minister inside Erbil's only functional hotel. Kurds universally want independence; by demographic necessity, this will become Kurdistan's policy. (Even in a federal Iraq, Kurds would accept nothing less than maximal autonomy while continuing to receive large volumes of donor assistance channeled through Baghdad.)

Kurdistan already exists more than Iraq does. Under the radar, habits of statehood are being codified on a daily basis. The Kurdistan Regional Government has created its own ministries for agriculture, development, education, and investment. At groundbreaking ceremonies in Erbil, politically incorrect lapel pins uniting the Kurdistan and British (and American) flags are distributed at events. The *peshmerga* guerillas have evolved into a united force fifty thousand strong, complete with military and police academies. The last foundation of independence would be control over the oil deposits around Kirkuk. Violently Arabized under Saddam—who denied Kurds power stations, railways, airports, and refineries—Kurds have since reversed Kirkuk's demographic balance in their favor, hoping eventually to secure its status through incremental referenda. Kurdistan has already signed huge oil exploration contracts with foreign energy companies and plans to complete a major refinery on Kirkuk's outskirts. "When the Baghdad government refuses to honor our deals, it only reminds us how important independence still is," one official declared. With or without Kirkuk, all that remains is a new currency, Kurdistan passports, and United Nations membership.[11]

"Even my brother is not my brother until he is cleared at the border," declared a translator ferrying visitors around Kurdistan's main cities in a large Japanese jeep. Along the frontier with Iraq, *peshmerga* steadfastly guard against any undesired infiltration, with Arabs and Arabic speakers routinely subjected to racial profiling, even including the thousands of Iraqi Arabs who fled to Kurdistan for safety. Arabs see this as ethnic cleansing, citing Israeli support for Kurdistan as yet more Western-backed divide and rule. Loyalty to the Kurdistan project supersedes even family bonds, with Kurds tacitly participating in a national neighborhood-watch program to report suspicious activity.

Since their own civil war in the 1990s, Kurds have begun to practice nonviolent governance in ways that are simply absent in any of their Arab neighbors. "We and the Arabs are both Sunni, but Kurdish fundamentalism is an oxymoron," a journalist in quaint, placid Sulaymaniyah proudly asserted. The two ruling parties—or rather, families—Barzani's KDP and Talabani's PUK, still divide and rule Kurdistan, maintaining mafia-like control over businesses and making it exceedingly difficult to form a third party. But the civility that has settled in Kurdistan is noticeable at airports and other public facilities, where guns are routinely checked in, like coats or umbrellas. While churches are being destroyed elsewhere in Iraq, Kurds are building them. Erbil has a new shopping mall, and Sulaymaniyah's Azaadi ("Freedom") Park, once an Iraqi army base, has a London-style Speaker's Corner next to a memorial etched with the names of the Kurds executed there by the Baathist regime in 1963. Around the park, large, modern homes are springing up, built with stone from large marble quarries. The growing presence of the Kurdish diaspora is a leading indicator of their success to date. Unlike brain-draining Syria and Iraq, Kurds are bringing back their money and talent. Many are conversant in German and could potentially do for Kurdistan what Turks from Germany have done for Turkey. Other expat Kurds are helping establish a new university in Sulaymaniyah, which already hosts visiting European and American faculty.

The birth of Kurdistan is not likely to be taken well by insecure neighbors Iran and Syria, who violently suppress their own Kurdish minorities. But Kurdistan's creation would only damage their egos, not their security, for they could simply expel their small Kurdish populations to an independent Kurdistan.* Turkey is even more hesitant

---

*Having Kurds remain as minorities in neighboring states—rather than entirely consolidating into Iraqi Kurdistan—actually serves Kurdistan's interests. A pure Kurdistan could be isolated by malevolent neighbors, whereas minority status helps to build international pressure for greater rights. For example, after a wave of Kurdish protests across Turkey in 2006, a Kurdish TV station filed a case before the European Court of Human Rights against Turkey for restricting its airtime and content.

about Kurdistan's independence—not that its emotional obsession constitutes a valid strategic assessment. Turkey will never see its flimsy claims on Kirkuk fulfilled merely because a small number of Turkmen live there, and it has little to fear from an independent Kurdistan, since it would be able to control whether Kurdistan amounted to more than a Mashreq Bolivia: resource-rich but geographically trapped. Turkey has long profited from illicit trade over the Habur Bridge, near Kurdish Zakho, which has been the only safe border crossing out of Iraq. The endless miles of trucks lining up to deliver gas to Iraq will need to drive in the opposite direction for landlocked Kurdistan to export Kirkuk's oil.

Eventually, Turkey's strategy toward Kurdistan may gradually take on the tenor of the EU's relations with Turkey: binding it closer and making it dependent. Turkish companies, the master construction engineers of the region, are already speedily building both of Kurdistan's international airports, as well as tunnels, overpasses, and ring roads, while the Kurdistan government protects oil flows to Turkey's strategic port of Ceyhan. Though Turkey's powerful military, amassed on Kurdistan's northern border, still routinely crosses into Kurdistan to snuff out PKK activity, a sovereign Kurdistan would have greater responsibility to rein in such groups than the quasi-independent province of a failed state. The smuggling of fuel, tea, sugar, and drugs has for centuries linked the markets of Turkey, Syria, Jordan, Iraq, Iran, and Afghanistan—with Kurdistan right in the middle. As Turkey's trade with Iran and Syria grows, Kurdistan would happily continue to play its part as a commercial conduit servicing all four. The famed Hamilton Road along the magnificent Zagros Mountains, built by New Zealand engineer A.M. Hamilton from 1928 to 1932, can once again become the primary artery for this branch of the Silk Road.

If geopolitics has an end state, it is when borders, populations, resources, and interests find equilibrium. When Iraq's civil war ends, the region may have lost a country—yet an independent Kurdistan not only corrects a major injustice of the post-Ottoman settlement, it also contributes to transcending the hostile divisions among Mashreq states. Kurds will undoubtedly have all the freedoms they deserve—the only question is when.

CHAPTER 25

IRAN:

VIRTUES AND VICES

IRAN IS NOT synonymous with Persia, for Persia harkens to a sophisticated and powerful civilization that flourished from the Sinai to India. Persian conquerors Cyrus, Darius, and Xerxes built the Achaemenid empire, the technical and cultural equal of anything in the West.[1] Despite Alexander the Great's sacking of Persepolis and the Arab subjugation of Persia in the eighth century, the Alborz, Zagros, and Mekran mountain ranges largely protected it from the total dominance Europeans and Ottomans exercised over the Arabs. At its seventeenth-century peak, the Safavid dynasty spread from Anatolia and the Caucasus across Mesopotamia to the Oxus River (today's Amu Darya). European maps of the eighteenth century referred to Persia as "Farsistan," and the Baluch tribes of what is today southeastern Iran and southwestern Pakistan speak a Farsi-derivative language. Though Iran today occupies prime strategic geography straddling the Caspian Sea and the Persian Gulf, the fundamental question remains whether Iran can become Persia again.

In 1934, Reza Khan renamed his country Iran to emphasize its Aryan "noble origin," a state no less committed than ancient Persia to radiating influence in all directions. Yet Iran's goals have traditionally not been military hegemony but rather strategic independence from the great powers. The Red Army's occupation of Iran during World War II sparked several decades of maneuvers between Russia and the West, including the removal of Reza Shah in favor of his son Mohammed Reza Pahlavi as shah in 1941, an attempted coup and assassination against him by the Communist (Tudeh) Party, a CIA-backed coup in 1953 against the nationalist prime minister Mohammed Mossadegh in response to his nationalization of the Anglo-Iranian Oil Company, and CIA and Mossad support for the creation of the fearsome SAVAK security service.[2] As a result, the shah, America's most loyal ally in the region, used the oil boom of the 1970s to buy ever more weapons from the United States, with the explicit goal of increasing autonomy from America.[3]

In considering himself the king of kings, however, the shah alienated his own people past the breaking point. After a century of nationalist and Communist revolutions, the only major religiously inflected revolution of the modern world was staged in Iran in 1979.[4] The revolution was directed against the existing order far more than it was pro-Islamic, thus the Ayatollah Khomenei's rise above the fray of nationalists and socialists contending for power stunned Iranians as much as it did the rest of the world. Iran's revolution was so unpredicted precisely because it was a strong and prospering state at the time, and indeed the shah fashioned himself a Persian Atatürk.[5] In the 1970s, Iran had the same GDP as Spain and optimistically compared itself to first-world Germany. In the quarter century since, however, Turkey's economic absorption by the European Union has brought it far closer to the economic achievement, military muscle, and political stability to which Iran aspires. By the 1980s, Iran was instead hailing its estimated three hundred thousand martyrs who had perished in the war with Iraq; only oil kept the country on the world's economic map. From smugglers traversing the switchback passes at Kermanshah to the criminal drug runners on the frontiers with Afghanistan and Pakistan, millions of Iranians live hand to mouth, getting by with multiple jobs on the black market. Iran still receives World Bank loans, however insignificant, for sewage, health care, emergency earthquake relief, and water supply and land management, showing how difficult it is to complete the final ascent into the first world without political stability.

Iran all but sets the standard for second-world schizophrenia. The radical path on which Khomenei took the country threw open the most fundamental questions as to whether to honor the country's pre-Islamic and pre-revolutionary history, with implications for the status of Zoroastrianism, Judaism, and even Muslim Sufism (Rumi attained his enlightenment in Iranian Tabriz in 1244), and the treatment of a shrine venerating the shah, whose debased secularism Khomenei detested.[6] His parallel system of dual government, which attempted to reconcile Islamic theocracy and republican statehood, created tensions with which the country continues to struggle: Iranians themselves grasp for terms such as polyarchy, elective oligarchy, semi-democracy, or neo-patrimonialism to describe what is simultaneously an authoritarian regime and perhaps the most democratic country in the region, with elections for president and for its parliament, the Majlis.[7] Though Khomenei's humiliating settlement with Saddam Hussein forced Iranians to reconsider their divinity as "pioneers of Islam," Iran's Revolutionary Guards have never ceased to challenge Western liberalism through maintaining the dominance of religion in the public realm and sponsoring Islamist fundamentalism from Palestine to Pakistan.

During the Cold War, the United States managed special relations with Saudi Arabia, Israel, and Iran as its anti-Communist bulwark. In 1977, President Carter flew to Tehran and toasted the shah as the leader of an "island of stability." Two years later, the shah fled the revolution. Since that time, American dealings with Iran can best be described as hostage politics, because the 1979 revolution and taking of hostages at the American embassy has clouded all relations—or rather, nonrelations—ever since. The former embassy became a training compound for the elite Revolutionary Guards, and Iran's reward for assisting in the ouster of the Taliban in Afghanistan was inclusion in President Bush's "Axis of Evil."

One consequence of this continued acrimony has been the election of Mahmoud Ahmadinejad—yet another former mayor of the capital of a second-world country, in this case Tehran—as Iran's president in 2005. By identifying himself with the common man's welfare and an anticorruption agenda, he amassed greater power than his clerical predecessors. Though Iran still suffers from suboptimal oil production and sporadic plane crashes, both due to outdated technology, Ahmadinejad wasted no time in flexing Iran's oil-slicked muscles from

Lebanon to Palestine to Iraq, seeming to merge the Persian imperial tradition with contemporary Islamic fervor.[8] Iran's vast oil and gas reserves, strong military (including a sound navy), and advancing nuclear program make it a strategic power in the Persian Gulf as well, seeming to justify the body of water's contested name.

America's childish silent treatment of Iran ignores the reality that in the geopolitical marketplace, attempting to isolate a country is about as effective as ignoring its existence. Like other second-world anchors Brazil, Kazakhstan, and Saudi Arabia, Iran is diplomatically sophisticated enough to derive benefits from multiple powers simultaneously —particularly if those powers have competing motivations. The United States has focused strictly on the military potential of Iran's nuclear program, ignoring its civilian uses and Iran's other commercial needs; the EU for many years ignored Iran's illicit nuclear and terrorist activities, undercutting American sanctions as it became Iran's largest trading partner; and Russia has sold nuclear reactor technology to Iran with little regard for the chain reaction it could set off.[9]

As befits two proud civilizations linked by Silk Road history and suspicion of America, China also helps Iran to transcend the tension between its desire for strategic influence and its need for greater investment. For China, Iran is the final square on its hopscotch path to the Persian Gulf, meaning that it could eventually avoid shipping Iranian oil by tanker through the Straits of Hormuz and Malacca and instead transport it by road, rail, and pipeline across Afghanistan. China and Iran have signed a vast array of energy, infrastructure, and arms deals: a $70 billion contract for natural gas from Iran's South Pars field (the world's largest); development of a massive oil field in Iran's Kurdish-populated region; construction of oil terminals on the Caspian Sea; construction of the Tehran metro; and shipment of ballistic missile technology and air defense radars to Iran. Iranian hardliners already believe that their country can rely on a mix of China and Russia for the technology, weapons, and trade they need without giving any ground to the West—even if Europe agrees to throw its immense economic weight behind sanctions.[10]

"Telling us to give up our nuclear program is as insulting as saying we cannot order something in a restaurant which everyone else is having," an Iranian analyst insisted, speaking for the majority of Iranians who intuitively support the country's atomic aspirations. New rial currency notes celebrate atomic fission, and Iran's nuclear program could provide a shield under which to expand its revolutionary influence. But surrounded by the vice of American troops in Iraq and Afghanistan (and, allegedly, Turkmenistan and Pakistan), Iran could also rationalize nuclear weapons for self-defense. Indeed, even though an Iranian nuclear program is permitted under the Nuclear Non-Proliferation Treaty (NPT), it could always justify crossing the nuclear threshold by citing a threat from Israel or Pakistan—two non-NPT signatories who have nuclear arsenals.

Like the country's signature powdery *gaz* pastry, Iranian diplomacy can be deceptively unsweet. The United States and the EU were slow to expose the false piety of Iranian nuclear rhetoric, which reflects the cultural hypocrisy of intentional vagueness honed over centuries. Though the West cannot oust the Iranian regime, its sanctions have instead given the government an excuse *not* to fulfill its domestic obligations and to deflect attention away from its human rights violations. When the United States pledged merely $40 million to promote political change, it was a "kiss of death" for reformers, on whom the crackdown was immediate. But unlike Saddam Hussein, Iranian leaders prefer controlled confrontation to the humiliation of war. A regional structure including every state falling between Israel, Iran, and Saudi Arabia (with the United States, the EU, China, and Russia as patrons) could serve to keep Iran in its place, even inspire a grand bargain in which normalized relations and the lifting of sanctions are offered in exchange for reduced support for terrorism and a monitored civilian nuclear program—with energy contracts conditional on upholding the bargain. Opening the flood gates of investment, tourism, and international media would overwhelm the Iranian regime's strategy of self-isolation and break the cleric-*bazaari* economic collusion. Though revolutions are the watched pot that never boils, they are more likely once the intelligentsia and masses can afford to think beyond basic welfare.[11]

Iran's diplomatic sophistry actually masks deep insecurities about its meager socioeconomic status. Flush with oil and gas reserves but still mired in underdevelopment, the country has far more pressing concerns than uranium. "We are a confused nation, and the *Basijis* are blurring public and private even further," a struggling entrepreneur in Tehran complained, referring to the fearless militiamen of the Iran-Iraq War who now ruthlessly enforce the revolution's agenda. Protesting students have disappeared and been tortured. A more democratic Iran might be less vehement in its nuclear quest, recognizing the trade-off between nuclear weapons and a sound economic policy.[12] Like the Arab neighbors to whom it condescends, Iran similarly lacks a shared national vision among its clerical, business, and technocratic factions, amplified by its fractious and self-serving exiles, ranging from monarchists to disaffected elites as far as "Tehrangeles." Its bureaucracy is an inefficient and inept cesspool of corruption, and it has so ritualized religion that it has alienated much of the postrevolution generation, which constitutes most of the seventy million population and most of the unemployed.[13] The already severe brain drain of Iran's technical class is common to second- and third-world countries, where entering the diaspora is the only possible route to success; lobbying for work permits at the Canadian embassy in Damascus has been described as a generational pilgrimage.[14] And despite its agricultural potential, manufacturing capacity, and heritage of ancient ruins to rival Greece or Turkey, Iran's main exports remain the same as before the revolution: carpets, pistachios, and, of course, petroleum.

Tehran itself best embodies Iran's socioeconomic degeneration. Only two hundred years old, it evokes none of the historical grandeur of Shiraz and Isfahan, with their imperial gardens and shrines. An ever-expanding, overpopulated, underplanned, and polluted morass, Toynbee recalled that when one enters Tehran, it actually feels as if "you are leaving the country of which this is the official capital."[15] Millions of economic migrants flock to Tehran from a countryside that suffers from the same aridity that ended Persia's golden age in the twelfth century. Unable to control its long border with Afghanistan, Iran is the transit route for much of the $65 billion annual trade in heroin and refined opium, to which an estimated one million Iranian adults are addicted. For all of its social taboos, drug abuse, prostitution, temporary marriages (*sigheh*) for consensual sex, and plastic surgery flourish in Iran as much as anywhere.[16] A country where the elite have to flee to have fun while suppressing those who can't afford to leave is hardly capable of governing itself, let alone dominating its neighbors. Globalization alone has Iran's regime cornered.

Ultimately, the American and Arab militaries prevent Iran from ever achieving the territorial reach of imperial Persia. Iran can stoke

Shi'ite unrest and dispute Persian Gulf islands, but as circumstances stand it cannot have the Gulf in any sense other than name. More immediately, though Khomenei famously said that the 1979 revolution was about more than the price of watermelons, three decades later the unfolding counterrevolution is about just that.

CHAPTER 26

GULF STREAMS

Even with all of the world's current and projected oil and gas taps flowing, the Persian Gulf will still provide 40 percent of the total energy supply well into the future, ensuring that its geopolitical centrality will continue to match its geographic centrality at the crossroads of Europe and Asia.[1] For over a century, Britain asserted imperial control over this "British lake" while managing independent Gulf sheikhdoms as two sides of the same coin. American legitimacy in the region—based on protecting regimes and ensuring the continuous flow of oil—is now struggling with the same balancing act.

Money alone cannot buy security. "We do not *want* American forces, but we feel we *need* them," an adviser to the government of Qatar emphasized. Fearful of Saudi Arabia's unpredictability and cultural austerity, the littoral statelets of Kuwait, Qatar, Oman, the United Arab Emirates, and Bahrain are emerging like vassals in different stages of revolt against their Saudi master.[2] They view the Saudi kingdom the same way the former Soviet republics in the Baltics and the Caucasus view Russia: a giant black hole attempting to suck them back in by any means at its disposal. Economic integration within the

Gulf Cooperation Council masks this continuous effort at differentiating individual identities few outsiders even know exist. Each is becoming a globalized city-region to ensure itself against Saudi domination. Saudi Arabia still requires visas of its Gulf neighbors even as they don't from one another, and it has sought to prevent them from circumventing this regulation altogether by trying to block construction of a bridge linking Bahrain to Qatar and an even longer bridge linking Qatar to the Emirates. When oil-less Bahrain signed a free trade agreement with the United States, Saudi Arabia cut off its oil supply from the Abu Safah field they technically share.

"It's close enough to see," a Dubai-based strategic analyst said, gesturing across the Gulf toward Iran. "And even if you can't, you know it's there." The Gulf Cooperation Council's internal animosities opened a window for the United States to renew massive conventional arms sales and disperse its heavy military forces on the promise to protect the Gulf's smaller sheikhdoms from both Saudi Arabia *and* Iran. During the Gulf War, only Kuwait was clearly pro-American due to its own occupation by Iraq, and it remains today a supply depot for America's Iraq occupation. But now tiny Qatar, which controls a nearly eternal supply of natural gas, serves as the forward headquarters of America's Central Command (CENTCOM) and has even abolished its own military forces to emphasize its reliance on the United States. The longest military runway outside the United States points directly at Iran. The minuscule island monarchy of Bahrain, a World War II forward base for the British navy, now hosts America's Fifth Fleet. While all the Gulf statelets criticize American diplomatic and military arrogance, they still prefer to import American hardware rather than the radical software of Saudi Wahhabism or Iranian Shi'ism. And it is not only America's heavy artillery and warships but also thousands of burly ex-military security contractors who patrol Gulf installations like a network of praetorian guards. Their exorbitant fees are, for the sheikhs at least, merely incidental. If the United States were to want to depose any of its new micro-allies, it would ironically have to pay off these Americans first to get to them.

President Jimmy Carter declared that the United States would protect the flow of oil "by any means necessary," but today there is no more risk of a Cold War Soviet invasion of Arabia (for which America planned dramatic contingencies, such as blowing up Saudi oil facilities). Yet America's Iraq invasion adversely affected both stability and oil prices, making Europeans and Asians far less willing to cede responsibility to the United States for securing their energy flows. At the same time, the Gulf regimes' priorities are stability and wealth generation, with backing the United States at their own expense a distant third. Both Europe and China have thus quietly moved into the Gulf through energy markets and investment deals. Europe has established a free trade area with the Gulf Cooperation Council, while Arabs increasingly deposit their oil wealth in European banks (and price it in Euros), list their companies in London instead of New York, and buy Airbus aircraft for top-rated airlines such as Emirates and Gulf Air. Not only does the term *petrodollar* seem increasingly antiquated, so does the cliché that Arabs denounce America while wanting green cards.[3]

At the same time, the Prophet's *hadith* to "seek knowledge, even as far away as China" has instead brought China to the Gulf. Asians consume far more Gulf oil (which meets 70 percent of their demand) than North Americans, a demand so large that it has changed every aspect of the industry, from pricing to the size of tankers to the width and depth of canals. Indeed, given Asia's massive growth rates, OPEC doesn't need to worry about the slowing of the U.S. economy to ensure its continued high profits. Furthermore, China's vulnerability to price spikes and blockages also justifies its development of Pakistan's Gwadar port to give it a naval foothold on the Arabian Sea. It is a sign of China's geopolitical maturity that it manages the superpower paradox of maintaining strong ties with mutual antagonists Iran and Saudi Arabia.[4] An alliance between the Middle East and the Middle Kingdom has been evolving under the radar since the 1960s when China began to sell missiles to Saudi Arabia.[5] More recently, Saudi Arabia has actively courted Chinese investment while reciprocally financing a massive petrochemical complex in China's Fujian province.[6] Unlike politically radioactive dealings with America, the royal family actually admires China for having achieved power without subjugating others, as the West did, and for its similar style of centralized decision making and absence of human rights concerns in diplomacy. "Instead of American dominance over the Gulf, a new maritime Silk Road is emerging between Gulf and East Asian countries. It's a highly complementary relationship in which Asians construct the Arabian Dream of twenty-first-century cities while purchasing an ever-growing share of its energy," said one Dubai-based analyst of regional trends. As one Saudi official noted, Saudi Arabia will not divorce America, but it can always have multiple wives.[7]

Until the discovery of oil, Arabia was considered a barren wasteland, receiving none of the benefits of colonization such as a modern bureaucracy or sophisticated educational institutions. Wilfred Thesiger, the British military adventurer famous for his crossings of the endless Empty Quarter, commented that the "changes which occurred in the space of a decade or two [roughly 1950 to 1970] were as great as those which occurred in Britain between the early Middle Ages and the present day."[8] In the 1970s, oil became the Arab second world's geopolitical lever, making the Gulf monarchies the world's nouveau riche. But in Saudi Arabia, oil money simply sponsored bloated government, with members of the royal family arbitrarily designated as heads of countless idle ministries. The catapult ride from mud huts to mansions lasted less than a decade: OPEC lost control of its members' output in the 1980s, as oil prices plunged and Gulf populations boomed. Saudi Arabia's per capita income plummeted, dropping it far below its status as the world's richest country into a modest tier alongside Mexico.

The enormous windfall from skyrocketing oil prices after September 11, 2001, inspired a pattern familiar from the 1970s oil boom: lavish military spending, which topped $40 billion in 2005.[9] But subjected to heightened scrutiny by Western banks, Arab capital is no longer blind. While African countries take foreign investment and recycle it right back into the first world, 70 percent of Arab oil revenues are now being heavily reinvested *within* the Arab world itself.[10] Gulf states have committed a trillion dollars to infrastructure projects ranging from water desalination, universities, and hospitals to new ports and export-driven cities rising out of the desert. The Arab business community is pushing a professionalized reform that is reminiscent of other intra–second world collective bootstrapping from Eastern Europe to East Asia, lifting tourism in Tunisia and Egypt, agricultural growth from Morocco to Sudan, and other entrepreneurial ventures that create jobs and even liberate many women into the workforce, changing the pattern by which Gulf countries were "richer than they are developed."[11]

Yet just because they are rich (again) today doesn't mean they won't blow it. The tribal aspects of monarchic control that made prosperity fleeting very much remain in place today.[12] "The medieval social structures are regressive even by Arab standards," pitied one Gulf monarchy watcher in Dubai. The rentier model of pure familial control in exchange for welfare precludes any notion of a balance of power between state and society.[13] In both Qatar and the Emirates, numerous bloodless coups within the royal families have involved sheikhs ousting and sacking one another out of pride or boredom. Prosperity derives from patronage, not labor, resulting in the debilitating effect of unearned privilege: a decadent society enjoying free welfare, but whose laziness can be combustible when oil process dwindle.* Will history repeat itself in Arabia?

SAUDI ARABIA: MONEY TALKS

Much of the Arab world's fortune rests on the Gulf's wealthiest monarchy, Saudi Arabia. Strategically located between the Red Sea and Persian Gulf, it has the world's largest oil reserves, and buttressed by replenished coffers, the kingdom now proactively mediates in Lebanon, Iraq, and in the Arab-Israeli dispute, with Egypt and Jordan as secondary partners. Even with the largest stock market in the region, Saudis have been known to drive overnight through the desert to take advantage of IPOs in Dubai and Doha. They have started to launch major hedge funds and to pool their investments and deposit them around the region. Saudi royals also own the region's major progressive newspapers and satellite TV stations such as Al Arabiya and are beginning to finance economic diversification and job creation to convert the Arab youth bulge from threat to opportunity.[14]

Saudi Arabia could be praised for the constant calibration it maintains among OPEC diplomacy, the heavy-handed demands of the United States, constantly stinging public opinion, and internal security

---

*Only first-world Kuwait, the wealthiest Gulf monarchy, which all of the others love to hate, is advanced enough politically and economically for the term *constitutional monarchy* not to be an oxymoron. The Majlis even ousted the emir in 2005. Literacy stands at over 90 percent, women's suffrage became universal in 2006, and a woman was recently appointed to the cabinet. The government spends far more per capita on salaries, housing, and developing businesses to employ its own citizens than other Gulf states. The country has for decades been the leading (and the quietest) Arab aid donor to Africa and Asia, financing airports, schools, hospitals, and fisheries. Oman, by contrast, is the region's tortoise. With its Indian Ocean climate, Oman's monsoonal weather keeps it milder than the rest of scorching Arabia, and it profits more from the oyster shell trade than from oil. Oman's Indian dhow builders are still the region's best and sell to seafaring merchants all over the Gulf. Indian Ocean culture and low oil reserves have made Oman a mellower monarchy, yet its Grand Mosque sets a new standard for religious aesthetic.

threats. Saudi Arabia, Bahrain, and Qatar together account for close to 70 percent of OPEC oil production, and the Saudi Abqaiq refinery and Ras Tanura terminal pump 10 percent of the world's daily oil consumption. To protect its economic heart, it has built an impenetrable energy infrastructure run by professional elites (which largely exclude members of the royal family)—which Al-Qaeda nonetheless tried to destroy with a suicide attack on the Abqaiq perimeter in 2006.

But oil price volatility, whether from political instability or supply disruptions, is the economic equivalent of an ulcer, a painful nuisance that weakens the entire body and can potentially be fatal.[15] Energy consumers are eager for Saudi oil but are grievously concerned about the dysfunctional family that controls it. From petty chiefs in central Arabia, the al-Saud ascended the tribal ranks through a 1744 alliance with Mohammed ibn Abd al-Wahhab, whose religious authority bestowed credibility on Mohammed ibn Saud, a forefather of Prince Abdul Aziz ibn Saud, who marched through the fortress gate of Riyadh in 1902 and secured control of the nation. The Saudi flag depicts the might of the Saudi sword and Koranic verses symbolizing Wahhabi fervor—the twin elements defining the state. Since the anti-Soviet jihad in Afghanistan, Saudi Arabia has been second to none in bankrolling Islamic radicalism from Pakistan to Indonesia, spending that was once considered essential to its Islamic credibility. While Egypt and Jordan expelled radicals in the 1970s, Saudi Arabia accepted them as teachers and pushed Islamism as an alternative to Arabism. More recently, thousands of Saudi jihadists have poured into Iraq to fight the American occupation.

The Wahhabist establishment is locked in a power struggle with the al-Saud rulers as well. America's cozy alliance with the royal family appalled Wahhabist clerics, who called on the likes of Osama bin Laden to resist not only the Soviet occupation of Afghanistan but also Arabia's own occupation by Western infidels, spawning a new generation of radicals that spread like cancer cells on the Arab body politic. In this religiously cloaked blowback, both the "near" and "far" enemies—autocrats at home and superpowers abroad—have been merged.[16] Much like Yemen—the narrow third-world southern edge of the Arabian Peninsula with a population equal to Saudi Arabia's—the regime has constantly paid off tribal chiefs and clerics, inadvertently making them more powerful. However, in Saudi Arabia there is no conceivable mechanism for the succession of power beyond the only family that has ever ruled the country. But while its efficient security apparatus pacifies the small and confined Shi'a population in the country's eastern provinces, it is far more difficult to contain homegrown Sunni fundamentalists.[17] "How can you tell one of them apart? They are among us, they move freely in the cities and villages," a royal family member fretted in his ornate office overlooking Riyadh.

Globalization appears to accelerate history, but in Saudi Arabia, history moves at two completely different speeds, one for the head and another for the heart. There are limits to how far a civilization can advance when people pray five times a day and live in the paralyzing heat of an endless desert. During Ramadan, day and night are switched, as people fast and rest all day and eat at night. As the custodians of Islam's holiest sites, Wahhabis consider themselves the only true practitioners of Islam. Saudi culture has been intentionally held back by their effort to return the country to a pure Islamic golden age by destroying all pre-Muhammed artifacts, in some cases burying entire villages. For the Prophet and his disciples, there was no distinction between secular and divine authority, thus even the Wahhabist partnership with the Saudi royal family is an unholy alliance that the *Ikhwan* (Brethren) must bear since they cannot raise an army.[18] Wahhabist radicals' bombing of oil facilities and declaring fatwas against IPOs are mere symptoms of a far deeper struggle *both* they and Saudi society at large are enduring to either resist or adjust to global modernity.

"Who is worse, master, he who claims divinity through ignorance or he who exploits the Quran for his own ends?" asks the traveler of Nobel Prize–winner Naguib Mahfouz's parable *The Journey of Ibn Fattouma*. Moral *conditioning* is a sensible strategy when a society seeks to maintain religious traditions, and sharia provides just such prohibitions and deterrents. But austere Saudi (and Iranian) moral *policing* has hardly been effective against the declared scourges of adultery, drug trafficking, and crime. Indeed, the false piety exposed through observing Saudis' transgressions of their own moral code eclipses even that of Iran, revealing the untenable contradictions of the simultaneous coexistence of two distant centuries.* Saudi public life belongs mostly to

---

*Qataris, who are also Wahhabi, view Saudi Arabia as a cultural iron ball weighing it down. While Saudi Arabia has gutted its own cultural heritage in the name of Wahhabi puritanism, Qatar now loans its treasures for display in the Louvre (which in turn loans them to Saudi Arabia).

the ten million foreign laborers in the kingdom who do most of the work, while private life is traditional and reclusive—but not enough to cover up Saudis' dysfunctional encounters with modernity: The black market for liquor is huge, resulting in drunk driving and road racing, which frequently lead to grisly crashes into sand dunes. Speed limits are considered recommendations. Forbidden from driving or straying outside alone, Saudi women have been known to rape household repairmen. Meanwhile, male homosexuality flourishes, despite the religious prohibitions, including lashings. Except at prayer time, materialistic indulgences are the order of the day among elites who worship their diamond-crusted mobile phones as if they were religious icons. The rhythmic movement of white-clothed pilgrims inside the Grand Mosque in Mecca is literally overshadowed by a ring of unsightly luxury hotels. Foreign women are imported for sexual servitude, while foreign labor is exploited under conditions of virtual slavery—but weekly public beheadings regularly feature poor guest workers (themselves often Muslim) whose heinous crimes include the theft of basic medication from pharmacies. However, neither executing nor quarantining foreign laborers will induce apathetic Saudis to replace them in the workforce, for much of the time Saudis overrun the rest of the Gulf from Bahrain to Dubai (where Saudis once imposed a ban on alcohol) in search of hedonism without limits, and conquer the boutiques of London and Geneva each summer.

The hypocrisies evident in Saudi Arabia's internal culture war have encouraged a Western smugness that assumes that Muslim Arabs are bereft of values, as if faith and modernity are antithetical, with modernity racing ahead and leaving faith to wither. Yet the reality is quite different: Modernity is a phase, while faith is eternal. It is modernity, not Islam, that is on trial as Muslims decide how to adapt their religion to modernity's choices—or to reject them altogether. Islam became a global religion by nomadic adaptation, and it is spreading rapidly today in both modern and nonmodern regions through high birthrates and mass appeal to converts. Banks in the United States and the United Kingdom now offer sharia-compliant financial instruments to their Muslim customers. More superficial innovations such as al-Quds brand jeans, Nike-designed sports *hijabs,* and beach-going female *burqinis* also show how Western style adapts to Islamic substance, rather than forcing the reverse. Because so many European Muslims have weathered this adaptation through a spiritual communitarianism, they may become a model for Muslims worldwide grappling with the changing roles of women, sectarianism, and secular education. But rejecting Islam is out of the question, which means that understanding Islam's aesthetics—its customs, philosophy, art, language, and music—is as important as decoding its scripture.[19] Samuel Huntington argued that the essence of Western civilization is "the Magna Carta, not the Big Mac"—it is good to remember that biting into the latter does not imply swallowing the former. Saudi editor Khaled al-Maeena knows this sentiment well, for even his American-educated daughter told him, "If you go to Starbucks, I'll bite you."[20]

Culture becomes history the moment parents change how they raise their children. Wahhabists have for generations taught only selective and rote recitation of the Koran, not Islam itself. Toynbee gushed about Islam's "extinction of race consciousness," saying there is "a crying need for the propagation of this Islamic virtue."[21] And never has Islam's emphasis on charity (*zakat*) and fraternity been more necessary in overpopulated Muslim countries. "Particularly in London and here in the kingdom, we urge young Muslims to seek social integration and promote these humanitarian foundations of Islam," an activist of the World Assembly of Muslim Youth in Riyadh explained. Toynbee predicted that the United States might overthrow the Wahhabis at any time of its choosing if their "zealotism became a sufficient nuisance to make the trouble of suppressing it seem worthwhile." But it is Saudi society's own conservatism that may be the best hope against radicalism. Much as exporting fundamentalism has discredited Saudi Arabia as a global Sunni leader, Wahhabists' own violence has eroded their popular resonance. King Abdullah has used his pious credentials to promote major television programs aimed at deradicalization and is reining in the thousands of decadent princes who have squandered the country's wealth.[22] He denounces extremists as "deviants," a term far more condemning than the Western "fundamentalist." He works with "Muslim democrats" to strengthen Shura councils, a move that paid off in the 2005 municipal elections in which Saudis voted not for radical candidates but rather for Islamists campaigning on pragmatic so-

cial agendas. More Islam, not less, may be the antidote to both Wahhabist extremism and Western materialism.*

This Saudi social apotheosis is occurring just as the country is getting a second chance to climb into the first world. During the 1970s oil
boom, no Gulf states created significant manufacturing or service sectors to employ the growing ranks of city dwellers who became what
Fouad Ajami called the "angry sons of a failed generation."[23] And if high
Saudi birthrates continue, Riyadh could become a megacity of ten million mostly underutilized citizens. Riyadh's ministry buildings are still
dilapidated, and the city is but a cleaner version of Cairo. But this time
around, Saudi Arabia is globalization-savvy, bringing in international
banks and consultants to modernize smartly.[24] It has the space, labor,
and money to construct four entirely new industrial cities as tax-free re-
export zones that create jobs while spreading the population away from
dense Riyadh and Jeddah to reverse the inward migration that also
plagues third-world countries. King Abdullah Economic City may itself
be listed on the stock market. "Some of us Gulf businessmen are learning fast, working hard, and taking risks like the Asians," a Riyadh businessman promised confidently. "We focus on big payoffs and real
delivery to shareholders and citizens." Wealthy Saudi industrialists now
commit portions of their fortunes toward grafting a vocational education system onto archaic universities, and even lobby for press freedom,
women's education, judicial independence, budget transparency, parliamentary legislative powers, independent electoral commissions, and diverse political parties. Witnessing the commercial success of Bahrain's
Formula One auto race, one remote village in northern Saudi Arabia decided to host a desert grand prix for sand-dune racing, earning more in
a week than it otherwise would in a year. "Keeping our political cart stable will require a sturdy economic chariot," a Saudi prince suggested.
The same is true of the entire Arab world.

---

*There are widespread calls for an Islamic reformation such as Christianity experienced in the sixteenth cen-
tury, but the Reformation cleaved Christianity into two major traditions and many splintered sects; each grew
independently of the others, eroding any hope of a Christian center that could rein in extremes. After its early
division into Sunni and Shi'a, Islam has come to suffer enough from this segmentation without a modern reformation. Indeed, Islam is a democratic religion, so thoroughly decentralized that even *muftis* are elected. Many
Muslims are interested not in further schisms but rather in reconciliation among the competing doctrines and
their extremist messengers, ultimately reducing the violence carried out against each other and other civilizations. As Gilles Kepel argues, though the rise of militant Islamism has been spectacular, its hyperviolence has
proved to be a liability rather than an asset. See Kepel, *Jihad*.

THE UNITED ARAB EMIRATES:
WHERE LAS VEGAS MEETS SINGAPORE

In the early 1990s, when Eastern Europe's postcommunist transition began, Dubai had no drainage system. Foreigners unfamiliar with the Arabian climate were puzzled at the need for cars to drive in knee-deep water due to flooding from seasonal rain. Sheikh Zayed Road, Dubai's main thoroughfare, was a short paved strip with a handful of buildings, with desert stretching in all directions right up to the Persian Gulf shore. Today, what used to be a hardship post for multinational employees has become the Arab world's only global city, the ultimate desert oasis and a flashy capitalist metropolis. In few cities in the world do so many people live in such wealth and comfort as in a Abu Dhabi, the sedate capital of the United Arab Emirates, while Dubai has quickly become the capital of the entire Arab civilization.

The motto for the Burj Dubai tower—a skyscraper standing so tall it will end other cities' petty rivalries for quite some time—is "History Rising," implying the birth of a glorious chapter in Arab affairs but also the emergence of something where for centuries there had been nothing. The United Arab Emirates was a confederation of poor, unrelated sheikhs surviving on smuggling and piracy until British Petroleum financed their entire oil-sector development, which Abu Dhabi now mostly controls while distributing a fair share of the spoils to the other six emirates. The vision of Sheikh Rashid, the most powerful of the Gulf smugglers, kickstarted Dubai's astonishing rise. Beginning with its Jebel Ali Free Zone in 1985, Dubai intentionally neglected taxes, visas, local ownership requirements, and other hassles on the premise that re-export alone would bring in vast sums of cash. Almost three-quarters of global trade is still conducted through shipping, and a significant percentage of the world's daily oil needs passes through the narrow Straits of Hormuz. Dubai's twin Jebel Ali and Rashid ports are today the world's most advanced alongside Singapore and Hong Kong.

Money, not Arabic, is the official language of Dubai. Television news from the imploded Iraq to the north competes for attention with the stock market ticker. Dubai's shiny financial district is built along the Creek, which for centuries has been the channel through which goods flowed in and out of the Persian Gulf to Africa and South Asia, and where still today teetering dhows are loaded with millions of tons of cigarettes, vegetable oil, tea bags, refrigerators, tires, and entire automobiles, bound for Pakistan and Iran's Bushehr and Bandar-e-Abbas. Dubai is the best example of globalization quietly thawing the geopolitical freeze between the Gulf states and Iran. Iran's free trade zone of Kish Island is the country's largest entrepôt for goods, mostly delivered and sold by Gulf Arabs. Thousands of Iranians have taken advantage of Dubai's equation of "property equals residency," buying into its booming real estate market as an exit strategy from stagnant Iran. Behind the scenes, Saudis, Iranians, and Emiratis aren't posturing over pan-Islamic leadership but rather gaming one another's stability and cultivating all sides as customers.

Much like resourceless Singapore, the geopolitical role of the Emirates stems from constantly finding a fresh global niche, and attracting foreign money and talent to capitalize on the inefficiencies around it. Abu Dhabi's investment authority (like Singapore's Temasek) responsibly controls well over $500 billion as the city builds a special island to house spectacular branches of the Louvre and Guggenheim museums, and it has invested heavily in renewable solar-power projects despite its oil reserves. Dubai's skyrocketing real estate, construction, hospitality, finance, media, consumer goods, and entertainment sectors receive more foreign investment and tourists than all of India. Billions of dollars of repatriated Arab money have allowed Dubai to leverage its local comparative advantage in sharia-compliant banking, attracting even more Muslim capital. The quest to triumph over the poor hand nature has dealt the Arabs is also big business, with Japanese plants producing desalinated water, allowing irrigation far into the desert. "Why should we settle for the oil curse when oil can pay for water?" a beaming Dubai official said in his blindingly shiny glass office space. Man-made Islands shaped like palm trees and continents rise from the sea, and posh lifestyle properties are sprouting faster than in Las Vegas, itself America's fastest growing city. New business ventures from export-ready pottery to solar cell production are under way, and its scenic setting for Indian cinema has led some to label it "Dollywood." Bedouin charm is now something foreigners purchase in the form of desert excursions, but they are equally likely to try out its indoor ski slope. With year-round conventions, sporting events, and shopping festivals, it is nearly impossible to get a hotel room in Dubai or any Gulf capital.

Europeans may fear Arab migration, but Arabs capitalize on the misfortune of other Arabs. Though London-based Arab intermediaries have for decades served as the proxy banks for Gulf finance, Dubai began to rise as Lebanon crumbled into civil war, and it took off with Saddam's 1990 invasion of Kuwait. The influx of Lebanese capitalist flair and Kuwaiti capital that began then continues today with as many as thirty thousand Lebanese relocating annually and filling roles ranging from banking executives to television news anchors, joining Egyptian engineers, Jordanian accountants, and Tunisian drivers who seek higher wages and a better life.

Dubai is the new Arab melting pot, a city where Arabs from all over the region and the world most easily mingle and integrate, fueling a new bottom-up rather than top-down Arabism based on economic interdependence and a vibrant media sector. Dubai's largest shopping mecca pays tribute to Abu Abdullah Muhammed ibn Battuta, the Arab Marco Polo who in the early fourteenth century traveled seventy-five thousand miles in caravans from Tangier to East Africa, Mecca, Syria, Central Asia, India, and China—without ever leaving the *Dar al Islam*. The goal of the most popular Arabic-language television channel, Al Arabiya, is contained in its name, addressing all Arabs through educational programs to promote proper Arab home-making and sound investment. Like the more politically pointed, Qatar-based Al-Jazeera, its Dubai headquarters is a mini-Brussels of cosmopolitan Arabs from over a dozen countries working together even when their countries don't. Satellite television is even harmonizing the previously dissonant dialects of spoken Arabic: As T. E. Lawrence observed nearly a century ago, "Patriotism, ordinarily of soil or race, was warped to a language."[25] "With all the low-cost Arab airlines, hostels have become perpetual slumber parties among new friends," said a young female journalist jet-setting to cover Arab business stories. "This first generation of young Arab women working alone in Gulf cities is developing class-consciousness as females with clear aspirations for financial success and social status."

Dubai is also the ultimate proof that the Arab realm is not cut off from globalization but is rather a proving ground for it. Its dystopian cosmopolitanism nakedly exposes the Arab world's divide between those who crave images of scantily clad Lebanese women on satellite television and those who are repulsed by their depravity. While by day Dubai is an emerging model of technology clusters such as Media City and Internet City staffed by sprightly young Arabs, by night it is perhaps the world's capital of the global sin industry, so embodying raw capitalism that it tests the notion that anything—or anyone—can be bought. Chinese and Russian mafias operate sex-trafficking rings, allegedly with government complicity through taxes on large whorehouses and hotels. Foreign businessmen stridently indulge in the global meat market where elsewhere they might sheepishly remain in the shadows. Dubai is so divorced from its cultural environs that many Arab men go there to forget that they are in a Muslim country. Brothels are where citizens and expatriates most closely mingle. Capitalism's triumph over Islam in Dubai is also noticeable in the companies that dock workers' pay for taking time to pray and in plans to build islands far enough out in international waters to allow for gambling.

Dubai is appropriately pronounced "Do buy." From the finest German automobiles to biometric scanners at the airport, the sheikhs have bought themselves modernity, much as Saudi Arabia did in the 1970s. Gold was once used to buy everything; now gold is bought with plastic. It seems as though the increasingly confident Arab civilization can force globalization into its cultural parameters, taking advantage of its late development by purchasing the best the rest of the world has to offer with none of the demands of research and innovation. The base of the Burj Dubai tower was designed by American architects to resemble an Arabian desert flower, and the Al-Qasr bungalows blend modern design with Bedouin ventilation shafts that channel breezes downward into spacious chambers. Dubai can even buy brains: Its Knowledge Village features micro-campuses of the world's top universities, and the current ruler, the benevolent Sheikh Mohammed, has pledged $10 billion to an education fund that promotes the region's knowledge economy.* The

---

*Like Dubai, Qatar also has a booming commercial real estate sector, is building islands shaped in Islamic patterns, and offered citizenship to athletes in order to perform well in the Asian Games it hosted in 2006. But Qatar's model lies in its aggressive pursuit of broad social development through education, rights for women (who are allowed to drive), and vocational training. The enormously endowed Qatar Foundation's Education City is the region's showpiece knowledge cluster, a collection of satellite campuses of the world's elite universities training study-abroad Americans and Europeans and Qatari students in engineering, medicine, and public policy while hosting high-profile conferences to bring the world's knowledge to them. By creating a space for government, entrepreneurs, civil society, and academia to synergize, Doha is attempting to replicate America's enviable mix of Silicon Valley and the Ivy League. Qatar's own schools have elected school boards and modern textbooks, reflecting a desire to put its entire population through a crash course in modernity by achieving universal secondary education.

hip Gulf male today sports his spotless white dishdasha, wears an American baseball cap, drives a Porsche or a Range Rover, and eats sushi in fine Asian fusion restaurants.

But even with all the money in the world, Arab states seem to consciously avoid investing in replicating the indigenous capacity that has fueled East Asia's rise to the pinnacle of the global economy. Instead, they allow bad habits to thrive in the new limitless context of globalization. Whereas a seven-star hotel rating such as the Burj al Arab can be bought, money alone cannot buy the cultural strengths a world-class university represents. Gulf sheikhs need Western know-how to cultivate new economic sectors, much as they needed them in the oil industry a half century ago. Foreign consultants today operate in the background producing studies and reports, while leaders recite their mantras at high-visibility events like "Ideas Arabia." To avoid threatening entrenched bureaucracies, Sheikh Mohammed has had to set up parallel agencies to run transportation and financial services, with Dubai Holding operating out of business towers and working a full week rather than taking off on Friday, the Muslim holy day. Gulf Arabs themselves mostly provide capital but rarely do any work—and are in fact often paid not to come to work at all, which suits them just fine. A Gulf think tank might have twenty times the budget of its Cairo equivalent but produce a quarter as much analysis. With wanton construction unguided by a macro urban design plan, Dubai remains a place where couriers must guide themselves by mosques, pharmacies, and trees in order to make deliveries.

"I wondered if any other race was as avaricious as the Arabs, with such an intense love of money," pondered Thesiger while crossing the empty Arabian desert with incessantly bartering Bedouin.[26] Dubai's horrendous traffic jams are a metaphor for finance in a freewheeling economy that sometimes resembles a game of Monopoly, with investments based on speculation and ultimately subject to the throw of the dice. The sheikhs who control the major contractor firms regularly dump their own stock when it gets too high, buying again at lower prices, hurting the many small investors who have no shareholder rights. Dubai's businesses are a selective sponge for absorbing international standards, seeking multinational assistance only where regulations serve their interests. WTO rules on money laundering are conveniently neglected to keep the real estate market soaring with cash from Russia, Iran, and the Afghan drug trade. More recently, it has also become a transit zone for antiquities stolen from Lebanon and Iraq.

Dubai represents the union of the first and third worlds at their geographical meeting point: the knowledge and technology of Europe combined with the limitless labor pool of Asia. With virtually free labor, billions of dollars of fresh and recycled money, and unclaimed desert spaces, Dubai is set to triple in size by 2015. The Eiffel Tower was built by only three hundred steelworkers, while Dubai today has no less than three hundred thousand Asian laborers at its disposal. As in Shanghai, over the past decade 20 percent of the world's commercial cranes have been working overtime in Dubai, putting up corporate towers, posh residential communities, and ornate hotels in a New Dubai satellite city ten miles west, where a Shanghai-like skyline now rises above the Gulf shore.

Wealth is always relative. During the British Raj, many Gulf Arabs traveled to India for work and sent remittances back to Arabia, where the rupee was also the currency. Now the migration flow has been completely reversed. For millions of poor Indians, Pakistanis, and Filipinos, Dubai's airport is a slick fortress of legal passage into the promised land. Yet if these Asian laborers were counted in their populations Arab states would forever remain in the third world, their first-world opulence a thin veneer over the deplorable conditions under which their vast worker populations live. But the emphasis in Arab legal and social codes on citizens over migrants—despite the latter constituting more than half the populations of Gulf countries—creates a peculiar form of apartheid, for which a triple standard is required: A half million citizens of Dubai live at arm's length from the rest, with intermarriage with foreign nationals considered taboo; hundreds of thousands of expatriate professionals from Ireland to India are law-abiding residents; and over a million guest workers are a case study in postmodern slavery for the globalization era—they are "less than human."[27] To date, the organized exploitation of foreign labor has left little cruelty to the imagination. Labor laws don't really exist, so ministries charged with overseeing guest workers' fate claim ignorance as the reason for their negligence. Driving through workers' tent and trailer camps on the fringes of an Arab Manhattan requires the same suspension of shame one feels in remote African villages.* For many foreign laborers, the confiscation of passports on arrival and late (under)payment of wages ultimately make the journey seem wasted when measured against the cost to personal well-being and pain of absence from families who receive far less remittances than originally hoped for and promised. The ultimate irony of their dashed expectations comes when fifty of them sleep in a luxury home they are constructing but will never come close to owning: Dubai the oasis is a mirage, for some.

The situation of third-world workers in Dubai is the best evidence that the city is run like a modern corporation: It responds not to political pressure, only to threats to its profits. As international media scrutiny focused on workers' deplorable conditions and spasmodic unrest, the Dubai sheikhs promised to act for the sake of shoring up their image, realizing that their dream could be undone at the hands of the very people who built it (a scenario depicted in the Hollywood film *Syriana*). But even as the sheikhs threatened contractors who had failed to treat their workers better, their heavy stake in these firms virtually guarantees inaction. More responsive processing of workers' complaints has been promised, an improvement on the previous tactic of collecting written suggestions in a hanging placebo box. All Gulf countries are also violators of international human-trafficking prohibitions, a status that WTO membership has altered on paper only. But to their credit, they now use robots instead of little boys as camel jockeys. As the hypocrisy of the Gulf states' labor systems is exposed, their denunciations of Western foreign policy injustices may begin to fall on deaf ears. For every Muslim humiliated or subjugated around the world in a Western prison, at least one non-Muslim (and many Muslims as well) is exploited in Dubai's labor camps and brothels. But the sheikhs' confidence continues to grow. "Even terrorism will not hurt tourism now," a real estate executive stridently claimed at his luxurious ranch-style villa on the outskirts of the city.

Voting with one's feet is the most important kind of election for the sheikhs in the Emirates. Sunny weather, friendly tax laws, and a virtu-

---

*In Qatar as well, the 150,000 natives are far outnumbered by foreigners, with no less than eight grades of citizenship for under one million people. While guest laborers are allowed to petition and complain without fear of physical violence, Qatar's official daily temperature seems intentionally set at forty-eight degrees Celsius, two degrees below the temperature at which workers would be officially relieved from laboring in the grotesque heat.

ally crime-free climate have lured thousands of European professionals to settle in Dubai, where their banking and engineering skills makes them the leading partners in Dubai's commercial growth. Every day planeloads of spiffy East Asians deplane in Dubai from Hong Kong as well. Evolving on the British and then American protection-for-oil model, China is additionally offering what other superpowers cannot: hordes of commercial vendors and low-cost goods. Unlike South Asian workers who rely on shady brokers, Chinese enter the market at a much higher status level since their sponsors are Chinese or Arab-Chinese companies that operate their own import channels. Organized Chinese cohorts have built a massive Chinatown residential compound and work in the thriving shops of the mile-long Dragon Mart export depot, saving Gulf merchants a trip to Shenzhen by selling everything from wigs to tractors, but of such poor quality that they might as well be labeled "designed to disintegrate." Much as Chinese contractors often bid half the rate of Western firms, Chinese prostitutes, now equaling their counterparts from the former Soviet Union in number, charge half as much as the competition as well. Dubai is for sale, and so is Arab geopolitical loyalty.

CONCLUSION:
ARABIAN SAND DUNES

SOME WESTERN COMMENTATORS go to great lengths to portray Arab societies as backward or feeble. American conservatives argued that the Iraq invasion was necessary because repressive Arab regimes and Islamic fundamentalists "only understand the language of force." But the West's inability to deal productively with the allegedly simplistic Arab culture actually highlights the feebleness of the West's own condescending logic. In reality, there is no naïveté in the Arab world about its centrality in the future success or failure of globalization, both geographically and geologically. It will not be, as some commentators claim, left behind.

While the West frets over Arab disorder, an emerging Arab order is defining the region's future. The combination of massive oil wealth, mass media, shared grievances, and the painful awareness of the arbitrary Western-imposed borders are transforming the Arab political landscape into one of remarkably consistent public opinion that is suspicious of American foreign policy and contests the legitimacy of un-elected rulers. The younger generation of Arabs is spreading these sentiments through student exchanges, activist conferences, and Internet blogs. This broad, concerted, and bottom-up push for political change is a trend not seen with any such consistency anywhere else. A new cohort of leaders that embodies liberal rather than military education may even bring policy change without violent regime change. As the editor of Beirut's *Daily Star,* Rami Khoury, pithily remarked, "We can't be the world's last undemocratic region forever!"

Where Arabism prevails, religious tolerance does as well. But Arab democrats are competing for the next generation's soul with Al-Qaeda's Voice of the Caliphate news program, which aids jihadist recruiters by glorifying anti-Western violence.[1] There is no guarantee that the West will continue its engagement with the Arab world despite the far-reaching impact of Islamist agitations. The West is sweating as a civilization, constantly alert to thwart every micro-plot to destroy its airplanes and cities. If the cultural stress of fighting radicalism continues a decade hence, the United States and the EU may decide to cut their losses and attempt to contain the region and allow an Arab-Islamist civil war to sap its virulent energies.

Whether Arabism or Islamism prevails, however, America loses, for both seek to solve problems with their own means and on their own terms.[2] America considers the region strategically important, but that does not guarantee it a right to military interventions, particularly since its blunders, not Arab genetic defects, are widely held to be the chief cause of terrorism, proliferation, and conflict. Reckless armament has been a far more consistent American policy than democracy promotion. The United States has not learned from T. E. Lawrence's revelation that although he could not assume an Arab character, "I could at least conceal my own, and pass among them without evident friction, neither a discord nor a critic but an unnoticed influence."[3] Lawrence's aspiration was a humble admission of cultural difference as well as a canny strategy to shape Arab affairs. America's present neoimperialism appears a blunt and messy improvisation, still ignorant of the most basic Arabian axiom that the best way up a sand dune is sideways. With Europe and China now actively pursuing their own agendas, America is unlikely to get its way without the active support of one or the other of its superpower counterparts. The only region where it is even more obvious that one superpower cannot manage the world alone—and where others have alternative visions for it—is East Asia.

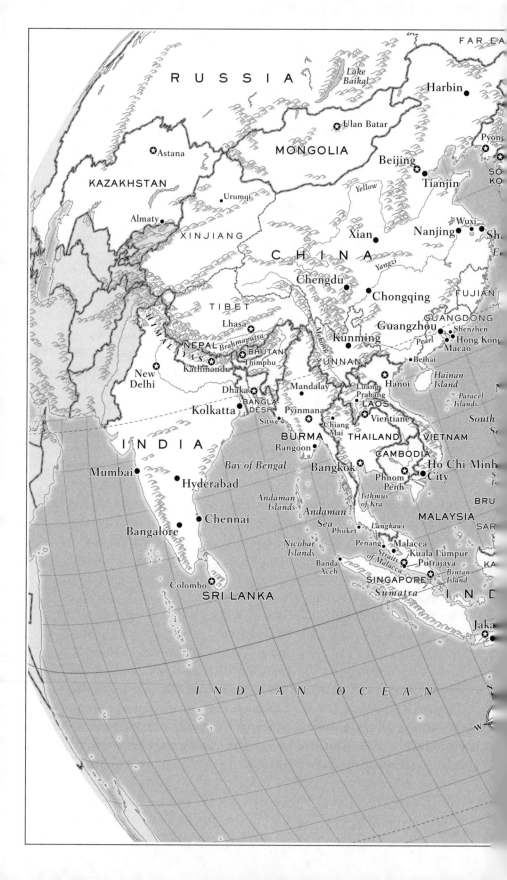

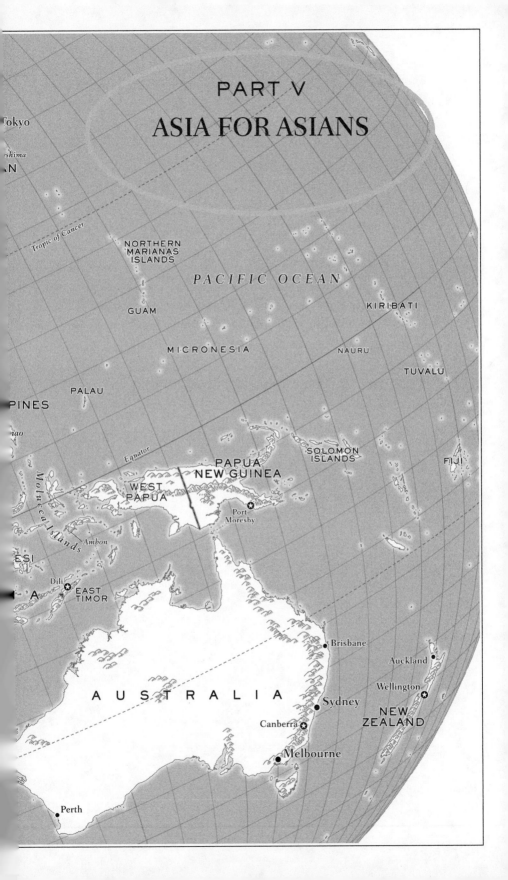

PART V
ASIA FOR ASIANS

CHAPTER 27

FROM OUTSIDE IN
TO INSIDE OUT

A CENTURY AGO, Theodore Roosevelt boldly claimed that "the Atlantic Era is now at the height of its development and must soon exhaust the resources at its command. The Pacific Era, destined to be the greatest of all, is just at its dawn." The Atlantic Era was led by Europe, then America. The Pacific Era will be led by China—and no one else.

China has only recently risen into the second world, but it has long been able to act like a global power, even when it lacked the military and economic prerequisites. It was the only third-world country given a permanent seat on the UN Security Council, and during its angry 1960s Cultural Revolution, China split from the Soviet Union and competed with it for regional allies and leadership of the international Communist movement. President Nixon warned of the need to pull China into the community of nations rather than have it remain the "epicenter of world revolution" and pursued a thaw to check the USSR. But when the Soviet Union collapsed, China's potential to become that revolutionary power was assured—and the United States could do nothing about it.

"It's not just on our maps. It's in our minds: China is the center of all the action here," explained a Singaporean journalist, pointing to the growing Chinese staff in his office. China sits at the core of the most populous and economically dynamic pan-region in the world, encompassing Russia's Far East, Japan, the Korean peninsula, India, Southeast Asia, and the Pacific islands, including Australia and New Zealand.[1] No nation within this India-Japan-Australia triangle—whether of the first, second, or third world—can withstand China's economic, demographic, political, and cultural encroachment. Some Americans believe it is their own preponderance that guarantees Asian stability, but the half of the world population that resides in Asia increasingly sees its stability as occurring under Chinese hegemony.[2] "America can come and go, but our fate ultimately hinges on China's decisions and behavior," remarked a Thai diplomat during a conference at a five-star Bangkok hotel.

Like the United States and the EU, China has become an empire that dare not speak its name. The reemergence of a Pax Sinica is the Asian equivalent of EU expansion, its diplomatic model a hybrid of ancient principles and modern institutions.[3] Centuries before the Westphalian nation-state system in Europe, Asia was governed by imperial hierarchy, with China the central heart and peripheral kingdoms paying tribute. Trade and diplomacy were synonymous: China demonstrated its generosity by actually giving larger gifts and tribute to its vassals than it received, an elegant façade to mask the reality of dominance.[4] Loyalty was bought, then earned. State sovereignty, the greatest legal shift since the tribute era, is simply a modern tool to maintain the fiction of autonomy from Chinese supremacy. The tribute model never required territorial domination; it was a means of extending influence to realms beyond direct Chinese control. Thus while powerful capitals like Tokyo, Seoul, and Singapore play roles today like London, Moscow, and Ankara do in relation to the EU—as dikes against the Chinese imperial tide—they are also tacitly aware of their increasingly subsovereign status vis-à-vis China. The UN does not matter in East Asia, for it ensures neither stability nor wealth—Asians' two main concerns.

China's protocol-obsessed emotiveness has revived the diplomatic theater of the tribute era. When its policies are criticized by neighbors, China pouts that such statements "hurt the feelings of the Chinese people." China's minimalist oratory gives the impression of reasoned consideration while allowing others to suffuse its every word with sophisticated historical symbolism and gravitas. But those who view China based solely on its cautious rhetoric are focused on words rather than numbers. As far back as 1968, scholar A. F. K. Organski predicted that China would supplant the United States as the world's leading power due to the incalculable potential of its population. In the globalization age, the amplifying power of diasporas must also be factored in. The fifty-five million overseas Chinese, mostly settled in the Asian periphery, are the demographic equivalent of climate change: imperceptibly advancing, knowing no boundaries, and affecting everyone.[5] Organic Chinese links are rekindling across political borders, fueling a demographic *blending* no less significant than that of the Americas or across the Mediterranean. Historical ties between China's northeast and South Korea and Japan, the Pearl River delta region and Hong Kong, the Yangzi River delta and Taiwan, and the southeast and the greater Mekong subregion all form natural economic territories that transcend peace and conflict.[6] China's massive gender imbalance (stemming from the one-child policy and pronounced boy bias) has led it to import women from Vietnam and North Korea, further diluting diverse bloods into a Chinese-based mongrel race.

China finds ways to manage contradictions that seem untenable in the West: It is an empire that at times has sealed itself off, expanding only to the point of ensuring self-defense; it settles its border disputes rather than using them as a specter to rouse nationalism; it has a tightly regulated capitalist economy; it is an authoritarian state practicing widespread local democracy; and its most fundamental strategic doctrine contains what may be the two most oxymoronic words in history: "peaceful rise."* Throughout history, rising powers have become increasingly belligerent, but the more confident China becomes, the more it cooperates.[7] "They have learned what lines cannot be crossed," a Malaysian strategic analyst confidently asserted over dinner at an up-

---

*The phrase *peaceful rise* (*heping jueqi*) was coined by Zheng Bijian of the elite Central Party School. Officially, this doctrine was later rephrased as "peaceful development" to sound more benign and emphasize China's domestic focus while also not sending any mixed signals of tolerance for Taiwanese independence. The policy implies an understanding that overconsumption and pollution are dangerous and inefficient, that expansion and aggression are ultimately self-defeating, and that economic and social development must be balanced.

scale Chinese restaurant in Kuala Lumpur. "Asian nations are gradually perceiving China as less of a threat, especially since its rise creates major economic opportunities for each of them, and has become a rallying point of Asian cultural pride."

America has ruled the waves since its seizure of the Philippines from Spain a century ago, and its Pacific Command (PACOM) is by far its largest military force, greater than all of the others combined and capable of sinking all the rest of the world's navies simultaneously.[8] America hangs on the Pacific Rim because American grand strategy is governed by Nicholas Spykman's Rimland theory. For Spykman, in contrast to Mackinder's thesis that the Central Asian heartland is the pivot of global power, the Eurasian coastal region stretching from the Persian Gulf around the Indian subcontinent to the Pacific Rim is the most important zone of industrial and population growth. He thus revised Mackinder's famous epigram about the heartland: "Who controls the Rimland rules Eurasia; who rules Eurasia controls the destinies of the world."[9] During the Cold War, America's *outside-in* system of "hub-and-spoke" alliances with Australia and New Zealand (known as ANZUS), Japan, South Korea, Singapore, and the Philippines discouraged regional cooperation, and America still has strong bilateral economic ties to East Asian states (which account for 40 percent of its total trade)—specifically signing free trade agreements with most of China's neighbors with the aim of maintaining their loyalty.

But America is losing its grip on the Rimland, one finger at a time. Rather than inspiring great awe, many Asians see America's offshore naval presence as a historical accident, now antiquated, superfluous, and even dangerous.[10] "We are still waiting to hear what America means when it says its 'strategic interests' require it to menacingly park a fleet of aircraft carriers and destroyers in our seas," a Chinese military analyst in Beijing sarcastically remarked. "We in the region can manage our own affairs, but we worry it is America that will overreact." Even more than in the Persian Gulf, America's weaknesses are most clearly exposed in East Asia precisely because this is where its maximum strength is visible. Its diminished credibility has reduced it from its status as the ultimate guarantor of Asian stability to a more minor role as Japan and Taiwan's protector and troubleshooter of crises from Malaysian-Indonesian naval skirmishes to the North Korean nuclear standoff.[11] By 2001, China stopped referring to the United States as a "hegemon" in East Asia not out of politeness, but simply because America had ceased to be able to function as one.

Not only is China encroaching on Mackinder's heartland, but its vast Pacific coastline makes it the largest nation on Spykman's Rimland as well. Just as the Silk Road is the land route from China to the West, the South China Sea and the Straits of Malacca are the region's sea lines of communication (known as SLOC), the maritime passageway to the energy resources and markets of the Persian Gulf and Europe. The East Asian strategic picture is thus evolving on the sea, with China working tirelessly to co-opt Southeast Asia's littoral states through trade pacts and naval cooperation. Where diplomatic pendulums once swung between the United States and China, many countries are preparing for the latter to eclipse the former. An *inside-out* Asian strategic culture has emerged, governed by a consultative diplomacy (known as *musyawarah*) that identifies common interests likely to yield face-saving decisions while marginalizing controversial or outside (read: U.S.-imposed) topics.[12]

"What we have now is a Chinese 'Monroe Doctrine,'" the Malaysian analyst declared. "We should get it over with and accept this Chinese order. That way we can peacefully resolve the problems of Taiwan, North Korea, and the South China Sea." Could a benign Chinese hierarchy prevent rivalries from escalating beyond the psychological and economic level? Even though serious disputes remain over land and sea boundaries, as Singaporean diplomat Kishore Mahbubani points out, "guns have fallen silent" in the region due to a "tidal wave of common sense" by which Asians are rejecting the Western historical pattern of militarism in favor of shared prosperity.

Asians do, however, welcome Europe's soft comeback to East Asia after its colonial presence came undone in Indochina and with the peaceful British handover of Hong Kong to China in 1997. "Europe is a 'strategic partner' for China, and its role in shaping our new regional order is a powerful endorsement of it," a Chinese academic explained. "We have been witness and victim of Western history, and only the stable order of the EU is a good guide for us." Asians who once turned to America for security now turn to Europe for capacity, since everything the EU does makes the region more modern, prosperous, educated, and professional, bolstering Asian confidence and weakening American dominance.* Regional organizations, chambers of commerce, eminent person "brain trusts" and student exchanges all take their intellectual cue from the EU.[13] Europe is a larger market for Asian exports than America, and Asians are increasing the Euro share of their massive foreign exchange reserves to hedge against America's imbalanced economy. Chinese academics, students, journalists, musicians, and tourists are all over Europe. Waves of Chinese businessmen stay in low-cost hotels in Germany and Eastern Europe, spending weeks in search of partnerships to export still more Chinese goods.

But China and Asia are merely absorbing Western knowledge to accelerate the construction of an Eastern order. American skeptics argue that a "Concert of Asia" is impossible due to simmering rivalries, but Asian confidence has already evolved to the point where America may speak only when invited—when the East Asian Summit first convened in Kuala Lumpur in 2005, the United States was not invited at all.[14] As this community evolves from a geographical club into the leading forum for Asia's priorities, most regional players see it as a chance to shun Western influence once and for all. As one senior Malaysian diplomat cheekily put it, but without a hint of jest, "Creating a community is easy among the yellow and the brown—but not the white."

How did East Asia become the cockpit of global change, a world region on a par with North America and Europe? Europeans long admired Eastern cultures until the Industrial Revolution massively expanded the material gap between them. Marx and Weber then argued that East Asia was doomed to stagnation: China was too large and feudal, other Asians too prone to the "despotism of custom."[15] Spengler saw it differently. What relevance do the Western philosophical concepts such as Dionysian ideals and the *Übermensch* have for Confucianism, he wondered, knowing that mankind both lives and thinks in unique cultural systems. For Spengler, the West was already in its autumn, withering as the gap between its ideal and its reality grew. By contrast, a large population, properly equipped, could have martial confidence. As the French sociologist Auguste Comte argued, demog-

---

*Ever eager to play all sides, Singapore hosts the Asia-Europe Meeting (ASEM), which has become focused on enhancing Europe's commercial strength to overtake the American-led Asia Pacific Economic Cooperation (APEC)—which was always joked to be "four adjectives in search of a noun." APEC's demise is also visible in China's preference for bilateral trade agreements, from Canada to South America.

raphy is destiny. Asia has the oldest cultures, the most people, and, by certain measures, the most money of any region in the world.[16] Asia is shaping the world's destiny—and exposing the flaws of the grand narrative of Western civilization in the process. Because of the East, the West is no longer master of its own fate.

The Cold War is often referred to as the East-West conflict, but the West's "deeply habituated condescension" prevented it from appreciating the rise of the *real* East, which now represents the true challenge to the West.[17] Asians saw America's post–Cold War hegemony as an attempt to maintain a Western grip on the leading instruments of technology and finance, and they responded by seeking to master these dialects of power faster than any other people in the world.[18] Today's unstoppable globalization is on their side, spreading knowledge faster than any single empire can control it, recalling Spengler's prophetic argument in *Der Mensch und die Technik* that technology quickly divorces from the culture that created it. Modernization and Westernization have the same starting point but two very distinct destinations. If "the West was the West long before it was modern," the East, too, shall remain the East, even after it captures modernity.[19]

"Asia's breakneck growth makes the very notion of risk aversion antiquated," beamed a Hong Kong investor, congratulating himself on moving there from New York. "East Asia now embodies the unbridled ambition that once characterized the West and is taking Western investment as those markets become saturated." East Asia has seized only the best technologies and standards from the West and made them its own. Bangkok, Shanghai, and Kuala Lumpur have monorails that glide effortlessly above the ground, while New York and London's subways sputter below it. The West may have invented the automobile, but 40 percent of cars bought in America today are from East Asia, which also boasts higher 3G cellular penetration than America and sets its own telephony standards, with which others must then compete. East Asians also have the advantage of relative mastery over the two global languages as well: English and Chinese. Success in American cinema increasingly comes from importing Japan-imation techniques and Hong Kong plots and cinematographic style, demonstrating that even the flow of cultural clout could be reversing.

History is being rewritten from the Eastern point of view, and the "End of History" looks very different in East Asia than it does in the

West.* Japan's nineteenth-century blending of Western means with Eastern ends was an indigenous model for the twentieth-century rise of Asia's "tigers": Taiwan, Korea, and Singapore. Combining inspiration and perspiration, East Asians' cultural proclivities called for high savings rates and good education.[20] Their ability to protect domestic sectors with export-led growth created enormous wealth and provided an alternative style of capitalism that appealed to the next wave of Asian dynamos, including China, Malaysia, and Vietnam. "Keynes is our man!" a well-educated Singaporean taxi driver exulted. Previously denigrated as tantamount to Marxism, government interference in the economy is viewed as an important counterpoint to laissez-faire economics in East Asia. Since the 1997–98 financial crisis, the Asians' explicit goal has been to shun the IMF, whose onerous conditionality made it a tool of the U.S. Treasury.[21] After the crisis, Asians rebounded by adopting fiscal discipline and global market standards—but without sacrificing the centrality of government. While in the West government is seen as stifling innovation, East Asian governments today are heavily reinvesting their massive capital liquidity in innovation. And as intra-Asian trade now exceeds transpacific trade, Asians can set their own rules.†

There is no reason for Asians to leave Asia. Asian travelers today effortlessly hop on and off low-cost airlines to explore over a dozen distinct and inviting cultures. "East Asian nations are rooted in precolonial history, so we are far more stable than postcolonial African or Arab

---

*Liberalism insists on its own universality, but its application across space and time shows that it works best where it already exists. As Amartya Sen argues, no political system supports anarchy and disorder, so the question is which system allows freedom to flourish to the maximum extent. The most economically developed countries in East Asia are those with concurrent individual rights and democracy—South Korea, Taiwan, and Japan—thus their success can hardly be attributed to authoritarianism. But there is little that is liberal about the policies that brought about this achievement. Instead, bureaucratic elites called the shots in all political and economic arenas, as they largely do today. Tight business-government cooperation with interlocking relationships between banks and suppliers were the key to closing the gap between these nations and the West. Bribery and family-run conglomerates are not Asian inventions, they have been part of the universal story of capitalist evolution the world over. Democracy works best with a sufficiently large middle class, and the democratization of the economy that is a prerequisite to a broad and sustainable liberal order did not emerge until later.

†Trade between ASEAN and China grew fivefold between 1997 and 2005, to $105 billion. China's purchasing of $15 to $20 billion per month of its own currency holds the renminbi artificially low while also allowing other countries in the region to opt out of the global currency adjustment process in favor of retaining their competitive position vis-à-vis China. By running trade deficits with its ASEAN neighbors, it has them on its side as its increasingly voracious export market. Though the Chinese manufacturing juggernaut sucks up 80 percent of the region's foreign direct investment (FDI), Southeast Asia still stands to gain in long-term manufacturing potential as China, Japan, and Korea age rapidly.

states. We see no reason for one's prosperity to cause rivalry with others," a Malay-Chinese historian argued during a small seminar of Southeast Asian academics at the University of Malaya. China and Japan, often viewed as eternal antagonists, are in fact East Asia's economic co-pilots.[22] Together with Singapore and South Korea, they hold over two-thirds of the world's foreign-exchange reserves, valued at over $2 trillion (held mostly in U.S. dollars), allowing them to pursue the mercantilist policies that fueled the rise of the West. A century ago President Warren Harding urged Americans to "go on the peaceful commercial conquest of the world" in order to stave off social conflict at home. East Asians are now following his advice, buying up companies, assets, and natural resources on every continent. "The world may be shrinking, but our fair share is larger than the West's," noted a Shanghai journalist on the bustling news floor of his paper's headquarters.

Beginning with British Hong Kong and Singapore, Western colonialism gave East Asia the head-start gift of the global city. Since the 1950s, Tokyo, Taipei, Seoul, and Shanghai have also become global cities, annually channeling billions of dollars of investment inward into their respective countries and around the region. Each is so powerful that they are better understood as "region-states," cities that operate like business units, as connected to the global economy as their own countries, while increasingly linked into a growing Asian network of economic nodes irrespective of political and cultural distinctions.[23] Asia also has more than half the world's megalopolises, which are home to most of Southeast Asia's five hundred million people. Third-world mega-cities in Africa and India contain bustling downtowns surrounded by rings and pockets of residential and squatter neighborhoods as far as the eye can see. As villages rapidly depopulate, urbanization means not modernization and development but squalor and depravity. Southeast Asia today is rising out of this third-world scenario as its per capita income rises above $3,000 and the poverty rate falls below 25 percent. In Malaysia and Thailand, there are still shantytowns perched on sewers and millions of stateless laborers, but not much in the way of disease-infested slums and mass homelessness. A rapidly growing number of people wake up each day eager to build their Asian dream.

"What is now the Asian dream was the American dream before," proclaimed Singapore's foreign minister, George Yeo. No cloud of self-doubt hangs over East Asia, where culture has been an asset in creating a virtuous circle of economic growth and cultural pride. East Asia accounts for much of the world's predicted growth in consumer demand, but its people are not like stocks; their values do not change daily. States with money are accorded status and respect, just as with wealthy people, meaning that the increasingly prosperous East can now more vocally challenge the universality of Western values, an "Occidentalism" that responds to the "offensive display of superiority by the West."[24] The "Asian values" of unified leadership, consensus, and social harmony could hardly be more discredited than American democracy, capitalism, and individualism today, multiplying the alternate models that exist for the rest of the second world. China is so confident in America's lack of appeal that U.S. presidential elections are televised live, perhaps for entertainment. An *American Idol*–style program for Chinese youth rewards knowledge of English idioms with miniature Statue-of-Liberty torches—without even a hint of irony. China doesn't bother to release political prisoners to appease the United States anymore. "We see how materialism has led to overconsumption and the erosion of American democracy," a Chinese student leader of a Party youth organization argued. "What we want is governance by consent and the rule of law." The West's democratization efforts have hit a wall even higher in East Asia than they have in the Arab world. Western scholars predict that economic openness will lead to democratization, but not only do Asian governments collude with elites to prevent any challenge to their control over public goods and the law, but democracy is even less in demand because many Asian countries actually have good leaders (*junzi*) who do not want to become the prince of a Confucian maxim who is wrong but not contradicted, thus bringing ruin to his country.*

The "Asian compact" features open societies but closed polities, restoring democracy to its place as a means to an end—not the highest virtue, but just one agenda item among many. It is ironic that the West's great rival should come from a Confucian-based meritocracy of elites, since this idea is firmly rooted in Plato's *Republic*, which calls for rule by wise philosopher kings.[25] Singapore and Malaysia's liberal-

---

*Rather than structure government to limit state power, Chinese, Japanese, and Korean history is characterized by rulers who have had supreme authority over political, social, and cultural life, with the moral authority to root out corruption and "cleanse" society even by extralegal measures. See Bell, *East Meets West*, 127, 153.

izing quasi-democracy is the preferred East Asian model today. There are opposition parties and elections, but not for the highest office. Succession proceeds by selection, not election.[26] This collective egocentrism prevents the state from being hijacked by majority ethnic group interests, which would lead to the unraveling of multiethnic states like Malaysia. Single-party leadership has made the governments of Malaysia and Singapore far more accountable and responsive to their people than that of the Philippines, where each week brings fresh coup rumors against the democratically elected but illiberal government. From Thailand to Taiwan, democracy has resulted in winner-take-all systems with constant extralegal maneuvering, impeachments, and coups. Thailand's democracy is like its boxing, in which fists, feet, knees, and elbows are all fair game, and democratic Indonesia's political instability and corruption hardly make its system admirable to others. "Western democracy is a waste of our time," spat a Malaysian diplomat.

East Asian communitarian traditions also challenge American notions of human rights by prioritizing social and economic rights over civic and political rights, justifying the denial of constitutional protections of individual liberty and free speech.[27] The early Confucian scholar Mencius argued that violating the right to food and material well-being is a greater crime than denying political rights. Humility and compassion (*ren*), not flamboyance and egoism, are the cherished virtues. In Confucian cultures, the family name comes first, then the given name. Filial piety is a cherished and legally enforced principle in numerous East Asian countries, and many believe that the ideal society is structured like a family rather than based on individuals.[28] Children are much more a center of family attention as well. "Because of the one-child policy in China, the child is synonymous with hope for the future," explained a Beijing intellectual, highlighting the effort he puts into managing well-rounded social, musical, and athletic activities for his only son. Like Europeans, East Asians focus more on subsistence and economic equality, rights that are far more enshrined in the European legal tradition than in the American. The German constitution, with provisions for health care and education, was the template for Korea. Lifetime employment is still taken very seriously and is cherished across East Asia; for the region's migrant workers, employment is far more important than citizenship. State-sponsored poverty eradication funds demonstrate a commitment to the redistribution of wealth.[29] Asians want to use globalization to build a middle class, not to erode it, as is happening in the United States. They board the globalization plane, but with their seatbelts on. And on that plane, they often practice tai chi stretches together, hundreds of hands moving in synchronization all through the cabin, sharing the joys of flying.

Asian values too have their flaws. "In some countries, the progress of the few has been used immaturely to mask inadequate improvements in the quality of life for many more," conceded the Malay-Chinese academic. Confucianism has certainly not proved to be a bulwark against Maoism and Marxism either, which from China to Cambodia to Vietnam claimed close to a hundred million lives in the past fifty years alone. Organized criminals operating in China, Taiwan, and Japan are hardly modest: Their ruthlessly efficient drug, weapon, and money-laundering operations make American gangs seem amateurish. And paternalistic privilege in the Asian state-business nexus is widely abused, with rather loose interpretations of the Confucian duty to help family and friends by personal—not professional—means. Yet even these flaws have inspired more confidence in Asians' own process of trial and error. "Now that we have economic growth and social stability, there is no more excuse to not have responsible leaders, police forces, and business executives," he continued. But guided by the Confucian idea of reciprocity between rulers and the ruled, even Western-educated elites in Malaysia, Singapore, and China remain loyal to this hierarchical system, which preserves both stability and their personal interests. As one Singaporean parliamentarian bluntly put it, "We take risks with our money, not with our beliefs."

CHAPTER 28

CHINA'S FIRST-WORLD
SEDUCTION

FAR BEYOND ITS second-world predecessor the Soviet Union, China can exploit globalization to co-opt not only the third world but the entire first world as well, particularly in its own region.[1] Japan, Korea, Australia, and Singapore are slowly but perceptibly shifting their grand strategies as they become more interdependent with China. The first world is not an American-dominated club: The very allies America relies on to hedge China's rise are contributing the most to fueling it.

Since Japan surrendered to the United States in World War II, America has viewed it as the bulwark of the "free world" in Asia.[2] But as the world's most technologically and organizationally sophisticated country, Japan has been a chief architect of the Asian order, investing heavily across the region to save on manufacturing costs in the automobile and other industries—nowhere more so than in China. The four hundred thousand overseas Chinese in Japan helped awaken early interest in China, and the thousands of Chinese students who flock to Japan each year help sustain it. Beijing's airport was built with Japanese aid, and Japanese investment in China has never been higher than during times of tension between them. Japan's imports from

China have skyrocketed, including half of its annual fruit consumption. Over one hundred thousand Japanese now live in Shanghai, many
facilitating the over $30 billion in Japanese investment as well as work-
ing in Japanese call centers.[3]

Japan remains a global economic powerhouse and the world's
largest provider of humanitarian aid, and its alliance with the United
States, its high-tech navy, and its missile-defense program together
allow for a very small defense budget that has provided enough security to satisfy this most humble of great powers. (Nationalist voices in
Japan's establishment are as concerned with Japan's unequal status
vis-à-vis the United States as they are with China.) Even if it acquires
nuclear weapons, Japan's cultural uniqueness means that it cannot
garner broad allegiance in Asia and must be content to play second fid-
dle to China, which has blocked its bid for a permanent seat on the
UN Security Council. Yet a bilateral dynamic of "new thinking" has
emerged as leaders on both sides appreciate that normalizing Japan's
relations in Asia is a task similar to Germany's rehabilitation in Europe,
a prerequisite to pursuing the "twin wheels" of economic and political regionalism to which both countries are committed.[4] In a shift
from fearing cooperation, China, Japan, and South Korea have moved
toward joint oil and gas exploration in the East China Sea, petroleum-
sharing agreements, strategic oil reserves, and a common program to
exploit the fisheries and gas deposits around the disputed Dokdo (or
Takeshima) islands.[5]

Next to Japan, South Korea is Asia's great success story, moving
from a classic aid client to a first-world state.[6] But even more than
Japan, South Korea's allegiance to America is under great strain. Rising
Korean confidence has led to confrontation with the United States
over the utility of its more than half century of military presence on the
peninsula, with Korea pushing for troop reductions. American bases,
once a bastion of extraterritoriality, now exist very much at the tolerance of host societies that are increasingly suspicious of American mo-
tives.[7] At the same time, many young Koreans are falling under the
spell of "Red Fever" and favor closer ties with China.[8] Almost all of
South Korea's economic growth is dependent on China, which has surpassed the United States as Korea's largest trade partner.[9] When
China indicated that its growth might slow in 2004, the Korean stock

market took a nasty hit. China has all but caught up to Korea's electronics standards but with far lower labor costs, meaning that Korea's current role in adding value to Chinese assembled goods could evaporate as China moves up the supply chain.

Nonetheless, China and South Korea are cooperating in the capitalist colonization of the nuclear-armed but destitute North Korea, which lies between them. China has already bought up North Korea's mines and railways, while South Korea, through various iterations of its "sunshine policy," has opened joint production and export zones there; the two countries now field a common Olympic team. Ultimately, China's and South Korea's contacts with North Korean dissidents and officials, and the weight of its crushingly poor population, mean that if and when the "hermit kingdom" collapses, both China and South Korea will share in Finlandizing it.[10]

China has all but neutered America's Anglosphere alliance with Australia as well. During World War II, the United States and Australia combined strength to defend against a potential Japanese invasion. But China's expansion is not like Japan's was; it is silent and economic, provoking not military counterstrategies but rather generating enormous goodwill.[11] Australians know that their historical ally is a rival of their most rapidly growing trade partner, causing foreign policy schizophrenia between geography and tradition.[12] China is Australia's largest consumer of uranium, iron ore, manganese, and liquid natural gas (which is shipped from the Northwest Shelf to a refinery in Guangdong).[13] The gas deal with China was the largest in Australia's history, bringing with it a muting of criticisms of China's human rights record. To retain its credibility as a trusted leader of Asian peacekeeping operations, Australia has committed to ASEAN's Treaty of Amity and Cooperation, a nonaggression pact that undermines its commitment to the United States. Like Korea, Australia now claims it can play a mediating role between the United States and China while not taking sides. For Australia's business community and diplomats, Beijing has for some time been the destination for success, while 75 percent of tour groups in Australia are from China. The United States must now turn to its only true ally: geography. From Palau to Guam to Hawaii, America's navy is devising an entirely sea-based network of logistics and access channels to allow it to operate militarily in a region where few want it to.[14]

SINGAPORE: ASIA'S FIRST-WORLD INSPIRATION

Built on an unpopulated backwater by the British East India Company, mostly Chinese-populated Singapore is the first country in the world to defy the notion of equatorial malaise that has become the third-world norm. When the Malaysian Federation expelled Singapore in 1965, it left Lee Kuan Yew and his band of migrants with no army, a "Chinese island in a Malay sea."[15] Lee inculcated self-reliance by organizing tree-planting contests, building Singapore into the very archetype of a global city, using foreign capital to finance a world-class infrastructure of roads, airports, hospitals, and schools—and a civil service to administer them. As one swerves along its perfectly paved, leafy avenues, tardiness is impossible. "America is third-world compared to us," Singaporeans frequently joke.

"Singapore is virtually synonymous with globalization," a multinational businessman reminded, pointing out how frequently he has changed jobs with the times. For decades it has constantly shifted its place in the global supply chain, becoming a center of oil-refinery and oil-rig construction even though it has no oil. Its new Biopolis for life sciences (including stem cell) research attracts Western scientists seeking hassle-free employment. The world-class port management, controlled prostitution, casinos, and simplified citizenship for professionals that Dubai envies are all already a reality in "Singapore, Inc." In the precious little space of Singapore, acreage is zoned years in advance to anticipate future housing and industry needs; high-tech industrial areas are referred to as "estates." Lacking other resources, currency reserves have been Singapore's force multiplier. Through the state company Temasek, Singapore holds shares in major conglomerates across Asia, and it invested in China long before others, earning it long-term credibility and leverage. "Since Asia produces such technically skilled workers these days," the businessman continued, "affirmative action in Singapore means hiring more Caucasians."

Singapore is the most successful avatar of the Asian way—and a model packaged for export. Lee's one-word answer to explain Singapore's success is "confidence," for he has sought to be "correct, not politically correct."[16] Under Lee's "Nothing is free" value system, rich and poor alike adjust to incentives—fares, fines, fees, penalties—for excessive consumption or even multiple car ownership. (The city's famous caning policy, a punishment in addition to prison time for a wide variety of crimes, was actually introduced by the British.) For Lee, democracy has no intrinsic value; results always trump process.[17] The government's meritocracy is based on the model of Royal Dutch Shell. Singaporean parliamentarians are the world's highest-paid, making them virtually corruption-free. They travel to capitals around the region emphasizing accountability, effectiveness, pragmatism—but not democracy. Singapore's constituency councils operate underneath, but feed indirectly into, the ruling party structure, a preferred model for much of Asia. Lee also imposed a firm stricture against physical coercion that many other countries in the region would do well to adopt as a big step toward cleaning up their politics. With enough humility not to govern until his death, Lee stepped down and became "Minister Mentor"—not least to his son, the current prime minister. Once Lee passes from the scene completely, however, government legitimacy will rest not on name recognition but rather on whether it cares for its people, rules by law, delivers economic growth and education, maintains infrastructure, cultivates the national culture, and upholds high standards of integrity.[18] Singapore's success has resulted in a level of public satisfaction that could allow it to lighten up on its paternalism and allow more freedoms as a social release valve, which incidentally would set a good example for the rest of the region. "We may be the envy of the world," a young academic explained on a florid university campus, "but we have a decadent sense of entitlement like people living in a five-star hotel." Indeed, Singapore is considered so boring that its own people don't want to procreate, instead divorcing at the world's highest rate.

Lee originally rejected the idea of Singapore as a "third China," instead making it a place where Chinese weren't allowed to be Chinese. He dismantled their businesses and substituted English as the national language. "Like most of the diaspora, we were Sinophobic during the Cold War," a Singaporean historian explained over lunch at the National University. "The Communist mainland was suspicious of our alien ideologies." Most Singaporean Chinese don't even speak the modern, constructed dialect of Mandarin but rather the vernacular "Singlish." To be more global than Asian, Singapore has reached far and wide to maintain a regional balance. Israel and India train its army, and its massive new harbor was built with America's navy in mind as it transitioned away from the Philippines, prompting some analysts to describe Singapore as an "anchored American battleship." At its annual Shangri-La defense dialogue, military officials from all the region's governments are invited—except China.

"The deep, cultural bond of Chineseness is becoming very real as of late," a newspaper editor explained. "Chinese affinity has returned to Singapore in a big way." Ethnic Chinese show growing interest in making Singapore a bilingual city, sending their English-speaking children to Chinese schools and traveling and investing far more in China. Also, the Chinese government has been softening its image with overseas Chinese—without undermining its official governmental relations (which could ironically provoke anti-China sentiment)—by relaxing investment laws and, potentially, offering dual citizenship to overseas Chinese. "Notice how the American and Chinese embassies are equidistant to the Foreign Ministry," a young diplomat nonchalantly pointed out during a drive through the city's broad, winding boulevards.

Singapore is the exception to the notion that China is shaping the rest of Asia, for the overseas Chinese of Singapore not only run their own country but are also shaping China itself. The question is thus not whether China will dominate Asia, but rather which model of China will prevail. Singapore can already claim some credit for the major changes in Chinese decision making over the past two decades. Deng Xiaoping opened China after visiting Singapore, where he saw that Chinese were smarter and more successful than at home. Toynbee's impression seems more valid now than it did a half century ago: "Singapore may have been founded by British enterprise, but today it is a Chinese city: The future capital of a Chinese 'Co-prosperity Sphere' which is likely to last, because it will have been established by business ability and not by military force."[19]

INDIA LOOKS EAST

The devastating 2004 tsunami, which centered on Indonesian Sumatra and swelled over islands and coasts from India to Somalia, reinforced the reality of a seamless oceanic space in the world's Eastern Hemisphere.[20] As lunar gravity dictates the tides, however, the Indian Ocean increasingly serves as the western bay of a greater Pacific space centered on East Asia. Its western shores—Africa, Arabia, and Iran—increasingly send their natural resources eastward, even as the area provides investment and export markets for booming Asia. The majority of the world's shipping now traverses this integrated Indo-Pacific realm, making all of South Asia the third-world western subsystem of the China-centered Asian order. Over 50 percent of India's trade is with East Asia, while Japan, South Korea, and Singapore are its largest foreign investors.

Under the British Raj, India was the most powerful territory between the Suez Canal and the Straits of Malacca, but its influence in the Arab world and Central Asia also ended with the Raj. Hemmed in by the world's highest mountain range and a vast ocean, power projection (even with nuclear weapons) is highly circumscribed for India's modest army and navy. The United States explicitly seeks to sponsor India's rise as "the first large, economically powerful, culturally vibrant, multiethnic, multireligious democracy outside of the geographic West"—not to mention as a hedge against China.[21] But India has transitioned from its Cold War nonalignment to multi-alignment. It declares itself and the United States to be the "twin towers of democracy" while announcing with China plans to "reshape world order."[22] To lure India, America has offered high-tech investment, civilian nuclear technology, defense agreements such as joint F-18 production, and more visas for immigrants. China has emphasized their common positions in trade negotiations, joint oil exploration, commercial corridors through the Himalayas, $20 billion in annual trade, and a civilian nuclear deal as well. Indian IT firms must import hardware from China to produce their software; that the largest outsourcing operations in China are Indian-owned shows its growing integration with China.[23]

But China's soft cooperation with India has facilitated its grand strategic goal of encircling and containing it through a naval "string of pearls" in order to reach the Arabian Sea without relying on the Straits of Malacca. Once part of colonial India, Burma is now entrenched in China's orbit, with India's proposed east-west gas pipelines dropped in favor of north-south pipelines to China. Where India has built a fence to prevent Bangladeshi migration, China has built a modern Bangladesh-China Friendship Conference Center in Dhaka. While India threatens to divert the Brahmaputra River (on which Bangladesh depends) into the Ganges, China has muscled in, since it is the source country of the Brahmaputra. Against Indian wishes, China has become an observer in the South Asian Association for Regional Cooperation (SAARC), while Indian influence in the evolving East Asian Community is marginal. "Nobody in the region really cares what India thinks," confided a Malaysian diplomat involved with regional diplomacy.

India is big but not yet important. Outsourcing has made it a leading back office for Western firms, but except for a few segregated twenty-first-century oases of development, India is almost completely third-world, most of its billion-plus people living in poverty.[24] In Mumbai (once known as Bombay), which accounts for over one-third of the national economy, some residents pay among the world's highest rents while the city's slums of over ten million inhabitants are also the world's largest. Clogged Indian cities still have three-way streets: Two directions for automobiles, with pedestrians and stray cattle meandering in between. India's bonanza of IPOs, impressive corporate profits, and billionaires galore show the dynamic potential of its private sector, but its growth will remain spectacularly uneven until the government catches up—perhaps over the next two decades—with its promises of infrastructure development. India's continued high population growth ensures that even with high economic growth it will remain the poorest large country in the world for decades to come. Though agriculture constitutes only 30 percent of the economy, seven hundred million people depend on seasonal monsoons and harvests—yet India's groundwater is depleting rapidly. Unable to pay their debts, many farmers have committed suicide, while indentured servitude continues in many backward areas. Most of India's population growth is occurring in the northern states, which have the weakest infrastructure, the worst governance, the poorest education, and the highest rate of HIV/AIDS infection, all while also being the epicenter of a resurgence of the polio epidemic.

China has order and may one day have democracy. India has democracy but achieves less because it is chaotic. The link between trade and development that China exemplifies is almost absent in India. Relative to its geographical and population size, India's government is almost invisibly weak, with a federal budget the size of Norway's. Unlike China, unified India is a British creation, and its unity often appears more geographical than psychological; it is a cramped peninsula where Tamils and Assamese have nowhere else to go—yet still they try. It could also be argued that China is a freer country than democratic India: Literacy is far higher, the poverty rate far lower. Also, it takes longer to start a business in India, one-third as many Indians have Internet access, and only one-fifth as many have cell phones. India's democracy may never have experienced a famine, but over half of India's children are malnourished. Because most Indians lack economic freedom, other freedoms are that much more difficult to enjoy. The difference between India and China is thus not just the time lag between the advents of their current economic reform eras but also a fundamental matter of national organizational ability. Even if India rises, it will be according to Chinese rules.

CHAPTER 29

MALAYSIA AND INDONESIA:

THE GREATER CHINESE
CO-PROSPERITY SPHERE

INDOCHINA'S POSTCOLONIAL LEADERS dreamt up the Association of Southeast Asian Nations (ASEAN) on a golf course in 1967, holding its first meeting in Bangkok because Thailand was the only country with which none of the founding members was fighting at the time. Because defiant militaries carried national legitimacy, ASEAN's inauspicious beginnings saw it grappling with Sukarno's aggressive Indonesian "Konfrontasi" policy toward Malaysia, followed by conflicts in Vietnam and Cambodia.[1] For decades, it remained an anticolonial bloc in which the United States boosted military rule to counter agrarian Marxism (tripling the size of the Thai military, for example). Like the EU, ASEAN experienced its Bosnia-like moments after the Cold War: the Asian financial crisis, Indonesian forest-fire haze, the East Timor intervention, and the SARS outbreak. Each tested the coherence and utilty of ASEAN, and spurred the rapid development of collective mechanisms for trade integration and combating terrorism, environmental decay, transnational crime, and disease. Mutual interference has become as much the norm as visa-free travel among its five hundred million citizens.[2] Some ASEAN countries still have defense agreements with the United States, which now hopes to shape the multilateral bloc into an anti-China hedge.[3]

But the ASEAN club lies in China's backyard. To break free of America's strategic encirclement, China is picking off ASEAN members one by one and pulling them into its neotribute system such that the individual ties each enjoys with China are now more powerful than the ties among themselves. "ASEAN countries kowtow to China not only to avoid being on China's bad side," a Thai diplomat and former ASEAN official explained, "but on the promise that China will not abandon them in times of need, as the U.S. did during the Asian financial crisis." ASEAN is now synonymous with China's multitiered periphery: Singapore, Malaysia, and Brunei as the wealthiest partners; Thailand, Indonesia, and Vietnam as economic and strategic assets; and Burma, Cambodia, Laos, and the Philippines as third-world clients. With all of them, China is granting greater market access and sustaining trade deficits (which have brought record profits to ASEAN businesses) in exchange for raw materials, defense agreements, and diplomatic pledges to lean its way.[4] Like Europeans in the Maghreb, Chinese baby-boomers are buying retirement properties from Penang to Bali, enlarging a greater Chinese co-prosperity sphere for the twenty-first century.

MALAYSIA: FRIENDS AND NEIGHBORS

There is no need to wait for the planned high-speed train connecting Singapore and Malaysia's capital, Kuala Lumpur, to see signs of the Singapore effect all the way up the country's tropical, clawlike peninsula. Driving north along Malaysia's national highway, palm oil and rubber plantations give way to industrialized zones, then signs appear for Putrajaya—the immaculately planned twin capital city—and Cyberjaya, part of the Multimedia Super Corridor that makes Kuala Lumpur East Asia's answer to Dubai, only with Singapore-quality planning. Both neocities are symbols of Asian risk-taking paying off, while the motorway on which they lie is supreme evidence of the centrality of infrastructure in connecting and building a first-world nation.

Malaysia has understood the physical side of development better than any other postcolonial country: Its currency notes even glorify trains and buildings more than individual leaders. Rather than allow its colonial infrastructure to decay like Egypt's, Malaysia's independence-era leaders capitalized on the inheritance of the British civil administration style (and athletic and leisure clubs). Singapore's example also showed Malaysia how to compete for global industry from aviation to port facilities. Putrajaya was built where plantations once stood, and it now produces textiles and other goods for Western markets. It has modern European architecture but in a distinctive Muslim style, with ornate mosques and bridges inspired by those in Iran. The national highway now stretches north all the way to Penang, which has also emerged as a high-tech hub.

There is no greater icon of Malaysia's success than Kuala Lumpur's Petronas towers, widely referred to as the "Twin Towers," until recently the tallest in the world. Their floor plans are based on Islamic geometry: an eight-pointed star symbolizing unity, harmony, stability, and rationality. One tower, occupied by the Petronas state oil company, stands for triumph over oil's corrosive effects on governance, while the other tower is occupied by multinational corporations. The double-decker sky bridge linking them forty-five stories above the ground signifies the bond between state-run companies and foreign capital—Asia's winning formula. "We are the only non-Western country not stricken by the oil curse," a Malaysian public relations executive proudly pointed out in his office with a view of the towers.* Though its oil boom began in the 1970s, it still diversified to refining and built a comparative advantage in electronics assembly, all the while exploiting but not eviscerating its massive timber and rubber resources. By keeping up with technology and wisely managing its reserves, Malaysia remains the only oil exporter in all of East Asia. Even when projected oil reserves run dry over the next two decades, it will still have massive deposits of natural gas. Urban-rural inequality and weak primary education have kept it from attaining the level of South Korea, but the highest share of its massive long-term budget is devoted to education, pushing the country to compete more actively in both the manufacturing and knowledge economies. The former spice route sultanate of Malacca now blends Portuguese colonial architecture with computer assembly plants, while Kuala Lumpur resi-

---

*Another is tiny Brunei, the Qatar of Southeast Asia, which lies safely ensconced between Malaysia's provinces of Sarawak and Sabah on the island of Borneo.

dents can purchase gourmet foods at Carrefour, the paragon brand of first-world grocery shopping.

Leadership can make much of the difference anywhere in the world, and while Venezuelans are stuck with Hugo Chávez, Malaysians had Mahathir bin Mohamad. Mahathir and his advisers were convinced that globalization was dangerous unless it was steered. During the Asian financial crisis, they bucked the international strictures that ravaged the Thai and Indonesian economies, instead imposing capital controls to keep the Malay ringgit afloat. As second-world leaders increasingly realize that globalization requires strong management to avoid uncontrollably exacerbating existing disparities, they are more likely to emulate Malaysia than Argentina.

"Dr. M," as Mahathir's supporters call him, is a Muslim Lee Kuan Yew, second only to Lee as a defender of Asian values, who argues that there are common virtues between Islam and Confucianism, such as reciprocity and loyalty. "Westerners believe that economic growth automatically means cultural liberalization, but Malaysia will prove there is an Asian path," claimed a Muslim scholar at the Masjid Negara (national mosque). Given the distance Islam has traveled over the centuries—Muslim missionaries and Arab traders reached all the way to the Philippines by the thirteenth century—Mahathir's analogy likening it to the children's game of whispering around a circle is appropriate: What the first person says and the last person hears can be completely different. Rather than engage in sinister doctrinal infighting over the will of the *Ulama,* Mahathir and his successor, Abdullah Badawi, realized that countries on the periphery of the Islamic world have always had to adapt to settings more ethnically heterogeneous than that of Arabs, thus dogmatism would be destructive. Malaysian euphoria over Islamic revolution withered as Iran sank; viewing the Islamic modernism of the Gulf as materialistic and corrosive, they invented *Islam Hadhari* ("Civilizational Islam"), which emphasizes social development, just leadership, moral integrity, personal freedom, environmental protection, and scientific education. They allow groups such as the Sisters of Islam to rail against conservative Islamic strictures by which women are deemed submissive and obedient, arguing that Islam promises gender equality and Malaysia must deliver it to be a respectable society. Malaysia thus presents itself as a mellow alternative to Saudi Arabia for Muslim education as well as a sharia-compliant venue for wealthy Arabs. Its pragmatic approach to Islamic leadership is most visible in the Organization of the Islamic Conference (OIC), which Malaysia is steering away from ideological diatribes and toward common trade projects and investments, and the use of *zakat* as a vehicle for poverty alleviation within the Muslim world.[5] "There can be Muslim geopolitical views," the scholar continued, "so long as they are led by us and not the Gulfies."

"If anything, Malaysia has become more Muslim rather than less, despite our economic growth," an indigenous Malay academic pointed out. With most of the world's Muslims residing in Asia rather than the Arab world, Malaysia's success in modernizing without sacrificing Islam makes it a pivotal Asian bulwark against the fundamentalist forces emanating from the west. Like Jordan, Malaysia is open and tolerant but conservative. Its success derives from the separation of mosque and state, the latter consulting the former without being dictated by it. Sharia trumps constitutional law for the majority Muslim population, while a secular legal system working in parallel exists for other groups, such as Chinese and Indians. Since Malaysia's indigenous population growth is far greater than that of the local Chinese population, its continued success cannot be attributed solely to the Confucian ethic of the minority Chinese population. But many Malay Muslims are being lured by the second wave of Arabian Islam—seven centuries after the first—visible in the increase in head scarves around the country. Where divorce via text-messaging was once allowed, it has now been banned. Sharia councils wield increasing power, and sharia police have even raided Zouk, Kuala Lumpur's most popular nightclub.

Anwar Ibrahim, a pioneer of Islamist politics and a former deputy prime minister, still believes that Islam can be a purifier against corruption in government, agitating the way the Muslim Brotherhood does in Egypt. "Islam will not be sacrificed in the name of democracy," he insisted. "The impunities of Asian values must end for success to continue." Malay politics have become more transparent, but not more open. Periodic multiparty elections give opposition parties a chance to win seats, but the dominant Barisan Nasional Party maintains a built-in advantage. For his part, Mahathir seems to appreciate democracy slightly more since retiring to become chairman of Petronas, the epicenter of the business-politics nexus. Ironically, he now attacks his successor, Badawi, for not giving greater voice to the opposition and not taking responsibility for awarding contracts and influential postings to his relatives.

But Mahathir never believed that democracy was worth the price of destabilizing the country's fragile ethnic balance, and most Malays agree, becoming more supportive of a strong state even as they become wealthier.[6] Malaysia is a case of interracial tolerance—but not necessarily harmony—underpinned by economic growth. Colonialism brought many Indians and Chinese to the peninsula, and Malaysia has managed to maintain stability despite its 50 percent Malay, 40 percent Chinese, and 10 percent Indian mix. (Mahathir's ancestors hail from the Indian state of Kerala, while Badawi's are Arab mixed with Chinese from Yunnan province.) Chinese and Indians were granted citizenship at independence, and efforts were made to unite non-Chinese Malays to avoid domination by the mostly urban Chinese—hence the expulsion of Singapore in 1965.

Asian values, Islam, and democracy are all stirring together in the Malaysian pot, but without yet coming to a boil. "Many wonder if an economic crisis would precipitate ethnic violence as it did in 1969, but we would rather achieve income equality than test the notion," remarked a conservative politician privately. Like South Africa, Malaysia has a unique affirmative action scheme for its majority Malay population—referred to as the Bumiputra ("sons of the soil")—which has created a stable middle class by providing low-interest loans to companies they own. The tension between ethnic Malays and the powerful Chinese population is nearly invisible, but it is still palpable. V. S. Naipaul compared the presence of the Chinese in Malaysia to injecting a 220-volt current into a country equipped for 110 volts only. For the Chinese, a garden is a commercial plot, while for Malays it is part of the home and the earth.[7] Today some joke that "if the Chinese became Muslim, the Malay would convert to Buddhism."

Nonetheless, as a former official whispered in his humble home office, "We won't admit it, but without the Chinese we might still be an economic backwater." Despite Mahathir's tough pro-Malay stance, his closest business associates are Chinese. He even created a special economic zone off the coast of Borneo to lure Chinese investment, cleverly attracting their funds while limiting their control. China's growing ties with Malaysia test the proverb that "a close neighbor is more important than a distant relative." Over the centuries, Chinese migrants have clus-tered around Kuala Lumpur and Penang, the former still very much a Chinese city with Chinese architecture and a lively annual Chinese pa-rade. Yet despite the overseas Chinese dominance of the economy—which has earned them the label "Jews of Asia"—Malaysians perceive no strategic threat from China. Malaysia was the first country in the region to establish relations with China in 1974. Malaysian exports of gas, palm oil, and electronics to China have boomed, accelerating China's program of catching up to Malaysia's other top trade partners, Japan and the United States. Like South Korea, much of Malaysia's economy is now moving in tandem with China's. In exchange, Malaysians have been given preferential access in China and are allowed to fully own real es-tate and even more sensitive investments like power plants. Petronas and various Malaysian timber companies hide behind Chinese state-run firms in their global resource hunt from Libya and Sudan to Indonesia.

"We have long viewed the U.S. as a comfort power," one Malaysian strategist explained of the country's strong military and naval coopera-tion with America. Precisely because U.S.-Malaysian relations have been close, Mahathir's anti-American potshots have been tolerated, for instance his argument that America cannot lead a "war on terror" against Islamist fundamentalism when it is not itself a Muslim country. Malaysia even convened a mock war crimes tribunal to shame Amer-ican leaders for the suffering of Iraqis and Palestinians. But like some other Muslim oil-producing states (Saudi Arabia, Libya, and Kazakh-stan), Malaysia has craftily mastered the art of multi-alignment, be-coming good friends with everyone. And like South Korea, Australia, Thailand, and India, Malaysia quietly assures the United States that it is on the U.S. side while not doing anything to offend China, effec-tively recusing itself from their rivalry by pledging to remain neutral if "the elephants wrestle."

INDONESIA: LESS IS MORE

Indonesia is perpetually under attack by both nature and man. It is prone to volcanic eruptions, earthquakes, tsunamis, infectious dis-eases, financial crises, and ethnic strife—and it is powerless against all of them. It is not a failed state, but it is perpetually at risk of becoming one with the next seismic shift in the earth or in the markets. In early 2007, Jakarta seemed to all but disappear in a torrential flood that displaced much of its population, swept away thousands of homes, and caused mass illness. It is a miracle that Indonesia exists at all, and it will be a greater miracle if it survives in its present form.

The Indonesian subsystem of islands is Southeast Asia's shield to the outside world. When imperial Japan occupied Indonesia during World War II, it freed imprisoned guerrilla leader Sukarno, who unleashed an independence struggle against Dutch colonizers and forced their surrender and eviction. But aside from its recognition under international law, Indonesia appears to have little right to exist as a sovereign state: An archipelago of some fourteen thousand islands stretching from Malaysia to the Philippines is impossible to govern, by either dictatorship or democracy.

Jakarta's armored ministries are the most visible symbol of a military-government nexus that acts as a postcolonial colonizer in its own country. For decades, the strongman Suharto and his nonaligned "New Order" regime focused more on profiteering than sovereignty, placing his children at the helm of numerous military-commercial monopolies. With only 12 percent of the country's budget derived from tax revenue, the military's for-profit ventures (comprised of some fifteen hundred companies) operate with impunity across Indonesia's semi-autonomous regions.[8] Unlike in Thailand, where military rule brought limited modernization and a strong state, since Indonesia's independence the military has been so preoccupied with maintaining its economic stakes that stable civilian government has been an afterthought. It has been difficult enough to remove the military from leadership; extracting it from the country's real estate, timber, and mining industries, to name a few, has proven impossible—not that it has really been tried.

With its vast geography and the world's fourth-largest population, over two hundred million, Indonesia has frequently inspired the epithet "sleeping giant." But while it sleeps, it is being hacked to pieces. The country is actually a sprawling waterborne golf course in which a mix of foreign companies and countries claim ownership of different holes. Where the interests of energy companies overlap with the state, Indonesia appears to work well. Samarinda, the capital of East Kalimantan province, on Borneo, has smooth roads and Western-style suburbs for international oil workers. Further from the center, however, exploitation of resources (and of minority populations) is far more the norm. In Papua province (former Irian Jaya), mining companies have colluded with the Indonesian military, resulting in massive river pollution and human rights violations. In 1997, brush-fire land clearing on Sumatra created a haze so vast and toxic (covering Malaysia, Papua New Guinea, and even parts of Australia) that the Malaysian government declared a state of emergency and asked clerics to pray for rain as thousands of infants asphyxiated and $10 billion in revenue was lost.

The government's constant gerrymandering and tweaking of provinces' status aim to sap the strength of autonomy movements while military-corporate fiefdoms continue to divide and rule. The parceling out of resource control to former military officers only accelerates the plunder of forests and fisheries among Chinese, Malaysian, American, and military-owned companies. But the more the center hordes economic benefits at the expense of the periphery, the more the periphery wants to secede. The independence of East Timor in 1999, growing autonomy for Aceh and Papua provinces, and the loss of two islands to Malaysia in a legal dispute are all indications that Indonesia may not last in its current form. Economically, ethnically, and religiously, Indonesia's main island clusters are already gravitating toward more stable kin: Sumatra, West Kalimantan, and even western parts of Java increasingly fall within prosperous Malaysia's sphere of influence; Christian-populated Sulawesi identifies more with the Philippines; and failing eastern provinces such as Papua may go the way of Melanesian cousin Papua New Guinea, managed more by Australia than Indonesia.* Singapore all but owns Bintan Island already, operating resorts while taking mountain soil for its own land reclamation.

"We're becoming like the Philippines," a Jakarta businessman observed derisively from the safety of his high-rise office. "Poorer and less stable each year." Failure hurts that much more when success has been close enough to taste. Toynbee described Sumatra as an "island of hope" where "oil, soil, and toil" would lift the country.[9] But Indonesia remains a perpetual "nation in waiting," suffering from the same missed opportunities today as in the 1960s.[10] Suharto oversaw three

---

*Indonesian Papua and Papua New Guinea are separated by perhaps the world's most artificial border, a vertical line through a dense jungle that nobody patrols. East Timor, now an independent country, will also remain a third-world speck on the map unless Australia fairly shares the oil fields lying between them.

decades of liberalization and regional fence mending, but, never learning that bigger does not always equal better, he frequently conde-
scended to tiny Singapore—until the 1997 financial crisis crippled
Indonesia and forced him to accept massive loans from it.

Suharto also had no choice but to turn to Islamist groups to fulfill
basic functions. For 350 years, Dutch colonizers were unable to penetrate Indonesia's milieu of cultures in which Christianity, Buddhism,
Hinduism, and Islam coexisted across disparate geography. Ancient
kingdoms in Java, Thailand, Malaya, and Cambodia derived their religions from India, a heritage that produced intricate monuments of
Hindu-Buddhist spirituality such as the giant temple and stupas of
Borobudur. "Scratch an Indonesian and find a Hindu," it was once
said. Indonesia's national symbol and airline, Garuda, is named for the
Hindu deity Vishnu's winged steed.

But missionaries cease their work at neither political nor spiritual
shores. As V. S. Naipaul argued in *Beyond Belief*, Islam is an Arab faith
and thus makes Arab-like social demands on its believers, crushing plu-
ralist histories and using modern technology to replace both local culture
and national identity with Islam. Many Indonesians now say that while
their brains looks east, their hearts looks west, to Mecca. Indonesia's
inner weaknesses make its massive Muslim population fertile ground for
globalized, radical Islam. While Malaysia receives Muslim investments,
tourists, and students, Indonesia is being turned into a "Jihad archipelago" by the nexus of Arab and domestic extremist groups, affording ex-
combatants from Afghanistan an anonymous space in which to plot and
conduct attacks against Western corporations and embassies.[11] Young
Arab Islamists have fanned out across Indonesia and Thailand preying
on impressionable, ignorant, and unemployed youth, recruiting them as
foot soldiers for Islamist armies such as Abu Sayyaf or the Moro National Liberation Front in the Philippines and inciting Muslim-Christian
violence in Sulawesi province. "Malaysians contribute bomb-making
skills, Thais and Filipinos do the smuggling, and Indonesians are the suicide bombers," a local analyst of fundamentalist movements explained.
In the close to fourteen thousand *pesantren* schools and mosques sponsored by the fundamentalist Jamaat Islamiyya, which are similar to the
madrasahs in Pakistan, students are taught they are good Muslims because they learn Arabic and memorize verses of the Koran.

In the Islamic world, wherever there is top-down corruption, one can expect bottom-up Islamicization. A corrupt state and economy with mass marginalization gives jihad the luster of a progressive force to salvage the relevance of the individual. "Islamist networks provide much of what the government should," an Islamic scholar turned politician pointed out. Like the Muslim Brotherhood in Egypt or the AKP in Turkey, Indonesia's Islamists live modestly, take little pay, and campaign on anticorruption platforms. Though they have faired poorly in national elections, they are achieving in substance what their election would only codify legally. In over a dozen districts across Indonesia, Muslim activist groups have pushed to ban alcohol and prostitution, require proof of ability to read the Koran before marriage or entering university, force female public servants to wear the *hijab*, forbid the holding of hands in public, and—in the same month that an Indonesian edition of *Playboy* magazine was released—declare pornographic the exhibiting of the female navel in public, which would make even traditional Indonesian dances difficult to execute. If shariatization continues across Indonesia, only the Hindu island of Bali, with its Australian hippie colony, could remain as a liberal bastion—but not necessarily a safe one given the major suicide bombings at nightclubs there in 2002 and 2005.

Indonesia's liberals are too removed from grassroots activism either to reassert Indonesia's indigenous, syncretic Islam or to foster alternatives such as teaching English. Educated abroad with jobs in Singapore, they live like globalized separatists in air-conditioned Jakarta villas. The remaining forces for moderation—and the most likely to succeed—are Islamists themselves. If Islamist fundamentalism is a virus, then the antibiotic must contain a small amount of it in order to help the body build up resistance. Indonesia is home to the world's two largest Muslim organizations: Nadhlatul Ulama and Muhammadiyah, today the country's most credible voices against shariatization. They argue for the preservation of the secular state because if unqualified state courts were to impose sharia, Islam would lose its divine character. "Our peasantry has been seduced by ideologies from communism to radical Islamism, so different from our traditions that they are entirely new religions," fretted an Islamist working within the government.

As Indonesia's national identity withers, its democracy becomes ever more like a car losing parts on a bumpy road. Indonesian leaders would like to brand the country as a synthetic center for democracy and Islamic discourse, but it's hardly clear that Indonesia's brand of these virtues is worth having. Since Suharto's 1998 ouster, corruption, income disparity, ethno-religious divides, and secessionist violence have all increased.[12] His handpicked successor, B. J. Habibie, was a clueless cleric whose referendum on East Timor resulted in its independence and his own impeachment. Political drift continued under Sukarno's daughter Megawati Sukarnoputri: The more powerful Islamist parties become, the more scared the rest get. The price of Indonesian democracy is unity, as near-total autonomy bordering on self-rule has become the model of choice for many provinces. Even mainstream Indonesians now clamor for real leadership, demanding a Lee Kuan Yew or Mahathir figure to restore unity and dignity. Short of this, Indonesia may very well continue to splinter in everything but name, a victim of its status as the most far-flung and ethnically unnatural state in the world. All that may be left of national substance would be the island of Java, where 70 percent of the population resides (including the dominant ethnic Javanese), with Jakarta as its capital.

The unsightly obelisks commemorating independence cannot mask Jakarta's reality that its continued functionality is owed to its new colonizers: the Chinese. Indonesia's relations with China are primordial, a perpetual dance of love and hate, life and death. During the Dutch East Indies era, Chinese workers arrived en masse to toil on sugar plantations. From the start, they had to be crafty to mitigate anti-Chinese sentiment, bribing politicians to set up "Ali Baba" companies in which Indonesians stood up front and Chinese ran things behind the scenes.* Indonesia's 1965 coup was actually anti-Chinese, for China had provided weapons to the Indonesian Communist Party. Five hundred thousand Chinese were expelled and returned to the mainland, many of whom had never even been there before. The small Chinese population, which controls 70 percent of Indonesia's economy, would have long ago been wiped out if the country had been a democ-

---

*Toynbee best captured this persistent reality of non-Chinese unable to run economies on their own wits: "The Chinese shopkeeper perpetually advances without ever receding. . . . [They] are no swashbucklers. They live on the defensive, behind iron shutters and bars, in 'China towns' that are the counter-parts of the ghettos of medieval Western Christendom. They are in constant fear of frantic reprisals on the part of the economically incompetent South-East Asia peoples whom they serve and at the same time exploit. . . . Neither pogroms nor discriminatory legislation can halt the flow of this gentle but persistent Chinese flood. . . . European empire-builders and Japanese conquerors and South-East Asian nationalists alike, we have all been working, in spite of ourselves, to further the interests of the insinuating Chinese huckster." Toynbee, *East to West*, 48, 58.

racy.[13] But Suharto remained cozy with the Chinese, whose superior business instincts and conglomerates built most of the banks that today make up Jakarta's impressive skyline—a vista designed very much to remind people of Singapore. Even after violent pogroms in 1998, during which Jakarta's Chinatown was torched out of existence and thousands of Chinese were brutally killed, intra-Chinese banking networks bailed out Chinese businesses—after which they shifted trillions of rupiah to Singapore. Still, absent Chinese wealth Indonesia would be completely third-world.

Given this precarious existence, it is no surprise that the overseas Chinese in Indonesia have been more loyal to China than to their adopted home. After the 1998 riots, China forcefully demanded that the government protect its Chinese minority. Yet because there is no more Chinatown in Jakarta, the Chinese are blending in more than ever. "The young generation of Chinese is much more humble about their wealth," one of them revealed, himself a successful businessman. "They drive Japanese rather than German cars." The requirement to mark Chinese origin on passports has been dropped, and as they grow to 8 percent of the population (making them the fourth-largest minority), civil rights groups have come to the aid of Chinese who seek citizenship. There has also been an awakening to China's economic and cultural importance, with far more Indonesian students now studying in China than in the United States.

Indonesia is gradually becoming China's chain-link buffer—the role Japan intended for the archipelago in World War II. The narrow window during which America temporarily suspended defense cooperation with Indonesia due to human rights concerns was precisely the moment at which Chinese defense agreements with Indonesia surged, making it a Chinese reef along China's expanding naval perimeter. China and Japan are the primary users of the Straits of Malacca, the busiest choke point (just a bit wider than a mile at its narrowest point) between major ports, with half the global flow of oil and one-third of other global trade passing through each year.[14] Regional initiatives to protect transiting vessels from piracy and terrorism have gradually elbowed out American proposals to increase its own patrols—which are viewed not only as clogging the straits but also as presenting provocative targets in their own right. Using sophisticated Japanese navigational technology, Singapore, Malaysia, and Indonesia now patrol the straits themselves, and the new International Maritime Organization based in Kuala Lumpur monitors and reports on suspicious activity in the area—all without American intervention.

"The benevolent American response to the [2004] tsunami was crucial for us," an Indonesian diplomat explained over breakfast in Jakarta's stately Borobudur Hotel. "But the goodwill was short-lived because aid is short-term and our people perceive America's policies as anti-Muslim." China is also replacing declining American investment in Indonesia, pumping a projected $30 billion into its extractive industries over the coming decade as it pumps oil and gas (and coal and timber) out of the country. As in Russia's Far East, Chinese front companies have raped the forests of Borneo and Kalimantan, which have half-disappeared.[15] Indonesia's very ecosystem is now threatened, home to the highest number of endangered species following Brazil. But unlike Brazil, environmental consciousness and enforcement lag far behind ecological depletion. Even as the United States, the EU, Japan, and Australia invest in Indonesian agriculture, support peaceful Islamist institutions, train the police force, and push their own companies to practice corporate citizenship (by paying higher wages and providing health benefits for workers), it still may not be enough to keep Indonesia a stable constellation of islands rather than a fractured belt of comets orbiting China.

CHAPTER 30

MYANMAR, THAILAND, AND VIETNAM:

THE INNER TRIANGLE

ALONGSIDE CHINA'S SEDUCTION of first-world Japan, South Korea, Australia, and Singapore, neutralization of populous rival India, and co-optation of geographically strategic Malaysia and Indonesia, its expansionist project in the Asian pan-region continues with the former British and French colonies of Indochina, once crucial sources of wealth for Europe. The region's endowments once moved east to west across the oceans to Europe; now they move south to north, into China. In third-world Cambodia and Laos, volumes of unconditional Chinese aid have quickly displaced the trickles of Western assistance and the democratization pressures that came with them, easily winning over their wayward regimes.[1] While China practices checkbook diplomacy, America is seen as being overly focused on ancillary issues such as military reform and counterterrorism. Chinese slash-and-burn logging in Cambodian collusion with the Cambodian military has led to extensive farmland loss, soil erosion, diminished water quality, and a potential food crisis. But low-cost Chinese goods such as cell phones flood local markets as well, allowing a growing number of people to enjoy middle-class comforts. "China's strategy is to build economic bonds that can withstand even tumultuous leadership transitions," a regional analyst based in Bangkok explained. "It does not matter who is in power, China will do business with them."

BURMESE DAYS (ARE NUMBERED)

Burma (renamed Myanmar by its reigning junta regime) has been an isolated, antiquated, and underdeveloped society for decades, but its location on the Bay of Bengal makes it a crucial strategic littoral for China to circumvent the Straits of Malacca. Since 1988, the military-corporatist clique known as the State Law and Order Restoration Council (SLORC) has turned the country's British and then Japanese colonial order into the world's only militant Buddhist state. In 1997, the junta renamed itself the State Peace and Development Council; a decade later, it is hard to tell the difference. In 2007 it unveiled a new capital city halfway between Yangon and Mandalay, allegedly to mark the establishment of its dynasty, as past Burmese kings have done, and yet suffered crippling protests by thousands of monks and citizens due to its absurd economic policy. The SLORC sustains its rule by fueling perceptions of an ongoing external threat, yet the principal threat to Burma's autonomy comes from China, the power the regime welcomes most.

Like Sudan and Uzbekistan, Burma's diplomatic isolation makes it a willing Chinese client state. Drug production and trafficking earn the SLORC hard currency to buy Chinese military hardware, yet what Burma gets in return is not just Chinese diplomatic support but also the Chinese themselves. In the late 1950s, Toynbee described Burma as a "population vacuum next door to China which cries out to be filled."[2] The untracked seasonal migrations of Chinese into northern Burma via the road, rail, and river channels of the Irrawaddy Corridor have created a minority (in many cases with historical family links) that will be able to make legal claims to rights beyond residency. Intermarriage and Chinese land acquisition have resulted in entire villages in Burma's north becoming Chinese-populated, with all signs in Chinese. In Mandalay, Chinese firms build large, bland hotels—not to prepare for Burma's opening to the world, but for Chinese visitors, whose numbers show no sign of ebbing.[3] Some already refer to Burma as "Yunnan South" after the once restive southern Chinese province on the Burmese border. Burma is an integral part of China's strategy to help its third-world interior regions such as Yunnan catch up with the booming coast. As part of this strategy, China has virtually economically annexed its southern neighbor. China has bought up most of Burma's timber and pillaged its forests, purchased and plundered its gem deposits, and plans to acquire 6.5 trillion cubic feet of Burmese natural gas over the next thirty years, much of it pumped via pipeline from Sitwe to Yunnan. The border between China and Burma hasn't changed, and no shots have been fired, but Burma has all but become a Chinese province.[4]

China has easily outmaneuvered ASEAN's pressure on the junta in Burma, which is still a fellow member, and thwarted U.S. and EU sanctions as well. China could potentially suffer blowback in Burma, however. If China doesn't do more to benefit the Burmese themselves, rising resentment could lead even the heartless junta to construe China as a threat rather than a lifeline. Always traveling in tandem, drugs and disease also flow in greater volumes from Afghanistan through China into the Golden Triangle and back, spreading addiction and AIDS. Southeast Asian youth are now hooked on *yaba,* a drug that keeps them perpetually alert. The highest AIDS infection rates are also in Thailand, Cambodia, and Burma, the same countries that export the most sex workers to China and elsewhere. For organized smugglers, people and drugs are equally lucrative commodities, and China is no more capable of policing its vast borders than Europe or the United States are. Finally, as if the region's dissipated civil wars did not leave enough small arms, China makes sure there remain enough weapons and ammunition for any criminal or insurgent cause that should arise—guns and grenades that could eventually find their way back onto Chinese streets.

As the source of both South and Southeast Asia's major river systems, China has the luxury of damming the mighty Mekong River for hydroelectric power generation while using it to transport goods downstream to the five hundred million Southeast Asians whose livelihoods depend on its flows. Though Chinese dams dramatically affect the Mekong's and its tributaries' water levels in Burma, Thailand, Laos, Cambodia, and Vietnam, China accepts no criticism for its manipulation of the river.[5] What remains of the Mekong when it reaches Laos allows for a small dam to generate electricity, which is then sold to Thailand for cash. For the people of Indochina's third-world nations like Burma, being downstream from China doesn't make life any easier.

THAILAND: SMILING NORTH

For second-world countries, diplomatic prowess lies in both fending off *and* maximizing benefit from superpowers, an art that the kingdom of Thailand has mastered over centuries of avoiding colonization. Toynbee explained that Thailand was spared devastation in World War II by luck of geography as a "buffer state between the British dominions in India and Burma and the French dominions in Indochina."[6] What saved the "land of smiles" was its monarchy, aristocracy, and military's strategy of smiling in all directions while "bending with the wind."[7] Fearing the Chinese after the 1949 civil war, it took huge amounts of military aid from the United States and served in the 1960s as a staging area for the Vietnam War. Quickly adjusting to America's diminished standing after the war, Thailand immediately normalized relations with China in 1975, creating a strategic partnership to contain North Vietnam.[8] As a reward, China sold oil to Thailand at reduced "friendship prices" after OPEC's price hikes.

U.S.-Thai friendship goes back two centuries to King Rama IV's offer of elephants to Abraham Lincoln for use in the Civil War, and the U.S. embassy in Bangkok is America's second-largest in the world, behind only Baghdad. But already in 1994, Thailand turned down a U.S. request to station six military ships in Thailand's ports, a decision backed by Malaysia and Indonesia. Complaints have steadily mounted on the economic front as well. Thailand was deeply insulted at not being bailed out by the United States during its 1997 currency crisis, just three years after the United States had rescued Mexico. The reason given was that Thailand was not America's border.

At the same time, Thailand is bending with the Chinese wind more than ever. "Because job creation and stability are our citizens' top priorities, we will respond to the best economic and political package offered," a Thai diplomat in Bangkok explained. During the 1997 financial crisis, Western institutions forced a selloff of assets, which Westerners bought at rock-bottom prices while the economy collapsed and poverty rose. By contrast, China delivered rapid tariff reduction under its "Early Harvest" program, hugely boosting its image as a benevolent power. In the decade since, Sino-Thai trade has nearly caught up to U.S.-Thai levels, and Chinese tourists now outnumber American tourists. Thanks to a major artery cut through Laos, China and Thailand now virtually border each other, and Thailand has become a leading re-exporter of Chinese goods.

In Thailand, China is embarking on a project so ambitious that it alters geography itself: It is carving a deep canal across Thailand's narrow Kra Isthmus.[9] The canal would give Thailand strategic port facilities of its own to rival those of Singapore (which vehemently opposes the project), while Malaysia's ports of Langkawi and Penang would also benefit greatly as logistics depots for canal users. Were it not for the Malay Muslim insurgency in southern Thailand—three small provinces that would be cut off by the canal from the country's torso—the project would already have begun.

Remapping Sino-Thai relations is not merely a geographic and economic affair but also a profoundly cultural and psychological one. As elsewhere in East Asia, the Chinese diaspora in Thailand operates provincial commercial centers from coastal Phuket to interior Maha Sarakham, and China considers Thailand's assimilation of its large Chinese population the model for other nations to follow. Since the nineteenth century, the Chinese population in Thailand have been key drivers of financial institutions, protected by the military in exchange for banking services.[10] By 1850, half of Bangkok's population was Chinese, submissive to the Thai royal family but also intermarried with it. Even in the era when Westerners controlled the companies, it was the Chinese whose intimate knowledge of Thai culture and customs kept business moving.[11] Today the Chinese have it both ways, controlling Thailand's key rice, timber, and tin exports. Chinese and Thai businessmen don't just cooperate, they bond, declaring that they are "none other than brothers."[12] "The Chinese are rewriting history here, framing the diaspora as a part of the Greater China," explained a Thai cultural historian. Reminiscent of the ages when Thai monarchs paid tribute to imperial China, the Thai royal family frequently visits Beijing, as did Thailand's former prime minister Thaksin Shinawatra, who actually *is* Chinese and publicly displays Chinese ancestral pride. Thaksin once opined that "democracy is just a tool. . . . The goal is to give people a good lifestyle, happiness, and national progress."[13] That his overly illiberal ways led to his ouster in a 2006 military coup hardly bothers China, however, whose arms sales and contacts with the Thai military have boomed in recent years. Thailand is smiling north more than ever.

VIETNAM: A NEW TUG OF WAR

America's two wars in East Asia—Korea and Vietnam—have been stalemates at best. The United States failed to become a land power in mainland Southeast Asia precisely because it was ousted by the North Vietnamese and held below the 38th parallel by the North Koreans— both backed by China. As with North Korea, China still believes that Vietnam falls within its civilizational boundaries, and many wealthy Chinese live in stately homes in the more developed south of the country. However, from the fifteenth century until their violent border clashes in 1979, Vietnam remains the only country China has invaded yet failed to conquer. But having lost its Soviet patron, Vietnam had no choice but to open its heavily mined border with China in 1988, signaling a modern resumption of the tribute-and-emissary pattern of Sino-Vietnamese relations in the globalization era.

"Vietnam remains staunchly anticolonial, but certainly not anticapitalist," summed up a Vietnamese political analyst on a sweltering day in Hanoi. Most Vietnamese have a charming innocence about globalization, unaware that what is happening to them is occurring all over the world as well, with uncertain consequences. And yet, many believe that they stand the best chance among their second-world peers of capitalizing on it. "The smart money is on Vietnam," a Chinese-American regional financial analyst in Hong Kong predicted. "It's like a miniature of China: communism, agriculture, and industry. And with their discipline they'll sail past Thailand and Indonesia." As manufacturing costs in coastal China rise, Japan and China have become massive investors in Vietnam, helping to southernize the country's rural north by building factories and importing modern tractors to boost rice and coffee exports, all of which is rapidly raising its per capita income. With one of the world's fastest-growing economies, it now uses more cement annually than its former colonial master France. Vietnam's California-length coastline of deep harbors makes it the future gateway for regional maritime exports, while its California-based diaspora plays an increasingly active role as educators and managers.[14] Hanoi today roars with motorcycles driven by a generation of eager youth born after the "American War," while along the city's quaint lakes, healthy retirees sip tea and play badminton.

Vietnam's regime clearly favors the China model of centralized political control while liberalizing the economy, even as it is concerned about the consequences: inequality, corruption, and demands for transparency and freedom. But despite their similarities, Vietnam shows no desire to be absorbed into the region's Sinocentric order, ironically reaching out to the United States to prevent this fate. American military contractors are selling the country hardware and satellites, while Intel's microchip plant has graduated Vietnam from shoe manufacturing to the high-tech arena. While the waxy, embalmed body of triumphant "Uncle Ho" Chi Minh still inspires awe in his grand Hanoi mausoleum, Uncle Sam has been invited back by both the economic and defense establishments.

Though it is much harder to draw lines in water than in sand, the South China Sea is a tripwire for exposing any Chinese transgressions toward its maritime neighbors—but also the best venue to witness China's maritime "smile diplomacy" at work. The potentially oil-rich Spratly and Paracel island clusters are claimed in whole or part by Taiwan, Vietnam, Malaysia, Indonesia, and the Philippines. The last three decades of the twentieth century witnessed many militarized reconnaissance incidents, naval skirmishes, oil rig installations, and flag plantings, all meant to assert Chinese sovereignty over the appropriately named Mischief Reef, after which China realized it would benefit more from calming the waters than making waves.[15] "China knows it can't seize the islands outright," the political analyst explained. "Instead it wants to become the trusted mediator while gaining the most usage of the sea." China signed an ASEAN code of conduct agreement aimed at peacefully settling the disputed islands' status, and Chinese, Philippine, and Vietnamese oil companies now jointly explore their hydrocarbon resources in the area, with China sweetening the deal through promises of greater investment in each country. China may never conquer Vietnam or vanquish its neighbors in the South China Sea, but it is learning how to get what it wants without having to.

THE INNER TRIANGLE   299

THE OCEANIC PERIPHERY

Just as underdeveloped Asian countries are straining to meet
the needs of growing populations, China's ravenous appetite for
their resources is cresting. China's conversion of arable land
into urban factory terrain has led to a premodern twist on outsourcing whereby it has literally off-shored substantial agricultural production to the Philippines, where the Chinese minority
controls much of the economy. If Indonesia is turning into a
Chinese reef, then the Philippines is becoming a Chinese rice
paddy.

Beyond Indonesia and the Philippines, Oceania is the second ring in China's strategy both to acquire resources and to
build friendly relations to support its eventual blue-water navy.
But China does not have to conquer weak island nations in the
Pacific—it buys them. Evading foreign investment restrictions
is no problem for Chinese state companies, which rather than
seeking to *own* the means of production, distribution, and exchange (as Marx would dictate), simply maneuver to *control*
them through financing mine exploration and the supporting infrastructure of roads, railways, and vehicles. In Papua New
Guinea, China has drastically accelerated deforestation of the
virgin jungle, which at present rates of logging will be mostly
gone by 2030. Irrespective of which country's firms are doing
the logging, most of the logs still wind up in China, where they
are used for everything from cottages to chopsticks.

Targeting the same island clusters Japan did during World
War II—Melanesia (Papua New Guinea and the Solomon Islands, both traditionally tied to Australia), Polynesia (micro-
states historically linked to New Zealand), and Micronesia
(Pacific island nations allied with the United States)—China
has overtaken Japan as the largest aid donor as well.[16] On the
island of Kiribati it has built a satellite tracking facility to advance its space program. How much longer will America "rule
the waves"?

CHAPTER 31

SIZE MATTERS:

THE FOUR CHINAS

CHINA AND THE United States share an imperial geography of size, latitude, and spectacular topology: China's southern and central provinces are battered by seasonal cyclones and flooding, its northeast receives heavy snowfall, and its west is a moonlike landscape of deserts and mountains. In a pattern somewhat like that of the United States, China grew from a few clusters of city-states along the Yellow River into a continental-scale empire, which according to the Tang Dynasty credo could have a height as great as heaven and the width of the earth itself. Within their similar spaces, however, China has three times the population of Europe and five times the population of the United States, combining third-world feudalism, a massive industrial base, and a first-world elite. Dividing China into four quadrants, the southeast region contains 60 percent of China's wealth due to the economic roles of Taiwan, Hong Kong, and Shanghai and is almost equal in development with the United States and the EU. The northeast quadrant, including Beijing, has been lifted solidly out of the third world through rapid industrialization and impressive infrastructure construction. China's two western quadrants—including its interior provinces,

Tibet and Xinjiang—are still a vast third-world realm of natural resources and a peasantry of seven hundred million feeding the empire.
These quadrants of China, as well as its diaspora of fifty-five million
people, constitute the four Chinas merging into one massive second-
world superpower.

Millennia of Chinese history have been a virtually continuous
struggle to unite under a single order. Its self-feeding mix of despotism
and patriotism has retained a strong sense of anti-Western feeling as it
seeks to overcome the humiliating extraterritoriality imposed by the
British during the mid–nineteenth century Opium Wars and the additional resentment of German colonies being handed to Japan in the
post–World War I Versailles settlement.[1] Though the United States
never colonized China—at that time, the State Department did not
even have a Far East division—its Open Door policy was at best a half-
benevolent impulse, seeking equal rights for all foreign commercial
powers in China so as not to lose out in Europe's sphere-of-influence
game.[2]

The Chinese are not known for halfhearted effort, and the twentieth century was to a great extent the intensified search for a workable
economic system for such an unprecedentedly large population. Ideas
such as Marxism-Leninism took hold with the establishment of the
Communist Party in Shanghai in 1921, where the horrors of industrial
capitalism were most visible. The resulting socialist agricultural collectivization that accelerated with Communists' victory in the civil war
was truly revolutionary—as Mao famously articulated, "A revolution is
not a dinner party, nor a literary composition, nor a painting, nor a
piece of pretty embroidery; it cannot be carried out softly, gradually,
carefully, considerately, respectfully, politely, plainly, and modestly."*
In the name of modernization and the "victory of the world revolution,"
he was willing to sacrifice all three hundred million of China's population at the time. Ultimately, over seventy million perished due to the
Great Leap Forward, the Cultural Revolution, and constant internal
purges in which more people died of starvation and overwork than
were killed by Hitler and Stalin combined. Deng Xiaoping continued

---

*Mao also stated in 1949, "China has always been a great, courageous, and industrious nation; it is only in mod-
ern times that they have fallen behind. And that was due entirely to oppression and exploitation by foreign imperialism and domestic reactionary governments. . . . Ours will no longer be a nation subject to insult and
humiliation. We have stood up."

the focus on development as the vehicle for overcoming insecurity, launching the "four modernizations" of agriculture, industry, defense, and technology and initiating the internal reform and external opening necessary to achieve them.[3] But it is the current leadership's continuation of both experimental and accumulative development that assures China's rise out of the third world. The thirty-year period ending in 2010 is meant to be remembered as one in which China reclaimed territories wrongfully seized by the West, delivered massive economic growth and development, and had its greatness recognized by hosting the 2008 Summer Olympics.

Progress is a mechanical necessity for China's leaders, who are keenly aware of previous eras of superlative glory. China has always been "a civilization pretending to be a nation," wrote eminent scholar Lucian Pye.[4] Communism was merely a fleeting ambition, but it erased ethnic nationalisms and paved the way for a far grander and more intrinsic goal: recapturing a glorious past destroyed during the shameful humiliations of the nineteenth century. Having otherwise been the region's dominant empire, there is no trepidation about embarking on that path again; for China, it is simply back to the future. The latest planned date for China's superpower coming-out party is 2049—the centennial of its national unification. Empires begin with the self-belief in the right to rule, and restoring China's status as the Middle Kingdom has meant shifting from contentment with isolation to rebranding itself as a boundless civilization.

CONSTRUING A SUPERPOWER

If America is the greatest nation on earth, then someone forgot to tell the Chinese.

China is a universe unto itself, the world's widest and deepest self-contained cultural space, with its own literature, philosophies, and dramatic forms—and with a civilization's worth of TV channels to match. It has no need to import culture from anywhere, nor to translate itself for others. As has been the case for most of the past three thousand years, China today attracts streams of traders, emissaries, and scholars, once again becoming Asia's cultural magnet.[5] At the same time, it exports teachers and nannies and is establishing dozens of branches of the Confucius Institute around the world to promote Chinese culture. Chinese cinema, art, and traditional medicines have all gone global, as has Weiqi, also called Go, a game older than chess.

A thousand years ago, globalization had Chinese characteristics, for it was the printing press, gunpowder, and the compass that had spread from east to west. Today China portrays itself like a great merchant ship once again navigating globalization's waters—in marked contrast to an American aircraft carrier. The iconic inspiration for China's new image is Admiral Zheng He, whose seven naval voyages in the early fifteenth century dwarfed those of Columbus and Vasco da Gama, shuttling Ming Dynasty ambassadors as far as the east coast of Africa, seeding the Chinese diaspora from Malacca to Kenya, and returning with sulfur from Indonesia and spices from India's Malabar coast.[6] Were it not for Emperor Zhu Gaozhi's decision to ban costly foreign excursions, China could have become the greatest continental and maritime superpower of the age. Because Zheng's voyages were considered commercial and cultural, his story implies that China today is a peaceful and well-intentioned power; as Zheng was himself a Muslim who died after a pilgrimage to Mecca, he represents the cosmopolitan China. And as captain of the first major wave of Chinese immigrants to Southeast Asia, many temples still honor and commemorate his landing in Malaysia, Indonesia, and Thailand.

On closer examination, Zheng He's story opens a window to both the justified and the warped sides of Chinese nationalism. Fabrications of Chinese history have stepped up in recent years to bolster a Sinocentric view of East Asia. In a speech to the joint session of Australia's parliament in 2003, Chinese premier Hu Jintao apocryphally declared that Zheng He's voyages touched off centuries of Sino-Australian contact, a fiction that might later be used to justify dominance over Australia. Furthermore, Zheng was not merely an "ambassador of friendship" but was involved in wars from Java to Sri Lanka, at one point enslaving the latter's king. He not only set up bases on the Straits of Malacca but also collected massive tributes to the Ming from Burma and Yunnan and instigated brutal violence against resistance in Vietnam. As the example of Zheng He attests, China's ancient strategic culture integrally involves the use of force.[7]

The world is already watching Chinese politics and economics exactly as it watches America's or Europe's—and China has an equal ability to confound experts. It issues keenly scrutinized strategic doctrines and even publishes a human rights report that criticizes America's incarceration rate, income inequality, and violent crime. Attached to China's universities and ministries, official and semiofficial research institutes all contribute to China's global policy formulation. "With the collapse of the Soviet Academy of Social Sciences, the Chinese Academy of Social Sciences is by any measure the largest think tank in the world today," boasted a Beijing intellectual. Its internal debates about global integration and confrontation are as heated and controversial as those in Washington or Brussels—with an equally profound impact on global order.

Some believe that China's "peaceful rise" represents the birth of a "Beijing Consensus," a new logic of governance based on leveraging new technology, presciently preempting crises, and righteously elbowing its way to global status in the face of entrenched powers.[8] But what would a Beijing Consensus look like in practice if it were indeed the vision statement for a Chinese-led world order, an alternative to American "hegemonism"? The only doctrine to judge is Premier Hu Jintao's "Harmonious World," a statement that is at once bold and flawed, ambitious yet hollow. In the "Harmonious World" there is complete respect for national sovereignty—a principle that even most of the third world has guardedly abandoned as global threats become transnational and domestic conflicts spill over borders. For Hu, "multilateralism" does not connote collective problem-solving but is rather code for the "democratization of international relations" by which new powers rise to check the United States. Finally, the "Harmonious World" supports shared economic development, particularly through interregional trade.[9] China's multiplying projects and low-interest loans in Africa have undoubtedly become important for growth in many poor countries, but they have also advanced a Chinese mercantilism that could be environmentally devastating while perpetuating third-world resource dependency. It seems that a Chinese-led "Harmonious World" may not necessarily be a much better place.[10]

But the "Harmonious World" is as much for domestic as international consumption, meant to pacify a restless population through latent nationalism. Rather than using China's growing openness to sublimate the people's energy toward commerce, prosperity, and leisure, the government has amplified national pride (through images such as that of Zheng He) as a means to replace discredited communism and specifically steered nationalism in a particularly anti-American direction. Indeed, America ranks as the most disliked country in China year after year.[11]

For over a century Americans have been in China, first as missionaries, businesspeople, and oil drillers and now as students, scholars, diplomats, architects, and artists, while Chinese have become a major brain gain for the United States.[12] At the same time, Chinese spies in America steal billions of dollars' worth of secrets, while U.S. foundations sponsor advanced scientific research in China itself. "Without America, China would be many years behind where it is today," an American scholar who regularly visits China pointed out.

But the United States is also the only power capable of upsetting China's plans for restoring its undisputed greatness, so for many Chinese it is public enemy number one. Despite all the deferential rituals of diplomacy, American humiliations of China—covert support to the Tibetans (which ended in 1971), arms supplies to Taiwan, missile defense deployments, the 1991 bombing of the Chinese embassy in Belgrade, the 2001 EP-3 spy plane incident, and (according to its leaders) diminished status during state visits—all contribute to an apotheotic sense of rivalry.[13] Many Asians suspect that America actually *wants* to awaken the Chinese dragon. Thus when former U.S. defense secretary Donald Rumsfeld asked why China would spend so much on building its military when it faces no overt threat, he seemed to miss the point that America's military *is* the principle threat to China. Because it was the West that invaded China in the nineteenth century—not vice versa—China will not sacrifice armaments necessary for self-defense.[14] The process is interminable, however, because there is no military strong enough to defeat the United States directly. After its manned space flight missions and planned lunar landing, China's tightly interwoven civilian and military space programs could attempt to field space-based weapons capable of evading American missile defense systems—and have already proven their ability to shoot down orbiting satellites.[15] America's deflated credibility in the region means it can no longer accuse China of being at fault.[16]

The Chinese language has no tenses, heightening both the sense of the past and the timeless character of Chinese views and expressions.[17] Seeing itself as the guardian of the truth, compromises with other powers (such as its alliance with the Soviet Union) are considered tactical rather than acts of moral equivalency.[18] Similarly, China's recognition of America's superpower status in no way signals acceptance of the status quo. Is China's strategy to "hide its ambitions and disguise its claws," as Mao advised, until it reaches the "comprehensive national strength" it seeks?* Or will it remain true to the "peaceful rise" doctrine, commensurate with Sun Tzu's aphorism that counsels achieving victories without ever engaging in battle? China has already deployed and proliferated nuclear weapons, cruise missiles, drones, satellites, and other technologies to raise the cost of America's regional military presence—without ever actually attacking it.† At the same time, as China's trade dependence on the United States decreases, so too do the incentives for restraint. An energy embargo against Japan helped spark World War II in the Pacific; a similar strategy toward China would push the region toward World War III.

Sino-U.S. mutual knowledge and interpenetration exist to such an extent that they know almost everything possible about each other—except what the other will do next. A Cold War–style military hotline may help clarify that. In the meantime, the United States has come to see China less in good-versus-evil terms and more through a humane lens that Oscar Wilde described as charming versus tedious. Washington has settled on a multilevel policy of "constrainment" or "congagement"—containment plus engagement—with the hope that the latter succeeds in shaping China into a "responsible stakeholder."[19] For the foreseeable future, however, China wants only to organize its own region and peripheries—not the entire planet.[20] If by 2020 the United States is still able to surround China militarily, while China continues to build an economic co-prosperity sphere, the re-

---

*The Chinese term for comprehensive national strength is *Zonghe guoli*, which arises out of natural resources, economic capabilities, external trade and investment capabilities, high levels of social development, military capabilities, high levels of government efficacy, and diplomatic capabilities.

†All is fair when geopolitics and globalization intersect. In an unauthorized and highly provocative text titled *Unrestricted Warfare*, two Chinese colonels gave maximum interpretation to the reality of a world in which governmental and nongovernmental divides are fading, strategic shape can be formless, individuals can wield as much power as countries, and the existence of so many technological means erases the rules of war. "There is nothing in the world today that cannot become a weapon," they write, and whatever weapons are available—money, the Internet, the environment, the media, the law—should be used to shape the battle and invisibly control a rival's fate through deception and obfuscation, the Asian equivalents of Arab dissimulation. Such "combination warfare" is the only—and a legitimate—means for weaker powers to defeat stronger ones, which they must rightfully do to overcome their inferiority. See Ling and Xiangsui, *Unrestricted Warfare*.

sult could be a stable holding pattern—but the United States will not have changed China from the *inside*.

Europe believes it can change China through soft power in ways American hard power cannot—or least achieve more with its strategy than America does. European trade with China exceeds Sino-U.S. trade, and China's exports to Europe now exceed America's. Europe has made clear that China will have to accept its interference if China is ever to attain the coveted "market economy" status.[21] China is now impervious to American pressures on democratization, human rights, and economic reform, but it implicitly welcomes European guidance on all such matters. Indeed, the state that China hopes to build is modeled on European norms of state capitalism and social democracy, the same source as their current official socialist ideology.[22] "We send far more diplomats, experts, and double the number of students to the EU than the U.S. to understand their welfare states," a Shanghai academic pointed out. It is better that China has the fruits of such exchanges than not—and Europe is providing them. Some European nations also viewed their 2005 effort to lift the EU arms embargo on China as a gesture of respect that would advance these constructive reform programs. Europe in fact already sells high-tech weaponry to China and has included China in its Galileo commercial satellite navigation system (even though China plans its own Beidou-2 global satellite system), which the United States fears could assist its weapons targeting systems. But by not imposing any conditions or penalties on China for its reckless arms sales to unsavory regimes—such as improving military transparency, increasing press freedom, curbing the death penalty, or signing the UN Covenant on Civil and Political Rights—Europe demonstrated its weakness as a moral leader when commercial interests are at stake. Since America itself is not party to many such treaties, only Europe could do this with any credibility. But China's greatest ally in the emerging balance of power is not Europe—it is globalization.

GLOBALIZED GREATNESS

China is experiencing a second Great Leap Forward, and it is already countless times more advanced than during the last one. While China's

"Harmonious World" rhetoric seems antiquated, its globalization strategy is anything but. While the American political establishment warns of a "China threat," most of the world—and most Americans—have bought into the idea of a "China opportunity." Unlike Japan and Korea, whose impressive growth was driven by a closed-state model, China's spectacular rise has come because it has abandoned the pretense of separating the domestic from the international. It has surpassed the United States as the largest recipient of foreign investment and overtaken Japan as the world's most trade-oriented nation. Holding over $1 trillion in currency reserves (more than Japan), it invests ever more in foreign markets through a Temasek-like agency to ensure against its own economic volatility while feeding its insatiable quest for raw materials. To acquire leading-edge technology, China has endowed state-owned firms with enough assets to go on Fortune 500 buying sprees.

Another pillar of China's strategy is to hijack first-world vessels, steer them to shore, and make their captains walk the plank. When Singapore's Temasek oversaw the construction of the Suzhou Industrial Park in China, China had already begun to lure investment away toward a nearly identical facility it was copying all along. Far from the days of extraterritoriality, China now insists that multinationals set up operations in China to further acquire top-tier technology. For the right to construct the Maglev high-speed train (the world's fastest) connecting Shanghai's Pudong airport to downtown, Siemens had to also build a Maglev research institute, assisting China to master the technology it will eventually use to connect Shanghai to Beijing. To strengthen its nonfunctional equity markets, China has outsourced raising capital for its banks to Hong Kong and Singapore. And to deal with vast nonperforming assets resulting from years of reckless lending, it allows major foreign banks to buy ever-larger stakes—and thus share the risk while using their expertise to clean up the mess.[23]

China benefits from foreign know-how, and the first world sweats to keep up. In the past foreign firms subcontracted only low-wage component assembly to China, but the "race to the bottom" is over: China now competes with first-world Singapore and Taiwan for electronics assembly and modular manufacturing. Germans workers now put in overtime to compete with the very Chinese workers they once trained—that is, if their entire design and manufacturing units have not already been moved to China. China has even reverse-engineered

European weapons and then dumped the supplier.[24] Shanghai Automotive may eventually put both General Motors and Volkswagen out of business in China, upgrading its models with their technology and then selling its cars for less—soon in the United States.

But keeping multinationals in China to create millions of jobs has been no trouble: Most don't have an exit strategy to begin with.[25] State-owned enterprises were once synonymous with the interior industrial dustbowls in which they lay, and their closures have been a major contributor to urban migration and unrest. In some areas, the government has forced urban to rural resettlement, turning workers into farmers and filling villages abandoned by urban migrants. But equally important is Wal-Mart, which has the vast majority of its goods produced in China and employs close to two hundred thousand people. But no matter whose factory or mine Chinese laborers work in, minimal rights often translate into *guolaosi*—"death from overwork."[26] Nonetheless, over a billion Chinese can have all the basic aspects of material welfare covered, because unlike third-world countries, they produce all those basics themselves. And with its high savings rate, China is building a mega-economy based both on mass production *and* consumption. From fruit juice to electronics to car insurance, everything Chinese buy can be scaled to an ever-expanding middle class, meaning that foreign companies will accept almost any conditions to gain access to a ripening market too big to ignore. People who used to earn twenty dollars a month in factories have suddenly become nouveau riche. China's three hundred thousand millionaires (going by the U.S. dollar) will make China the third-largest consumer of luxury goods behind Europe and the United States within a decade. "To get rich is glorious," Deng famously remarked.

Globalization is happening on China's terms. Rather than accepting Western pressure to open its markets before the United States and EU did, China has been highly selective about its internalization of WTO standards.[27] Nowhere is this more visible than in the sphere of intellectual property rights (IPR), an international regime currently being washed away in a flood of pirated music, movies, cigarettes (making them even deadlier), pharmaceuticals, batteries, watches, apparel, even cars: BMW's X5 sports sedan appears on Shanghai's streets as the "CEO." Quantity dwarfs quality on Nanjing Road and Beijing's Silk Road, where the massive trade in pirated DVDs pauses only periodically for symbolic events in which government tractors crush piles of them to appease American and European complaints. But the ruse impresses no one, for the government won't clamp down on one of the most prolific for-profit pirates of intellectual property—the People's Liberation Army—whose dispersed factories pump out counterfeit multimedia items to supplement its budget.[28] If left to its own opaque decision making, China would respect IPRs only after it has pirated its way to the first world.* Yet when its own patents are infringed, China has proven remarkably swift at enforcement, protecting its market in flat-screen televisions, computer hard drives, webcams, and all manner of 2008 Olympics paraphernalia, which only Chinese authorities are allowed to produce and sell.[29] The United States and the EU are increasingly fighting back with trade war threats due to their massive trade deficits with China, but as one Chinese economist in Shanghai speculated, "If we really wanted to flout the IPR regime completely, there would be absolutely nothing left for the West to produce."

A TIDE TO LIFT ALL RAFTS

China's real development miracle is actually still in its infancy. In 1980, China was a post–Cultural Revolution wasteland, with two-thirds of its people living in a blighted and barren dustbowl of punishing loneliness, chronicled by writer Ma Jian in his despondent memoir *Red Dust*. But from five hundred million people living in absolute poverty, now there are only fifty million surviving on a dollar per day, and China no longer accepts international aid to reduce poverty. China does not have to lift a billion people, however; it is more a question of rafts, each symbolizing a family.[30] On each raft family members take care of one another, with the result being significantly less homelessness and begging—and far more order and dignity—than in third-world India.

---

*Chinese/Confucian culture centers more on transmission than creation; learning by doing necessarily leads to infringements. Also, Western corporations have gone overboard in their patenting binge, which in some cases amounts to legally veiled theft of ancient medical knowledge such as plant-based Ayurvedic medicines. By this logic, it is the West whose pirates use hegemonic legal frameworks to steal from the East and punish others for doing what they had done for centuries before the West. See Philip J. Ivanhoe, "Intellectual Property and Traditional Chinese Culture," in *Topics in Contemporary Philosophy*, Campbell, O'Rourke, and Shier, eds., 125–42.

China's coastal provinces have to date received an overwhelming proportion—four-fifths—of total foreign investment, but this dazzling statistic is by design: Capitalism has come in stages to China as a way to manage it gradually. The cost of this approach, however, has been inequality.[31] Migrants show up in big coastal cities as if arriving in a new world the likes of which they have never imagined. Many rummage through trash dumps to earn more money than they would as farmers, while elites casually ignore them like hordes of animals. Like Brazil, inequality has correlated to rising crime in China. The city of Guangzhou has deployed hundreds of additional policemen to patrol the streets. But because China is tackling its inequality problem head-on rather than getting hung up about crime, it has become the model that Brazil is watching most closely. Halting the rural migration of over three hundred million Chinese is not possible, but China's efforts at providing housing, electricity, water, health care, and even education and pensions, will gradually bring down overall inequality.[32] Rather than debate statistics, however, Chinese leaders know that even as the top rises like a skyrocket, the key is to raise the bottom. China has sought to bridge its coastal-interior and east-west divides in terms of wealth, infrastructure, technology, and legal and social norms, through a $40 billion rural social investment program including government offices, schools, and hospitals, all intended to "build a new socialist countryside"—a wise slogan for the country's heartland, where agrarian socialist ideals remain strong.[33] In addition to state investment, internal remittances from the coast to the interior have played a huge rule in alleviating poverty for over eight hundred million peasants. Village renovation has meant demolishing huts and replacing them with sturdier structures, as well as building two-story villas with solar-paneled roofs as weekend homes for urban Chinese. Fifty thousand miles of major roads are being paved to connect remote villages to highways, with fiber-optic cables connecting them to the information superhighway as well—both decades faster than supposed IT powerhouse India.

With its innermost regions accessible by air, land, and river, the rapid development of China's mini-Shanghai "second cities" naturally follows. It is no coincidence that Chongqing, near the geographic center of the country in Sichuan province, has become the world's largest municipal area with over thirty million residents. As the hub of the Three Gorges Dam region, workers and residents are building entire new towns for those resettled by the dam's construction. At the same time, it is the site of over $40 billion in planned industrial renovations, making it the hub of an economic zone that encompasses thirty-five cities and one hundred million people—larger than any European country. There are now more than one hundred midsize Chinese cities with over a million residents, many with skylines starting to resemble Frankfurt's. (By contrast, America has only ten cities of greater than one million people, and Europe about thirty.) Most Americans have never heard of cities like Wuxi, which will soon be as wealthy as some of their own cities—but with a population of seven million. It's no surprise that although China produces far more steel than any other country (a third of the world's total) and consumes twice as much as the United States or the EU, it still requires more.

The toxins accumulated in an urban Chinese person's lungs are like the layers of sediment investigated by a paleontologist, telling the story of the most rapid industrialization the world has ever known. China's massively inefficient coal mines and steel plants have created smog so thick it blocks planes from landing and makes falling snow black in the winter. Six of the ten most polluted cities in the world are in China, with a full third of Chinese cities suffering from unbearable air pollution.[34] Like its economic picture, China's environmental race has no opponent but globalization itself: Can China go green through technology, efficiency, and conservation before it goes black—taking other parts of the world with it as the very straw that breaks the global ecosystem's back?

As China goes, so goes the world: It will soon be responsible for one-third of California's air pollution.[35] Like Americans, Chinese want to enjoy the good life and the great outdoors, taking road trips across their vast and scenic country. An official from the Chinese National Oil Offshore Corporation (CNOOC) actually argued that "human rights mean guaranteed access to energy."[36] The problem with the belief that China is simply repeating Western history and will become greener in lockstep with its growing wealth is that, like everything else in China, the scale of the problems is bigger and appearing much faster—and is heaped on top of two hundred years of corrosive Western industrialization. China is already the second-largest global polluter behind the United States, a status to which the rest of the world gleefully contributes by using China as its central factory.* But environmental NGOs are trying to promote ecological consciousness *before* a Chernobyl-like disaster. All of this is well suited to China's culture of cleanliness and order. Even in old *hutong* neighborhoods of Beijing, trash is neatly collected and cyclists pedal through to collect bottles set aside for recycling, balancing them in enormous plastic sacks as they navigate the narrow alleys.

Clusters of wind farms have appeared in China's western provinces all the way to the Kazakh border. When China is motivated to act on a challenge, it proves that no society can adapt on a large scale with such velocity. Growth is the cornerstone of the government's legitimacy, but environmental degradation costs China perhaps $200 billion a year.[37] China has thus become home to most of the world's hydroelectric and nuclear power projects and is building more liquid natural gas terminals both to take advantage of its own large gas reserves (and those of Malaysia and Indonesia) and to mitigate its excessive dependence on coal and oil.[38] Like a giant Singapore, China is now off-shoring pollutants to remote regions, raising the price of water, and publicly shaming, blacklisting, and fining excessive polluters. China already uses more solar power for water heating than the rest of the world, and has begun to sell those technologies abroad as well.[39] The Celestial Empire is even working to control the weather, using cloud-seeding technology to increase rainfall and clear up Beijing's near perpetual sunless haze.

SHANGHAI AND BEIJING: IMPERIAL CAPITALS

Located at the mouth of the Yangtze River, Shanghai subsumes China's best and brightest into a culture of doing in the way New Yorkers are known for, its first-world urban culture and cosmopolitan design already earning it the status of a global hot spot. Ironically, the city where

---

*China has only half the world's average resource base per capita, yet uses seven times as much energy for the same volume of production as Japan, six times as much as the United States, and three times as much as India. Some have discussed the scenario of China forcing foreign companies to pay for the fuels they require for production in China, which would cleverly recruit them to support China's case to secure foreign resources and keep sea-lanes to China open. But the reality is that China's own township factories are the greatest source of inefficient production, not multinationals.

the Communist Party was founded to put an end to corporatist owner-ship has displaced Hong Kong as the new epicenter of Chinese capi-talism. This is only fair, since it was Shanghai's millionaires who fled to Hong Kong in 1949 and mastered Western business practices under British tutelage. But Shanghai has none of Hong Kong's gangs, smut, or criminality. Taxi drivers sit in plastic cocoons, yet there is virtually no crime, and police are unarmed. White-gloved traffic officers coach citizens in pedestrian manners with stern whistles and gestures. Swarms of gardeners trim flowers and cut grass. Unlike the open la-trines of third-world cities, public toilets are ubiquitous. A single elec-tronic card can be used to pay for all transport—the metro, the buses, even taxis.

China's national bird is most certainly the crane. Alongside Du-bai, Shanghai has the largest share of the world's commercial cranes, which are hard at work clearing hundreds of thousands of traditional and colonial-era homes and building the city of the future. For the 2010 World Expo, an area the size of Manhattan is being developed with fancy pavilions and residences. Shanghai already has more skyscrapers than New York, with some, like the Jin Mao Tower for instance, blend-ing the best of the old and the new in its design, which resemble a bam-boo shoot in spring. The Bund, its well-known riverfront, was built at the turn of the century to resemble European art deco, but rather than let colonial contributions crumble, the Chinese have integrated mod-ern glass façades to modernize its grandeur. Every luxury car dealer has a showroom in Shanghai, and young yuppies party in art galleries con-verted to discos. Concept restaurants have sprouted to rival London and Los Angeles—and since it is Asian food that increasingly inspires global cuisine, it is as much the East as the West that now defines in-ternational chic.

Shanghai is being built into the world's largest metropolis, dwarf-ing New York, London, or São Paulo. City officials have planned fifty years ahead, meaning that despite its population of twenty-six million (thirteen million locals and an equal number of migrants) and growing, it will not descend into the chaotic sprawl of Latin America's mega-lopolises but rather remain in the orderly ranks of cities like Tokyo. Neighborhoods are zoned and color-coded, and millions live in podlike apartment capsules. New districts have sprouted that resemble Swiss villages or British towns to appeal to middle-class Chinese—whose empire imports the world to itself. Shanghai is also the hub of a massive city-region of rising prosperity stretching to Nanjing and encompassing multiple cities of five million people each.

Once the city of bicycles, Beijing now seems to have more cars—while bicycles are being recycled. Dozens of five-star hotels and gated communities of full-service condominiums now augment what has always been a city of ancient palaces and sprawling parks whose grandeur was awe-inspiring as far back as Marco Polo. Elderly couples learn to tango at night by the illuminated Ming-era city walls. Although, as in Shanghai, many old neighborhoods are being cleared for modern developments, numerous old *hutong* are refurbished and capitalize on the constant tourist influx.

TAIWAN AND HONG KONG: BECOMING CHINA

If there were any lingering doubt that no inherent faith in Marxist-Leninist dogma exists in the Chinese soul, one need only visit Taiwan and Hong Kong to have it quickly dispelled.

Sun Yat-sen explicitly elevated China toward Enlightenment ideals, and Chiang Kai-shek, his successor as head of the Kuomintang, presided over a flowering of economic and cultural liberty until 1949. Mao Zedong then leveraged mass agrarian impulses during the civil war's Long March to force the Nationalists' retreat to Taiwan and denounced the Chang Kai-shek era as "bureaucratic capitalism." But if Mao were alive today, he surely would be able to come up with a better description of what mainland China has become.

The Communist victory in the civil war sparked great capital flight from China, money that spread and multiplied across the region in the hands of scrupulous overseas Chinese investors. Ironically, it was particularly the Yueh—the people of China's southern coastal region—whom northern Chinese leaders most disparaged and expelled to Taiwan and elsewhere. Yet in the past decades, the Yueh have done the most to propel China's economy, investing billions through their Shanghai financial links.[40]

From an island of undesirables, Taiwan has become, in the words of former Chinese foreign minister Li Zhouxing, "A matter of life or death for China."[41] Any Chinese leader who lost Taiwan would be considered eternally guilty. Taiwan is actually a stateless economic node, so central to the global economy that almost no electronic instrument is lacking a Taiwanese component. A disruption in its economy—whether due to war or natural calamity—would be disastrous for everyone equally, taking a large chunk of the global economy off-line.[42] Washington protects Taiwan as much for its microchips as for its military dignity, but it privately opposes Taiwanese independence, hoping that a grand bargain can be reached whereby Taiwan promises not to secede and China de-escalates. After years of Chinese lobbying around the world, Taiwan has become so isolated diplomatically that its independence would be recognized by no country—perhaps not even by the United States. Despite the massive armaments on both sides and America's looming presence, what is really at stake is political face and economic control. China knows that the eventual incorporation of Taiwan will give it a world-class center of high-tech industries in addition to a manufacturing juggernaut. To this day, Taiwan is the largest foreign investor in the mainland's factories and enterprises, far larger than the United States, the EU, or Japan. Pragmatists in Taiwan want an ever-deeper common market with China to facilitate such investments, and China has responded by cleverly offering $4 billion in loans to small and medium-size Taiwanese enterprises (SMEs) operating in China. China is already Taiwan's largest export market, so it has no desire to attack the very island that serves its economic growth so dutifully.[43]

Despite the occasional cross-strait saber rattling, the reality of China and Taiwan's mutual colonization proceeds apace. Yet today it is clear that Taiwan will not politically absorb China any more than the earth will swallow the heavens. Mainland Chinese show little respect for Taiwan's democracy, which has been prone to nationalist hijacking and the marginalization of mainland immigrants.[44] "We are only copying Taiwan's economic and social model," explained a Chinese businessman in Beijing. "After a wild early phase of capitalism, they too focused on development and became first-world."

Even more than Taiwan, Hong Kong has perennially been rated the world's freest economy, and it has been seen as a model of how the Chinese might just be malleable into Western civility or democracy. In 1997, when the "last British colony surrendered to the last Communist tyranny," in the words of the island's final British governor, Chris Patten, China was gifted this global financial capital where now less than one in ten people work in manufacturing despite an annual export value greater than India's or Russia's.

Land reclamation on both Hong Kong island and mainland Kowloon have narrowed the grand Victoria Harbor between them—a symbol for the closing gap between Hong Kong and the upper Pearl River delta cities of Shenzhen and Guangzhou (Canton), which together form the wealthiest Chinese region.[45] The delta was Britain's entrepôt on the maritime Silk Road, and now it is the channel on which ancient Yueh cities have reclaimed modern glory as export-processing zones. In nearby Macao (China's own Las Vegas) and Hainan Island, Chinese mega-infrastructure projects are paving the way for Taiwanese, Korean, and Hong Kong investors to build hugely profitable hotels and resorts; buy up real estate; and launch low-cost airlines to ferry Chinese there from all over the mainland, while Beihai offers an ideal location for the coastal trade with Vietnam. But the shrinking harbor metaphor travels in the opposite direction as well: The upper delta's pollution has traveled downstream, clouding Hong Kong's air and water, and since the handover, Hong Kong's politics have suffered from greater corruption and violations of property rights. Like Taiwan, Hong Kong becomes more Chinese and less an independent system with each passing year.

ONE COUNTRY, TWO SYSTEMS

The phrase "one country, two systems" no longer refers as much to the China-Taiwan divide as to the dualism of "Market Leninism." For the West it is an axiom of history that no country can sustain the paradox of a capitalist economy paired with an authoritarian government—yet this is precisely China's sturdy reality.[46] Outside powers have never penetrated China's inscrutable imperial politics and so must come to terms with "China as it is, not as we want it to be."[47]

When China's last emperor, Pu Yi, was demoted from head of the Celestial Empire and integrated into the Communist ranks, he allegedly said of his reeducation: "The Communist Party is so great that it does not annihilate the person physically in the flesh, but rather annihilates mistaken ideas." The Party has had no shortage of mistaken ideas of its own in the past half century, but it has not suffered a revolution, which Chinese euphemistically term a "withdrawal of mandate." The Party's singular goal is to retain this mandate by any means necessary. In fact, it faces little competition, for in five thousand years, never once have "the people" been a candidate to assume the "mandate of heaven." Maoism may be discredited, but Mao's dictum remains beyond dispute: "Political power grows out of the barrel of a gun—therefore the Party must control the gun."

Since the nearly simultaneous Tiananmen Square uprising and the disintegration of the Soviet Union, China and Russia have followed two very different trajectories. Chinese communism has been abandoned by strategic choice, replaced not with Russian-style neo-authoritarianism and apocalyptic capitalism but rather with a transition toward the "Asian compact." The Party apparatus was hastily built after a civil war power grab and now touts its oxymoronic "democratic centralism" as if it were the legacy of thousands of years of received wisdom. In a way, it is: Confucianism is making a comeback in its own homeland, just in time to legitimize the Party the way it does other East Asian regimes. Confucianism broadly justifies the Party's twin pillars of state capitalism and social democracy, emphasizing stability, respect for authority, meritocracy, and leadership by example.[48] A statue of Confucius now stands in a lotus lake on the campus of Beijing's elite Tsinghua University.

No matter what ideological adjustments the Party makes, there remain several inviolable "no-nos": no religious freedom for China's estimated forty million Christians and thirty million Muslims (known as *Hui*), which no emperor has ever allowed. China has already experienced mass opium addiction and will not allow Marx's "opiate of the masses" to spread freely. No compromises will be made on territorial integrity, including Taiwan, Tibet, and Xinjiang—all of which the government has more strength to subdue than ever before. The sublime action propaganda film *Hero*, one of the most widely viewed movies across Asia in recent years, artistically captures the visceral importance of unity across China's kingdoms.

The Party is more powerful, sophisticated, and complex than any Chinese dynasty in history. Rather than child emperors for whom the nation itself was a personal asset, today there are MBA emperors who think in terms of business plans—and are co-opting the business elites into consulting roles. In the post-Deng era, there are no more totemic figures whose aura is bestowed on obsequious acolytes, but instead a new generation of technocrats competing more or less meritocratically for influence—and with greater accountability than ever before. Term limits may soon be imposed on Party officials.[49]

Of course, the only regimes more corrupt than ones where multiple parties contend for power are those where one party has all the power. China's systemic corruption has been likened to a rotten tree that still stands but bears no fruit.[50] The selling of government positions, the meddling in enterprises large and small, the siphoning of funds for grand public squares, the nonexistent product-safety standards, the confiscation and sale of peasant property to developers, the mismanagement of banks, and the operation of low-quality hotels and hospitals by provincial ministries and the army to raise funds are just a few examples of the nexus of Chinese politics and capitalism gone awry. Even Beijing's Imperial Palace is not immune: The American Express logo appears on brass plaques scattered throughout its pavilions.

Yet Chinese people still believe they are better off with a strong state than a weak one that can be exploited by foreign powers. While in the West the law serves to protect the lower classes from the elites, historically in China the law is dictated from above and passed down to the people. The seventy-four thousand reported demonstrations that took place across China in 2004 were largely against price changes and land seizures and for workplace rights—not a revolutionary groundswell against the Party.[51] Peasant revolts are a common feature of Chinese history, with frequent protests not against the ideals of redistribution but rather poor execution by government cadres.[52] Self-sacrifice remains a strong cultural trait, and steadily cultivated state loyalty still prevails. Despite everything, the Party's popularity even seems to be increasing.*

China is no democracy, but the transition from comrade to citizen, and from rule by law to rule of law, began even before Tiananmen Square.[53] Millions of families now have property rights for the first

---

*For the Chinese, democracy is a tool to curb corruption and increase transparency, not a mode of competitive politics. In a population so large, petitioning remains a weapon more effective than democracy. See Bell, *East Meets West*, 138–41.

time, liberating entire regions into the realm of credit and consumption. The flogging of errant officials is no longer hidden behind the vermillion walls of the Imperial City but rather takes place in public and is publicized by the media, which widely reported the execution of the country's top food-safety official in 2007 as a warning to others cutting corners and taking bribes. Corrupt governors have been sacked, rogue police officers reined in, ethics handbooks distributed, and ministerial budgets posted online. More than one million villages have already had elections for committees to administer local affairs, a process that remains experimental only because insiders too often come out ahead—a flaw that the government hopes to correct before it makes a mockery of democracy. City officials now use polling companies to canvas public opinions and priorities.

China will heed no calls for democratization or any other systemic change until it reaches its goal of a medium-income population by 2050.[54] In fact it may take a century or more for full democracy to appear in China—if ever—but the race is purely internal, giving no ground to foreign demands.[55] Chinese take growing pride in their social and civic order, something that liberalization of the information environment could actually increase further—again, contrary to Western logic. The Chinese state is strong enough that it can afford to allow the media to be critical without becoming an independent power base, but as in Singapore, the Party is not confident enough yet. For the growing millions of Chinese Internet users, many Web sites remain restricted and Orwellian rewards are given for self-censorship; media reporting on natural disasters without prior approval is banned.[56] Yet a free media environment is a vehicle for healthy debate, transparency, and public education. China can hardly command unmitigated international respect when many of its prize-winning filmmakers and writers live in exile from a country where telling the truth and telling lies are equally dangerous. In this area, at least, China would far more commendably lead the East if it adapted more lessons from the West.

CONCLUSION:
THE SEARCH FOR EQUILIBRIUM
IN A NON-AMERICAN WORLD

A RACE TO THE TOP

It is hard to overestimate the fluidity of the early twenty-first-century landscape. As America vacillates between shunning and embracing the international community, the Chinese Politburo remains a black box, and the EU cautiously exercises strategic leverage, alternative scenarios to a world dominated by these three powers must be entertained. America may not be able to afford its excessive consumption, nor Europe its expansion, nor China its environmental and social burdens. All three superpowers might retrench if they are unable to maintain present commitments, or if blending with their peripheries proves too cumbersome.[1] Yet it remains a safe bet that history's fatalistic cycles of rise, fall, and conflict will continue.[2]

Much of America's global esteem and self-promotion has been based on its status as the military defender of freedom, the wealthiest society and the most vibrant democracy in a Hobbesian and Darwinian world.[3] But America has misunderstood both Hobbes and Darwin.[4] Though Hobbes believed that man is driven by what Hans Morgenthau later called an *animus dominandi* ("a desire for power"), he called not for a single, tyrannical Leviathan standing above the people, but rather "the Matter, Forme, and Power of a Commonwealth Ecclesiastical and Civil."[5] Darwin too never argued that brute force guarantees longevity. He wrote: "It is not the strongest of the species that survive, nor the most intelligent, but the one most responsive to change." The real lessons of Hobbes and Darwin are that no single power will dominate others; rather, the most adaptive system will prevail.

A superpower doesn't last a minute longer that it has to. America has long had the military capacity to pulverize its competitors into dust, but despite President Bush's repeated claims that America must "go on the offensive and stay on the offensive," between the "war on terror" and the "Axis of Evil," America has failed on every single count to resolve the major threats it has identified, revealing the impotence of military power.[6] Furthermore, American influence has diminished most quickly where its posture is the most militarized: the Arab world and East Asia. Some Americans counsel a limited grand strategy of offshore balancing in strategic regions, but even this is just a passive-aggressive form of the same utterly failed doctrine. Even under the most benign hegemony, it is difficult to sugarcoat bunker-buster nuclear warheads and preemptive wars while rejecting the treaties that regulate them. As Henry Kissinger wrote, "Force might conquer the world but it cannot legitimize itself."

Ironically, even if America is merely a benign "accidental empire," it increasingly feels that it must act imperially to defend its vision against those of the EU and China.* While it admonishes others for playing power politics, those others nonetheless continue to counter America's own attempted power monopoly.† America's false assumptions of dominance are laid bare in every second-world region: The EU *can* stabilize its East, the Chinese-led SCO *can* organize Central Asia,

---

*America is anticolonial but still imperial. The proof is winsomely captured by Niall Ferguson's imitation of Americans at war overseas: "Can we, like, go home now?" But American imperialism is a tradition dating back to its westward expansion through its antihegemonic engagements in the twentieth century to its current interventions in the name of human rights, democracy, counterterrorism, or oil. Debates among Democrats and Republicans to this day are not a matter of *if* America should intervene, only *when* and *where*. As John Quincy Adams predicted, America never runs out of justifications for "going abroad in search of monsters to destroy," by launching what Andrew Bacevich formulates as "Operation [Insert Name Here] Freedom."

†As E. H. Carr wrote of the interwar geopolitical waltz, "Utopian writers from the English-speaking countries seriously believed that the establishment of the League of Nations meant the elimination of power from international relations. . . . What was commonly called the 'return to power politics' in 1931 was, in fact, the termination of the monopoly of power enjoyed by the status quo powers." See *The Twenty Years' Crisis*.

South America *can* reject the United States, Arab states *can* refuse American hegemony, and China *cannot* be contained in East Asia by military means alone. The geopolitical mutiny is well under way.

Does the world no longer need the United States?[7] Anti-Americanism continues even as America's dominance fades.[8] Americans frequently state that China's uncertain course is the key "X factor" of the future, but it is the United States that has become the equivalent of the uncertainty principle: From different perspectives there is no agreement on where it stands. America now holds the mantle of Perfidious Albion. Neither democratic idealism nor hegemonic messianism holds much promise for restoring trust in America, which has gone from the invisible hand incarnate to merely one of several competing vendors or brands on the catwalk of credibility. The question for Americans has changed from "What's in it for us?" to "Why aren't we there?" International congresses and summits are being held elsewhere with none of the hassles of America's arbitrary visa restrictions. From hedge funds to online gambling, London and Hong Kong are increasingly preferred to New York for listing companies. In 2006, Al Jazeera International launched its English-language TV station worldwide—but not in the United States. The world's sports—cricket and soccer—remain largely absent in America. Soft power only worked for America when it was ahead.

With neither its hard power nor its soft power functioning effectively, the United States is learning that history happens to everyone—even Americans. Much as rubber bands snap far more quickly than they stretch, empires collapse not long after they reach their fullest extent. America would like to remain safely distant from—but able to dictate to—the European and Asian powers on either end of the Eurasian "world island," much as it did nearly a century ago at the Paris peace conference, after which Sir Harold Nicolson chastised, "America, eternally protected by the Atlantic, desired to satisfy her self-righteousness while disengaging her responsibility."[9] But detached geography is an advantage only if allies will share the burdens. Raymond Aron called America's system of indirect global rule an "imperial republic," but its return on investment has shrunk considerably as it loses allies around the world and its "coalitions of the willing" appear more dalliances of self-serving convenience. The United States today must go it alone far more often than befits a true leader—not coincidentally, just as its military, fiscal, and moral leverage diminishes.[10] Transforming NATO into an underresourced "Axis of Democracy" will not turn things around: The failed venture in Iraq has cost America the unquestioned loyalty of Great Britain, and Japan is more and more cautious in East Asia, making both little more than Potemkin allies for America. Many other states once solidly under the U.S. security umbrella are also "leash-slipping," building their own forces to gain autonomy from the United States.[11] As the organs of the world body reject America's surgical insertions, Americans have become unable to decide whether the costs and consequences of global engagement are worthwhile.[12] This domestic discontent and the inability to uphold global commitments alone are the key indicators of imperial overstretch. As Toynbee warned, "There is no armor against fate."[13]

American foreign policy is often described as distracted or overwhelmed by its many agendas: counterterrorism, trade expansion, energy security, and conflict resolution—and a preoccupation with crisis management is a sure sign that it is failing in these grand strategic priorities. Yet imperial diplomacy requires multifaceted reasoning, not clinically separated bureaucratic stovepipes and one-size-fits-all policies that more befit a management consulting firm.[14] George Kennan wrote of the tension between representing one's own system while being a knowledgeable sympathizer of others, aware that they cannot be remade in one's own image. American diplomacy seems condemned to fail in both categories. The immense resources devoted to running the State Department as the world's largest travel agency do not befit an empire that requires deep and continuous regional expertise and personnel willing to spend their lives mastering the affairs of far-flung parts of the world. As counterinsurgency expert David Kilcullen has pointed out, "There are substantially more people employed as musicians in Defense bands than in the entire foreign service."[15] As "special envoy" troubleshooters replace expert career ambassadors, diplomacy by dilettantism has materialized.

In a world of alignments, not alliances, the diplomatic playing field pits America's *coalition,* Europe's *consensus,* and China's *consultative* imperial modes—each hardening in divergent ideological cement. The United States offers military and regime protection and aid, China offers full-service, conditionality-free relationships, and Europe offers deep reform and economic association with its union. Their imperial networks or spheres of influence increasingly overlap, with second-world countries multi-aligning: balancing and bandwagoning simultaneously to gain economic assistance from one power, military aid from another, and trade ties with the third.[16] The United States, the EU, and China increasingly act like "frenemies": friends and enemies at the same time.

A superpower has to be irresistible to succeed in such a competitive marketplace, where non-engagement is tantamount to abdication of influence.[17] For America to win over wayward second-world states, only the boldest publicly visible offers of massive economic, technical, and security inducements on the condition of immediate political overhaul can restore its stature. The race is on to deploy ever-larger cadres of what Toynbee called "marchmen," the multidimensional foot soldiers of empire who spread its way of life. America's new "transformational diplomacy" has dispatched more Foreign Service officers into hardship posts—sometimes alone—to boost America's presence. The European Commission has also initiated its own diplomatic corps of commercial, development, and political experts. China too has multiplied its global outposts and cadres of aid workers.

But even then, the second-world anti-imperial belt of Venezuela, Iran, Kazakhstan, Libya, Malaysia and others will continue to focus as much on building ties among themselves as with Washington, Brussels, or Beijing. Not only will these countries syncretize the best of what each superpower offers to achieve their own vision of success, they will also partner directly with one another to extract oil reserves, share intelligence, combat terrorism, reduce poverty, implement capital controls, and build modern infrastructure. They will use their sovereign wealth to buy Western banks, ports, and other strategic assests. Their regional groups will continue to construct their own economic zones, development banks, peacekeeping forces, and criminal courts. Airline connections have sprouted to connect Arabs, South Americans, and East Asians directly to one another. For the superpowers, having regional ambassadors will be more effective than working through global institutions.* But even as America confronts this seismic shift toward a non-American world, it must increasingly look inward, for the only direction from the apogee of power is down.

---

*Regional thinking has become so important that some proposals for reform of the UN Security Council suggest permanent regional seats that countries within each region would occupy on rotation. America could elevate its assistant secretaries to a rank similar to that of the Pentagon's CINCs, giving them greater decision-making and policy-coordination authority over their respective regions.

AMERICA: FROM THE FIRST WORLD TO THE SECOND?

China already is second-world, but is climbing up from the third. Europe is absorbing its second-world periphery, seeking to elevate it to the first world. Could America, long the first-world icon, slip into the second world? As with all empires, there is a certain cognitive dissonance when contemplating its demise. But civilization, Toynbee explained, "is a movement and not a condition, a voyage and not a harbour." To understand how civilizations break down, we must "extend our mental range of vision beyond its bounds." Toynbee's study of imperial personalities found that the most common causes of decline were militarism and the deterioration of the creative minority. Past empires were undone by the lies within, with each "getting the barbarians it deserved." Strong arms and strongmen cannot mask America's relative decline, since they are the chief symbols of it.*

America's imperial overstretch is occurring in lockstep with its declining economic dominance, undermining the very foundation of its global leadership. America may not be sacked by barbarians like Rome was, but, like imperial Spain, its dependency on foreign financing and defecting allies are nearly insurmountable vulnerabilities. The United States' share of the world economy has fallen from 50 percent to 25 percent since World War II—with Europe and Asia building the other two world-regions. During the Cold War, American allies tolerated the overvalued dollar, knowing it was necessary to sustain America's military commitment to protect them, but the goodwill on which that exceptionalism rests is quickly evaporating. Not only are China and Japan the two largest holders of U.S. dollar reserves, but for the first time in history, the world's main reserve currency belongs to a debtor nation—and one indebted to its rivals.[18] America's fiscal and trade imbalances make the dollar no longer the safest haven of investment, inspiring a gradual diversification of both currency holdings and the pricing of commodities such as oil. Though the world has several major currencies, there are three whose value all are constantly watching: the U.S. dollar, the Euro, and the Chinese renminbi. The more countries and investors diversify to the Euro, the less the United States can fi-

---

*Spengler warned that technological and cultural decay are the chief causes of civilizational decline. See *The Decline of the West.*

nance its deficits and costly military ventures. Because the deficits are the result of what Joseph Stiglitz calls a "consumption binge," America will have little to show for itself when the music stops.[19] And because America's debt payments already exceed the investment it receives, it is living beyond the wealth saved for the next generation, actually making the country poorer. America's fiscal adventurism clearly parallels that of its military—both symbolizing how America's imperial chariot is coasting on inertia rather than being propelled, for its tank is running out of gas.

America justifies its deviation from international conventions such as the Kyoto Protocol or the International Criminal Court either in the name of improving them or due to the demands of its global posture. But what can explain its domestic aberrations? It is not easy to psychoanalyze America, a country so encompassing of contradictions that the psychologist Erik Erikson once noted, "Whatever one may come to consider a truly American trait can be shown to have its equally characteristic opposite."[20] Generosity and selfishness, for example, are two intrinsic yet opposing American qualities. If it is true, however, that a society's way of warfare reflects its nature, then it is clear that self-restraint is not an American virtue.

America may claim to embody certain ideals for the world—liberty, happiness, opportunity—but it now actually has to prove this in comparison with others. The term *quality of life* sounds abstract, but in concretely measurable ways it is deteriorating, and America's continental size compounds the challenge. America ranks near the bottom of the OECD in average worker income and income inequality, similar to its ranking in individual happiness (to which inequality negatively correlates). America's median income is far less impressive than the mean income its individual wealth deceptively inflates. The super-rich live in economic bubbles, contributing as much to other countries' economies as their own, with the top 130,000 individuals earning as much as the bottom 40 percent of the entire population of three hundred million. Citibank analysts refer to the United States as a "plutonomy," in which the wealthy few fuel the economy more than the masses.[21] At the top, the market for gas-guzzling SUVs and diamonds has grown, while at the bottom, the materialist frenzy continues at dollar stores and Wal-Mart, where the annual stampede for holiday presents—sometimes even resulting in fatalities—begins each year at Thanksgiving (if not earlier).

America is ceasing to be a middle-class nation, becoming instead a classic second-world combination of extremes. For three decades now, America's working class has seen no increase in its wages in real terms, its share of the economy dwindling even as its numbers swell.[22] The very notion of "two Americas" raised in its 2004 presidential election campaign shows that it is lacking a middle. One-fifth of America's children grow up in poverty, with the total poor population close to forty million. In New York City, many low-income families have downsized into dormitories, unable to afford regular housing. Perhaps they will at least be sheltered as the country's real estate bubble bursts.

America is not a healthy country compared to its first-world peers. One is hard pressed to find people who would not want to have a guarantee of free or affordable medical care in times of need. America may live by a free market ideology, but that does not mean that the forty-five million Americans who lack health insurance like it that way. While scolding other nations for their overly bureaucratic ways, the astronomical administrative costs in America's health-care system are like its foreign aid programs, with more money going into overhead than to the intended recipients. Rising levels of child and adult obesity are symbols not of excessive health but of rather a widespread dependence on cheap, high-fat foods. Americans traveling on airlines are now accorded an automatic twenty-two pounds more weight when flight loads are calculated. And yet it requires the vast generosity of volunteers to mitigate the neglect of the elderly, who might otherwise perish of hunger.

Dominant powers retain their innovative edge over rivals through education in science and technology, but America's ranking in degrees awarded in these fields has plummeted. The United States has its elite universities, but most Americans now claim only a partial college education, and many take five to eight years to complete course work at local colleges while working to pay for it. America's high school dropout rate is 32 percent—and that from a great many failing and bankrupt public schools, in some of which America's military has even stepped in to run like military academies.

In a nation of privatized privilege, services that work well—fancy apartment buildings, hotels, restaurants, health clubs, private taxis—all cater to the elite and their private economy. For everyone else, things fall apart: Public transportation systems—roads, tunnels, trains, and buses—are in various states of disrepair; broadband Internet penetration has fallen behind Europe's; mobile telephone networks are substandard; and archaic taxi cabs don't accept electronic payment. Even worse, America may prove to be afflicted by the same oil curse as many second-world states. Much of its infrastructure was built during the post–World War II boom when America was the world's largest oil producer and exporter—but today its water pipes and power stations are run-down, causing lead and mercury poisoning and sporadic but massive blackouts.[23] During New York's transit strikes in the frigid winter of 2005, commuters trudging long distances through the snow declared that they felt like they lived in the third world.

Laissez-faire is a somewhat inaccurate way to describe America's social and economic principles when skewed societal structures actually favor the perpetuation of inequality. The social mobility that "equal opportunity" would entail is increasingly a myth, particularly for those already at the bottom: African Americans and Latinos, 50 percent of whom do not complete high school. From Los Angeles to Brooklyn, Latino minorities crowd crumbling districts and live at the mercy of despotic slumlords. Gentrification is a euphemism for urban renewal, which widely amounts to the same slum clearance seen in the second and third worlds. The influx of low-wage migrant labor has expanded the ranks of the poor, both due to their own numbers and because they reduce the wages of unskilled Americans.[24] Almost two decades ago Los Angeles was described as the "capital of the third world" due to its segregated immigrant communities seeking simply to stay afloat with little regard for the broader society.[25] Samuel Huntington also recently argued that America's Anglo-Protestant culture and melting pot creed have been undermined by nonintegrating Hispanic minorities, warning that there cannot be an "Americano dream" to substitute for the American Dream without America becoming a schizophrenic nation.[26] But it is hard to speak of a deep "community of values" in America when the primary reason Americans don't support a welfare state to support the poor is that the poor are disproportionately minorities.[27] In a country where recidivist violence seems never more than a few steps away, could white nativism reappear more regularly than it already does? The idea of homeland security seems to have as much to do with illegal immigration coming through the southern border as it does with the threat of terrorism.

Americans have shown a fear of the future, one that may only accelerate its arrival. In 2005, Europe, India, the United States, and China were all hit by major storms or flooding. In Germany and Poland, thousands of citizens had their livelihoods wiped away, but through immediate assistance from their governments, people worked together to restore homes and towns as quickly as possible. A monsoon also drowned much of downtown Mumbai, submerging the domiciles of millions of already destitute residents, but life carried on and damage was repaired. After America's Hurricane Katrina, which overwhelmed the antiquated levies of New Orleans, a variety of government agencies and charity groups hastily deployed, but so did gangs of armed looters, forcing the Louisiana governor to declare martial law. The region's minority residents learned the hard way how little their citizenship mattered.[28] Cases of government fraud and profiteering have run into the billions of dollars. Just two weeks after Katrina, Chinese authorities used cell phone messaging networks to warn and evacuate coastal populations in advance of an oncoming typhoon. Even a year after Katrina, much housing remained in ruins, some schools had not reopened, and the electricity supply was limited, prompting an enterprising Chinese contractor to offer to rebuild a number of dilapidated Mississippi towns, as their residents were still living in tents and trailers.

American socioeconomic attitudes would be laughable if they were not so scary. As in other countries, there is a general correlation linking low education, high income inequality, low living standards, and rising crime: America has an equal number of gang members as policemen (about 750,000). The relationship between inequality and homicide is airtight: "Societies that tolerate the injustices of great inequality will almost inescapably suffer their social consequences: they will be unfriendly and violent, recognized more for their hostility than their hospitality."[29] If every society gets the barbarians it deserves, as Toynbee argued, are Americans their own worst enemies? It remains a mystery why Americans, threatened physically by no one but themselves, require so many weapons, as they are mostly used to kill one another off. Not only do many communities live in fear of arbitrary shootings, but the state's purpose is widely redirected toward suppression of violence rather than rehabilitation of underdeveloped areas. At the same time, America has the highest incarceration rate in the world, with a rising number of life sentences. America, not China, is the world's largest penal colony. And together with Iran, Saudi Arabia, and China, America's death penalty—odious to most of the developed world—contributes to 80 percent of the world's executions. Americans seem to be entertaining themselves by death as well, with police car chases, wasteful motor sports, and human cock-fighting becoming the most popular spectator activities. It would be a step down for most Japanese and Germans to live like Americans, since their countries are the two wealthiest and most advanced—and least unequal—large countries in the world.

Early in the twentieth century, Supreme Court justice Louis Brandeis warned that America "can have democracy . . . or we can have great concentrated wealth in the hands of the few, but we cannot have both." Tocqueville and Nietzsche warned of democracy's natural degeneration, and by the 1990s the deteriorating quality of life and politics in America raised fundamental questions about whether American democracy could maintain a respectable social order at all.[30]

Vaclav Havel once observed that success in politics was a matter of tact and good taste; what would he say about the vulgarity of American politics today? American democracy appears to work better in theory than in practice. As populist politicians from the South gained political clout in Washington, they imported their aristocratic, dynastic, and underhanded ways, in which name recognition matters above all else.[31] From federal appointments to overseas ambassadors, presidents move in and out of office as a clique—emperor and coterie. Who actually won the 2000 election will be a subject of debate for years. A two-party system based on coastal versus heartland geographic loyalties ensures that there is little effort at power-sharing and coalitions; instead, political competition results in permanent gridlock and gerrymandering.[32] The parties are fund-raising shells with a veneer of semantics, promoting candidates not as individuals but as agents of their corporate interests, which have an invisible role in writing pivotal laws related to tax, energy, food safety, and other policies. Unlike even second-world countries such as Turkey, where high oil prices are used to subsidize strategic petroleum reserves, in America they are as much the result of corporate gouging as a risk premium; the common people suffer while energy company executives and shareholders reap the dividends. Like Russia's oligarchs, the financial scandals that have beset corporate America re-

veal a system of monopolistic capitalism that reduces distinctions between public and private—the former owned by the latter—to an "elegant escape from reality"[33] Politicians fighting over diminishing economic
spoils are a common symptom of hegemonic decline, and as America's
global corruption rating falls, it must be questioned whether Americans'
loyalty is to people or institutions, to profits or to progress.[34]

In *Common Sense,* Thomas Paine argued that the checks balancing the British monarchy, the aristocracy, and the Commons were a
farce. Today, the separation of powers articulated in Montesquieu's
Spirit of the Laws is becoming equally scarce in America. Because "enlightened statesmen may not always be at the helm," wrote James
Madison in Federalist No. 10, checks and balances are necessary. Yet
precisely when America needed to assuage the world's anxieties about
its power, the executive branch neglected both its obligation of truth
and its limitations under the law, undermining both the office and
respect for it. Whether or not America recovers from the unitary executive model of President Bush, the state of America's politicians
and population remain equally significant causes for concern. America's Patriot Act violates five of the ten cherished amendments of the
Bill of Rights: freedom of speech and assembly, protection from un-
reasonable search and seizure, due process, prompt public trial, and
protection from cruel and unusual punishment. Though this act was
passed by Congress, the executive branch's classification of secrets
demonstrates an evaporating desire to share information with the legislative branch. Even if subsequent administrations reverse these policies, the damage has already been done.

From the glorification of military power to the gladiator culture in
sport, what Polybius wrote of Rome applies well to America: Great
wealth and extravagance lead to the worst of all governments, namely
the mob rule of elites with little motivation other than preventing others
from gaining the upper hand. As Christianity brought down Rome,
might it not do the same to America? What Reinhold Niebuhr called
the "messianic consciousness of America" has inevitably seeped into its
foreign policy and eroded the strategic competence prescribed by realism.[35] The religious sanctification of foreign policy has led to a greater
rhetorical focus on human rights, religious freedom, and suffering from
mass diseases, but the policies corresponding to such ambitions has
had anything but their desired effect.[36] Religious revival has led to a na-

tional polarization and even "disenlightenment."[37] While Christian evangelists gained ground in American politics through grassroots social activism and federal tax breaks, Islam has spread rapidly in its prisons, with both groups promising an eternal community consisting only of themselves. When he addressed the ultimate question—"Does history repeat itself?"—Toynbee surmised, "There is nothing to prevent our Western civilization from following historical precedent, if it chooses, by committing social suicide," as Greco-Roman civilization had, decaying long before it was extinguished by turning itself "into an idol to which men paid an exorbitant worship."[38]

America's defining trait has been above all else a capacity for self-renewal—a political, economic, and cultural regeneration, even self-correction. But the combination of messianic leaders and corporate puppet masters, culture wars, fear of the outside world, and self-doubt about its leadership make a new domestic consensus unlikely. America's foreign policy elite is utterly divorced from citizens' concerns as well: Leaders are keen for the United States to fight more wars, push for free trade, and allow mass immigration, while the majority of Americans want fewer military interventions, less foreign aid, immigration restrictions, and some form of protectionism for American jobs and industries.[39] The era of the "Great Society" seemed to end definitively with President Reagan, never to return again. America has lost its momentum, and it cannot turn things around simply because it wants to—especially because it no longer seems to know what it wants. Because renewal is equal parts physical and ideological, America is a first-world country in need of a Marshall Plan to stay where it is.[40] Because Americans are so unfamiliar with the world beyond their shores, however, they continue to believe that their way of life is the de facto standard for the planet. Soon they may wake up to realize that the standard they set is more appropriate for the second world than for the first.

America has no policy to guarantee that it remains a first-world country—it leaves this fate to chance and globalization. America has always been geographically divided, its first-world Northeast absorbing the resource-rich colonies of the South. Today its heartland between the Mississippi River and the Rocky Mountains lacks the airports and labor base to make it a motor rather than a drag on the nation's economy.[41] While Silicon Valley stands for America's high-tech renaissance, Detroit is the symbol of its postindustrial rust belt and manufacturing obsolescence, embodied by the second-rate automobiles it produces— or rather produced.[42] Having lost hundreds of thousands of manufacturing jobs to second- and third-world competitors, America has not built the broader technological base of the EU and Japan to retrain its workforce.[43] The most productive states across Europe and East Asia have rejected the Anglo-Saxon values of individual rights and small government, and by focusing more on high-value labor and technology rather than low-skilled immigration, Europeans have been able to maintain high wages while automating their economies. By contrast, American companies are themselves going on the auction block, to be bought up by Asians and other cash-rich foreign conglomerates. Auto workers in America's heartland now beg for Japanese firms like Honda to set up plants in their districts to restore their incomes and dignity. Can America afford globalization?[44]

America's blind faith in its innovative capacity and the virtues of the free market are dangerous precisely because other countries aim explicitly to exploit America's weaknesses. Though America's economy grows with the world economy, its relative decline stems from second-world countries becoming smarter faster than it does.[45] Foreign powers are slipstreaming the United States, using its economy as a place to invest and its universities for technical training until their own markets, institutions, and infrastructure can deliver similar returns and absorb their capital and overseas talent. Chinese enrollment in American universities has recently fallen because of opportunities in Europe and China itself. First-world countries slow to adjust to the pace of global redistribution of labor and investment are vulnerable to competition from—and potentially displacement by—members of the second world.

A single world economy of competition across all sectors and regions has sparked a palpable global *middling* by which even more countries get pulled into the second world. The knowledge economy is no longer the special domain of the first world, meaning not only low-wage jobs but also such previously nontradable services as technology development, medical diagnostics, business consulting, and legal processing are off-shored to second- and third-world countries, where expanding incomes and consumption further strain the precious commons. But because no second-world state will voluntarily restrain its growth due to environmental concerns, rising commodity prices may harm growth for everyone. The first, second, and third worlds will persist, but the cast of characters is always changing.[46]

THE IMPERIAL BALANCING ACT

Imperialism, like leadership, is about finding a balance between fear and love. Machiavelli believed that bonds of gratitude expire quickly, abandoned when self-interest calls; thus the "dread of punishment" makes fear a stronger instrument of control than love. Taking the long view, America is decreasingly loved and increasingly feared, Europe is increasingly loved and decreasingly feared, and China is increasingly both loved and feared. Geopolitics doesn't play favorites; it doesn't care which power is in the lead or what its government structure is. Its essence outweighs the particular American claim of exceptionalism from geopolitical cycles. Only in America does one hear the argument that it is like the sun in the solar system, bestowing its radiance on all the planets.[47] Elsewhere America's self-touted exceptionalism has become a sarcastic euphemism for brattiness. Other powers quite rightly want their place in (or as) the sun, to be the world's *Ordnungsmacht*.* For the first time in history, there exists a multipolar and multicivilizational world of three distinct superpowers competing on a planet of shrinking resources.[48] When each acts, each creates its own reality. For each, mere *raison d'état* has become *raison du système:* The extension of their core rationality and vision of order constitutes the highest morality.[49] The more America considers itself exceptional, the more its rivals will seek to advance their own exceptionalism at America's expense.[50] China feels it upholds the burden of maintaining the tenets of international law such as sovereignty and noninterference, while Europe's approach to world order transcends the interstate system altogether.

Each in its own way undermines the international architecture of global governance, eroding the fiction that laws and institutions alone can restrain imperial competition. Three different American presi-

---

*Of course, imperial power does not equal moral rectitude. The five permanent members of the UN Security Council—the United States, Britain, France, China, and Russia—are also the world's top arms dealers. China has profited from selling nuclear and long-range missile technology to Iran, Pakistan, and North Korea and exporting small arms to the worst human rights violators in exchange for long-term energy contracts.

dents in the twentieth century proclaimed a new world order under shared institutions.[51] Early in the Cold War, Toynbee also argued that the advent of the nuclear weapons necessitated a geopolitical condominium between the United States and Soviet Union and a greatly strengthened United Nations. He believed that only a world government marrying mixed economies and religious virtues could salvage humanity, going so far as to declare, "It is a foregone conclusion that the world is in any event going to be unified politically in the near future."[52] But as Timothy Garton Ash points out, "The moral 'we' of all humankind is more important than ever, but it's not the same as our operational 'we.'"[53] Other states might have continued to support the imperfect United Nations as a common forum for authoritative global diplomacy if the United States had, but its abusive negligence of the UN gave others the excuse to do the same.* The United States is more responsible than any other country for creating the post–World War II international architecture, but it is now doing as much as any other country to fragment it. Double standards and legalistic isolationism have undone America's exemplary record of promoting human rights, and unsanctioned preemptive war has undermined the authority of the UN Security Council. When superpower interests collide, the UN has proven to be as catastrophically irrelevant as the League of Nations.

Many believe that deep globalization among the United States, the EU, and China portends a world of interdependent hemispheres. Yet given their fortunate geographies—lying between northern, resource-rich latitudes and more temperate southern zones—each empire's true priority is to establish and manage self-sufficient pan-regions from the Arctic to Antarctica in its *own* hemisphere, making all others in its space reliant on its imperial core.[54] As America reconnects with Latin America in its search for low-cost, competitive production centers and alternative energy, the EU deepens its economic ties with the Arab world for its energy resources, and China increasingly organizes the

---

*The UN is not viewed by any of the three superpowers as an overarching governance mechanism but as a forum in which to posture and, most importantly, block the others. It was never a central actor in geopolitical affairs, but instead has always been a stage. The UN is a *place* for consultation and joint declarations, but it is not *where* decisions are actually made. The UN operates at the mercy of the great powers and their budgets. The less they have in common in their approach to the world, the less they will use it. The UN has had many major humanitarian successes, from peacekeeping to providing food and medical aid around the world. It may create a democracy fund, a standing peacekeeping force, and a human rights council, but its standards for these will only matter where the superpowers don't bother to intervene, mostly in the third world.

trade and diplomatic patterns in the Far East, these pan-regions may harden into a planetary competition among world-islands eerily similar to what Orwell envisioned in *1984*.[55]

Even this scenario is optimistic, for superpowers are by definition willing to encroach on the turf of others—changing the world map in the process. Much as in geology, such tectonic shifts always result in earthquakes, particularly as rising powers tread on the entrenched position of the reigning hegemon.[56] The sole exception was the twentieth century Anglo-American transition in which Great Britain and the United States were allies and shared a common culture—and even that took two world wars to complete.[57] As the relative levels of power of the three superpowers draw closer, the temptation of the number-two to preemptively knock out the king on the hill grows, as does the lead power's incentive to preventively attack and weaken its ascending rival before being eclipsed.[58] David Hume wrote, "It is not a great disproportion between ourselves and others which produces envy, but on the contrary, a proximity."[59] While the density of contacts among the three superpowers makes the creation of a society of states more possible than ever—all the foreign ministers have one anothers' mobile phone numbers—the deep differences in interests among the three make forging a "culture of peace" more challenging than ever.[60]

As stealthy, globalized escalations continue, the potential sparks are manifold and growing: resource competition in the Caspian or South China seas, hyperterrorism with nuclear weapons, an attack in the Gulf of Aden or the Straits of Malacca. The uncertain alignments of lesser but still substantial powers such as Russia, Japan, and India could also cause escalation. Furthermore, America's foreign lenders could pull the plug to undermine its grand strategy, sparking economic turmoil, political acrimony, and military tension. War brings profit to the military-industrial complex and is always supported by the large patriotic camps on all sides. Yet the notion of a Sino-U.S. rivalry to lead the world is also premature and simplistic, for in the event of their conflict, Europe would be the winner, as capital would flee to its sanctuaries.

These great tensions are being played out in the world today, as each superpower strives to attain the most advantageous position *for* itself, while none are powerful enough to dictate the system *by* itself. Global stability thus hangs between the bookends Raymond Aron identified as "peace by law" and "peace by empire," the former toothless and the latter prone to excess.[61] Historically, successive iterations of balance of power and collective security doctrines have evolved from justifying war for strategic advantage into building systems to avoid it, with the post-Napoleonic "Concert of Europe" as the first of the modern era.[62] Because it followed rules, it was itself something of a societal system.* Even where these attempts at creating a stable world order have failed—including the League of Nations after World War I—systemic *learning* takes place in which states (particularly democracies) internalize the lessons of the past into their institutions to prevent history from repeating itself.[63] Toynbee too viewed history as progressive rather than purely cyclical, a wheel that not only turns around and around but also moves forward such that Civilization (with a big C) could become civilized.[64] But did he "give too much credit to time's arrows and not enough to time's cycle"?[65] Empires and superpowers usually promise peace but bring wars.[66] The time to recognize the current revolutionary situation is now—*before* the next world war.[67]

How could the next world war be averted?[68] There does exist a tripartite coalition to triumph globalization over geopolitics: The American working class supports Chinese workers by shopping at Wal-Mart, while its upper class spends on European cars and luxury items; both Europe and China buy American technology; and America's General Motors and Boeing and Europe's Airbus can attribute much of their profits to reduced costs derived from production in—and sales to—China. Capital markets allow for endless profit for all rather than a zero-sum competition. Furthermore, the "cult of the offensive" does not dominate military strategy today: In an age of nuclear weaponry, few believe that initiating conflict entails quick victory with minimal loss. Never has A.J.P. Taylor's adage been more true: If the goal of being a great power is to be able to fight a great war, the only way to remain a great power is not to fight one. The damage done to oneself through conflict has never been higher than in today's integrated world.

The tripolar world should be thought of as a stool: With two legs it cannot stand long; with three it can be stable.[69] The three-legged

---

*Rousseau praised the concert's dynamic, writing that "the balance existing between the power of these diverse members of the European society is more the work of nature than of art. It maintains itself without effort, in such a manner that if it sinks on one side, it reestablishes itself very soon on the other."

U.S.-EU-China stool is currently wobbling, and the new global strategy for the current turn of the geopolitical wheel is "equilibrium."[70] Equilibrium is dynamic, hence more difficult to keep in balance than the unchallenged hegemony of a single hegemon, but it nonetheless represents the next evolutionary stage beyond the laws of anarchy and balance of power. Equilibrium also inspires a more progressive psychology and vocabulary: The "multipolar" order rising powers seek is not the same as the "multilateral" order that is required to manage it in practice. Similarly, the idea of "checks and balances" connotes cautious reaction, while "division of labor" implies positive action toward common ends; "prudence" alone does not fulfill blithely made commitments, but "burden-sharing" could. Peace, justice, and order will only follow from equilibrium.[71]

There is as yet no clear vision for such a global concert of powers or a legitimate global division of labor among the three superpowers—but such multilateralism will be more a matter of imperial coordination than of channeling resources through common institutions.[72] A global strategy of equilibrium would transform the current power transition from a wrestling match of suspicious powers into a team cycling race in which the lead is alternately shared toward the same finish line. As Toynbee hoped, the West is not "doomed to make history repeat itself; it is open to us, through our own efforts, to give history, in our case, some new and unprecedented turn."[73] At present the term "international community" is little more than a euphemism for Western dominance; the West can expect no allegiance to a Western order masquerading as representative of global values decreed without global input. America has called on China to be a "responsible stakeholder" in the global system, but because it is implicitly an American order, China is naturally resistant to it. China will not exercise its enormous economic weight in the interests of antiquated and unrepresentative clubs like the G-8 that won't even let it in. Similarly, much as the efficacy of the UN Security Council today depends on the United States, the same is becoming true of China, which can also bribe the rotating Security Council members to vote its way. Without a new division of labor, Western institutions will diminish with America's power, leaving only classic geopolitical competition without even the veneer of diplomatic coordination. If the superpowers do not choose adaptation over fundamentalism, they will miss a chance to keep history permanently in the past.

Equilibrium requires that the United States, the EU, and China together determine the rules of the geopolitical game. Much as in a family, equilibrium entails a complex set of codes to domesticate international relations, with compromise a similarly crucial value.[74] The incentives in favor of creating institutions that intentionally diminish one's own power and elevate others are admittedly elusive; egotistical states need to be convinced that they would save costs through collaborations that serve their interests. But America could actually increase its influence if it tempers its power. The path between dominance and retrenchment is the active creation of an "international constitution" with broad allegiance, inspiring a collective maturation.[75]

Power is tamed by addressing core interests, not leapfrogging into utopia. Rather than the U.S.-Soviet-Chinese "strategic triangle" of the 1960s and 1970s, a G-3 institution of the United States, the EU, and China would be the most appropriate forum to establish deeper working relations among the superpowers.[76] By openly discussing specific countries where spheres of influence overlap and contradict one another such as Sudan, Iran, Uzbekistan, and Burma, their differences could be reduced from the strategic to the merely tactical. A broad agenda requiring active Chinese participation could go a long way toward softening Chinese suspicion of the United States and commit China to pooling resources with its peers. The further down the road one looks, the more global problems revolve around energy resources and fresh water rather than calculations of military power imbalances and territorial rivalry. Yet China's present exclusion from the deliberations of the International Energy Agency fuels its suspicion that there is an "invisible Western hand" keeping global oil prices high. Instead, key energy consumers can focus on bringing more oil to a free market, hence reducing prices, rather than locking in oil contracts with state-owned companies to secure it from others' reach.*

The world of the twenty-first century seems so complex and unpredictable that even the scientific genius Stephen Hawking pessimistically asked, "In a world that is in chaos politically, socially, and

---

*Even if China were to become a full player in the global energy market, its domestic demand would not allow it to cease its dealings with odious regimes. Peer pressure from the United States and the EU and threats of instability in its own oil-providing client states may gradually temper its full-service packages of arms shipments, debt forgiveness, aid, low-cost infrastructure projects, and diplomatic protection in the UN Security Council, but it will not support total sanctions or coerce regime change that could destabilize its energy supply. See David Zweig and Bi Jianhai, "China's Global Hunt for Energy," *Foreign Affairs*, September–October 2005.

environmentally, can the human race sustain another one hundred years?" The question echoes the realist pioneer Hans Morgenthau's admonition that "Scientism has left man enriched in his technical mastery of inanimate nature, but it has left him impoverished in his quest for an answer to the riddle of the universe and of his existence in it."[77] It is a great challenge to prognosticate on a world of diffusing power and contending empires, but Morgenthau was certain of this: Globalization (the "Scientism" of today) will not alone trump the geopolitical cycles of world war, for this ultimate task of history requires more than a blind belief in rationality. Indeed, history proves that mankind is often anything but rational, and often precisely when it needs rationality most.[78] Instead, altering our future course demands a deep knowledge of second-world political dynamics, a precise mutual understanding among the superpowers, and proactive and flexible statecraft to create and maintain stability among them.

Academics and former government officials have come up with no shortage of acronyms to embody their grand visions for managing global order—but reality always seems to have a different opinion.[79] The evolution of international laws and codes *without* war would undoubtedly serve the great powers most, but as the playwright Bertolt Brecht aphorized, "War is like love; it always finds a way."[80] Mankind will only progress systemically as far as it has progressed psychologically. Diplomacy is "the management of international relations by negotiation," wrote Sir Harold Nicolson.[81] War, in this sense, is not the continuation of politics by other means, but rather the cessation of negotiation.* A century ago, globalization was defeated by geopolitics, unleashing World War I. The question is whether history will repeat itself a century later. The answer remains unknown, for as the second world shapes both geopolitics and globalization, diplomacy becomes ever more an art.

---

*As Kissinger argued, "Diplomacy in the classic sense, the adjustment of differences through negotiation, is possible only in 'legitimate' international orders. . . . It is a mistake to assume that diplomacy can always settle international disputes if there is 'good faith' and 'willingness to come to an agreement.' For in a revolutionary international order, each power will seem to its opponent to lack precisely these qualities. . . . When the fate of empires is at stake, the convictions of their statesmen are the medium for survival." Kissinger, *World Restored*, 2, 8.

ACKNOWLEDGMENTS

OVERWHELMED AT THE experience of his round-the-world journey, Arnold Toynbee wrote, "Words of thanks are inadequate. The best way for us to show our gratitude will be by trying to turn to some account all that we have learnt through the disinterested help that we have received from a very large number of people all round the World. The memory of this kindness is the most precious part of the mental cargo that we have brought back with us. . . ."

Tracking global trends while traveling around the world is not something one can do alone. A wise friend once told me that "true insights come from reading and loneliness and reflection and travel." It must be added that the validation of the ideas that come from travel is impossible without the generosity and expertise of the countless individuals one encounters along the way. I am honored that this book may serve as a vehicle to spread their wisdom.

Thanks to Ian Bremmer, the charismatic founder of Eurasia Group, I was able to take advantage of the highly impressive expertise of a globe-spanning set of analysts. In particular, I am grateful to Tanya Costello, Kaan Nazli, Preston Keat, Patrick Esteruelas, Allyson Benton,

Christopher Garman, Geoff Porter, Rochdi Younsi, Peter Khalil, Simon Kitchen, Ben Faulks, Wolfango Piccoli, John Green, Ross Schaap, Sijin Cheng, Erik Tollefson, Robert Herrera-Lim, Bruce Klingner, and Amitabh Dubey.

Similarly, the International Crisis Group has a well-earned reputation for sharp analysis and proposals. Its president, Gareth Evans, and his far-flung staff has also been of great value to this project, particularly James Lyon, Sabine Freizer, David Lewis, Michael Hall, Shirin Amirkyzy, Joanna Nathan, Samina Ahmed, Markus Schultze-Kraft, Karim Sadjadpour, Hugh Roberts, Joost Hiltermann, Sidney Jones, and Francesca Lawe-Davies.

For assistance with thinking about Europe's East, I am particularly grateful to Robert Cooper of the European Union, who generously shared his time and ideas, as well as his colleagues Riina Kionka, Jukka Leskala, and James Moran. Manfred Stinnes, Frank Umbach, Alexander Rahr, Nadia Verjee, Joelle Fiss, Ann Mettler, Sebastian Kaempf, Agnes Gilka-Boetzow, Ulrike Guerot, and Dan Dombey were also very thoughtful. Thanks also to participants in the Global Atlanticists group of the Friedrich Ebert Stiftung, especially Thorsten Benner, Arnd Henze, Derek Chollet, Julianne Smith, and Michael Haltzel. Very useful insights, comments, and corrections came from Paddy Ashdown, Lane Greene, David Young, Neil Pyper, Aidan Manktelow, Giri Jadeja, Alex Wooley, Masha Rosner, Colin Temme, Tom Weston, Tom Melia, Andy Cohen, Rob Sobhani, Larry Wohlers, Matt Bryza, Cliff Gaddy, Bogdan Tereshchenko, Anatole Faykin, Eric Johnson, John Brown, Taras Kuzio, Richard Byrne, David Philips, Charles King, Hugh Pope, Mark Nichols, Jennifer Long, Stephen Kinzer, Omer Taspiner, Warren Valdmanis, Eric Green, Cory Welt, Jan Neutze, Soner Cagaptay, Trevor Gunn, Diego Osorio, Bob Simmons, Hamid Ladjevardi, Matt Spence, Ron Asmus, Ronald Steel, and Richard Giragosian. While traveling in Europe's East I was greatly assisted by Arnoldas Pranckevicus, Ramunas Vilpisauskas, Giedrimas Jeglinskas, Kostiantyn Kononenko, Viktor Nikitiuk, Rostyslav Pawlenko, Alexander Gladskyy, Igor Dir, Volodymir Makukha, Dimtry Kiselev, Yulia Mostova, Varvara Zhluktenko, Yulya Borisova, Kostyantyn Kvurt, Vlada Tkach, Mykolay Churylov, Olga Sych, Vitalij Sych, Vera Nanivska, Valeriy Chaly, Hryhoriy Nemyria, Christoph Saurenbach, Tim Fairbank, David Dettman, John Herbst, Juhani Grossman, Olya Smyrnova, Inna Bogoslovska,

Yulia Volosevych, Sara Pfaffenhofer, Katja Ardanyan, Gesine Stern, Rostislav Gavrilov, Yuri Arabski, Karl Wolfram, Sasa Rikanovic, Jadranka Jelincic, Nenad Djurdjevic, Srdjan Cvijic, Ivana Aleksic, Ivan Vejvoda, Bozidar Djelic, Timothy Collins, Jasna Matic, Andrew Vonnegut, Tanja Miscevic, Zeljko Komsic, Ognian Zlatev, Fekri Shaban, Tugba Kalafatoglu, Murat Ucer, Soli Özel, Cengiz Candar, Yilmaz Argueden, Suzan Benmayor, Hasan Cemal, Erkan Keremoglu, Edip Baser, Ali Babacan, Youssuf Alsharif, Suat Kiniklioglu, Roger Rigaud, Georgi Baramidze, Zurab Noghaideli, Giorgi Sumbadse, Avto Svadnize, Zeno Reichenbecher, David Absesadze, Alexander Rondeli, Theresa Freese, Tinatin Khidasheli, Elizabeth Owen, Elin Suleymanov, Ingrid Gossinger, Berit Linderman, Dennis Sammut, Jehangir Hajiyev, Lynn Sferrazza, Vafa Gulizade, Elman Salayev, Florian Schroeder, Elmar Jabarov, Fariz Ismailzade, Mehrnaz Davoudi, Ulvi Ismayil, Jyoti Swaroop Pande, Betty Blair, Dallas Frohrib, Leila Aliyeva, and Lynn Sferrazza. Special thanks for their warm hospitality go to Eugenia Klochko, Nenad Rava, Robert and Helena Finn, Mark Simakovsky, Sasha Bruce, Taleh Ziyadov, and Thomas Goltz.

For significant insights on Central Asia, I am thankful to James Millward, Daniel Burghart, Johannes Linn, Olya Oliker, David Hoffman, Barney Rubin, Roman Vassilenko, Murad Sharapov, Nurzhan Zhumbakov, Kevin Jones, Anders Aslund, Zeyno Baran, Chris Seiple, Bill Maynes, Ethan Wilensky Lanford, Xenia Dormandy, Dan Markey, Steve Cohen, Evan Feigenbaum, Judi Kilachand, Bama Athriya, Nicholas Swanstrom, Sartaj Aziz, and especially Matthew Oresman. While traveling in the region, I learned a great deal from Andrew Wilson, Berik Otemurat, Fabrizio Vielmini, Josh Machleder, Alexander Sosnin, Assel Rustemova, Oraz Jandosov, Azamat Ablazimov, Kassymzhomart Tokaev, Murat Auezov, Yerbol Suleimenov, Meiirzhan Mashan, Adil Abishev, Azamat Abdymomunov, Nikolay Kuzmin, Kadyr Toktogulov, Nicolas Ebnother, Rosa Oltambaeva, Edil Baissalov, Shakirat Toktosunova, Elbek Khojayev, Catherine Eldridge, Susan Carnduff, Farkhad Tolipov, Jeff Erlich, Steve Labensky, Jon Purnell, Ulugbek Ishankhodjaev, Abdujabar Abduvakhitov, and Ulugbeck Khasanoff.

As a Latin America neophyte, I am very thankful for the assistance of Moises Naim, Carlos Lozada, Javier Corrales, Kai Poetschke, Bill Hinchberger, David de Ferranti, Hernando de Soto, Shahnaz Radjy,

Meredith Davenport, Maria Hutcheson, Timothy O'Neil-Dunne, Jan Boyer, Andres Oppenheimer, Jenny Caplan, Jose Yunis, Juan Enriquez, Hillary Batjer-Johnson, Erica Breth, Moises Benamor, Michael Shifter, Lorena Barbaria, Gilberto Dupas, Paulo Roberto de Almeida, Rubens Barbosa, Eiiti Sato, Amado Cervo, Shepard Forman, Adriana Abdenur, David Henschel, Nathalie Cely, Cecelia Zarate, Maria Teresa Petersen, Peter Schechter, Blas Pérez Henríquez, Sylvie Naville, Joerg Schimmel, Pedro Burelli, Michael Penfold, Dante Pesce, Steve Reifenberg, and Katty Kauffman. While traveling in South America, I was fortunate to make the acquaintance of Alesia Rodriguez, Toby Bottome, Asdrubal Baptista, Carlos Romero, Phil Gunson, Lorenzo Mendoza, Alejandro Plaz, Juan Forero, Michael Rowan, Brian Ellsworth, Ramon Espinasa, Steve Ambrus, Mike Ceaser, Andrea Armeni, Cristina Lleras, Miguel Silva, Luis Guillermo Plata, Camilo Reyes Restrepo, Alberto Galán Sarmiento, Mike McCullough, Ricardo Avila, Jhoney Baracolo, Paula Boyce Castro, Charles Tang, Marina Stabile, Eliana Cardoso, Philip Yang, Nicolas Ducote, and Juan Tokatlian. Allan Oliver provided excellent, thorough research for which I am very grateful, and Julia Sweig was a patient and energetic tutor.

Essential background on the Arab world was provided by Ken Pollack, Tamara Cofman Wittes, Jeremy Shapiro, Shibley Telhami, Ammar Abdulhamid, Afshin Molavi, Nir Rosen, Jeremy Greenstock, Erik Petersen, Tarik Yousef, Yvonne Haddad, Dan Byman, John Esposito, Jon Alterman, Haim Malka, Charles King Mallory, Herro Mustafa, Alyse Nelson Bloom, Shamil Idriss, Lisa Anderson, Colin McCullough, Mohammed Alami, Sherif El Diwaney, Daniel Davies, Ayham Ammora, Cathy Bellafronto, Bill Dowell, Marin Strmecki, Ellen Jermaine, Brian Katulis, Nick Snyder, Michael Totten, Abdelwahab El-Affendi, Dan Runde, Tim Pounds, Randa Fahmy-Hudome, Ali Aujali, Mahmoud Shammam, Joe Saba, David Goldwyn, Scott Anderson, Steven Cook, Ed Girardet, Karim Chrobog, Alex Fox, Aaron Miller, Helima Croft, Maria Alzahrani-Sturgis, Ghassan Salamé, Sogand Zamani, Fadi Elsalameen, Emile El-Hokayam, Karim Kawar, Ziad Abdelnour, Hady Amr, Michael Rubin, Katherine Brown, Carol O'Leary, Faiz al-Gailani, Qubad Talabani, Heyrsh Abdul, Babak Yektafar, Jared Cohen, Najmeh Bozorgmehr, Negar Azimi, Ellen Laipson, Shereen El Feki, Robin Wright, Mahmood Sariolghalam, Anoush Ehteshami, Nail al-Jubeir, Karthik Nagarajan, and Mark Gerson. While traveling across the region, I benefited enormously from the thoughts of Saleh Abdul-salam Saleh, Hasouna Shawsh, Mohamed Taher Siala, Rajab M. Shiglabu, Greg Berry, Ethan Goldrich, Elizabeth Fristschlee, Ethan Chorin, Taher Ahmed Aboulkassim, Mustafa Onallah, Abdalla Othman Aburrahim, Salem Hamza, Ismail Serageldin, Karim Abdel Monem, Seif Fahmy, Hasan Abdalla, Dalia Abdel Kader, Michael Slackman, Karim Haggag, Abdel Monem Said Aly, Samer Shehata, Saad Eddin Ibrahim, Scott Macleod, Barry Iverson, Ezzat Ibrahim, Michael Corbin, Roger Kenna, Amany Asfour, David Selman, Max Rodenbeck, Asmaa Shalabi, Christine Spolar, Hemy Abouleish, Blake Hounshell, Josh Stacher, Bassem Awadallah, Fouad Ghanma, Marwan Jamil Muasher, Stephen Rivers, Emile Cubeisy, Khaldoon Tabaza, Sharif Al Zu'bi, Laith Arafeh, Sami Al-Jundi, Ziad Abu Amr, Akram Baker, Michael Tarazi, Marwan Aburdeneh, Mounir Kleibo, Jonathan Lincoln, Guy Raz, Rami Khoury, Michael Young, Gregory Marchese, Maha al Azar, Matt Pilcher, Juliet Wurr, Ryan Gliha, Muhamad Mugraby, Habib Malik, Hassan Fadlallah, Hisham Kassab, Oussama Safa, Paul Salem, Kate Brooks, Kaelen Wilson-Goldie, Irina Prentice, Joe Koayess, Katherine Zoepf, Diane King, Nabil Abou Charaf, Falah Mustafa Bakir, Rawand Darwesh, Sarko Mahmoud, Mohammad Sadik, Mohammed Ihsan, Aumeed Nouri Amin, Jawhar Sourchi, Bayan Sami Abdul Rahman, Khaled Salih, Abdul Kader Mustafa, Hassan Fattah, Nasser Saidi, Tamur Goudarzi-Pour, Anthony Shadid, Jamil El Hage, Michel Costandi, Sumant Sareen, Abdul Aziz al Sager, Christian Koch, Sunil John, Daria Prentine, Dergham Owainati, Roger Clayton, Maggie Steber, Alex Fowler, Lucy Martens, Ali Solaimani, Oula Ghawi, Khalil Matar, Siobhan Leyden, James Reardon-Anderson, Abdul Aziz al-Mahmoud, Elan Fabbri, Cherif and Lynn Hassouna, Richard Neu, John Lochner, Muna Abu-Sulayman, and Mohammed Khaled al-Faisal. I owe very special thanks to Bryan Gunderson and Karim Makdisi.

The following people provided excellent insight into East Asian affairs: Frank Richter, Ramesh Thakur, Elizabeth Economy, Pamela Mar, Bill O'Chee, Frank Blithe, Cobb Mixter, Michael Kulma, Anwar Ibrahim, Paul Frandano, Pranay Gupte, Yuan-Kang Wang, Jeff Bader, Richard Bush, James Clad, Ziad Haider, Roger Mitton, Ernie Wilson, Pietra Rivoli, Siddharth Mohandas, Karan Khemka, and particularly Banning Garrett. While traveling in East Asia, I was intellectually assisted by Varun Vig, Cheryl Mainland Hall, Cheong Yip-Seng, Penny Low, Wai Chiew Chik, Eric Teo, Wayne Arnold, Siew Hoon Yeoh, Bontosoglou Vassilis, Bertrand Fort, Chua Chim Kang, Michael Vatikiotis, Simon Tay, Geoff Wade, Tommy Koh, Koh Buck Song, Tan Tai Yong, Amitav Acharya, Rohan Gunaratna, John Harrison, Christoph Marcinkowski, Haseenah Koyakutty, Christopher Roberts, Rajeev Sawhney, Manjeet S. Pardesi, Kwa Chong Guan, RK Mishra, Raja Mohan, Shelley Thakral, Alex Perry, Gautam Adhikari, Rahul Singh, Sundeep Waslekar, Rich Howard, John Boomgard, Hadi Soesastro, Rizal Sukma, Bantarto Bandoro, Umar Hadi, M. C. Abad, Nono Makarim, Hasmy Aham, Emile Yeoh, Chandran Jeshurun, Khairy Jamaluddin, Justin Leong Ming Loong, Jawhar Hassan, Abdul Razak Baginda, Surin Pitsuwan, Emile Yu, Crystal Mo, Zhao Huasheng, Wu Xinbo, Pan Guang, Fang Xing-Hai, Stefan Donle, Fan Gang, Evan Osnos, Joshua Cooper Ramo, Eric Hagt, Wu Baiyi, He Fan, Wang Shuo, Huang Shan, Wu Jianmin, Qin Min, Hans Au, Rafael Wober, and Jennifer Welker. Very special thanks for their personal kindness and support to Kishore Mahbubani, Umej Bhatia, Daniel A. Bell, Kim Beng Phar, and Jeremy Jurgens.

Since this project began, weekday-weeknight and work-pleasure distinctions ceased to exist, reinforcing the ageless power of travel. However, the benefits of the far-flung Indian diaspora gave me the special advantage of cultural and culinary nourishment when I needed it most. For this I am most grateful to my loving relatives Sharat and Rashmey Seth, Manoj and Mala Chawla, and Arun and Sunita Seth.

Travelers bond faster than other breeds. I have had the pleasure of truly stimulating companionship for several portions of these voyages. Jan-Philipp Goertz, an inveterate "terrist," has been a dear friend on almost every continent, and his spontaneity was a great asset in Ukraine, Tanzania, and Egypt. Sebastian Strassburg, an incorrigible gentleman and adventurer, was the ideal mate for the "Bosnia to Baku Rally." It was my honor to be his navigator. Joel DeCastro in Jordan and Louise Brown in Libya enriched my own experiences through their unique missions. My new Tibetan friends Gamba and Losang led me up our common holy mountain and across thousands of miles of the world's most rugged frontier.

Were it not for the School of Foreign Service at Georgetown University, I would never have learned geopolitics under Professor Charles Pirtle. Between my undergraduate and graduate studies there, I have been inspired and mentored by faculty who supported my many phases of intellectual experimentation. In particular, Dean Robert Gallucci and Michael Brown have encouraged me since the beginning. Thomas Banchoff, Dan Nexon, Sally Ann Baynard, and Michael Mazaar provided both rigorous methodological coaching and opened interdisciplinary horizons. Georgetown's president, Jack DeGioia, not only introduced me to philosophy the fun way but also unhesitatingly lent his personal support to this venture. Doug Shaw provided memorable enthusiasm and useful contacts in every corner of the planet, both of which I am deeply thankful for. Jennifer Ward, Scott Fleming, and Lauren Rivkin also kindly opened Georgetown's impressive alumni database.

The World Economic Forum in Geneva, Switzerland, is a unique institution where the term "global thinking" has genuine meaning in both theory and practice. Under the guidance of Rick Samans, and colleagues Sven Behrendt, Sean Cleary, Lee Howell and Thierry Malleret, I have since 2000 benefited enormously from the forum's special perch at the intersection of public and private expertise, and its willingness to anticipate an uncertain future. I thank them all sincerely.

The intellectual firepower housed in Washington's think tank community remains second to none, and it has been my privilege to be a fellow at both the Brookings Institution and New America Foundation since returning to Washington in 2002. At Brookings, Strobe Talbott, Jim Steinberg, Fiona Hill, and particularly Ann Florini provided valuable guidance in shaping the vision of this project and marrying it with policy relevance. The New America Foundation is fearless in its willingness to challenge conventional wisdom and explore the world from unconventional angles. I am grateful to Ted Halstead, Steve Clemons, Sherle Schwenninger, Rachel White, and Simone Frank for bringing me on board and providing constant support during my long months away. In the final phase of writing, Ned Hodgman, Michael Lind, and Barry Lynn were ideal intellectual sounding boards, refining and correcting my thoughts with their vast knowledge. Alex Konetzki provided excellent feedback on several chapters as well as admirably shouldering the burden of "imperial grunt work." Danielle Maxwell, Leila Saradj, and Jeff Meyer cheerfully made many rounds to every library in Washington, carting the legal and physical limits of books each time. This manuscript was completed prior to my service as an adviser to United States Special Operations Forces and in no way reflects the views of the United States government or any of its employees.

Pico Iyer and Robert Kaplan, two renowned psychoanalysts of the world, the former spiritual and the latter strategic, stand out as perennial mentors. They have been perfectly unintrusive role models and correspondents for close to a decade and a constant source of wisdom through their devotion to portraying the world as the physical embodiment of ideas. I thank them here for kinship that goes well beyond the scope of this book.

I cannot thank enough so many dear friends who accepted the role of e-friend for most of the past two years. Jeremy Goldberg gave this project its most essential boost: the first. My cosmocratic brain trust of Rana Sarkar and Vijay Vaitheeswaran provided the constant incentive of high expectations as well as a nonstop flurry of ideas. From far and wide, Richard Ponzio, Maria Figueroa, Greg Lucas, Tom Sanderson, Eliza Griswold, David Rice, Paul Roberts, Lyndsay Howard, Verena Ringler, Lawrence Groo, Raj Kumar, and Ben Skinner have been refreshing sources of energy and relevant insights. The "Shakti All-Stars" are the most trusting and loyal friends one could hope for: Anna Beauregard, Alex and Samar Bloomingdale, Colin Browne, Justine Graham, Yasmin Ibrahim, Shilpa Mohan, and Brooks Rosenquist. A particular group of close friends also went above and beyond the call of duty to support my rent-free lifestyle, providing shelter and emotional support during my brief visits home. For all that and more I am grateful to Willy Pell, Krishna Kumar, Farah Pandith, Peter and Susan Singer, Joy de Menil and Laird Reed, Kate Taylor, Jim Clippard, Natasha Kohne, Karima Sagrani and Gaurav Burman, Swathi Kappagantula, and Asad Naqvi. I am especially grateful to my wife, Ayesha Khanna, for the world we have created together where I am always at home.

My agent, Jennifer Joel at International Creative Management, is a grand strategist in her own right, and very much a trusted friend. I thank her profusely, and Katie Sigelman as well, for investing their time and energy in me, and for convincing Random House to accept my proposal without even a sample chapter. The boost they provided gave new meaning to all my previous travels and all that was yet to come. Editors are to authors what coaches and instructors are to athletes and artists. Though accustomed to working with far superior intellects, Will Murphy showed great patience and just the right amount of steering to whittle down what began as an untenably voluminous manuscript. Helen Conford of Penguin U.K. rounded out my very own "Dream Team" with her keen sense of what makes a good book. At Random House, Evan Camfield was a sharp and efficient production editor, and Claire Tisne, Nicole Bond, Lea Beresford, and Joelle Dieu made generous promotional contributions. Martin Schneider was a superb and conscientious copy editor, and David Lindroth pushed mental horizons with his world-class, innovative cartography.

This book was written wherever I could find quietude: remote corners of China, an air-conditioned living room in Dubai, the Patagonian highlands, long transcontinental flights. But whenever possible, I have tried to write within the confines of the most caring and supportive household I could ever wish for. My parents, Sushil and Manjula Khanna, have survived fires and floods and never missed a beat in parenting, while my brother Gaurav, sister-in-law Anuradha, and niece Anisha have provided constant joy. My dad in particular read each chapter multiple times, never tiring of the successive drafts and never failing to find fresh errors and ways to improve the text. I am forever grateful to them.

BIBLIOGRAPHY

Adams, Richard H., Jr. *International Migration, Remittances, and the Brain Drain: A Study of 24 Labor Exporting Countries.* Washington, D.C.: World Bank, 2005.

Agnew, John, and Stuart Corbridge. *Mastering Space: Hegemony, Territory, and International Political Economy.* London: Routledge, 1995.

Aksyonov, Vasily. *The Island of Crimea.* New York: Vintage, 1984.

Alagappa, Muthiah, ed. *Asian Security Practice: Material and Ideational Influences.* Palo Alto, Calif.: Stanford University Press, 1998.

Alesina, Alberto, and Enrico Spolaore. *The Size of Nations.* Cambridge, Mass.: MIT Press, 2003.

Aly, Abdel Monem Said, and Shai Feldman. *Ecopolitics: Changing the Regional Context of Arab-Israeli Peacemaking.* Cambridge, Mass.: Belfer Center for Science and International Affairs, John F. Kennedy School of Government, 2003.

Anderson, Malcolm. *Frontiers: Territory and State Formation in the Modern World.* Cambridge, U.K.: Polity Press, 1996.

Andes 2020: A New Strategy for the Challenges of Colombia and the Region (A Center for Preventive Action Report). New York: Council on Foreign Relations Press, 2004.

Andrew, Christopher, and Vasili Mitrokhin. *The World Was Going Our Way: The KGB and the Battle for the Third World*. New York: Basic Books, 2005.

Andric, Ivo. *The Days of the Consuls*. Belgrade: Dereta, 2000.

Appadurai, Arjun, ed. *Globalization*. Durham, N.C.: Duke University Press, 2000.

Aron, Raymond. *Peace and War: A Theory of International Relations*. Garden City, N.Y.: Doubleday, 1966.

Aslan, Reza. *No god but God: The Origins, Evolution, and Future of Islam*. New York: Random House, 2005.

Aslund, Anders. *Building Capitalism: The Transformation of the Former Soviet Bloc*. New York: Cambridge University Press, 2002.

Avedon, John F. *In Exile from the Land of Snows*. New York: Alfred A. Knopf, 1984.

Ayoob, Mohammed. *The Third World Security Predicament: State Making, Regional Conflict, and the International System*. Boulder, Colo.: Lynne Rienner, 1995.

Bacevich, Andrew J. *The New American Militarism: How Americans Are Seduced by War*. New York: Oxford University Press, 2005.

Baiocchi, Gianpaolo. *Radicals in Power: The Worker's Party and Experiments in Urban Democracy in Brazil*. New York: Zed Books, 2003.

Barakat, Halim. *The Arab World: Society, Culture, and State*. Berkeley: University of California Press, 1993.

Baran, Zeyno. *Hizb ut-Tahrir: Islam's Political Insurgency*. Washington, D.C.: Nixon Center, 2004.

Barber, Benjamin. *Fear's Empire: War, Terrorism, and Democracy*. New York: W. W. Norton, 2004.

Barnett, Michael. *Dialogues in Arab Politics: Negotiations in Regional Order*. New York: Columbia University Press, 1998.

Barnett, Thomas P. M. *The Pentagon's New Map: War and Peace in the Twenty-first Century*. New York: Putnam, 2004.

Bartleson, James. *A Genealogy of Sovereignty*. Cambridge, U.K.: Cambridge University Press, 1995.

Beinert, Peter. *The Good Fight: Why Liberals—and Only Liberals—Can Win the War on Terror and Make America Great Again*. New York: HarperCollins, 2006.

Bell, Daniel A. *Beyond Liberal Democracy: Political Thinking for an East Asian Context*. Princeton, N.J.: Princeton University Press, 2006.

———. *East Meets West: Human Rights and Democracy in East Asia*. Princeton, N.J.: Princeton University Press, 2000.

Bergsten, C. Fred, Bates Gill, Nicholas Lardy, and Derek Mitchell. *China:*

The Balance Sheet—What the World Needs to Know Now About the Emerging Superpower. New York: Public Affairs, 2006.

Bernard, Cheryl. *Civil, Democratic Islam: Partners, Resources, and Strategies.* Santa Monica, Calif.: RAND Corporation, 2003.

Birdsall, Nancy, and Augusto de la Torre. *Washington Contentious: Economic Policies for Social Equity in Latin America.* Washington, D.C.: Carnegie Endowment for International Peace and Inter-American Dialogue, 2001.

Blank, Stephen. *After Two Wars: Reflections on the American Strategic Revolution in Central Asia.* Carlisle, Penn.: Strategic Studies Institute, U.S. Army War College, 2005.

Blustein, Paul. *And the Money Kept Rolling In (and Out): Wall Street, the IMF, and the Bankrupting of Argentina.* New York: Public Affairs, 2005.

Bose, Sugata. *A Hundred Horizons: The Indian Ocean in the Age of Global Empire.* Cambridge, Mass.: Harvard University Press, 2006.

Bracken, Paul. *Fire in the East: The Rise of Asian Military Power and the Second Nuclear Age.* New York: HarperCollins, 1999.

Bradbury, Ray. *Fahrenheit 451.* New York: Ballantine, 1950.

Bradley, John R. *Saudi Arabia Exposed: Inside a Kingdom in Crisis.* New York: Palgrave Macmillan, 2005.

Braudel, Fernand. *The Mediterranean and the World in the Age of Philip II.* 2 volumes. Trans. Sian Reynolds. London: Collins Sons and Harper and Row, 1972.

Bremmer, Ian. *The J Curve: A New Way to Understand Why Nations Rise and Fall.* New York: Simon and Schuster, 2006.

Bringing Down Barriers: Regional Cooperation for Human Development and Human Security. Central Asia Human Development Report. Bratislava: UNDP Regional Bureau for Europe and the Commonwealth of Independent States, 2005.

Bronson, Rachel. *Thicker Than Oil: The United States and Saudi Arabia—a History.* New York: Oxford University Press, 2006.

Brown, Chris. *Sovereignty, Rights, and Justice: International Political Theory Today.* Cambridge, U.K.: Polity Press, 2002.

Brown, Lester. *Plan B 2.0.* Washington, D.C.: Earth Policy Institute, 2006.

Brown, Michael, Sean Lynn-Jones, and Steven Miller, eds. *Debating the Democratic Peace.* Cambridge, Mass.: MIT Press, 1996.

Brzezinksi, Zbigniew. *The Grand Chessboard: American Primacy and Its Geostrategic Imperatives.* New York: Basic Books, 1997.

Bull, Hedley. *The Anarchical Society: A Study of Order in World Politics.* New York: Columbia University Press, 1977.

Burgat, François. *Face to Face with Political Islam.* London: I. B. Tauris, 2003.

Burghart, Daniel L., and Theresa Sabonis-Helf, eds. *In the Tracks of Tamer-*

lane: *Central Asia's Path to the Twenty-first Century.* Washington, D.C.: Center for Technology and Security Policy, National Defense University, 2005.

Buruma, Ian. *Bad Elements: Chinese Rebels from Los Angeles to Beijing.* New York: Random House, 2001.

Buruma, Ian, and Avishai Margalit. *Occidentalism: The West in the Eyes of Its Enemies.* New York: Penguin, 2004.

Buttimer, Anne. *Geography and the Human Spirit.* Baltimore: Johns Hopkins University Press, 1993.

Buzan, Barry. *The United States and the Great Powers: World Politics in the Twenty-first Century.* Cambridge, U.K.: Polity Press, 2004.

Buzan, Barry, and Ole Wæver. *Regions and Powers: The Structure of International Security.* Cambridge, U.K.: Cambridge University Press, 2003.

Byman, Daniel L. *Deadly Connections: States That Sponsor Terrorism.* New York: Cambridge University Press, 2005.

Campbell, Joseph Keim, Michael O'Rourke, and David Shier, eds. *Topics in Contemporary Philosophy.* Cambridge, Mass.: MIT Press, 2005.

Cardoso, Fernando. *Charting a New Course: The Politics of Globalization and Social Transformation.* Ed. Mauricio A. Font. Lanham, Md.: Rowman and Littlefield, 2001.

Cardoso, Fernando, and Peter Bell. *A Break in the Clouds: Latin America and the Caribbean in 2005.* Washington, D.C.: Inter-American Dialogue, 2005.

Carothers, Thomas, and Marina Ottoway, eds. *Uncharted Journey: Promoting Democracy in the Middle East.* Washington, D.C.: Carnegie Endowment for International Peace, 2005.

Carr, Edward Hallett. *The Twenty Years' Crisis, 1919–1939: An Introduction to the Study of International Relations.* New York: Harper Perennial, 1964.

Chang, Gordon. *The Coming Collapse of China.* New York: Random House, 2001.

Chase, Robert S., Emily Hill, and Paul M. Kennedy, eds. *Pivotal States and U.S. Policy: A New Strategy for U.S. Policy in the Developing World.* New York: W. W. Norton, 1999.

Chomsky, Noam. *Failed States: The Abuse of Power and the Assault on Democracy.* New York: Metropolitan Books, 2006.

Chua, Amy. *World on Fire: How Exporting Free Market Democracy Breeds Ethnic Hatred and Global Instability.* New York: Doubleday, 2003.

Clissold, Tim. *Mr. China.* New York: HarperCollins, 2004.

Cohen, Benjamin J. *The Geography of Money.* Ithaca, N.Y.: Cornell University Press, 1998.

Cohen, Saul. *Geography and Politics in a Divided World.* New York: Random House, 1963.

Cohen, Stephen P. *The Idea of Pakistan.* Washington, D.C.: Brookings Institution Press, 2004.

———. *India: Emerging Power.* Washington, D.C.: Brookings Institution, 2002.

Coker, Christopher. *Empires in Conflict: The Growing Rift Between Europe and the United States.* Whitehall Paper no. 58. London: Royal United Services Institute, 2003.

Collins, Allan. *Security in Southeast Asia: Domestic Regional and Global Issues.* Boulder, Colo.: Lynne Rienner, 2003.

Cooper, Robert. *The Breaking of Nations: Order and Chaos in the Twenty-first Century.* New York: Atlantic Monthly Press, 2003.

Cordesman, Anthony H. *Iran's Developing Military Capabilities.* Washington, D.C.: CSIS Press, 2005.

Cornell, Svante E., et al. *Regional Security in the South Caucasus: The Role of NATO.* Washington, D.C.: Central Asia–Caucasus Institute, Paul H. Nitze School of Advanced International Studies, 2004.

Crocker, Chester, ed. *Turbulent Peace.* Washington, D.C.: United States Institute of Peace, 2001.

Daalder, Ivo, Nicole Gnesotto, and Philip Gordon, eds. *Crescent of Crisis: U.S.-European Strategy for the Greater Middle East.* Washington, D.C.: Brookings Institution Press, 2006.

Dahrendorf, Ralf. *Reflections on the Revolution in Europe.* New York: Crown, 1990.

Danziger, Nick. *Danziger's Travels: Beyond Forbidden Frontiers.* New York: HarperCollins, 1987.

de Bellaigue, Christopher. *In the Rose Garden of Martyrs: A Memoir of Iran.* New York: HarperCollins, 2005.

de Blij, Harm. *Why Geography Matters: Three Challenges Facing America: Climate Change, the Rise of China, and Global Terrorism.* New York: Oxford University Press, 2005.

De Ferranti, David M., Guillermo E. Perry, Francisco H. G. Ferreira, and Michael Walton, eds. *Inequality in Latin America and the Caribbean: Breaking with History?* Washington, D.C.: International Bank for Reconstruction and Development, World Bank, 2004.

de Soto, Hernando. *The Mystery of Capital: Why Capitalism Triumphs in the West and Fails Everywhere Else.* New York: Basic Books, 2003.

Diamond, Jared. *Collapse: How Societies Choose to Fail or Succeed.* New York: Penguin, 2004.

Dobbins, James. *The UN's Role in Nation-Building: From the Congo to Iraq.* Santa Monica, Calif.: RAND Corporation, 2005.

Dominguez, Jorge I., and Byung Cook Kim, eds. *Between Compliance and Conflict: Between East Asia, Latin America, and the "New" Pax Americana.* New York: Routlege, 2005.

Doyle, Michael. *Empires.* Ithaca, N.Y.: Cornell University Press, 1986.

Drakuli, Slavenka. *Café Europa: Life After Communism.* London: Penguin, 1996.

Dresch, Paul, and James Piscatori, eds. *Monarchies and Nations: Globalization and Identity in the Arab States of the Gulf.* London: I. B. Tauris, 2005.

Dupont, Alan. *East Asia Imperilled: Transnational Challenges to Security.* Cambridge, U.K.: Cambridge University Press, 2001.

Easterly, William. *White Man's Burden: Why the West's Efforts to Aid the Rest Have Done So Much Ill and So Little Good.* New York: Penguin, 2006.

Ehteshami, Anoush. *Globalization and Geopolitics in the Middle East.* London: Routledge, 2007.

Eisenman, Joshusa, Eric Heginbotham, and Derek Mitchell, eds. *China and the Developing World: Beijing's Strategy for the Twenty-first Century.* Armonk, N.Y.: M. E. Sharpe, 2006

Elman, Colin, and Miriam Fendius Elman. *Progress in International Relations Theory: Appraising the Field.* Cambridge, Mass.: MIT Press, 2003.

Enriques, Juan. *The Untied States of America: Polarization, Fracturing, and Our Future.* New York: Crown, 2005.

Esposito, John L. *Unholy War: Terror in the Name of Islam.* New York: Oxford University Press, 2002.

Estevadeordal, Antoni, Dani Rodrik, Alan M. Taylor, and Andres Velasco, eds. *Integrating the Americas: FTAA and Beyond.* Cambridge, Mass.: Harvard University Press, 2004.

Etzioni, Amitai. *From Empire to Community: A New Approach to International Relations.* New York: Palgrave Macmillan, 2004.

Eurasia Economic Summit 2002 Report: Sustaining Growth in Uncertain Times. Cologny and Geneva, Switzerland: World Economic Forum, 2002.

European Defense Integration: Bridging the Gap Between Strategy and Capabilities. Washington, D.C.: Center for Strategic and International Studies, 2005.

Fairbank, John King, ed. *The Chinese World Order: Traditional China's Foreign Relations.* Harvard East Asian Series. Cambridge, Mass.: Harvard University Press, 1968.

Falcoff, Mark. *A Culture of Its Own: Taking Latin America Seriously.* New Brunswick, N.J.: Transaction Publishers, 1998.

Fandy, Mahmoun. *Saudi Arabia and the Politics of Dissent*. New York: St. Martin's Press, 1999.

Fay, Marianne, ed. *The Urban Poor in Latin America (Directions in Development)*. Washington, D.C.: International Bank for Reconstruction and Development, World Bank, 2005.

Feldman, Noah. *After Jihad: America and the Struggle for Islamic Democracy*. New York: Farrar, Straus and Giroux, 2003.

———. *What We Owe Iraq: War and the Ethics of Nation Building*. New York: Princeton University Press, 2005.

Ferguson, Niall. *1914: Why the World Went to War*. New York: Penguin, 1998.

———. *The War of the World: History's Age of Hatred*. London: Penguin, 2006.

Fishman, Ted C. *China, Inc.* New York: Scribner, 2005.

Fletcher, George P. *Romantics at War: Glory and Guilt in an Age of Terrorism*. Princeton, N.J.: Princeton University Press, 2002.

Foer, Franklin. *How Soccer Explains the World: An Unlikely Theory of Globalization*. New York: HarperCollins, 2004.

Forging a World of Liberty Under Law: U.S. National Security in the Twenty-first Century: Final Report of the Princeton Project on National Security. Princeton, N.J.: Woodrow Wilson School of Public and International Affairs, 2006.

Fort, Bertrand, ed. *Overcoming Vulnerability: Managing New Security Challenges in Asia and Europe*. Singapore: Marshall Cavendish Academic, 2005.

Frankel, Francine R., and Harry Harding, eds. *The India-China Relationship: What the United States Needs to Know*. New York: Columbia University Press, 2004.

French, Howard W. *A Continent for the Taking: The Tragedy and Hope of Africa*. New York: Vintage, 2005.

Freud, Sigmund. *Forgetting Things*. London: Penguin, 1941; reprint, 2002.

Friedman, Thomas L. *From Beirut to Jerusalem*. New York: Farrar, Straus and Giroux, 1989.

———. *The World Is Flat: A Brief History of the Twenty-first Century*. New York: Farrar, Straus and Giroux, 2005.

Fromkin, David. *A Peace to End All Peace: The Fall of the Ottoman Empire and the Creation of the Modern Middle East*. New York: Henry Holt, 1989.

Fukuyama, Francis. *America at the Crossroads: Democracy, Power, and the Neoconservative Legacy*. New Haven, Conn.: Yale University Press, 2006.

———. *The End of History and the Last Man*. New York: Avon Books, 1992.

———. *State-Building: Governance and World Order in the Twenty-first Century*. Ithaca, N.Y.: Cornell University Press, 2004.

Gachechiladze, Revaz. *The New Georgia: Space, Society, Politics*. Eastern European Studies no. 3. London: University College London Press, 1995.

Galbraith, John Kenneth. *The Economics of Innocent Fraud: Truth for Our Time*. New York: Penguin, 2004.

Galeano, Eduardo. *Open Veins of Latin America: Five Centuries of the Pillage of a Continent*. New York: Monthly Review Press, 1973.

———. *We Say No: Chronicles, 1963–1991*. New York: W. W. Norton, 1992.

Garrett, Laurie. *HIV and National Security: Where Are the Links?* Washington, D.C.: Council on Foreign Relations, 2005.

Garton Ash, Timothy. *Free World*. New York: Random House, 2005.

———. *History of the Present: Essays, Sketches, and Dispatches from Europe in the 1990s*. New York: Random House, 1999.

Garver, John W. *Protracted Contest: Sino-Indian Rivalry in the Twentieth Century*. Seattle: University of Washington Press, 2001.

Gill, Bates. *Meeting the Challenges and Opportunities of China's Rise*. Washington, D.C.: Center for Strategic and International Studies, 2006.

Gill, Bates, and Matthew Oresman. *China's New Journey to the West: China's Emergence in Central Asia and Implications for U.S. Interests*. Washington, D.C.: Center for Strategic and International Studies, August 2003.

Gilley, Bruce. *China's Democratic Future: How It Will Happen and Where It Will Lead*. New York: Columbia University Press, 2004.

Gilpin, Robert. *The Challenge of Global Capitalism: The World Economy of the Twenty-first Century*. Princeton, N.J.: Princeton University Press, 2000.

———. *The Political Economy of International Relations*. Princeton, N.J.: Princeton University Press, 1987.

———. *War and Change in World Politics*. Cambridge, U.K.: Cambridge University Press, 1981.

Goldstein, Judith, and Robert Keohane, eds. *Ideas and Foreign Policy: Beliefs, Institutions, and Political Change*. Ithaca, N.Y.: Cornell University Press, 1993.

Goltz, Thomas. *Azerbaijan Diary: A Rogue Reporter's Adventures in an Oil-Rich, War-Torn, Post-Soviet Republic*. Armonk, N.Y.: M. E. Sharpe, 1998.

Gregg, Gary S. *The Middle East: A Cultural Psychology*. New York: Oxford University Press, 2005.

Gregorian, Vartan. *Islam: A Mosaic, Not a Monolith*. Washington, D.C.: Brookings Institution Press, 2003.

Gress, David. *From Plato to NATO: The Idea of the West and Its Opponents*. New York: Free Press, 1998.

Gries, Peter. *China's New Nationalism: Pride, Politics, and Diplomacy*. Berkeley: University of California Press, 2004.

Guillermoprieto, Alma. *The Heart That Bleeds: Latin America Now*. New York: Alfred A. Knopf, 1994.

Hadar, Leon. *Sandstorm: Policy Failure in the Middle East*. New York: Palgrave Macmillan, 2005.

Hamdan, Gamal. *The Personality of Egypt: A Study on the Genius of Place*. Cairo: Al-Hilal, 1993.

Hanson, Victor Davis. *A War Like No Other: How the Athenians and Spartans Fought the Peloponnesian War*. New York: Random House, 2005.

Hart, B. H. Liddell. *Strategy*. New York: Praeger Paperbacks, 1954.

Held, David, and Mathias Koenig-Archibugi, eds. *American Power in the Twenty-first Century*. Cambridge, U.K.: Polity Press, 2004.

Hertsgaard, Mark. *The Eagle's Shadow: Why America Fascinates and Infuriates the World*. New York: Farrar, Straus and Giroux, 2002.

Hill, Fiona. *Energy Empire: Oil, Gas, and Russia's Revival*. London: Foreign Policy Centre, 2004.

Hill, Fiona, and Clifford Gaddy. *The Siberian Curse: How Communist Planners Left Russia out in the Cold*. Washington, D.C.: Brookings Institution Press, 2003.

Hinsley, F. H. *Power and the Pursuit of Peace: Theory and Practice in the History of Relations Between States*. Cambridge, U.K.: Cambridge University Press, 1963.

Hirst, Monica. *The United States and Brazil: A Long Road of Unmet Expectations*. New York: Routledge, 2004.

Hockenos, Paul. *Homeland Calling: Exile Patriotism and the Balkan Wars*. Ithaca, N.Y.: Cornell University Press, 2003.

Hoffman, David. *The Oligarchs: Wealth and Power in the New Russia*. New York: Public Affairs, 2003.

Holbrooke, Richard. *To End a War*. New York: Random House, 1998.

Hopkirk, Peter. *The Great Game: The Struggle for Empire in Central Asia*. London: Kodansha International, 1992.

Hosking, Geoffrey. *Russia and the Russians: A History*. Cambridge, Mass.: Harvard University Press, 2002.

Howard, Michael. *The Invention of Peace*. New Haven, Conn.: Yale University Press, 2000.

Hudson, Michael C., ed. *Middle East Dilemma*. New York: Columbia University Press, 1999.

Human Development Report 2002: Deepening Democracy in a Fragmented World. New York: United Nations Development Program, 2002.

Human Development Report 2005: International Cooperation at a Crossroads: Aid, Trade, and Security in an Unequal World. New York: United Nations Development Program, 2005.

Hunter, Shireen T., and Huma Malik, eds. *Modernization, Democracy, and Islam*. Westport, Conn.: Praeger, 2005.

Huntington, Samuel P. *The Clash of Civilizations and the Remaking of World Order*. New York: Simon and Schuster, 1996.

———. *Political Order in Changing Societies*. New Haven, Conn.: Yale University Press, 1968.

———. *Who Are We? The Challenges to America's National Identity*. New York: Simon and Schuster, 2004.

Ignatieff, Michael, ed. *American Exceptionalism and Human Rights*. Princeton, N.J.: Princeton University Press, 2005.

Ikenberry, G. John. *After Victory: Institutions, Strategic Restraint, and the Rebuilding of Order After Major Wars*. Princeton, N.J.: Princeton University Press, 2000.

———. *Liberal Order and Imperial Ambition: Essays on American Power and World Politics*. London: Polity Press, 2006.

Ikenberry, G. John, ed. *America Unrivaled: The Future of the Balance of Power*. Ithaca, N.Y.: Cornell University Press, 2002.

Ikenberry, G. John, and Anne-Marie Slaughter. *Forging a World of Liberty Under Law: U.S. National Security in the Twenty-first Century*. Final Report of the Princeton Project on National Security, September 2006.

Ikenberry, G. John, and Michael Mastanduno. *International Relations Theory and the Asia-Pacific*. New York: Columbia University Press, 2003.

Iklé, Fred Charles. *Every War Must End*. Rev. ed. New York: Columbia University Press, 2005.

International Commission on the Balkans. *The Balkans in Europe's Future*. Sofia, Bulgaria: Centre for Liberal Strategies, 2005.

Islamic Calvinists: Change and Conservatism in Central Anatolia. Berlin and Istanbul: European Stability Initative, 2005.

Ispahani, Mahnaz Z. *Roads and Rivals: The Political Uses of Access in the Borderlands of Asia*. Ithaca, N.Y.: Cornell University Press, 1989.

Jackson, Robert H. *The Global Covenant: Human Conduct in a World of States*. London: Oxford University Press, 2005.

———. *Quasi-States: Sovereignty, International Relations, and the Third World*. Cambridge, U.K.: Cambridge University Press, 1993.

Jervis, Robert. *System Effects: Complexity in Political and Social Life*. Princeton, N.J.: Princeton University Press, 1997.

Joffe, Josef. *Überpower: The Imperial Temptation of America*. New York: W. W. Norton, 2006.

Johnston, Alastair Ian. *Cultural Realism: Strategic Culture and Grand Strategy in Chinese History*. Princeton, N.J.: Princeton University Press, 1995.

Johnston, R. J., Peter J. Taylor, and Michael J. Watts, eds. *Geographies of Global Change: Remapping the World in the Late Twentieth Century.* Malden, Mass.: Blackwell Publishing, 2002.

Jones Luong, Pauline, ed. *The Transformation of Central Asia: States and Societies from Soviet Rule to Independence.* Ithaca, N.Y.: Cornell University Press, 2004.

Jones, Seth G. *The Rise of European Security Cooperation.* New York: Cambridge University Press, 2006.

Jung Chang and Jon Halliday. *Mao: The Unknown Story.* New York: Alfred A. Knopf, 2005.

Kagan, Robert. *Of Paradise and Power: America and Europe in the New World Order.* New York: Alfred A. Knopf, 2003.

Kahler, Miles, and David A. Lake, eds. *Governance in a Global Economy: Political Authority in Transition.* Princeton, N.J.: Princeton University Press, 2003.

Kamen, Henry. *Empire: How Spain Became a World Power, 1492–1763.* New York: HarperCollins, 2003.

Kant, Immanuel. *Kant: Political Writings.* Ed. H. S. Reiss. Cambridge, U.K.: Cambridge University Press, 1970.

Kaplan, Robert D. *Eastward to Tartary: Travels in the Balkans, the Middle East, and the Caucasus.* New York: Random House, 2000.

———. *Imperial Grunts: The American Military on the Ground.* New York: Random House, 2005.

———. *Mediterranean Winter: The Pleasures of History and Landscape in Tunisia, Sicily, Dalmatia, and Greece.* New York: Random House, 2004.

———. *Warrior Politics: Why Leadership Demands a Pagan Ethos.* New York: Random House, 2002.

Karl, Terry Lynn. *The Paradox of Plenty: Oil Booms and Petro-States.* Berkeley: University of California Press, 1997.

Katzenstein, Peter J., ed. *A World of Regions: Asia and Europe in the American Imperium.* Ithaca, N.Y.: Cornell University Press, 2005.

Keddie, Nikki R. *Iran and the Muslim World: Resistance and Revolution.* New York: New York University Press, 1995.

Keegan, John. *A History of Warfare.* New York: Vintage, 1993.

Kemp, Geoffrey, and Robert E. Harkavy. *Strategic Geography and the Changing Middle East.* Washington, D.C.: Carnegie Endowment for International Peace, 1997.

Kennan, George F. *American Diplomacy.* 1951; repr. Chicago: University of Chicago Press, 1984.

Kennedy, Hugh. *When Baghdad Ruled the Muslim World: The Rise and Fall of Islam's Greatest Dynasty.* New York: Da Capo Press, 2004.

Kennedy, Paul. *The Parliament of Man: The Past, Present, and Future of the United Nations.* New York: Random House, 2006.

———. *The Rise and Fall of the Great Powers.* New York: Vintage, 1989.

Keohane, Robert. *After Hegemony: Cooperation and Discord in the World Political Economy.* Princeton, N.J.: Princeton University Press, 1984.

Kepel, Gilles. *Jihad: The Trial of Political Islam.* Cambridge, Mass.: Harvard University Press, 2003.

———. *The War for Muslim Minds: Islam and the West.* Cambridge, Mass.: Harvard University Press, 2005.

Keynes, John Maynard. *The Economic Consequences of the Peace.* New York: Harcourt, Brace and Howe, 1920.

Kiesling, John Brady. *Diplomacy Lessons: Realism for an Unloved Superpower.* Dulles, Va.: Potomac Books, 2006.

Kim, Samuel, ed. *East Asia and Globalization (Asia in World Politics).* London: Rowman and Littlefield, 2000.

King, Charles. *The Black Sea: A History.* London: Oxford University Press, 2004.

Kinzer, Stephen. *Crescent and Star: Turkey Between Two Worlds.* New York: Farrar, Straus and Giroux, 2001.

Kissinger, Henry A. *Does America Need a Foreign Policy? Toward a Diplomacy for the Twenty-first Century.* New York: Simon and Schuster, 2001.

———. *A World Restored: Metternich, Castlereagh, and the Problems of Peace, 1812–1822.* Boston: Houghton Mifflin, 1973.

Kliot, Nurit, and David Newman, eds. *Geopolitics and Globalization: The Changing World Political Map.* London: Frank Cass, 1999.

Kohut, Andrew, and Bruce Stokes. *America Against the World: How We Are Different and Why We Are Disliked.* New York: Times Books, 2006.

Kotkin, Joel. *The City: A Global History.* New York: Modern Library, 2005.

Kotkin, Joel, and Delore Zimmerman. *Rebuilding America's Productive Economy: A Heartland Development Strategy.* Washington, D.C.: New America Foundation, 2006.

Krasner, Stephen D. *Structural Conflict: The Third World Against Global Liberalism.* Berkeley: University of California Press, 1985.

Krasner, Stephen D., ed. *Problematic Sovereignty: Contested Rules and Political Possibilities.* New York: Columbia University Press, 2001.

Kristof, Nicholas, and Sheryl Wudunn. *China Wakes: The Struggle for the Soul of a Rising Power.* New York: Vintage, 1995.

Kumar, Krishna, ed. *Post-Conflict Elections, Democratization and International Assistance.* Boulder, Colo.: Lynne Rienner, 1998.

Kupchan, Charles. *The End of the American Era: U.S. Foreign Policy and the Geopolitics of the Twenty-first Century.* New York: Alfred A. Knopf, 2002.

Lake, David A. *Entangling Relations: American Foreign Policy in Its Century*. Princeton, N.J.: Princeton University Press, 1999.

Lal, Deepak. *In Praise of Empires: Globalization and Order*. New York: Palgrave Macmillan, 2004.

Lampton, David. *Same Bed, Different Dreams: Managing U.S.-China Relations, 1989–2000*. Berkeley: University of California Press, 2001.

Lasch, Christopher. *The Revolt of the Elites and the Betrayal of Democracy*. New York: W. W. Norton, 1996.

Lawrence, T. E. *Seven Pillars of Wisdom: A Triumph*. New York: Anchor Books, 1935.

Lee Kuan Yew. *The Singapore Story: Memoirs of Lee Kuan Yew*. New York: Prentice Hall, 1999.

Legrain, Philipe. *Open World: The Truth About Globalization*. London: Abacus, 2002.

Legvold, Robert, ed. *Thinking Strategically: The Major Powers, Kazakhstan, and the Central Asian Nexus*. Cambridge, Mass.: American Academy of Arts and Sciences, 2003.

Leonard, Mark. *Why Europe Will Run the Twenty-first Century*. London: Fourth Estate, 2005.

Lepgold, Joseph, and Miroslav Ninic. *Beyond the Ivory Tower: International Relations Theory and the Issue of Policy Relevance*. New York: Columbia University Press, 2001.

Leverett, Flynt. *Inheriting Syria: Bashar's Trial by Fire*. Washington, D.C.: Brookings Institution Press, 2005.

LeVine, Steven. *The Oil and the Glory: The Pursuit of Empire and Fortune on the Caspian Sea*. New York: Random House, 2007.

Lewis, Martin W., and Karen E. Wigen. *The Myth of Continents: A Critique of Metageography*. Berkeley: University of California Press, 1997.

Lieber, Robert J. *The American Era: Power and Strategy for the Twenty-first Century*. New York: Cambridge University Press, 2005.

Lieven, Anatol. *America Right or Wrong: An Anatomy of American Nationalism*. New York: Oxford University Press, 2004.

Lieven, Anatol, and Dmitri Trenin, eds. *Ambivalent Neighbors: The EU, NATO, and the Price of Membership*. Washington, D.C.: Carnegie Endowment for International Peace, 2003.

Lieven, Anatol, and John Hulsman. *Ethical Realism: A Vision for America's Role in the World*. New York: Pantheon, 2006.

Lilley, James. *China Hands: Nine Decades of Adventure, Espionage, and Diplomacy in Asia*. New York: Public Affairs, 2004.

Lind, Michael. *The American Way of Strategy: U.S. Foreign Policy and the American Way of Life*. New York: Oxford University Press, 2006.

————. *Made in Texas: George W. Bush and the Southern Takeover of American Politics.* New York: Basic Books, 2003.

Linn, Johannes, and David Tiomkin. *Economic Integration of Eurasia: Opportunities and Challenges of Global Significance.* Warsaw: Center for Social and Economic Research, 2005.

Little, Allan, and Laura Silber. *Yugoslavia: Death of a Nation.* New York: Penguin, 1995.

Loh Kok Wah, Francis, and Khoo Boo Teik, eds. *Democracy in Malaysia: Discourses and Practices.* Richmond, U.K.: Curzon Press, 2002.

Lynn, Barry C. *End of the Line: The Rise and Coming Fall of the Global Corporation.* New York: Doubleday, 2005.

Mackinder, Halford. *Democratic Ideals and Reality: A Study in the Politics of Reconstruction.* London: Constable Publishers, 1919.

Maddison, Angus. *The World Economy: A Millennial Perspective.* Paris: OECD Development Centre, 2001.

Mahbubani, Kishore. *Beyond the Age of Innocence: Rebuilding Trust Between America and the World.* New York: Public Affairs, 2005.

Maier, Charles. *Among Empires: American Ascendancy and Its Predecessors.* Cambridge, Mass.: Harvard University Press, 2006.

Makdisi, Ussama. *The Culture of Sectarianism: Community, History, and Violence in Nineteenth-Century Ottoman Lebanon.* Berkeley: University of California Press, 2000.

Malka, Haim, and Jon B. Alterman. *Arab Reform and Foreign Aid: Lessons from Morocco.* Washington, D.C.: Center for Strategic and International Studies, 2006.

Mamdani, Mahmood. *Good Muslim, Bad Muslim: America, the Cold War, and the Roots of Terror.* New York: Pantheon, 2004.

Mandelbaum, Michael. *The Case for Goliath: How America Acts as the World's Government in the Twenty-first Century.* New York: Public Affairs, 2006.

Mango, Andrew. *The Turks Today.* London: Overlook Press, 2005.

Mansfield, Edward D., and Jack Snyder. *Electing to Fight: Why Emerging Democracies Go to War.* Cambridge, Mass.: MIT Press, 2005.

Mansfield, Edward D., and Helen V. Milner, eds. *The Political Economy of Regionalism.* New York: Columbia University Press, 1997.

Mapes, Rosemary S. *Russian Nationalism and Russian Historiography, 1725–1854.* Washington, D.C.: Georgetown University Press, 1961.

Mapping the Global Future: Report of the National Intelligence Council's 2020 Project. Washington, D.C.: Government Printing Office, 2004.

Mattern, Johannes. *Geopolitik: Doctrine of National Self-Sufficiency and Empire.* Baltimore, Md.: Johns Hopkins Press, 1942.

Maxwell, Kenneth. *Naked Tropics: Essays on Empire and Other Rogues.* New York: Routledge, 2003.

McNeill, William. *The Rise of the West: A History of the Human Community.* Chicago: University of Chicago Press, 1963.

Mearsheimer, John J. *The Tragedy of Great Power Politics.* New York: W. W. Norton, 2001.

Menkhoff, Thomas, and Gerke Solvay, eds. *Chinese Entrepreneurship and Asian Business Networks.* London: Routledge Curzon, 2002.

Menon, Raja. *The End of Alliances.* New York: Oxford University Press, 2007.

Merry, Robert W. *Sands of Empire: Missionary Zeal, American Foreign Policy, and the Hazards of Global Ambition.* New York: Simon and Schuster, 2005.

Meyer, Karl E., and Shareen B. Brysac. *Tournament of Shadows: The Great Game and the Race for Empire in Central Asia.* New York: Counterpoint, 2000.

Micklethwait, John, and Adrian Woolridge. *A Future Perfect: The Challenge and Hidden Promise of Globalization.* New York: Crown Business, 2000.

Migdal, Joel. *Strong Societies and Weak States: State-Society Relations and State Capabilities in the Third World.* Princeton, N.J.: Princeton University Press, 1998.

Milanovic, Branko. *Worlds Apart: Measuring International and Global Inequality.* Princeton, N.J.: Princeton University Press, 2005.

Minevich, Mark, Frank-Jürgen Richter, and Faisal Hoque. *Six Billion Minds: Managing Outsourcing in the Global Knowledge Economy.* Boston: Aspatore Books, 2006.

Mixin Pei. *China's Trapped Transition: The Limits of Developmental Autocracy.* Cambridge, Mass.: Harvard University Press, 2006.

Moaveni, Azadeh. *Lipstick Jihad: A Memoir of Growing Up Iranian in America and American in Iran.* New York: Public Affairs, 2005.

Modelski, George, and William R. Thompson. *Leading Sectors and World Powers: The Coevolution of Global Economics and Politics.* Columbia: University of South Carolina Press, 1995.

Molavi, Afshin. *The Soul of Iran: A Nation's Journey to Freedom.* New York: W. W. Norton, 2005.

Montaigne, Fen. *Reeling in Russia: An Angler's Paradise.* New York: St. Martin's Press, 1998.

Moravcsik, Andrew. *Europe Without Illusions: The Paul-Henri Spaak Lectures, 1994–1999.* Lanham, Md.: University Press of America, 2005.

More Than Humanitarianism: A Strategic U.S. Approach Toward Africa. New York: Council on Foreign Relations, 2006.

Morgenthau, Hans. *Politics Among Nations.* New York: Alfred A. Knopf, 1948.
———. *Scientific Man vs. Power Politics.* Chicago: University of Chicago Press, 1946.
Motyl, Alexander. *Imperial Ends: The Decay, Collapse, and Revival of Empires.* New York: Columbia University Press, 2001.
Mueller, John. *Retreat from Doomsday: The Obsolescence of Major War.* New York: Basic Books, 1989.
Nafisi, Azar. *Reading Lolita in Tehran: A Memoir in Books.* New York: Random House, 2003.
Naím, Moisés. *Illicit: How Smugglers, Traffickers, and Copycats Are Hijacking the Global Economy.* New York: Doubleday, 2005.
Naipaul, V. S. *Among the Believers: An Islamic Journey.* London: Penguin, 1982.
———. *Beyond Belief: Excursions Among the Coverted Peoples.* New York: Vintage, 1999.
———. *Return of Eva Peron.* New York: Alfred A. Knopf, 1980.
Nasr, Vali. *The Shia Revival: How Conflicts Within Islam Will Shape the Future.* New York: W. W. Norton, 2006.
Nau, Henry. *At Home Abroad: Identity and Power in American Foreign Policy.* Ithaca, N.Y.: Cornell University Press, 2002.
Nazarbayev, Nursultan. *Epicenter of Peace.* Hollis, N.H.: Puritan Press, 2001.
Nellis, John, Rachel Menezes, and Sarah Lucas. *Privatization in Latin America: The Rapid Rise, Recent Fall, and Continuing Puzzle of a Contentious Economic Policy.* Washington, D.C.: Center for Global Development, 2004.
The New Energy Security Paradigm. Cologny and Geneva, Switzerland: Energy Industry Community of the World Economic Forum, 2006.
Newman, Edward, Ramesh Thakur, and John Tirman, eds. *Mulitlateralism Under Challenge? Power, International Order, and Structural Change.* Tokyo: United Nations University Press, 2006.
Nicolson, Harold. *Diplomacy.* London: Oxford University Press, 1950.
Nye, Joseph. *Soft Power: The Means to Success in World Politics.* New York: Public Affairs, 2004.
O'Leary, Brendan, John McGarry, and Khaled Salih, eds. *The Future of Kurdistan in Iraq.* Philadelphia: University of Pennsylvania Press, 2005.
O'Tuathail, Gearoid. *Critical Geopolitics: The Politics of Writing Global Space.* London: Routledge, 1996.
Obolensky, Dimitri. *The Byzantine Commonwealth: Eastern Europe, 500–1453.* New York: Praeger Publishers, 1971.
Ohmae, Kenichi. *The End of the Nation State: The Rise of Regional Economies.* New York: Simon and Schuster, 1996.

Olcott, Martha. *Central Asia's Second Chance*. Washington, D.C.: Carnegie Endowment for International Peace, 2005.

———. *Kazakhstan: Unfulfilled Promise*. Washington, D.C.: Carnegie Endowment for International Peace, 2002.

Oliker, Olga, and David A. Shlapak. *U.S. Interests in Central Asia: Policy Priorities and Military Roles*. Santa Monica, Calif.: RAND Corporation, 2005.

Oliker, Olga, and Tanya Charlick-Paley. *Assessing Russia's Decline: Trends and Implications for the United States and the U.S. Air Force*. Santa Monica, Calif.: RAND Corporation, 2002.

Organski, A.F.K. *World Politics*. New York: Alfred A. Knopf, 1968.

Pape, Robert A. *Dying to Win: The Strategic Logic of Suicide Terrorism*. New York: Random House, 2005.

Pastor, Robert A. *A Century's Journey: How the Great Powers Shape the World*. New York: Basic Books, 1999.

Patten, Chris. *Cousins and Strangers: America, Britain, and Europe in a New Century*. New York: Times Books, 2006.

———. *East and West*. London: Pan Macmillan Publishers, 1998.

Paul, T. V., G. John Ikenberry, and John A. Hall, eds. *The Nation-State in Question*. Princeton, N.J.: Princeton University Press, 2003.

Paul, T. V., James J. Wirtz, and Michel Fortmann, eds. *Balance of Power: Theory and Practice in the Twenty-first Century*. Stanford, Calif.: Stanford University Press, 2004.

Pempel, T. J., ed. *Remapping East Asia: The Construction of a Region*. Ithaca, N.Y.: Cornell University Press, 2005.

Perkins, John. *Confessions of an Economic Hit Man*. San Francisco: Berrett Koehler, 2003.

Phillips, David L. *Losing Iraq: Inside the Postwar Reconstruction Fiasco*. Boulder, Colo.: Westview, 2005.

Phillips, Kevin. *American Theocracy: The Peril and Politics of Radical Religion, Oil, and Borrowed Money in the Twenty-first Century*. New York: Viking, 2006.

Pollack, Kenneth M. *The Persian Puzzle: The Conflict Between Iran and America*. New York: Random House, 2004.

Pond, Elizabeth. *Endgame in the Balkans: Regime Change, European Style*. Washington, D.C.: Brookings Institution Press, 2006.

Pope, Hugh. *Sons of the Conquerors: The Rise of the Turkic World*. London: Overlook Press, 2005.

Prestowitz, Clyde V. *Three Billion New Capitalists: The Great Shift of Wealth and Power to the East*. New York: Basic Books, 2005.

Priest, Dana. *The Mission: Waging War and Keeping Peace with America's Military*. New York: W. W. Norton, 2003.

Pye, Lucian W. *China*. New York: Harper Collins, 1990.

Qiao Ling and Wang Xiangsui. *Unrestricted Warfare: China's Master Plan to Destroy America*. Beijing: PLA Literature and Arts Publishing House, 1999.

Quandt, William B. *Peace Process: American Diplomacy and the Arab-Israeli Conflict Since 1967*. 3d ed. Washington, D.C.: Brookings Institution Press, 2005.

Ramadan, Tariq. *Western Muslims and the Future of Islam*. New York: Oxford University Press, 2004.

Ramo, Joshua Cooper. *The Beijing Consensus*. London: Foreign Policy Centre, 2004.

Rancour-Laferriere, Daniel. *The Slave Soul of Russia: Moral Masochism and the Cult of Suffering*. New York: New York University Press, 1995.

Rasler, Karen A., and William R. Thompson. *The Great Powers and Global Struggle, 1490–1990*. Lexington: University Press of Kentucky, 1994.

Reich, Robert B. *The Future of Success*. New York: Alfred A. Knopf, 2001.

Reid, Anne. *Borderland: A Journey Through the History of Ukraine*. Boulder, Colo.: Westview, 1997.

Reid, T. R. *The United States of Europe: The New Superpower and the End of American Supremacy*. New York: Penguin, 2004.

Reiter, Dan, and Allan C. Stan. *Democracies at War*. Princeton, N.J.: Princeton University Press, 2002.

Revel, Jean-François. *How Democracies Perish*. New York: HarperCollins, 1985.

Rieff, David. *Los Angeles: Capital of the Third World*. New York: Touchstone Books, 1992.

Rifkin, Jeremy. *The European Dream: How Europe's Vision of the Future Is Quietly Eclipsing the American Dream*. New York: Penguin, 2004.

Ringmar, Eric. *The Mechanics of Modernity in Europe and East Asia: The Institutional Origins of Social Change and Stagnation*. London: Routledge, 2004.

Rivoli, Pietra. *The Travels of a T-shirt in the Global Economy: An Economist Explores the Markets, Power, and Politics of World Trade*. New York: John Wiley and Sons, 2005.

Roberts, Adam. *The Wonga Coup: Guns, Thugs, and Ruthless Determination to Create Mayhem in an Oil-Rich Corner of Africa*. New York: Public Affairs, 2006.

Robertson, Robbie. *The Three Waves of Globalization: A History of Developing Global Consciousness*. London: Zed Books, 2003.

Rogers, Jim. *Adventure Capitalist: The Ultimate Road Trip.* New York: Random House, 2003.

Rosecrance, Richard A. *The Rise of the Trading State: Commerce and Conquest in the Modern World.* New York: Basic Books, 1986.

———. *The Rise of the Virtual State: Wealth and Poverty in the Coming Century.* New York: Basic Books, 2000.

Rosecrance, Richard A., and Arthur A. Stein, eds. *No More States? Globalization, National Self-Determination, and Terrorism.* Lanham, Md.: Rowman and Littlefield, 2006.

Rosen, Nir. *In the Belly of the Green Bird: The Triumph of the Martyrs in Iraq.* New York: Free Press, 2006.

Rosenau, James N. *Distant Proximities: Dynamics Beyond Globalization.* Princeton, N.J.: Princeton University Press, 2003.

Rosenberg, Tina. *The Haunted Land: Facing Europe's Ghosts After Communism.* New York: Vintage, 1996.

Rotberg, Robert I., ed. *Battling Terrorism in the Horn of Africa.* Washington, D.C.: Brookings Institution Press, 2005.

Rowan, Michael. *Getting Over Chávez and Poverty.* 2006. Available from michael.rowan.book@gmail.com.

Roy, Olivier. *The Failure of Political Islam.* Cambridge, Mass.: Harvard University Press, 1995.

———. *Globalized Islam: The Search for a New Ummah.* New York: Columbia University Press, 2004.

———. *The New Central Asia: The Creation of Nations.* New York: New York University Press, 2000.

Rubin, Barnett R. *The Search for Peace in Afghanistan: From Buffer State to Failed State.* New Haven, Conn.: Yale University Press, 1995.

Rubin, Barnett R., and Jack Snyder, eds. *Post-Soviet Political Order: Conflict and State-Building.* London: Routledge, 1998.

Rugh, William. *America's Encounters with Arabs: The "Soft Power" of U.S. Diplomacy in the Middle East.* Westport, Conn.: Praeger Security International, 2006.

Rumer, Boris, and Lan Sim Yee, eds. *Central Asia and South Caucasus Affairs.* Tokyo: Sasakawa Peace Foundation, 2003.

Rusi, Alpo. *Dangerous Peace: New Rivalry in World Politics.* Boulder, Colo.: Westview, 1998.

Russett, Bruce. *Grasping the Democratic Peace: Principles for a Post–Cold War World.* Princeton, N.J.: Princeton University Press, 1992.

Sageman, Marc. *Understanding Terror Networks.* Philadelphia: University of Pennsylvania Press, 2004.

Said, Edward W. *The Question of Palestine.* New York: Vintage, 1992.

Said, Kurban. *Ali and Nino: A Love Story.* New York: Anchor, 2000.

Salamé, Ghassan, ed. *Democracy Without Democrats? The Renewal of Politics in the Muslim World.* London: I. B. Tauris, 1994.

Schanzer, Jonathan. *Al-Qaeda's Armies: Middle East Affiliate Groups and the Next Generation of Terror.* Washington, D.C.: Washington Institute for Near East Policy, 2005.

Schell, Jonathan. *The Unconquerable World: Power, Nonviolence, and the Will of the People.* New York: Metropolitan Books, 2003.

Schwarz, Adam. *A Nation in Waiting: Indonesia's Search for Stability.* Boulder, Colo.: Westview, 2000.

Schweller, Randall L. *Unanswered Threats: Political Constraints on the Balance of Power.* Princeton, N.J.: Princeton University Press, 2006.

Seagrave, Sterling. *Lords of the Rim: The Invisible Empire of Overseas Chinese.* New York: Putnam, 1995.

Seiple, Robert A., and Dennis R. Hoover. *Religion and Security: The New Nexus in International Relations.* Lanham, Md.: Rowman and Littlefield, 2004.

Sen, Amartya. *The Argumentative Indian: Writings on Indian History, Culture, and Identity.* New York: Farrar, Straus and Giroux, 2005.

———. *Developent as Freedom.* Oxford, U.K.: Oxford University Press, 1999.

Shambaugh, David, ed. *Power Shift: China and Asia's New Dynamics.* Berkeley: University of California Press, 2005.

Shannon, Thomas R. *An Introduction to the World-System Perspective.* Boulder, Colo.: Westview, 1989.

Shaw, Martin. *Theory of the Global State: Globality as an Unfinished Revolution.* Cambridge, U.K.: Cambridge University Press, 2000.

Shenkar, Oded. *The Chinese Century: The Rising Chinese Economy and Its Impact on the Global Economy, the Balance of Power, and Your Job.* Philadelphia: Wharton School Publishing, 2005.

Shikaki, Khalil. *Building a State, Building Peace: How to Make a Roadmap That Works for Palestinians and Israelis.* Saban Center for Middle East Policy, Monograph no. 1. Washington, D.C.: Brookings Institution Press, 2003.

Siddiqa, Ayesha, *Military, Inc.: Inside Pakistan's Military Economy.* London: Pluto Press, 2007.

Simmons, Matthew R. *Twilight in the Desert: The Coming Saudi Oil Shock and the World Economy.* Hoboken, N.J.: John Wiley and Sons, 2005.

Simon, Sheldon W., ed. *The Many Faces of Asian Security.* Lanham, Md.: Rowman and Littlefield, 2001.

Simons, Thomas W., Jr. *Islam in a Globalizing World.* Stanford, Calif.: Stanford University Press, 2003.

Singer, Peter. *One World: The Ethics of Globalization*. New Haven, Conn.: Yale University Press, 2003.

Smith, Peter H. *Democracy in Latin America: Political Change in Comparative Perspective*. New York: Oxford University Press, 2005.

———. *Talons of the Eagle: Dynamics of U.S.–Latin American Relations*. New York: Oxford University Press, 1996.

Snyder, Jack. *From Voting to Violence: Democratization and Nationalist Conflict*. New York: W. W. Norton, 2000.

———. *Myths of Empire: Domestic Politics and International Ambition*. Ithaca, N.Y.: Cornell University Press, 1991.

Sokolsky, Richard, Angel Rabasa, and C. R. Neu. *The Role of Southeast Asia in U.S. Strategy Toward China*. Santa Monica, Calif.: RAND Corporation, 2000.

Sowell, Thomas. *Migrations and Cultures: A World View*. New York: Basic Books, 1996.

Speak No Evil: Mass Media Control in Contemporary China. Washington, D.C.: Freedom House, 2006.

Spykman, Nicholas John. *America's Strategy in World Politics: The United States and the Balance of Power*. New York: Harcourt, Brace and Company, 1942.

———. *The Geography of the Peace*. New York: Harcourt Brace, 1944.

Steinberg, David I., and Catharin Dalpino, eds. *Georgetown Southeast Asia Survey, 2002–2003*. Washington, D.C.: Georgetown University Press, 2004.

Stewart, Rory. *The Places in Between*. London: Harcourt, 2004.

Suisheng Zhao. *A Nation-State by Construction: Dynamics of Modern Chinese Nationalism*. Stanford, Calif.: Stanford University Press, 2004.

Suisman, Doug, et al. *The Arc: A Formal Structure for a Palestinian State*. Santa Monica, Calif.: RAND Corporation, 2005.

Sutter, Robert. *China's Rise in Asia: Promises and Perils*. Boulder, Colo.: Rowman and Littlefield, 2005.

Sweig, Julia. *Friendly Fire: Losing Friends and Making Enemies in the Anti-American Century*. New York: Public Affairs, 2006.

Talbott, Stobe. *The Russia Hand: A Memoir of Presidential Diplomacy*. New York: Random House, 2003.

Taylor, A. J. P. *The Struggle for Mastery in Europe, 1848–1918*. Oxford, U.K.: Clarendon Press, 1954.

Telhami, Shibley. *The Stakes: America and the Middle East*. Boulder, Colo.: Westview, 2002.

Tellis, Ashley J., and Michael Willis. *Strategic Asia, 2005–2006: Military Mod-

ernization in an Era of Uncertainty. Seattle: National Bureau of Asian Research, 2005.

Terrill, Ross. *The New Chinese Empire: And What It Means for the United States*. New York: Basic Books, 2003.

Thesiger, Wilfred. *Arabian Sands*. 1959; repr. London: Penguin, 1991.

Thucydides. *History of the Peloponnesian War*. Trans. Rex Warner. London: Penguin, 1954.

Todd, Emmanuel. *After the Empire: The Breakdown of the American Order*. New York: Columbia University Press, 2002.

Tokaev, Kassymzhomart. *Meeting the Challenge: Memoirs by Khazakstan's Foreign Minister*. Redding, Conn.: Begell House, 2004.

Toynbee, Arnold. *Civilization on Trial*. London: Oxford University Press, 1948.

———. *East to West: A Journey Round the World*. New York: Oxford University Press, 1958.

———. *A Study of History*. 12 volumes. Oxford, U.K.: Oxford University Press, 1934–1961.

Trenin, Dmitri. *The End of Eurasia: Russia on the Border Between Geopolitics and Globalization*. Washington, D.C.: Carnegie Endowment for International Peace, 2002.

Trofimov, Yaroslav. *Faith at War: A Journey on the Frontlines of Islam, from Baghdad to Timbuktu*. New York: Henry Holt, 2005.

Tulchin, Jospeh L., and Heather A. Golding, eds. *Environment and Security in the Amazon Basin*. Woodrow Wilson Center Reports on the Americas no. 4. Washington, D.C.: Woodrow Wilson International Center for Scholars, 2002.

Tunander, Ola, Pavel Baev, and Victoria Ingrid Einagel, eds. *The Geopolitics of Post-Wall Europe: Security, Territory, and Identity*. London: Sage Publications, 1997.

Unlocking the Employment Potential in the Middle East and North Africa: Toward a New Social Contract. Washington, D.C.: International Bank for Reconstruction and Development, World Bank, 2004.

Vandewalle, Dirk. *A History of Modern Libya*. Cambridge, U.K.: Cambridge University Press, 2006.

Viorst, Milton. *Storm from the East: The Struggle Between the Arab World and the Christian West*. New York: Modern Library, 2006.

Wallerstein, Immanuel. *The Modern World-System I: Capitalist Agriculture and the Origins of the European World Economy in the Sixteenth Century*. San Diego, Calif.: Academic Press, 1974.

———. *The Modern World-System II: Mercantilism and the Consolidation of the European World Economy, 1600–1750*. San Diego, Calif.: Academic Press, 1980.

———. *The Modern World-System III: The Second Era of Great Expansion of the Capitalist World Economy, 1730–1840s*. San Diego, Calif.: Academic Press, 1989.

Walt, Stephen M. *Taming American Power: The Global Response to U.S. Primacy*. New York: W. W. Norton, 2005.

Waltz, Kenneth N. *Theory of International Politics*. Reading, Mass.: Addison-Wesley, 1979.

Weatherford, Jack. *Genghis Khan and the Making of the Modern World*. New York: Crown, 2004.

Weimann, Gabriel. *Terror on the Internet: The New Arena, the New Challenges*. Washington, D.C.: United States Institute of Peace Press, 2006.

Weinstein, Michael M., ed. *Globalization: What's New?* New York: Columbia University Press, 2005.

Wendt, Alexander. *Social Theory of International Politics*. Cambridge, U.K.: Cambridge University Press, 1999.

West, Rebecca. *Black Lamb and Gray Falcon: A Journey Through Yugoslavia*. New York: Viking Press, 1941.

Wilkinson, Richard G. *The Impact of Inequality: How to Make Sick Societies Healthier*. London: Routledge, 2005.

Williams, William Appleman. *The Tragedy of American Diplomacy*. New York: W. W. Norton, 1959.

Wilson, Andrew. *The Ukrainians: Unexpected Nation*. New Haven, Conn.: Yale University Press, 2000.

Wolfe, Alan. *Return to Greatness: How America Lost Its Sense of Purpose and What It Needs to Do to Recover It*. Princeton, N.J.: Princeton University Press, 2005.

Wright, Robert. *Non-Zero: The Logic of Human Destiny*. New York: Vintage, 2000.

Yahuda, Michael. *The International Politics of the Asia-Pacific, 1945–1995*. London: Routledge, 1996.

Yang, Dali L. *Remaking the Chinese Leviathan: Market Transition and the Politics of Governance in China*. Stanford, Calif.: Stanford University Press, 2004.

Yergin, Daniel. *The Prize: The Epic Quest for Oil, Money, and Power*. New York: Free Press, 1993.

Yergin, Daniel, and Thane Gustafson. *Russia 2010 and What It Means for the World*. New York: Random House, 1993.

Yongjin, Zhang. *China Goes Global*. London: Foreign Policy Centre, 2005.

Yuan-Tsung Chen. *The Dragon's Village: An Autobiographical Novel of Revolutionary China*. New York: Penguin, 1981.

Zakaria, Fareed. *The Future of Freedom: Illiberal Democracy at Home and Abroad*. New York: W. W. Norton, 2003.

NOTES

INTRODUCTION: INTER-IMPERIAL RELATIONS

1. Michael Doyle defines an empire as "a system of interaction between two political entities, one of which, the dominant metropole, exerts political control over the internal and external policy—the effective sovereignty—of the other in the subordinate periphery." Doyle, *Empires* (Ithaca, N.Y.: Cornell University Press, 1986), 12. For a succinct academic overview of theories of imperial rise and decline, see Alexander Motyl, *Imperial Ends: The Decay, Collapse, and Revival of Empires* (New York: Columbia University Press, 2001). Empires are symbiotic and exploitative at the same time: They hoard resources but spread prosperity. Empires impose their laws and culture on their peripheries even as they extract talent from them. They set standards for goods in their markets, and they produce indigenous technology to protect against foreign control of their supplies. When empires collapse, new ones are born. As Robert Kaplan writes, "Since antiquity the collapse of empires has been a messy business, and the most benign antidote to the chaos unleashed has been the birth of new imperial domains." Kaplan, *Imperial Grunts: The American Military on the Ground* (New York: Random House, 2005), 7.

2. See Richard N. Rosecrance, "Who Will Be Independent?" in *No More States? Globalization, National Self-Determination, and Terrorism*, ed. Richard

N. Rosecrance and Arthur A. Stein (Lanham, Md.: Rowman and Littlefield, 2006).

3. Charles Maier defines *empire* as "a territorially extensive structure of rule" that subordinates "diverse ethnolinguistic groups" and is preponderantly governed by executive authority and associated elites. Maier, *Among Empires: American Ascendancy and Its Predecessors* (Cambridge, Mass.: Harvard University Press, 2006). See also Martin W. Lewis and Karen E. Wigen, *The Myth of Continents: A Critique of Metageography* (Berkeley: University of California Press, 1997). Toynbee wrote that as civilizations rise and fall, they "radiate and penetrate," encountering one another across space and time. The absorption of Greece into Rome; the contacts among Arab, Persian, and Indian civilizations; the late-medieval renaissance of Hellenism in Italy—these are all examples of what Toynbee called the process of "Apparentation-and-Affiliation" between dying civilizations and their infant successors. For a civilization-based approach to world politics, see Samuel P. Huntington, *The Clash of Civilizations and the Remaking of World Order* (New York: Simon and Schuster, 1996).

4. Alexander Wendt has argued that a world state is inevitable due to the self-organizing teleology of the global system in which the number of meaningful political units diminishes over time. Wendt, "Why a World State Is Inevitable," *European Journal of International Relations* 9, no. 4 (2003): 491–542.

5. Much as history is written by the victors, Kenneth Waltz once claimed that the very "theory of international politics is written by the great powers of the era." Waltz, *Theory of International Politics* (Reading, Mass.: Addison-Wesley, 1979), 73.

6. As Robert Gilpin notes, "No state has ever completely controlled an international system." Gilpin, *War and Change in World Politics* (Cambridge, U.K.: Cambridge University Press, 1981), 28.

7. John Maynard Keynes, *The Economic Consequences of the Peace* (New York: Harcourt, Brace and Howe, 1920), 14–15.

8. As Kenneth Waltz has written, "As nature abhors a vacuum, so international politics abhors unbalanced power." Waltz, "Structural Realism After the Cold War," *International Security* 25, no. 1 (Summer 2000): 28.

9. A superpower is dominant in its region and capable of pursuing its own interests globally. As Paul Bracken has argued, power is "the ability to initiate events on the world stage." Bracken, *Fire in the East: The Rise of Asian Military Power and the Second Nuclear Age* (New York: HarperCollins, 1999). Hard power is the exercise of military force, related forms of intimidation and coercion, or the deepening of military ties and weapons sales. Soft power is economic leverage and influence accrued through trade and aid; diplomatic

cooperation enhanced through treaties, pacts and organizations; and social integration resulting from migration and other forms of cultural exchange. See David A. Lake, "Hierarchy in International Relations: Authority, Sovereignty, and the New Structure of World Poltics," unpublished working paper, University of California at San Diego, 2005; and Joseph Nye, *Soft Power: The Means to Success in World Politics* (New York: Public Affairs, 2004).

10. Thomas Barnett similarly calls upon the United States to serve as a "Gap Leviathan," assuming that American-led solutions to regional problems are preferable (and superior) to collective or local approaches. Barnett, *The Pentagon's New Map: War and Peace in the Twenty-first Century* (New York: Putnam, 2004).

11. John J. Mearsheimer, "Back to the Future: Instability in Europe After the Cold War," *International Security* 15, no. 4 (Summer 1990): 5–56.

12. Josef Joffe, "'Bismarck' or 'Britain'? Toward an American Grand Strategy After Bipolarity," *International Security* 19, no. 4 (Spring 1995): 94–117.

13. According to Samuel Huntington, the creation of the European Union, not the rise of China, was the single greatest step toward a global anti-hegemonic (read: anti-American) coalition. Huntington, "The Lonely Superpower," *Foreign Affairs*, March–April 1999. See also Barry Buzan, *The United States and the Great Powers: World Politics in the Twenty-first Century* (London: Polity Press, 2004), 125–26.

14. Richard N. Rosecrance, *The Rise of the Trading State: Commerce and Conquest in the Modern World* (New York: Basic Books, 1986), 17–18.

15. For a discussion of the definitions of the terms *superpower, great power,* and *regional power,* see Buzan, *United States and the Great Powers,* ch. 5. A brief discussion of the pecking order of international relations is found in "A Geopolitical Detective Story," *The Economist,* January 3, 1998.

16. For a discussion of various forms of hard, soft, and asymmetric balancing in the post–Cold War world, see T. V. Paul, James J. Wirtz, and Michel Fortmann, eds., *Balance of Power: Theory and Practice in the Twenty-first Century* (Stanford, Calif.: Stanford University Press, 2004).

17. Johanes Mattern, *Geopolitik: Doctrine of National Self-Sufficiency and Empire* (Baltimore: Johns Hopkins Press, 1942).

18. Influential writings by Mackinder include "The Geographical Pivot of History," *Geographical Journal* 23 (1904): 421–37; *Democratic Ideals and Reality: A Study in the Politics of Reconstruction* (London: Constable, 1919); and "The Round World and Winning the Peace," *Foreign Affairs,* July 1943.

19. Geopolitical theories now combine the original, Olympian view of the power-space dynamic with a more modern, highly quantitative calculus of power that measures both polarity (the number of centers of power) and concentration (the distribution of power). Hegemonic stability theory, for exam-

ple, argues that a single dominant power in the system such as Rome or Great Britain controls the global supply of money, materials, and production, in particular the most profitable products, while also ensuring firm management of the global economy and providing public goods such as protection of sea transport lanes. But suffering from overextension abroad and economic decline at home, the hegemon cannot command the system it sustains forever and is eventually supplanted by another—but usually only after a major war. See Gilpin, *War and Change in World Politics*. For Gilpin, too, the state and the market are the two organizing principles of international society; see his *Political Economy of International Relations* (Princeton: Princeton University Press, 1987). World-system theory also focuses on the role of the hegemon and its allies in dominating the world capitalist economy but adds a horizontal schism of economic class to the vertical conflicts among states. This Marxist bent argues that the first-world core, the second-world semiperiphery, and the third-world periphery do not arise from any legacies of backwardness but rather exist due to exploitation that depends on an imbalanced global division of labor. Achieving modernization and autonomy from the hegemonic structures of control are the only means to escape the periphery and rise toward the core. At the same time, because hegemonic cycles follow from economic cycles, the erosion of the hegemon's economic dominance can be foreseen decades in advance, even its own potential slide from the first-world core. See Thomas R. Shannon, *Introduction to the World-System Perspective* (Boulder, Colo.: Westview Press, 1989). Much of world-system theory is grounded in the writings of Immanuel Wallerstein; see his three-part work, *The Modern World-System* (New York: Academic, 1974–89). A third school of geopolitics, with two variants referred to as long-cycle and long-wave theories, emphasizes naval power and commercial innovation in the key economic sectors, respectively, and the concentration of both in the hands of the single "world power." Over the past thousand years, the mantle of leading power has skipped westward from Sung China to the Mongols, the Mughals, the Ottomans, the Italian city-states, Spain, Portugal, the Netherlands, Great Britain, and then the United States—but each has been subject to the phases of ascending hegemony, victory, maturity, and decline. See George Modelski and William R. Thompson, *Leading Sectors and World Powers: The Coevolution of Global Economics and Politics* (Columbia: University of South Carolina Press, 1995); Karen A. Rasler and William R. Thompson, *The Great Powers and Global Struggle, 1490–1990* (Lexington: University of Kentucky Press, 1994); and John Agnew and Stuart Corbridge, *Mastering Space: Hegemony, Territory, and International Political Economy* (London: Routledge, 1995). The newest strand of so-called critical geopolitics challenges the traditional spatial ontology of other theories, pointing out that the state is not a given but rather only one form of political organization and that resources can be accumulated beyond a state's natural endowments. It also emphasizes symbolic as well as material forces, including new forms of soft power. There has never been only one form of power, and empires have always merged their various powers in different combinations. See Gearoid O'Tuathail, *Critical Geopolitics: The Politics of Writing Global Space* (London: Routledge, 1996).

20. Arnold Toynbee, *Civilization on Trial* (London: Oxford University Press, 1948), 8–9.

21. Technically defined, globalization comprises all cross-border interactions—economic, political, or cultural. Peter Marber, "Globalization and Its Contents," *World Policy Journal,* Winter 2004–05, 29.

22. For a discussion of system dynamics and complexity theory, see Robert Jervis, *System Effects: Complexity in Political and Social Life* (Princeton, N.J.: Princeton University Press, 1997), ch. 1.

23. See Michael M. Weinstein, ed., *Globalization: What's New?* (New York: Columbia University Press, 2005). Weinstein, as editor, shows no bias in favor of any particular definition of globalization.

24. See Pietra Rivoli, *The Travels of a T-shirt in the Global Economy: An Economist Explores the Markets, Power, and Politics of World Trade* (New York: John Wiley and Sons, 2005).

25. See Michael Doyle, "Kant, Liberal Legacies, and Foreign Affairs," parts 1 and 2, *Philosophy and Public Affairs* 12, nos. 3–4 (1983): 205–35, 323–53; Bruce Russett, *Grasping the Democratic Peace: Principles for a Post–Cold War World* (Princeton, N.J.: Princeton University Press, 1992); and Michael Brown, Sean Lynn-Jones, and Steven Miller, eds., *Debating the Democratic Peace* (Cambridge, Mass.: MIT Press, 1996).

26. Richard N. Rosecrance, *The Rise of the Virtual State: Wealth and Poverty in the Coming Century* (New York: Basic Books, 2000).

27. David Rothkopf, "Values Conundrum: Will the U.S. and China Play by the Same Rules?" *Washington Post,* July 11, 2005.

28. See Deepak Lal, *In Praise of Empires: Globalization and Order* (New York: Palgrave Macmillan, 2004).

29. See Doyle, *Empires,* 71.

30. Toynbee, *Civilization on Trial.*

31. The U.S. National Intelligence Council's most recent report makes the case most pithily: "How we mentally map the world in 2020 will change radically, rendering obsolete the old categories of East and West, North and South, aligned and nonaligned, developed and developing. Traditional geographic groupings will increasingly lose salience in international relations. A state-bound world and a world of mega-cities, linked by flows of telecommunications, trade and finance, will co-exist. Competition for allegiances will be

more open, less fixed than in the past." *Mapping the Global Future* (Washington, D.C.: U.S. National Intelligence Council, 2005).

32. Arnold Toynbee, *East to West: A Journey Round the World* (New York: Oxford University Press, 1958), 199. Theory itself is psychological, and the anthropomorphizing of states is built into international relations theory. The very model of the state actor used in the dominant rational-choice theory assumes that nations act like a value-maximizing *Homo economicus*. As Robert Keohane writes, however, rationality is "a theoretically useful simplification of reality rather than a true reflection of it." Keohane, *After Hegemony: Cooperation and Discord in the World Political Economy* (Princeton, N.J.: Princeton University Press, 1984), 108. In the 1940s, Hans Morgenthau wrote, "The philosophy of rationalism has misunderstood the nature of man, the nature of the social world, and the nature of reason itself. It does not see that man's nature has three dimensions: biological, rational, and spiritual. By neglecting the biological impulses and spiritual aspirations of man, it misconstrues the function reason fulfils within the whole of human existence; it distorts the problem of ethics, especially in the political field; and it perverts the natural sciences into an instrument of social salivation for which neither their own nature nor the nature of the social world fits them." Morgenthau, *Scientific Man vs. Power Politics* (Chicago: University of Chicago Press, 1946), 5. Rationality is appealing to social scientists because it allows them to presume that identities are fixed, that all people practice a similar cost/benefit calculus, and that weighty decisions must be made on the basis of such rational calculations, enhancing their powers of prediction. See Jonathan Mercer, "Rationality and Psychology in International Politics," *International Organization* 59 (Winter 2005): 77–106.

33. Alexander Wendt, *Social Theory of International Politics* (Cambridge, U.K.: Cambridge University Press, 1999), 194. Wendt also argues that states are organismic agents of collective cognition, supervening the individuals comprising them. See "The State as a Person in International Theory," *Review of International Studies* 30 (2004): 289–316. Elsewhere he explains that states "act differently toward enemies than they do toward friends because enemies are threatening and friends are not. Anarchy and the distribution of power are insufficient to tell us which is which." See "Anarchy Is What States Make of It: The Social Construction of Power Politics," *International Organization* 46, no. 2 (1992): 396–97.

34. See Abraham H. Maslow,"A Theory of Human Motivation," *Psychological Review* 50 (1943): 370–96.

35. Many scholars, Amartya Sen and the authors of the 2002 Human Development Report *Deepening Democracy in a Fragmented World* among them, argue that democracy is itself a component of sustainable political and so-

cioeconomic health. Amartya Sen, *Developent as Freedom* (Oxford, U.K.: Oxford University Press, 1999).

36. Robert Chase, Emily Hill, and Paul Kennedy have identified nine key states around the world that could collectively underpin a robust, global American presence. Their emphasis is on states that are sites of diplomatic contests between three distinct superpowers—that is, not so much pro- or anti-American states but rather potentially pro-EU or pro-China states. Of course, intraregional dynamics greatly affect how an entire region relates to the three superpowers. Chase, Hill, and Kennedy, eds., *Pivotal States and U.S. Policy: A New Strategy for U.S. Policy in the Developing World* (New York: W. W. Norton, 1999).

37. The French demographer Alfred Sauvy coined the term *third world* in 1952, saying that "this ignored, exploited, scorned Third World, like the Third Estate, wants to become something too." Like the French peasantry before the Revolution, the global underclass of poor societies has persisted through all modernizations, from the Industrial Revolution to the Information Revolution. The term implies not progression but dispossession. India's first prime minister, Jawaharlal Nehru, picked up on the term to distinguish and give voice to the already marginalized nations that chose not to align with either the West or the Soviet Union during the Cold War. In the 1970s, the third world demanded the New International Economic Order, which was to bring about equitable redistribution, including the relocation of industries from north to south, price supports for developing-country exports, lower tariffs, and a robust international food program. But the Non-Aligned Movement only cemented the third world's geopolitical irrelevance. (The successor to the Non-Aligned Movement today is the G-77 group within the United Nations.) Geographer Saul Cohen once described South America and Africa as the "quartersphere of marginality" for their detachment from the global economy. Today the third world encompasses Central America and the Caribbean, inner and Andean South America, most of Africa and South Asia, parts of the Arab world, the southern states of Central Asia, and a number of Southeast Asian countries—mostly falling outside the major geostrategic crossroads inhabited by second-world countries. See Mohammed Ayoob, *The Third World Security Predicament: State Making, Regional Conflict, and the International System* (Boulder, Colo.: Lynne Rienner, 1995); and Stephen D. Krasner, *Structural Conflict: The Third World Against Global Liberalism* (Berkeley: University of California Press, 1985).

38. On the bifurcation of the international economic order and upward/downward mobility within it as a result of globalization, see Branko Milanovic, *Worlds Apart: Measuring International and Global Inequality* (Princeton, N.J.: Princeton University Press, 2005), ch. 7.

39. One measure of progress up the ladder of modernity is "stateness." Stateness refers to a government's capacity to enforce its power, ranging from minimal functions (public goods, property rights, defense) to intermediate functions (addressing externalities, education, regulation, social insurance) to more activist roles (industrial policy, wealth redistribution). See Francis Fukuyama, *State-Building: Governance and World Order in the Twenty-first Century* (Ithaca, N.Y.: Cornell University Press, 2004). Four decades ago, Samuel Huntington wrote in *Political Order in Changing Societies* that "the most important political distinction among countries concerns not their form of government, but their degree of government. The differences between democracy and dictatorship are less than the differences between those countries whose politics embodies consensus, community, legitimacy, organization, effectiveness, stability, and those countries whose politics is deficient in these qualities."

40. Adam Przeworski and Fernando Limongi, "Modernization: Facts and Theories," *World Politics* 49, no. 2 (1997). In Seymour Martin Lipset's words, "The more well-to-do a nation, the greater its chances to sustain democracy."

41. As the National Intelligence Council warns, "Even as most of the world gets richer, globalization will profoundly shake up the status quo—generating enormous economic, cultural and consequently political convulsions." *Global Trends 2015* (Washington, D.C.: U.S. National Intelligence Council, 2000).

42. Spykman, *The Geography of the Peace* (New York: Harcourt Brace, 1944), 41.

43. Regions can be defined as geographic zones within which countries have sufficient interdependence to differentiate themselves from other regions, and each region is both a part of and relates to the collective dynamics of the world system. See Buzan, *United States and the Great Powers*, ch. 15.

I. BRUSSELS: THE NEW ROME

1. See Barry Buzan and Ole Wæver, *Regions and Powers: The Structure of International Security* (New York: Cambridge University Press, 2003), ch. 11; John J. Mearsheimer, "Back to the Future: Instability in Europe After the Cold War," *International Security* 15, no. 4 (Summer 1990): 5–56; and John O'Loughlin, "Ordering the 'Crush Zone': Geopolitical Games in Post–Cold War Eastern Europe," in *Geopolitics and Globalization: The Changing World Political Map*, ed. Nurit Kliot and David Newman (London: Frank Cass, 1999).

2. Ralf Dahrendorf, *Reflections on the Revolution in Europe* (New York: Crown, 1990).

3. As Malcolm Anderson explains, Europe's external frontiers have been

expanding as quickly as its internal barriers have collapsed. Anderson, *Frontiers: Territory and State Formation in the Modern World* (London, Polity Press, 1996), 178–91.

4. Graham Bowley, "EU Turns Its Attention and Resources to East," *International Herald Tribune,* July 18, 2005.

5. One unintended consequence of the rapid industrialization of Eastern Europe is that it has slowed the EU's collective reduction in greenhouse gas emissions.

6. Ann Mettler, "A Two-Speed Europe, at Last," *Wall Street Journal Europe,* June 9, 2005.

7. As Cooper writes, "The post-modern EU offers a vision of cooperative empire, common liberty and a common security without the ethnic domination and centralized absolutism to which past empires have been subject." See Cooper, "The New Liberal Imperialism," *Guardian* (Manchester), April 7, 2002. A century ago, H. D. Sedgwick similarly wrote that Rome's example proves that "not empire, but federation, is the true political step toward a cosmopolitan system . . . with its ethical laws, in place of our national system, with its individualistic laws."

8. As Franklin Foer explains, this transformation is best observed through football clubs like FC Barcelona that consider themselves superior but without the political aftertaste of domination. Foer, *How Soccer Explains the World: An Unlikely Theory of Globalization* (New York: HarperCollins, 2004).

9. The EU resembles a Roman *foederatio,* or federation, but features a neomedieval blend of supranational, national, and regional authorities. It functions like a compound republic, with vertical and horizontal separation of powers. See Andrew Moravcsik, "Despotism in Brussels? Misreading the European Union," *Foreign Affairs,* May–June 2001, and *Europe Without Illusions: The Paul-Henri Spaak Lectures, 1994–1999* (Lanham, Md.: University Press of America, 2005); and Ole Wæver, "Imperial Metaphors: Emerging European Analogies to Pre-Nation State Imperial Systems," in *The Geopolitics of Post-Wall Europe: Security, Territory, and Identity,* ed. Ola Tunander, Pavel Baev, and Victoria Ingrid Einagel (Oslo: International Peace Research Institute, 1997).

10. Richard N. Rosecrance, "Mergers and Acquisitions," *The National Interest,* Summer 2005. See also Robert J. Lieber, *The American Era: Power and Strategy for the Twenty-first Century* (New York: Cambridge University Press, 2005); and Chris Patten, *Cousins and Strangers: America, Britain, and Europe in a New Century* (New York: Times Books, 2006).

11. Timothy Garton Ash argues that there is about an 85 percent overlap between the values and beliefs of Americans and Europeans, and that even

anti-American Europeans "measure America against their own high ideal of Europe." Garton Ash, *Free World* (New York: Random House, 2005), 216.

12. R. Nicholas Burns, "A Renewed Partnership for Global Engagement," Remarks at the European Institute Annual Gala Dinner, Washington, D.C., December 15, 2005. At the level of diplomacy, Garton Ash explains that friendship is the name given to "relations between statesmen and stateswomen and, by the two-way symbolic extension, to relations between the states they represent." Garton Ash, *Free World*, 7. And as Christopher Coker points out, even the alleged philosophical divide between America's Hobbesian and Europe's Kantian worldviews only serves to demonstrate that both are ultimately of the West, with discrepancies occurring over the means, not the ends, of coercive force. See Coker, *Empires in Conflict: The Growing Rift Between Europe and the United States*, Whitehall Paper no. 58 (London: Royal United Services Institute, 2003).

13. Robert Kagan, "Power and Weakness," *Policy Review*, June 2002.

14. T. R. Reid, *The United States of Europe: The New Superpower and the End of American Supremacy* (New York: Penguin, 2004).

15. See Josef Joffe, *Überpower: The Imperial Temptation of America* (New York: W. W. Norton, 2006), ch. 3; and Jeremy Rifkin, *The European Dream: How Europe's Vision of the Future Is Quietly Eclipsing the American Dream* (New York: Penguin, 2004).

16. Toynbee, *Civilization on Trial*, 41.

17. See *European Defense Integration: Bridging the Gap Between Strategy and Capabilities* (Washington, D.C.: Center for Strategic and International Studies, 2005); and Seth G. Jones, *The Rise of European Security Cooperation* (New York: Cambridge University Press, 2006).

2. THE RUSSIAN DEVOLUTION

1. See Rosemary S. Mapes, *Russian Nationalism and Russian Historiography, 1725–1854* (Washington, D.C.: Georgetown University Press, 1961); and Daniel Rancour-Laferriere, *The Slave Soul of Russia: Moral Masochism and the Cult of Suffering* (New York: New York University Press, 1995).

2. See Dmitri Trenin, "Russia Leaves the West," *Foreign Affairs*, July–August 2006, and *The End of Eurasia: Russia on the Border Between Geopolitics and Globalization* (Washington, D.C.: Carnegie Endowment for International Peace, 2002). As Alexander Muzykantsky notes, "The ideological confusion of the elite has been the hallmark of Russia's mental continuum since the collapse of the Soviet Union." Muzykantsky, "A Yardstick for Russia," *Russia in Global Affairs* 3, no. 3 (July–September 2005).

3. Andrew E. Kramer and Steven Lee Myers, "Workers' Paradise Is Rebranded as Kremlin, Inc.," *New York Times*, April 24, 2006.

4. See Anders Aslund, "The Hunt for Russia's Riches," *Foreign Policy*, January–February 2006; and David Hoffman, *The Oligarchs: Wealth and Power in the New Russia* (New York: Public Affairs, 2003).

5. Steven Lee Myers, "In Russia, the New Year's Holiday Becomes a Long Winter's Nap," *International Herald Tribune*, January 8, 2007.

6. See Andrei Illarionov, "A Long-Term Project for Russia," and Vladimir Mau, "Lessons from the Spanish Empire," both in *Russia in Global Affairs* 3, no. 3 (July–September 2005).

7. Keith C. Smith, "Gaz Promises," *Georgetown Journal of International Affairs*, Winter–Spring 2007, 51–58.

8. See Rajan Menon and Alexander J. Motyl, "The Myth of Russian Resurgence," *The American Interest*, Spring 2007.

3. UKRAINE: FROM BORDER TO BRIDGE

1. In 1991, writes Anna Reid, "Ukrainians won independence by default. Many had dreamed of independence, but none had expected it; none had prepared for it." Reid, *Borderland: A Journey Through the History of Ukraine* (Boulder, Colo.: Westview, 1997), 217.

2. A litany of unfavorable initial conditions in Ukraine—noncompetitive heavy industry, a demoralized peasantry, energy dependence, an east-west regional divide, and elite incompetence—combined with ineffective and divided government, poorly designed reforms, widespread corruption, and popular apathy "to form a logically coherent system prone to stagnation and resistant to change." Alexander Motyl, "Ukraine, Europe, and Russia: Exclusion or Dependence?" in *Ambivalent Neighbors: The EU, NATO, and the Price of Membership,* ed. Anatol Lieven and Dmitri Trenin (Washington, D.C.: Carnegie Endowment for International Peace, 2003), 19.

3. One scholar refers to Kuchma's system as "competitive authoritarianism," in which informal patronage institutions allow rivals to accumulate capital and loyalties and eventually challenge authority. See Lucan Way, "Kuchma's Failed Authoritarianism," *Journal of Democracy* 16, no. 2 (April 2005).

4. Rudolf Kjellen, *Die politische Probleme des Weltkrieges* (Leipzig, 1916).

5. As Andrew Wilson explains, Russians are still raised to believe that the ancient Rus remains a single nation. Wilson, *The Ukrainians: Unexpected Nation* (New Haven, Conn.: Yale University Press, 2000).

6. Michael Meyer, "Ukraine: Stranded Between Two Worlds?" *World Policy Journal*, Spring 2005.

7. Vasily Aksyonov, *The Island of Crimea* (New York: Vintage, 1984), 40.

8. The United States has learned a similar lesson. The best democracy trainers on the National Democratic Institute staff turned out to be activists from countries that had just been through transitions, even failed or halting ones. Already in 1992, NDI was sending Filipinos to Zambia and Bulgarians to Yemen and Indonesia. NDI's staff is now thoroughly multinational.

9. Pamela Hyde Smith, *Moldova Matters: Why Progress Is Still Possible on Ukraine's Southwestern Flank,* Atlantic Council Occasional Paper, March 2005.

10. As quoted to Timothy Garton Ash and cited in Slavenka Drakuli, *Café Europa: Life After Communism* (London: Penguin, 1996).

4. THE BALKANS: EASTERN QUESTIONS

1. Cited in Nicholas Wood, "Can an Iron Fist Put Power in Bosnia's Hands?" *New York Times,* November 5, 2005.

2. Jack Snyder, *From Voting to Violence: Democratization and Nationalist Conflict* (New York: W. W. Norton, 2000); and Barnett R. Rubin and Jack Snyder, eds., *Post-Soviet Political Order: Conflict and State-Building* (London: Routledge, 1998).

3. "The Inflexibility Trap: Frustrated Societies, Weak States, and Democracy," UNDP Issues Paper, United Nations Development Program, Bratislava, 2002.

4. Despite Romania and Poland's similar economic and demographic structure, Romania does not border Germany, and thus received little EU engagement in the early 1990s. Romanian youth, like North Africans, had little desire to stay in their own country. Whereas Poland's trade did a complete one-eighty, to 70 percent with Europe and only 3 percent with Russia, Romania's strongmen governed through emergency ordinances and Latin American–style populism, returning the country to subsistence farming and entrenching its status as the largest peasant society in Europe. At the same time, the disenfranchised Roma nomads who have lived for generations in fetid encampments can now find a place in society under the EU's antidiscrimination laws and social aid programs. See Tom Gallagher, "Ceausescu's Legacy: Threats to Romania's Internal Security," *The National Interest,* Summer 1999; Georges de Menil, "History, Policy, and Performance in Two Transition Economies: Poland and Romania," March 2002; *Nations in Transit: Romania Country Report 2005,* Freedom House 2005; Alina M. Pippidi, "The Unbearable Lightness of Democracy," unpublished paper; and Charles King, "The Europe Question in Romania and Moldova," in *Ambivalent Neighbors,* ed. Lieven and Trenin, 247.

5. A millennium ago Bulgaria vied with Serbia for regional dominance before both succumbed to Ottoman rule. After switching sides during World War II, Bulgaria eventually became so loyal to the Soviet Union that it proposed to join it in 1973. Its first decade of independence was marred by stasis, with successive protest votes resulting in the return of the exiled king as prime minister. Unable to maintain Cold War levels of industrialization without Soviet subsidies, Bulgaria experienced what one analyst called "de-development," in which the "East became the South." Only through the EU's preaccession process did the situation begin to turn around. Wages rose and price stability resulted from pegging the currency to the euro. See Rossen Vassilev, "De-Development Problems in Bulgaria," *East European Quarterly*, September 22, 2003.

6. According to two experts on the Balkan wars, the Contact Group formed to settle the festering conflict "was reminiscent of nineteenth-century Great Power politics. The five nations gathered to dictate the future of the former Yugoslavia. . . . Talks on Bosnia were mere exercises in regulating relations among the Contact Group members and positioning themselves in the new political order [rather] than about the region or its inhabitants." Allan Little and Laura Silber, *Yugoslavia: Death of a Nation* (New York: Penguin, 1995), 336.

7. Timothy Garton Ash, "The Sultanate of Europe," *Los Angeles Times*, April 14, 2005.

8. See Ivo Andri, *The Days of the Consuls* (Belgrade: Dereta, 2000).

9. Europe could have done much more to back the anti-Milošević opposition, for the sheer unpopularity of incumbents is a far more important factor in ousting them than the existence or growth of a middle class. See Michael McFaul, "Transitions from Postcommunism," *Journal of Democracy* 16, no. 3 (July 2005): 5–19.

10. "A Tale of Two Slavic States," *The Economist*, June 3, 2006, 53.

11. E. Wayne Merry, "Therapy's End: Thinking Beyond NATO," *The National Interest*, Winter 2003–04.

12. This climate of malaise and frustration led the Third International Commission on the Balkans in 2005 to declare the region "as close to failure as to success," adding, "If Europe's neo-colonial rule becomes further entrenched, it will encourage economic discontent; it will become a political embarrassment for the European project; and, above all, European electorates would see it as an immense and unnecessary financial and moral burden." International Commission on the Balkans, *The Balkans in Europe's Future* (Sofia, Bulgaria: Centre for Liberal Strategies, 2005), 7, 11.

13. See Elizabeth Pond, *Endgame in the Balkans: Regime Change, European Style* (Washington, D.C.: Brookings Institution Press, 2006).

14. *Breaking Out of the Balkan Ghetto: Why IPA Should Be Changed,* European Stability Initiative, June 2005.

15. Dimitri Obolensky, *The Byzantine Commonwealth: Eastern Europe, 500–1453* (New York: Praeger Publishers, 1971), 4 (map).

5. TURKEY: MARCHING EAST AND WEST

1. See Christopher Caldwell, "The East in the West," *New York Times Magazine,* September 25, 2005. The populations of Turkey and Russia are projected to nearly equalize over the next thirty years.

2. Jacques Le Goff originated this use of the term. Cited in Jacques Pilet, "Geboren im Mittelalter," *Cicero,* November 2005, 24–26.

3. It is the EU, not NATO, that is helping resolve the Cyprus dispute by pressuring Turkey to allow ships and aircraft from Cyprus to land in Turkey.

4. Fiona Hill and Omer Taspinar, "Turkey and Russia: The Axis of Excluded?" *Survival,* Spring 2006.

5. Soner Cagaptay, "Why Are the Turks Hesitating on Iraq?" Policy Watch no. 704, Washington Institute for Near East Policy, January 27, 2003.

6. Mark Parris, "Allergic Partners: Can U.S.-Turkish Relations Be Saved?" *Turkish Policy Quarterly* 5, no. 1 (Spring 2005).

7. See the report *Islamic Calvinists: Change and Conservatism in Central Anatolia,* European Stability Initative, September 2005.

8. Quoted in Salman Rushdie, "How Can a Country That Victimizes Its Greatest Living Writer Also Join the EU?," *The Times* (London), October 14, 2005.

9. In both 1970 and 1980, the Turkish military seized power and then quickly restored civilian rule, thus strengthening its own popularity. See Ersel Aydinli, Nihat Ali Özcan, and Dogan Akyaz, "The Turkish Military's March Toward Europe," *Foreign Affairs,* January–February 2006.

10. See Stephen Kinzer, *Crescent and Star: Turkey Between Two Worlds* (New York: Farrar, Straus and Giroux, 2001). As Soli Özel explains, major Turkish leaders from the former prime minister and later president Turgut Ozal to the Islamist Recep Tayyip Erdoğan have cited EU membership as "the agent of Turkey's transformation from a spotty and in too many ways illiberal democracy into a fully fledged specimen of the liberal democratic breed." Özel, "After the Tsunami," *Turkish Policy Quarterly* 3, no. 1 (Spring 2003).

11. Andrew Mango, *The Turks Today* (London: Overlook Press, 2005).

12. As Hugh Pope writes, "Most Turkish Islamists rarely stray far from a national consensus that no longer wants Islamic *sharia* law. Indeed, the closer

they get to the consensus, the more successful they are." Pope, *Sons of the Conquerors: The Rise of the Turkic World* (London: Overlook Press, 2005), 277.

13. See Charles King, *The Black Sea: A History* (London: Oxford University Press, 2004).

14. Ronald D. Asmus and Bruce P. Jackson, "The Black Sea and the Frontiers of Freedom," *Policy Review*, June 2004.

6. THE CAUCASIAN CORRIDOR

1. Aleksander Rondeli, "Russia and Georgia: Asymmetrical Neighbors," in *Central Asia and South Caucasus Affairs*, ed. Boris Rumer and Lan Sim Yee (Tokyo: Sasakawa Peace Foundation, 2003).

2. Eduard Ponarin and Irina Kouznetsova-Morenko, "Russia's Islamic Challenge," *Georgetown Journal of International Affairs*, Summer–Fall 2006, 21–28.

3. The International Finance Corporation and the European Bank for Reconstruction and Development funded much of the $4 billion BTC pipeline. The main operator, British Petroleum, controlled a 30 percent stake, with American firms Unocal and Chevron (who later merged), Norway's Statoil, Italy's Eni S.p.A., Turkey's state-run TPAO, and Azerbaijan's own SOCAR also as major contributors.

4. Quoted in Kim Murphy, "Caspian Sea Pipeline Has Its Origin in Murky Waters," *Los Angeles Times*, June 27, 2005.

5. Fiona Hill, "Beyond the Colored Revolutions," keynote speech at Central Eurasia Studies Society 6th Annual Conference, Boston University, September 30, 2005.

6. Svante E. Cornell et al., *Regional Security in the South Caucasus: The Role of NATO* (Washington, D.C.: Central Asia–Caucasus Institute, Paul H. Nitze School of Advanced International Studies, 2004).

7. In the 1990s the Armenian diaspora also lobbied successfully to have Azerbaijan sanctioned by the United States under the controversial section 907 of the Iran Libya Sanctions Act (ILSA).

8. The Russo-Iranian wars of 1813 and 1828 split Azeris geographically. Azerbaijan today represents only a quarter of the Azeri nation, with twenty-five million Azeris living in northern Iran (representing a third of Iran's population). As Afshin Molavi explains, the benevolent Persian shah Safavid in the sixteenth century was Azeri, and his court city of Tabriz was the center of Iran's progressive constitutionalist movement in the late nineteenth and early twentieth centuries. Molavi, *The Soul of Iran: A Nation's Journey to Freedom* (New York: W. W. Norton, 2005), 211.

9. See Zbigniew Brzezinski, *The Grand Chessboard: American Primacy and Its Geostrategic Imperatives* (New York: Basic Books, 1997).

10. See Thomas Goltz, *Azerbaijan Diary: A Rogue Reporter's Adventures in an Oil-Rich, War-Torn, Post-Soviet Republic* (Armonk, N.Y.: M.E. Sharpe, 1998).

11. See *How Freedom Is Won: From Civic Resistance to Durable Democracy,* Freedom House, 2005.

7. THE SILK ROAD AND THE GREAT GAME

1. Peter Hopkirk, *The Great Game: The Struggle for Empire in Central Asia* (London: Kodansha International, 1992), 466.

2. As Jack Weatherford writes, the empire of Genghis Khan "stretched from the snowy tundra of Siberia to the hot plains of India, from the rice paddies of Vietnam to the wheat fields of Hungary, and from Korea to the Balkans. . . . [He] opened roads of commerce in a free-trade zone that stretched across the continents. . . . He took the disjoined and languorous trading towns along the Silk Route and organized them into history's largest free-trade zone." Weatherford, *Genghis Khan and the Making of the Modern World* (New York: Crown, 2004), xviii–xix.

3. Hopkirk, *Great Game,* 231; see also Karl E. Meyer and Shareen B. Brysac, *Tournament of Shadows: The Great Game and the Race for Empire in Central Asia* (New York: Counterpoint, 2000).

4. See R. James Ferguson, "China and the Emerging Eurasian Agenda: From Special Interests to Strategic Cooperation," Centre for East-West Cultural and Economic Studies, Research Paper no. 8, December 2001; Matthew Oresman, "Beyond the Battle of Talas" and "China's Reemergence in Central Asia," both in *In the Tracks of Tamerlane: Central Asia's Path to the Twenty-first Century,* ed. Daniel L. Burghart and Theresa Sabonis-Helf (Washington, D.C.: Center for Technology and Security Policy, National Defense University, 2005).

5. As Bates Gill has stated, "This is all about soft power and strategic and diplomatic relationships . . . with China reaching out and settling old scores, and trying to establish a benign kind of hegemony." Quoted in Howard W. French, "China Moves Toward Another West: Central Asia," *New York Times,* March 28, 2004.

6. Joseph F. Fletcher, "China and Central Asia, 1368–1884," in *The Chinese World Order: Traditional China's Foreign Relations,* ed. John K. Fairbank (Cambridge, Mass.: Harvard University Press, 1968).

8. THE RUSSIA THAT WAS

1. Fen Montaigne, *Reeling in Russia: An Angler's Paradise* (New York: St. Martin's Press, 1998).

2. Geoffrey Hosking, *Russia and the Russians: A History* (Cambridge, Mass.: Harvard University Press, 2002).

3. See Fiona Hill and Clifford Gaddy, *The Siberian Curse: How Communist Planners Left Russia out in the Cold* (Washington, D.C.: Brookings Institution Press, 2003); and Harm de Blij, *Why Geography Matters: Three Challenges Facing America: Climate Change, the Rise of China, and Global Terrorism* (New York: Cambridge University Press, 2005), 240.

4. The affected Russian oblasts include Krasnoyarsk, Amur, Irkutsk, Trans-Baikal, and Magadan. See Friends of the Earth, *Plundering Russia's Far Eastern Taiga: Illegal Logging, Corruption, and Trade,* July 2000.

5. For a discussion of Sino-Russian demographic scenarios in the Far East, see Olga Oliker and Tanya Charlick-Paley, *Assessing Russia's Decline: Trends and Implications for the United States and the U.S. Air Force* (Santa Monica, Calif.: RAND Corporation, 2002), ch. 5. Early in the Cold War, George Kennan viewed the Russia-China relationship as one in which "a great military power which is coterminous for over 4,000 miles with the land frontier of China . . . is never likely to be without its due share of influence on the councils of that country." But those roles are reversed today. Kennan, *American Diplomacy* (1951; repr. Chicago: University of Chicago Press, 1984).

6. Michael Schuman, "The New El Dorado," *Time,* August 7, 2006.

7. Mikhail Alexseev, "The Chinese Are Coming: Public Opinion and Threat Perception in the Russian Far East," PONARS Policy Memo no. 184, January 2001.

8. Christopher Andrews and Vasili Mitrokhin, *The World Was Going Our Way: The KGB and the Battle for the Third World* (New York: Basic Books, 2005), 279–80.

9. Gaye Christoffersen, "The Dilemmas of China's Energy Governance: Recentralization and Regional Cooperation," *China-Eurasia Forum Quarterly* 3, no. 3 (November 2005): 55–80.

10. Pauline Jones Luong, ed., *The Transformation of Central Asia: States and Societies from Soviet Rule to Independence* (Ithaca, N.Y.: Cornell University Press, 2004).

11. Oliver Roy, *The New Central Asia: The Creation of Nations* (New York: New York University Press, 2000).

12. Gregory Gleason, "Reform Strategies in Central Asia: Early Starters,

Late Starters, and Non-Starters," in *In the Tracks of Tamerlane*, ed. Burghart and Sabonis-Helf.

13. Mancur Olson, "Dictatorships, Democracy, and Development," *American Political Science Review* 87, no. 3 (September 1993).

14. See Anders Aslund, *Building Capitalism: The Transformation of the Former Soviet Bloc* (New York: Cambridge University Press, 2001); and *Sustaining Growth in Uncertain Times*, Eurasia Economic Summit 2002 Report, World Economic Forum.

9. TIBET AND XINJIANG: THE NEW BAMBOO CURTAIN

1. Mahnaz Z. Ispahani elaborates, "Roads and railroads still can define the territorial reach and physical capabilities of the state and are integral to the achievement of its political, economic and military potential." Ispahani, *Roads and Rivals: The Political Uses of Access in the Borderlands of Asia* (Ithaca, N.Y.: Cornell University Press, 1989), xii, 3.

2. As a recent Chinese government manifesto declares, "Since the Western Han dynasty (206 B.C.–24 A.D.), Xinjiang has been an inseparable part of the unitary multiethnic Chinese nation."

3. Ross Terrill, *The New Chinese Empire: And What It Means for the United States* (New York: Basic Books, 2003), 54.

4. Mackinder, *Democratic Ideals and Reality*. See also Robert Harkavy, "Strategic Geography and the Greater Middle East," *Naval War College Review*, Autumn 2001.

10. KAZAKHSTAN: "HAPPINESS IS MULTIPLE PIPELINES"

1. Many scholars now refer to the region as "Inner Asia." See the contributions in Robert Legvold, ed., *Thinking Strategically: The Major Powers, Kazakhstan, and the Central Asian Nexus* (Cambridge, Mass.: American Academy of Arts and Sciences, 2003).

2. Kassymzhomart Tokaev, *Meeting the Challenge* (Redding, Conn.: Begell House, 2004).

3. Stephen Blank, "China, Kazakh Energy, and Russia: An Unlikely Menage à Trois," *China-Eurasia Forum Quarterly* 3, no. 3 (November 2005): 101.

4. Steve LeVine, *The Oil and the Glory: The Pursuit of Empire and Fortune on the Caspian Sea* (New York: Random House, 2007).

5. Taleh Ziyadov, "Prospects of Caspian Gas and Its Potential Markets," *Central Asia and the Caucasus Journal* 29, no. 5 (2004).

6. Johannes Linn and David Tiomkin, *Economic Integration of Eurasia:*

Opportunities and Challenges of Global Significance (Warsaw: Center for Social and Economic Research, 2005).

7. See Paul Starobin, "Sultan of the Steppes," *Atlantic Monthly,* December 2005.

8. For a discussion of economic trends and scenarios for the region, see Malcolm Dowling and Ganeshan Wignarajan, "Central Asia's Economy: Mapping Future Prospects to 2015," Central Asia–Caucasus Institute, Silk Road Paper, July 2006; Alan Rousso, "Escaping the Resource Trap: Market Reform and Political Governance in the Resource Rich Countries of Eurasia," *China-Eurasia Forum Quarterly* 4, no. 3 (Autumn 2006): 3–14; and *Republic of Kazakhstan: Selected Issues,* IMF Country Report no. 04/362, November 2004.

9. Fiona Hill, "Whither Kazakhstan?" *In the National Interest,* September 20, 2005.

10. See *Kazakhstan: Reducing Nuclear Dangers, Increasing Global Security,* Nuclear Threat Initiative, 2004; and Nursultan Nazarbayev, *Epicenter of Peace* (Hollis, N.H.: Puritan Press, 2001).

11. He ultimately received 90 percent of the vote, with a 75 percent turnout.

11. KYRGYZSTAN AND TAJIKISTAN: SOVEREIGN OF EVERYTHING, MASTER OF NOTHING

1. Alexander Cooley, "Depoliticizing Manas: The Domestic Consequences of the U.S. Military Presence in Kyrgyzstan," PONARS Policy Memo no. 362, February 2005.

12. UZBEKISTAN AND TURKMENISTAN: MEN BEHAVING BADLY

1. Assel Rustemova, "National Identities of Central Asia States and Their Impact on the Prospects for Regional Integration," unpublished paper presented at the International Studies Association, San Diego, March 2006.

2. Naqshbandi Sufi orders eventually played an important role in nationalist movements. See Chris Seiple and Joshua White, "Uzbekistan and the Central Asian Crucible of Religion and Security," in *Religion and Security: The New Nexus in International Relations,* ed. Chris Seiple and Dennis R. Hoover (Lanham, Md.: Rowman and Littlefield, 2004).

3. Martha Olcott, *Central Asia's Second Chance* (Washington, D.C.: Carnegie Endowment for International Peace, 2005), 207.

4. See "The IMU and the Hizb-ut-Tahrir: Implications of the Afghanistan

Campaign," Central Asia Briefing, International Crisis Group, January 30, 2002; Zeyno Baran, "Fighting the War of Ideas," *Foreign Affairs*, November–December 2005, 68, and *Hizb ut-Tahrir: Islam's Political Insurgency* (Washington, D.C.: Nixon Center, 2004).

5. Martha Brill Olcott and Bakhtiar Babajanov, "The Terrorist Notebooks," *Foreign Policy*, March–April 2003.

6. Tiffany Petros, "Islam in Central Asia: The Emergence and Growth of Radicalism in the Post-Communist Era," in *In the Tracks of Tamerlane*, ed. Burghart and Sabonis-Helf.

7. Chris Seiple, "Uzbekistan and the Bush Doctrine," *Review of Faith and International Affairs* 3, no. 2 (Fall 2005).

8. Dana Priest, *The Mission: Waging War and Keeping Peace with America's Military* (New York: W. W. Norton, 2003), 108.

9. Sylvia W. Babus, "Democracy-Building in Central Asia Post–September 11," in *In the Tracks of Tamerlane*, ed. Burghart and Sabonis-Helf.

10. Alexander Cooley, "Base Politics," *Foreign Affairs*, November–December 2005, 79–92.

11. Olcott, *Central Asia's Second Chance*, 100.

12. Theresa Sabonis-Helf, "The Rise of the Post-Soviet Petro-States: Energy Exports and Domestic Governance in Turkmenistan and Kazakhstan," in *In the Tracks of Tamerlane*, ed. Burghart and Sabonis-Helf.

13. In 2005, a feasibility study by the Asian Development Bank concluded that the pipeline is commercially viable.

14. Kathleen J. Hancock, "Escaping Russia, Looking to China: Turkmenistan Pins Hopes on China's Thirst for Natural Gas," *China-Eurasia Forum Quarterly* 4, no. 3 (Autumn 2006): 67–87.

13. AFGHANISTAN AND PAKISTAN: TAMING SOUTH-CENTRAL ASIA

1. See Olga Oliker and David A. Shlapak, *U.S. Interests in Central Asia: Policy Priorities and Military Roles* (Santa Monica, Calif.: RAND Corporation, 2005), v. It took until 2006 for America to sort out its geographic schizophrenia, however, with the Pentagon including the region in its Central Command (CENTCOM) and the State Department leaving it in its European bureau.

2. Cited in Ispahani, *Roads and Rivals*, 117.

3. Rachel Morajee, "Narcotecture in Afghanistan," *Monocle*, no. 5, 2007.

4. Elizabeth Rubin, "In the Land of the Taliban," *New York Times Magazine*, October 22, 2006.

5. By breaching the mountain barrier, the Karakoram "altered the bal-

ance of geographical politics in the subcontinent." Ispahani, *Roads and Rivals*, 151, 201. Furthermore, the Soviet Union no longer exists as India's diplomatic ally to protest Sino-Pakistani military cooperation along the Karakoram.

6. See Husain Haqqani, "Counter-Terrorism or Bounty Hunting," *Nation* (Pakistan), November 8, 2006; and Mansour Ijaz, "Musharrafistan," *Wall Street Journal*, September 19, 2006.

7. Ziad Haider, "Sino-Pakistan Relations and Xinjiang's Uighurs: Politics, Trade, and Islam Along the Karakoram Highway," *Asian Survey*, July–August 2005, 522–45.

8. Ayesha Siddiqa, *Military, Inc.: Inside Pakistan's Military Economy* (London: Pluto Press, 2007).

CONCLUSION: A CHANGE OF HEART

1. See S. Frederick Starr, "A 'Greater Central Asia Partnership' for Afghanistan and Its Neighbors," Central Asia–Caucasus Institute Silk Road Studies Program, March 2005.

2. Mackinder, *Democratic Ideals and Reality*, 144.

3. Bates Gill and Matthew Oresman, *China's New Journey to the West: China's Emergence in Central Asia and Implications for U.S. Interests*, report of the CSIS Freeman Chair in China Studies, August 2003.

4. Linn and Tiomkin, *Economic Integration of Eurasia*, fig. 17.

14. THE NEW RULES OF THE GAME

1. Eduardo Galeano, *Open Veins of Latin America: Five Centuries of the Pillage of a Continent* (New York: Monthly Review Press, 1973), 11.

2. Peter H. Smith, *Talons of the Eagle: Dynamics of U.S.–Latin American Relations* (New York: Oxford University Press, 1996), 17.

3. New states were consolidated from the remnants of the Spanish empire by the principle of *uti possidetis* ("as you possess"), meaning borders would be defined as those controlled at the end of conflict.

4. John Hay's "Open Door" notes articulated the goal of ensuring equal rights of foreign commercial access overseas, particularly in China, while preserving territorial and administrative integrity. See William Appleman Williams, *The Tragedy of American Diplomacy* (New York: W. W. Norton, 1959), 50.

5. As William Appleman Williams points out, Wilson's ideology was fundamentally liberal rather than mercantilist because it assumed a harmony of interests. Williams, *Tragedy of American Diplomacy*, 95n.

6. Smith, *Talons of the Eagle*, 62.

7. Ibid., 134.

8. Ibid., 151.

9. Fernando Henrique Cardoso, *Charting a New Course: The Politics of Globalization and Social Transformation*, ed. Mauricio A. Font (Lanham, Md.: Rowman and Littlefield, 2001), 122.

10. Moises Naim, "The Lost Continent," *Foreign Policy*, February 2004.

11. Galeano, *Open Veins of Latin America*, 255.

12. See Tomoe Funakushi and Claudio Loser, *China's Rising Economic Presence in Latin America*, Inter-American Dialogue, 2005, 2; and "Magic, or Realism?" *The Economist*, December 29, 2004.

13. Andrew and Mitrokhin, *World Was Going Our Way*, 27.

14. See Cynthia A. Watson, testimony before the Western Hemisphere Subcommittee of the House of Representatives Committee on Foreign Affairs, April 6, 2005.

15. Anywhere from 60 to 90 percent of Latin America's GDP (depending on the country) derives from primary commodity exports. As a recent UNDP report notes, "Oil and mineral wealth generated through exports can be bad for growth, bad for democracy and bad for development." *Human Development Report 2005*, United Nations Development Program, 124.

16. Funakushi and Loser, *China's Rising Economic Presence*, 3, 8.

17. For a discussion of perceptions and realities of Chinese involvement in Latin America, see Sam Logan and Ben Bain, "China's Entrance into Latin America: A Cause for Worry?" *IRC Americas*, August 24, 2005.

18. See Antoni Estevadeordal, Dani Rodrik, Alan M. Taylor, and Andres Velasco, eds., *Integrating the Americas: FTAA and Beyond* (Cambridge, Mass.: Harvard University Press, 2004); Pamela K. Starr, "Pax America in Latin America: The Hegemony Behind Free Trade," in *Between Compliance and Conflict: Between East Asia, Latin America, and the "New" Pax Americana*, ed. Jorge I. Dominguez and Byung Cook Kim (New York: Routlege, 2005), 85–86.

19. Unlike the EU, the FTAA creates no formal linkages between open markets, democratic governance, and social equity. Despite the low bar they set, FTAA discussions continue simply because no side wants to be seen as lacking commitment—and they continue to fail because of pick-and-choose "cafeteria model" terms, which have created a complex maze of regulations rather than a truly free market. See Jorge I. Dominguez, "Bush Administration Policy: A View Toward Latin America," *ReVista*, Spring–Summer 2005, 4.

20. Across Latin America, real per capita GDP in 2003 was essentially the same as in 1980, and poverty actually increased over the same period. See Marianne Fay, ed., *The Urban Poor in Latin America (Directions in Development)* (Washington, D.C.: International Bank for Reconstruction and Development, World Bank, 2005); and De Ferranti et al., eds., *Inequality in Latin*

America and the Caribbean: Breaking with History? (Washington, D.C.: International Bank for Reconstruction and Development, World Bank, 2005).

21. Nancy Birdsall and Augusto de la Torre, *Washington Contentious: Economic Policies for Social Equity in Latin America* (Washington, D.C.: Carnegie Endowment for International Peace and Inter-American Dialogue, 2001), 6.

22. Since the tumultuous IMF stabilization programs of the 1990s, trade, foreign investment, and social expenditure have all grown while inflation is under control, and Latin countries are actively pursuing a mix of free trade agreements—with the United States, Europe, Asia, and one another. See Dominguez and Kim, ed., *Between Compliance and Conflict*, 2, 11.

15. MEXICO: THE UMBILICAL CORD

1. Though tourism revenues have also increased by $1 billion per year, oil revenues continue to provide up to 40 percent of Mexico's budget.

2. In 2003, China had 25 percent of the U.S. clothing market and Mexico 10 percent; by 2005, China had 56 percent and Mexico only 3 percent; Funakushi and Loser, *China's Rising Economic Presence*, 5.

3. Juan Enriques, *The Untied States of America: Polarization, Fracturing, and Our Future* (New York: Crown, 2005), ch. 6.

4. Joseph Contreras, "Losing the Battle," *Newsweek*, July 11, 2005; and James C. McKinley Jr., "With Beheadings and Attacks, Drug Gangs Terrorize Mexico," *New York Times*, October 27, 2006.

5. Tamar Jacoby, "Immigration Nation," *Foreign Affairs*, November–December 2006.

6. *Building a North American Community*, Report of an Independent Task Force Sponsored by the Council on Foreign Relations, 2005.

7. Enriques, *Untied States of America*, 154.

8. "10 Questions for Pat Buchanan," *Time*, August 28, 2006, 6.

9. "Applauding the CAFTA 15," *New York Times*, July 29, 2005.

10. Fernando Cardoso and Peter Bell, *A Break in the Clouds: Latin America and the Caribbean in 2005* (Washington, D.C.: Inter-American Dialogue, 2005), 8.

16. VENEZUELA: BOLÍVAR'S REVENGE

1. Ricardo Hausmann, "A Case of Bad Latitude: Why Geography Causes Poverty," *Foreign Policy*, January–February 2001.

2. Alma Guillermoprieto, *The Heart That Bleeds: Latin America Now* (New York: Alfred A. Knopf, 1994), x.

3. Terry Lynn Karl, *The Paradox of Plenty: Oil Booms and Petro-States* (Berkeley: University of California Press, 1997), 3.

4. Karl, *Paradox of Plenty*, 32.

5. Michael Rowan, *Getting Over Chávez and Poverty* (2006; available from michael.rowan.book@gmail.com).

6. Michael Rowan, "A Strategy for Success in Venezuela," *VenEconomia*, December 2, 2005.

7. Charles S. Shapiro, "Venezuelan Labor Struggles to Find Autonomy," *Georgetown Journal of International Affairs*, Winter–Spring 2007, 19–26.

8. "Oil, Missions, and a Chat Show," *The Economist*, May 14, 2005, 23–25.

9. Michael Penfold-Becerra, "Social Funds, Clientelism, and Redistribution: Chávez's *'Misiones'* Programs in Comparative Perspective," working paper, Instituto de Estudios Superiores de Administración (IESA), November 2005.

10. According to Javier Corrales, Chávez has "eliminated the contradictions between autocracy and political competitiveness." See "Hugo Boss," *Foreign Policy*, January–February 2006, 32–40; and Javier Corrales, "In Search of a Theory of Polarization: Lessons from Venezuela, 1999–2005," *Revista Europea de Estudios Latinamericanos y del Caribe*, October 2005, 79.

11. Asdrúbal Baptista, "El Estado y el capitalismo rentístico," paper presented at the Conferencia José Gil Fortoul, Academia Nacional de la Historia, Caracas, 2005, 25.

12. Josep M. Colomer and Gabriel L. Negretto, "Can Presidentialism Work Like Parliamentarism?" *Government and Opposition* (2005); 60–89.

13. Eduardo Galeano, *We Say No: Chronicles, 1963–1991* (New York: W. W. Norton, 1992), 195. Alvaro Vargas Llosa is less discreet, referring to leftist-populist leaders like Chávez as "idiots." See his "The Return of the Idiot," *Foreign Policy*, May–June 2007.

14. Alma Guillermoprieto, "The Gambler," *New York Review of Books*, October 20, 2005.

15. Alma Guillermoprieto, "Don't Cry for Me, Venezuela," *New York Review of Books*, October 6, 2005.

16. Quoted in Jens Erik Gould, "Plans for South American Pipeline Has Ambitions Beyond Gas," *New York Times*, December 2, 2006.

17. COLOMBIA: THE ANDEAN BALKANS?

1. Toynbee, *East to West*, 1–3.

2. See International Crisis Group, *Colombia's Borders: The Weak Link in Uribe's Security Policy*, Latin America Report no. 9, September 23, 2004, and *War and Drugs in Colombia*, Latin America Report no. 11, January 27, 2005.

3. International Crisis Group, *Colombia: Presidential Politics and Peace Prospects,* Latin America Report no. 14, June 16, 2005, 12.

4. International Crisis Group, *Coca, Drugs, and Social Protest in Bolivia and Peru,* Latin America Report no. 12, March 3, 2005.

5. Guillermoprieto, *Heart That Bleeds,* 19.

6. Toynbee, *East to West,* 3.

7. International Crisis Group, *Uribe's Re-election: Can the EU Help Colombia Develop a More Balanced Peace Strategy?* Latin America Report no. 17, June 8, 2006.

8. It is widely claimed that the United States, through the IMF and World Bank, intentionally encouraged heavy loans for narrow projects undertaken by American contractors across the Andes that would bring little public benefit, particularly during the 1980s, resulting in massive debt burdens. See Jorge Castenada, "Latin America's Left Turn," *Foreign Affairs,* May–June 2006; William Finnegan, "The Economics of Empire: Notes on the Washington Consensus," *Harper's,* May 2003; Adam Isacson, "12 Elections in Twelve Months," DemocracyArsenal.org, January 12, 2006; John Nellis, Rachel Menezes, and Sarah Lucas, *Privatization in Latin America: The Rapid Rise, Recent Fall, and Continuing Puzzle of a Contentious Economic Policy* (Washington, D.C.: Center for Global Development, 2004); John Perkins, *Confessions of an Economic Hit Man* (San Francisco: Berrett Koehler, 2003); and David Rieff, "Che's Second Coming?" *New York Times Magazine,* November 20, 2005.

9. "Democracy's Ten-Year Rut," *The Economist,* October 29, 2005, 60–62.

10. Heinrich Kreft, "The EU and Latin America Should Forge a Strategic Partnership," *European Perspectives,* Summer 2005.

18. BRAZIL: THE SOUTHERN POLE

1. It was America's independence struggle that inspired Brazil to break the chains that bound it to Portugal, and the Parisian mobs of the French Revolution provided tactical guidance for Brazil's revolutionaries. Two centuries ago, Brazil considered slavery a social ill that could be replaced by excess laborers and European immigrants. See Kenneth Maxwell, *Naked Tropics: Essays on Empire and Other Rogues* (New York: Routledge, 2003), ch. 7–8.

2. Cardoso, *Charting a New Course,* Mauricio A. Font's introductory essay and ch. 21.

3. Amaury de Souza, "Cardoso and the Struggle for Reform in Brazil," *Journal of Democracy* 10, no. 3 (July 1999): 49–63.

4. Gianpaolo Baiocchi, *Radicals in Power: The Worker's Party and Experiments in Urban Democracy in Brazil* (New York: Zed Books, 2003), 5; and "Taming an Urban Monster," *The Economist*, January 29, 2005, 45–46.

5. See Paulo Roberto de Almeida, "Two Foreign Policies from Cardoso to Lula," presentation at Florida International University, March 4, 2004; and Monica Hirst, *The United States and Brazil: A Long Road of Unmet Expectations* (New York: Routledge, 2004).

6. Rubens Antonio Barbosa, "Why the Group of 20 Was 'Suddenly' Formed," remarks at the Cordell Hull Institute Trade Policy Roundtable, Washington, D.C., November 25, 2003.

7. See Larry Rohter, "Brazil Weighs Costs and Benefits of Alliance with China," *New York Times*, November 20, 2005; and Charles Tang, "Brazil-China: A Strategic and Commercial Alliance," paper presented at the ITAMARATY conference on "Brazil-Asia in the Twenty-first Century: A Meeting of Horizons," Brasilia, June 8, 2001.

8. Cardoso and Bell, *Break in the Clouds*, 11.

9. For incisive discussions of Amazon security issues from a variety of perspectives, see Jospeh L. Tulchin and Heather A. Golding, eds., *Environment and Security in the Amazon Basin* (Washington, D.C.: Woodrow Wilson International Center for Scholars, 2002).

19. ARGENTINA AND CHILE: VERY FRATERNAL TWINS

1. V. S. Naipaul, *Return of Eva Peron* (New York: Alfred A. Knopf, 1980), 103, 153.

2. Mark Falcoff, *A Culture of Its Own: Taking Latin America Seriously* (New Brunswick, N.J.: Transaction Publishers, 1998), 255.

3. According to Paul Blustein, the financial meltdown exposed Argentina as a country no more capable of managing huge sums of hot money than a teenager put behind the wheel of a sportscar. Blustein, *And the Money Kept Rolling In (And Out): Wall Street, the IMF, and the Bankrupting of Argentina* (New York: Public Affairs, 2005).

4. See Monica Herz, "Brazilian Foreign Policy Since 1990 and the Pax Americana," in *Between Compliance and Conflict,* ed. Dominguez and Kim; and Laura Gomez Mera, "Explaining Mercosur's Survival: Strategic Sources of Argentine-Brazilian Convergence," *Journal of Latin American Studies* 37 (2005): 109–40.

5. June Erlick, "Chile: A Changing Country," *ReVista*, Spring 2004.

6. See Peter H. Smith, *Democracy in Latin America: Political Change in Comparative Perspective* (New York: Oxford University Press, 2005), 231; and

"Writing the Next Chapter in a Latin American Success Story," *The Economist*, April 2, 2005, 32–33.

7. Larry Rohter, "Debating the Course of Chile's Rivers," *New York Times*, August 6, 2006.

8. Smith, *Democracy in Latin America*, 327.

20. THE SHATTERED BELT

1. Cohen defined a "shatter-belt" as "a large, strategically located region that is occupied by a number of conflicting states and is caught between the conflicting interests of adjoining Great Powers." Cohen, *Geography and Politics in a Divided World* (New York: Random House, 1963). See also Geoffrey Kemp and Robert E. Harkavy, *Strategic Geography and the Changing Middle East* (Washington, D.C.: Brookings Institution Press, 1997).

2. As Halim Barakat has argued, the Arab world should be viewed as "a single, overarching society rather than a collection of several independent nation-states." Barakat, *The Arab World: Society, Culture and State* (Berkeley: University of California Press, 1993), xi.

3. See the Arab Human Development Reports commissioned by the United Nations Development Program.

4. Edward N. Luttwak, "The Middle of Nowhere," *Prospect*, May 2007.

5. See Anoush Ehteshami, *Globalization and Geopolitics in the Middle East* (London: Routledge, 2007).

6. François Burgat, "French and U.S. Approaches to Understanding Islam," lecture given to the France-Stanford Centre on Interdisciplinary Studies, September 2004.

7. See de Blij, *Why Geography Matters*, 123. The U.S. National Intelligence Council argues that "political Islam will have a significant global impact, rallying disparate ethnic and national groups and perhaps even creating an authority that transcends national boundaries." *Global Trends 2020*, National Intelligence Council, 2005.

8. See John L. Esposito, *Unholy War: Terror in the Name of Islam* (New York: Oxford University Press, 2002); George P. Fletcher, *Romantics at War: Glory and Guilt in an Age of Terrorism* (Princeton, N.J.: Princeton University Press, 2002); "Islamic Extremists: How Do They Mobilize Support?" United States Institute of Peace, Special Report no. 89, July 2002; George Perkovich, "Giving Justice Its Due," *Foreign Affairs*, July–August 2005, 83; Guy Raz, "The War on the Word 'Jihad,'" National Public Radio, October 31, 2006, available at www.npr.org; and Jonathan Schanzer, *Al-Qaeda's Armies: Middle East Affiliate Groups and the Next Generation of Terror* (Washington, D.C.: Washington Insti-

tute for Near East Policy, 2005). The manifesto of dozens of prominent Islamic scholars, titled "How We Can Co-exist," was published at www.islamtoday.net.

9. As Francis Fukuyama has written, "Conceiving the larger struggle as a global war comparable to the world wars or the Cold War vastly overstates the scope of the problem, suggesting that we are taking on a large part of the Arab and Muslim worlds. Before the Iraq war, we were probably at war with no more than a few thousand people around the world who would consider martyring themselves and causing nihilistic damage to the United States. The scale of the problem has grown because we have unleashed a maelstrom." Fukuyama, *America at the Crossroads: Democracy, Power, and the Neoconservative Legacy* (New Haven, Conn.: Yale University Press, 2006).

21. THE MAGHREB: EUROPE'S SOUTHERN SHORE

1. Fernand Braudel, *The Mediterranean and the World in the Age of Philip II,* trans. Sian Reynolds (Glasgow: Fontana–Collins, 1975), 1:276.

2. Robert D. Kaplan, *Mediterranean Winter: The Pleasures of History and Landscape in Tunisia, Sicily, Dalmatia, and Greece* (New York: Random House, 2004).

3. See Tamara Cofman Wittes and Sarah Yerkes, "The Middle East Partnership Initiative: Progress, Problems, and Prospects," Saban Center Middle East Memo no. 5, November 29, 2004; and Mona Yacoubian, "Promoting Middle East Democracy: European Initiatives," United States Institute of Peace, Special Report no. 127, October 2004.

4. The region's labor force, slightly greater than one hundred million workers, is expected to double in the next decade due to the youth bulge in the Arab world, where 60 percent of the region's population is age twenty-four or younger. In Morocco, Algeria, and Egypt, population growth rates are either rising or at least not yet declining from their present high rates. With regional unemployment standing at an average of over 15 percent, Arab economies would need to grow at more than double their present rate (about 7 percent versus their current 3 percent) in order to absorb the youth population. See Graham E. Fuller, *The Youth Factor: The New Demographics of the Middle East and the Implications for U.S. Policy,* Analysis Paper no. 3, Saban Center for Middle East Policy at the Brookings Institution, June 2003; *Unlocking the Employment Potential in the Middle East and North Africa: Toward a New Social Contract* (Washington, D.C.: World Bank, 2004).

5. Toynbee, *East to West,* 155.

6. A century ago, America also targeted Morocco in its Open Door policy, aiming to encourage the evolution of orderly administration for the sake of

making the country a stable market for American goods. Much as in Latin America, the Open Door policy ultimately failed in its quest to engineer dramatic social change and take credit for it—yet stop it before it became unfavorable to the United States. See William Appleman Williams, *Tragedy of American Diplomacy*, 67. For an overview of Western relations with Morocco, see Haim Malka and Jon B. Alterman, *Arab Reform and Foreign Aid: Lessons from Morocco* (Washington, D.C.: Center for Strategic and International Studies, 2006).

7. Gary S. Gregg, *The Middle East: A Cultural Psychology* (New York: Oxford University Press, 2005); and Heather Deegan, "Culture and Development," in Shireen T. Hunter and Huma Malik, eds., *Modernization, Democracy, and Islam* (Westport, Conn.: Praeger, 2005).

8. See Daniel Brumberg, "Liberalization Versus Democracy," in *Uncharted Journey: Promoting Democracy in the Middle East*, ed. Thomas Carothers and Marina Ottoway (Washington, D.C.: Carnegie Endowment for International Peace, 2005), 16; Mehran Kamrava, "Development and Democracy: The Muslim World in a Comparative Perspective," in Hunter and Malik, eds., *Modernization, Democracy, and Islam*, 53; and Thomas W. Simons Jr., *Islam in a Globalizing World* (Palo Alto, Calif.: Stanford University Press, 2003), 62.

9. See François Burgat, *Face to Face with Political Islam* (London: I. B. Tauris, 2003), 170–72.

10. See the following surveys: Public Opinion Survey, TNS Sofres, March 2005; and German Marshall Fund, *Transatlantic Trends 2005*.

11. Marcus Noland and Howard Pack, "Globalization and Economic Performance in the Middle East," *In the National Interest*, June 30, 2004.

12. Geoff D. Porter, "Tourism Meets Terrorism in Morocco," *Daily Star* (Beirut), April 24, 2007.

13. Dirk Vandewalle, *A History of Modern Libya* (Cambridge, U.K.: Cambridge University Press, 2006), 1.

14. Libya's oil reserves are estimated at thirty-nine billion barrels, the largest in Africa.

15. Vandewalle, *History of Modern Libya*, 1.

16. See Joshua Eisenman and Joshua Kurlantzick, "China's Africa Strategy," *Current History*, May 2006, 219–24; James Traub, "China's African Adventure," *New York Times Magazine*, November 19, 2006; and Ernest J. Wilson, "China's Influence in Africa: Implications for U.S. Policy," testimony before the Subcommittee of Africa, Human Rights and International Operations, U.S. House of Representatives, July 28, 2005.

17. A quarter of China's natural gas imports comes from a bloc consisting of Algeria, Angola, Chad, Sudan, Nigeria, and Equatorial Guinea.

18. Karby Leggett, "China Flexes Economic Muscle Throughout Burgeoning Africa," *Wall Street Journal,* March 29, 2005.

19. See *More Than Humanitarianism: A Strategic U.S. Approach Toward Africa,* report of an independent task force of the Council on Foreign Relations, New York, 2006; and "No Questions Asked," *The Economist,* January 21, 2006, 53–54.

22. EGYPT: BETWEEN BUREAUCRATS AND THEOCRATS

1. Egypt was given privileged control over Nile waters through a 1929 treaty with Britain, signed before the East African states were granted independence. The Nile Basin Initiative of ten countries has been convened to secure more equitable distribution and management of the Nile's waters.

2. Scott Anderson, "Under Egypt's Volcano," *Vanity Fair,* October 2006.

3. Andrews and Mitrokhin, *World Was Going Our Way,* 148.

4. Andrew Batson and Shai Oster, "Egypt Sees China Replacing U.S. as Top Trade Partner by 2012," *Wall Street Journal,* September 12, 2006.

5. Gamal Hamdan, *The Personality of Egypt: A Study on the Genius of Place* (Cairo: Al-Hilal, 1993).

6. Paul Berman, "The Philosopher of Islamic Terror," *New York Times Magazine,* March 23, 2003.

7. See Graham Fuller, "Islamists and Democracy," in *Uncharted Journey,* ed. Carothers and Ottoway, 41–42; and "Islam and Democracy," United States Institute of Peace, Special Report no. 93, September 2002.

8. See Olivier Roy, *Globalized Islam: The Search for a New Ummah* (New York: Columbia University Press, 2004), 80–81. Islamist parties have evolved four main approaches to confronting modern challenges: fundamentalism (which rejects democracy and Westernization but uses technology to advance the cause of an authoritarian Islamic caliphate), traditionalism (which is suspicious of secularism and favors conservative social norms), modernism (which seeks a reconciliation between Islamic principles and international norms), and secularism (which prefers that religion be relegated to the private sphere, as in Western liberal democracies). It is difficult to argue that Islam is not pluralistic when such diversity clearly exists within Islamist politics today, as views on major political and social issues such as democracy, jihad, polygamy, and *hijab*-wearing differ sharply across this spectrum. Furthermore, because each camp has an established power base and support network, none can be ignored. In fact, the modernists whom Western leaders prefer to engage have little of the resources traditionalists derive from tax collection, subsidies and donations, business and foundations, mosques and schools, and radio and television stations. See Cheryl Bernard, *Civil, Democratic Islam:*

Partners, Resources, and Strategies (Santa Monica, Calif.: RAND Corporation, 2003). A slightly different typology can be found in International Crisis Group, *Understanding Political Islam*, Middle East–North Africa Report no. 37, March 2, 2005.

9. See Ghassan Salamé, *Democracy Without Democrats? The Renewal of Politics in the Muslim World* (London: I. B. Tauris, 1994); Burgat, *Face to Face with Political Islam*, 180; Amr Hamzawy, "The Key to Arab Reform: Moderate Islamists," Carnegie Endowment for International Peace, Policy Brief no. 40, August 2005; and Judy Barsalou, "Islamists at the Ballot Box: Findings from Egypt, Jordan, Kuwait, and Turkey," United States Institute of Peace, Special Report no. 144, July 2005.

10. Saad Eddin Ibrahim, "Islam Can Vote, If We Let It," *New York Times*, May 21, 2005.

11. Lawrence Groo and Parag Khanna, "The Regime Change We Need," *The National Interest*, Winter 2006.

12. Steven A. Cook, "The Promise of Pacts," *Journal of Democracy* 17, no. 1 (January 2006).

13. "The U.S. Project for Democracy in the Greater Middle East—Yes, but with Whom?" *Al-Hayat*, February 23, 2004.

14. Shibley Telhami, "In the Middle East, the Third Way Is a Myth," *Washington Post*, February 17, 2006.

15. As Ray Takeyh points out, "The central dilemma of the Arab political order is not unfamiliarity with the process of political competition, but an entrenched elite that is determined to retain power." Takeyh, "Close, but No Democracy," *The National Interest*, Winter 2004–05, 58.

16. See F. Gregory Gause III, "Can Democracy Stop Terrorism?" *Foreign Affairs*, September–October 2005; and John M. Owen, "Democracy, Realistically," *The National Interest*, Spring 2006, 40.

17. As T. E. Lawrence wrote, "Arab civilization has been an abstract nature, moral and intellectual rather than applied; and their lack of public spirit made their excellent private qualities futile." Lawrence cites the 1905 *Encyclopedia Britannica*, which declares that mentally, Arabs surpass most races but "are only held back in the march of progress by the remarkable defect of organizing power and incapacity for combined action." Lawrence, *Seven Pillars of Wisdom: A Triumph* (New York: Anchor Books, 1935), 44.

18. See Barakat, *The Arab World*, ch. 10.

19. See Fouad Ajami, "The End of Pan-Arabism," *Foreign Affairs*, Winter 1978–79; and Michael Barnett, *Dialogues in Arab Politics: Negotiations in Regional Order* (New York: Columbia University Press, 1998). To this day, all Arab militaries suffer from weak manpower, poor training, politicized leadership, and old technology and have little experience in fighting together in co-

ordinatcd fashion. See Daniel Byman, "The Future Security Environment and the Middle East," testimony before the Defense Review Threat Panel of the House Committee on Armed Services, September 28, 2005.

23. THE MASHREQ: ROAD MAPS

1. See David Fromkin, *A Peace to End All Peace: The Fall of the Ottoman Empire and the Creation of the Modern Middle East* (New York: Henry Holt, 1989).

2. See Fromkin, *Peace to End All Peace,* 24, 96.

3. See Robert D. Kaplan, *Eastward to Tartary: Travels in the Balkans, the Middle East, and the Caucasus* (New York: Random House, 2000).

4. Toynbee, *East to West,* 214.

5. According to the National Insurance Institute, Israel's poverty rate is 28 percent; one in three children is undernourished.

6. As American scholars John Mearsheimer and Stephen Walt pithily note, "Israel is a liability in the war on terror and the broader effort to deal with rogue states. . . . Saying that Israel and the U.S. are united by a shared terrorist threat has the causal relationship backwards: the U.S. has a terrorism problem in good part because it is so closely allied with Israel, not the other way around." Mearsheimer and Walt, "The Israel Lobby," *London Review of Books,* March 23, 2006.

7. Terrorist acts are the final link in a much longer chain of social humiliation, political disenfranchisement, economic grievance, and radical seduction. The most famous terrorists and ringleaders are often educated professionals using their skills and mobility to pursue what they believe is a noble cause, sacrificing others and sometimes themselves in the process. As Michael Mazaar elaborates, "The security threats the United States faces today have everything to do with the pressures of modernity and globalization, the diaphanous character of identity, the burden of choice, and the vulnerability of the alienated. That is not *all* that they have to do with, and the influence of psychological factors lies in a larger context of socioeconomic, cultural, demographic, and other realities. Yet those material issues become most relevant, and most dangerous, when they are breathing life into latent psychological distress." Mazaar, "The Psychological Sources of Islamic Terrorism," *Policy Review,* June 2004. See also Robert A. Pape, *Dying to Win: The Strategic Logic of Suicide Terrorism* (New York: Random House, 2005); and Marc Sageman, *Understanding Terror Networks* (Philadelphia: University of Pennsylvania Press, 2004).

8. According to geographer and demographer Jan Je Jong, under present territorial divisions the Palestinian population only has effective usage of 55

percent of the West Bank due to the irregularities of access created by disparate settlements. Furthermore, Israel siphons up to 85 percent of the water from West Bank aquifers and could potentially deplete them before Palestinians ever gain sovereign control of the territory.

9. Doug Suisman et al., *The Arc: A Formal Structure for a Palestinian State,* Santa Monica, Calif.: RAND Corporation, 2005. See also Abdel Monem Said Aly and Shai Feldman, *Ecopolitics: Changing the Regional Context of Arab-Israeli Peacemaking* (Cambridge, Mass.: Belfer Center for Science and International Affairs, John F. Kennedy School of Government, 2003); Khalil Shikaki, *Building a State, Building Peace: How to Make a Roadmap That Works for Palestinians and Israelis* (Washington, D.C.: Brookings Institution Press, 2003).

10. In spending over $100 million per year on education, Jordan spends more on education per student than almost any country in the world.

11. Muhamad Magraby, "Some Impediments to the Rule of Law in the Middle East and Beyond," *Fordham International Law Journal* 26, no. 3 (March 2003): 777.

12. Thomas L. Friedman, *From Beirut to Jerusalem* (New York: Farrar, Straus and Giroux, 1989), 214.

13. P. W. Singer, "Mike Tyson and the Hornet's Nest: Military Lessons of the Lebanon Crisis," Brookings Institution, August 1, 2006.

14. Muhamad Mugraby, "Lebanon, a Wholly Owned Subsidiary," *Middle East Quarterly,* March 1998.

15. Lawrence, *Seven Pillars of Wisdom,* 131.

24. THE FORMER IRAQ: BUFFER, BLACK HOLE, AND BROKEN BOUNDARY

1. Hugh Kennedy, *When Baghdad Ruled the Muslim World: The Rise and Fall of Islam's Greatest Dynasty* (New York: Da Capo Press, 2004).

2. Andrews and Mitrokhin, *World Was Going Our Way,* 193.

3. Quoting U.S. congressman David Bonior. "U.S. Congressmen Criticize Iraqi Sanctions," BBC News Online, February 17, 2000.

4. Quoted in Fromkin, *Peace to End All Peace,* 453.

5. During the early phases of its occupation many American officials watched *Battle of Algiers* prior to service in Iraq, yet they seemed to re-create the heavy-handed tactics and menacing behavior that led to France's shameful ouster from Algeria. The British colonial administrator Gertrude Bell had warned in 1920 of the difficulty of simultaneously occupying a country and establishing a local government with any legitimacy. Much like the British, America attempted to sustain such "bloody and inefficient" politics (in the words of T. E. Lawrence), which inevitably degenerated into what Churchill once called

"miserable, wasteful, sporadic warfare." With very few Arabic speakers inside the "Green Zone," where America's largest embassy in the world is located, American diplomats mostly served as a logistics center for the U.S. military, whose footprint was anything but light. Whatever the acronym for postconflict stabilization (PCRU in the United Kingdom and SCRS in the United States), coordination across the continuum of stabilization and reconstruction was abysmal both within and across governments. Once the U.S. Army finally came up with its ideal manual to handle counterinsurgencies—dubbed "armed social work"—it relied heavily on British lessons it should have learned much earlier: the importance of safeguarding civilians, restoring local utilities, building domestic security services, and restructuring the national army as soon as possible. See Noah Feldman, *What We Owe Iraq: War and the Ethics of Nation Building* (New York: Princeton University Press, 2005).

6. See Amatzia Baram, "Who Are the Insurgents?" United States Institute of Peace, Special Report no. 134, April 2005; Peter Bergen and Alec Reynolds, "Blowback Revisited," *Foreign Affairs,* November–December 2005; Rik Coolsaet and Teun van de Voorde, "The Evolution of Terrorism in 2005: A Statistical Assessment," University of Ghent, February 2006; Andrew F. Krepinevich Jr., "How to Win in Iraq," *Foreign Affairs,* September–October 2005; Vali Nasr, *The Shia Revival: How Conflicts Within Islam Will Shape the Future* (New York: W. W. Norton, 2006); and Kenneth Pollack, "A Switch in Time: A New Strategy for America in Iraq," Saban Center Analysis Paper no. 7, Brookings Institution, February 15, 2006.

7. See Nir Rosen, "The Exodus," *New York Times Magazine,* May 13, 2007. Iraq now has the largest refugee population living in neighboring countries since the Palestinian refugee crisis resulting from the creation of Israel in 1948.

8. See Geoffrey Kemp, "Iran and Iraq: The Shia Connection, Soft Power, and the Nuclear Dilemma," United States Institute of Peace, Special Report no. 156, November 2005.

9. As former State Department official Richard Haas writes, "It is one of history's ironies that the first war in Iraq, a war of necessity, marked the beginning of the American era in the Middle East and the second Iraq war, a war of choice, has precipitated its end." Haas, "The New Middle East," *Foreign Affairs,* November–December 2006.

10. See Brendan O'Leary, John McGarry, and Khaled Salih, eds., *The Future of Kurdistan in Iraq* (Philadelphia: University of Pennsylvania Press, 2005).

11. Or rather, their old currency. The Kurds used their own currency for eleven years until the "Bremer dinar" and then the Iraqi dinar were reintroduced. For a discussion of the regional implications of Kurdish dynamics

within Iraq, see Henri J. Barkey and Ellen Laipson, "Iraqi Kurds and Iraq's Future," *Middle East Policy* 12, no. 4 (Winter 2005).

25. IRAN: VIRTUES AND VICES

1. It was Cyrus the Great who liberated Persians from Babylonian rule, even resettling the Israelites to Palestine in the sixth century B.C., seeking to create a buffer between itself and Egypt.

2. Andrews and Mitrokhin, *World Was Going Our Way,* 169.

3. Iran's oil revenues skyrocketed from less than $1 billion in 1971 to $18 billion in 1975.

4. Unlike all other Muslim societies, they experienced modernization, parliamentary politics, and socialist intellectual traditions as early as the nineteenth century during the Qajar dynasty. See Shireen T. Hunter, "Islam, Modernization, and Democratization: The Case of Iran," in Hunter and Malik, eds., *Modernization, Democracy, and Islam,* ch. 16.

5. Nikki R. Keddie, *Iran and the Muslim World: Resistance and Revolution* (New York: New York University Press, 1995), 13–15; and Molavi, *Soul of Iran,* 13.

6. See Molavi, *Soul of Iran.* As Azar Nafisi wrote, "The truth of Iran's past became immaterial to those who appropriated it." Nafisi, *Reading Lolita in Tehran: A Memoir in Books* (New York: Random House, 2003), 37.

7. Timothy Garton Ash, "Soldiers of the Hidden Imam," *New York Review of Books,* November 3, 2005.

8. Estimates of Iran's natural gas reserves are twenty-six trillion cubic meters (behind only Russia), and 130 billion barrels of oil (behind Saudi Arabia and Canada). In the Iranian system, state interests actually supersede sharia in many instances, and the state controls the clergy's finances. The Ayatollah Khamenei, however, heir to the mantle of Khomenei's revolutionary spirit and supreme religious guardian of the country, is also a driving force behind the country's radical foreign policy and faces none of the accountability of other leaders. See Michael Ignatieff, "Iranian Lessons," *New York Times Magazine,* July 17, 2005; and Henry A. Kissinger, "Now Tehran's Choice Is Cast in Starker Terms," *International Herald Tribune,* August 1, 2006.

9. See Philip Gordon, "America, Europe, and the Challenge of Bringing Democracy to Iran," paper presented at the Aspen Berlin Conference on "Iran and Democracy in the Greater Middle East," Amman, Jordan, May 23 and 24, 2005; Robin Niblett and Derek Mix, *Transatlantic Approaches to Sanctions: Principles and Recommendations for Action,* Center for Strategic and International Studies, October 10, 2006.

10. See Justin Bernier, "China's Strategic Proxies," *Orbis,* Fall 2003,

629–43; Afshin Molavi, "Buying Time in Tehran," *Foreign Affairs*, September–October 2004; and Kenneth M. Pollack, *The Persian Puzzle: The Conflict Between Iran and America* (New York: Random House, 2004).

11. See Neil MacFarquhar, "Exiles in 'Tehrangeles' Are Split on How U.S. Should Sway Iran," *New York Times*, May 9, 2006; Michael McFaul, Larry Diamond, and Abbas Milani, "Beyond Incrementalism: A New Strategy for Dealing with Iran," Hoover Institution, 2005; Afshin Molavi, "Our Allies in Iran," *New York Times*, November 3, 2005; Molavi, *Soul of Iran*, 175; and Mahmood Sariolghalam, "Cutting a Deal with Tehran," *Newsweek*, April 24, 2006.

12. See Karim Sadjadpour, "How Relevant Is the Iranian Street?" *Washington Quarterly*, Winter 2007.

13. Jared Cohen and Abbas Milani, "The Passive Revolution," *Hoover Digest*, Winter 2005; Mohsen Sazegara, "Iran's Road to Democracy," November 4, 2005, available at www.OpenDemocracy.net.

14. See Molavi, *Soul of Iran*.

15. Toynbee, *East to West*, 221.

16. Christopher de Bellaigue, *In the Rose Garden of Martyrs: A Memoir of Iran* (New York: HarperCollins, 2005).

26. GULF STREAMS

1. World energy demand is projected to rise by 35 percent to 120 million barrels per day by 2030.

2. Olivier de Lage, "Saudi Arabia and the Smaller Gulf States: The Vassals Take Their Revenge," CERI Colloquium on Gulf Monarchies in Transition, Paris, January 10–11, 2005.

3. "Economic Relations with Regions Neighboring the Euro Area and in the 'Euro Time Zone,'" European Central Bank, December 2002.

4. China–Saudi Arabia bilateral trade surpassed $14 billion in 2005, and overall trade with the Arab world is over $50 billion. See Chu Shulong, "The Middle East in China's National Strategy," speech given at the Center for Strategic and International Studies conference on "The Vital Triangle: China, the United States, and the Middle East," Washington, D.C., September 14, 2006; and Jin Liangxiang, "Energy First: China and the Middle East," *Middle East Quarterly*, Spring 2005.

5. Samuel Huntington wrote that this alliance "could materialize, not because Muhammed and Confucius are anti-West but because these cultures offer a vehicle for the expression of grievances for which the West is partly blamed—a West whose political, military, economic and cultural dominance increasingly rankles in a world where states 'feel they don't have to take it anymore.'" Huntington, *Clash of Civilizations*, 239.

6. Kuwait, too, is investing $8 billion in building a major refinery in Guangzhou province.

7. Hassan Fattah, "Avoiding Political Talk, Saudis and Chinese Build Trade," *New York Times,* April 23, 2006.

8. Wilfred Thesiger, *Arabian Sands* (1959; repr. London: Penguin, 1991), preface to the second edition, 7.

9. *The Military Balance,* International Institute for Strategic Studies, 2005.

10. Bank of International Settlements, 2006.

11. See the United Nations, *Arab Human Development Report.*

12. Yaroslav Trofimov, *Faith at War: A Journey on the Frontlines of Islam, from Baghdad to Timbuktu* (New York: Henry Holt, 2005), 4.

13. See Paul Dresch and James Piscatori, eds., *Monarchies and Nations: Globalization and Identity in the Arab States of the Gulf* (London: I. B. Tauris, 2005).

14. See Afshin Molavi, "The Real 'New Middle East,'" *Washington Post,* August 20, 2006; and Nawaf Obaid and Khalid al-Rhodan, "Saudi Arabia's Sustainable Capacity and Security Issues," Center for Strategic and International Studies, September 27, 2005.

15. There is constant debate over the longevity of Saudi Arabia's oil reserves based on whether or not it has reached its peak production point, the number of years of oil remaining in its fields based on global demand, and the volume of oil contained in new discoveries. See Matthew R. Simmons, *Twilight in the Desert: The Coming Saudi Oil Shock and the World Economy* (Hoboken, N.J.: John Wiley and Sons, 2005); and Peter Maass, "The Breaking Point," *New York Times Magazine,* August 21, 2005.

16. Peter Bergen and Alec Reynolds, "Blowback Revisited," *Foreign Affairs,* November–December 2005, 2–6. As the U.S. Defense Science Board notes, "Muslims do not hate our freedoms, but rather they hate our policies."

17. See John Bradley, *Saudi Arabia Exposed: Inside a Kingdom in Crisis* (New York: Palgrave Macmillan, 2005); and International Crisis Group, *The Shiite Question in Saudi Arabia,* Middle East Report no. 145, September 19, 2005.

18. See Michael Scott Doran, "The Saudi Paradox," *Foreign Affairs,* January–February 2004; and Simons, *Islam in a Globalizing World.*

19. See "*Ijtihad:* Reinterpreting Islamic Principles for the Twenty-first Century," United States Institute of Peace, Special Report no. 125, August 2004; Vartan Gregorian, *Islam: A Mosaic, Not a Monolith* (Washington, D.C.: Brookings Institution Press, 2003); Tariq Ramadan, *Western Muslims and the Future of Islam* (New York: Oxford University Press, 2004); and Olivier Roy, *Globalized Islam: The Search for a New Ummah* (New York: Columbia University Press, 2004), 18–19.

20. Quoted in "Verbatim," *Time Magazine*, May 5, 2003.

21. Toynbee, *Civilization on Trial*, 205.

22. "A Long Walk," survey of Saudi Arabia, *The Economist*, January 7, 2006.

23. "A Thwarted Civilization," *Wall Street Journal*, October 16, 2001.

24. Kito de Boer and John M. Turner, "Beyond Oil: Reappraising the Gulf States," *The McKinsey Quarterly*, special issue, 2007.

25. Lawrence, *Seven Pillars of Wisdom*, 336.

26. Thesiger, *Arabian Sands*.

27. "Building Towers, Cheating Workers," Human Rights Watch, 2006.

CONCLUSION: ARABIAN SAND DUNES

1. Gabriel Weimann, *Terror on the Internet: The New Arena, the New Challenges* (Washington, D.C.: United States Institute of Peace Press, 2006).

2. As Milton Viorst writes, "For the West to imagine it can impose its values on the East is a huge miscalculation. For the East to imagine the zealotry of its warriors can intimidate the West is naïve. Another lesson is that neither has the power to choose the other's course. . . . Notwithstanding its military superiority, unless the West accepts the East's right to determine its own future, the bloodshed that currently marks the contest will continue. Both civilization will clearly be the poorer for it." Viorst, *Storm from the East*.

3. Lawrence, *Seven Pillars of Wisdom*, 30.

27. FROM OUTSIDE IN TO INSIDE OUT

1. David Shambaugh wastes no words: "Asia is changing, and China is a principal cause." Shambaugh, "China Engages Asia," *International Security* 29, no. 3 (Winter 2004–05): 64–99. See also David Shambaugh, "The Rise of China and Asia's New Dynamics," in *Power Shift: China and Asia's New Dynamics*, ed. David Shambaugh (Berkeley: University of California Press, 2005), 1. While East Asia is traditionally defined as the zone between Japan and Burma, much as with Europe, T. J. Pempel argues that "no map is so uncontested that there are no alternatives; can be expanded to include–exclude any number of countries–zones." See "Introduction," in T. J. Pempel, ed., *Remapping East Asia: The Construction of a Region* (Ithaca, N.Y.: Cornell University Press, 2005), 25; see also Buzan and Wæver, *Regions and Powers*, 98.

2. Milton Osborne, *The Paramount Power: China and Countries of Southeast Asia*, Lowy Institute Paper no. 11, 2006. As Samuel Huntington wrote, "China's history, culture, traditions, size, economic dynamism, and self-image

all impel it to assume a hegemonic position in East Asia. This goal is the natural result of its rapid economic development." Huntington, *Clash of Civilizations,* 229.

3. See David C. Kang, "Hierarchy, Balancing, and Empirical Puzzles in Asian International Relations," *International Security* 28, no. 3 (Winter 2003–04): 165–80; "Hierarchy in Asian International Relations: 1300–1900," *Asian Security* 1, no. 1 (January 2005).

4. The Sinic order began during the third millennium B.C. under the Xia Dynasty, when an imperial process of integration and subjugation expanded the empire in concentric rings. The tribute model became the meta-narrative for interpreting Chinese foreign relations during the Ming Dynasty from the fourteenth through the seventeenth centuries. The empire's Inner Asian zone contained Tibetans and Central Asians, the Outer zone included Southeast Asians, and the direct Sinic core included nontributaries such as Korea, Vietnam, and part of Japan. See Fairbank, ed., *Chinese World Order.*

5. See Thomas Sowell, *Migrations and Cultures: A World View* (New York: Basic Books, 1996), ch. 5.

6. Softening the border region creates an insurance policy against domestic overcrowding. The nineteenth century Taiping Rebellion resulted from such involution, in which the people-to-land ratio became too high. The Qing Dynasty was later besieged as China's size had not grown to accommodate such a rapidly growing population. Should another set of economic troubles hit the Chinese countryside and periphery, more open borders would allow a migration valve for people to flee to countries like Burma and Laos to begin their lives again and work their way up—reproducing a now ancient pattern of Chinese demographic expansion, spread, and control. See Robert F. Ash, "China's Regional Economies and the Asian Region," in *Power Shift,* ed. Shambaugh, 96–131.

7. In geopolitical terms, the emerging Sinocentric order represents a mix of concepts including hegemony, condominiums, spheres of influence, suzerain systems, and complex interdependence. See David C. Kang, "Getting Asia Wrong," *International Security* 27, no. 4 (Spring 2003): 57–85; David A. Lake, "Beyond Anarchy: The Importance of Security Institutions," *International Security* 26, no. 1 (Summer 2001): 129–60; and Shambaugh, "Rise of China," 12–17.

8. In the early Cold War, the Truman administration defined its defense perimeter as stretching from the Aleutian Islands through Japan to the Philippines; Korea, then under UN protection, was not considered of strategic value. The extension of America's security guarantee to Taiwan began in the Eisenhower administration and only after China's shelling of Quemoy and

Matsu. See Robert S. Ross, "The U.S.-China Peace: Great Power Politics, Spheres of Influence, and the Peace of East Asia," in *Between Compliance and Conflict,* ed. Dominguez and Kim.

9. *America's Strategy in World Politics: The United States and the Balance of Power* (New York: Harcourt, Brace, 1942).

10. See Robert Sutter, *China's Rise in Asia: Promises and Perils* (Boulder, Colo.: Rowman and Littlefield, 2005), introduction; and Avery Goldstein, "The Diplomatic Face of China's Grand Strategy: A Rising Power's Emerging Choice," *China Quarterly* (168), 2001: 837.

11. For a discussion of the contrast between balancing and protecting, see Buzan, *United States and the Great Powers,* 178–79.

12. See Muthiah Alagappa, ed., *Asian Security Practice: Material and Ideational Influences* (Stanford, Calif.: Stanford University Press, 1998), ix; and "Introduction," in Pempel, ed., *Remapping East Asia,* 5. Alastair Iain Johnston defines strategic culture as an "ideational milieu which limits behavioral choices." Alastair Iain Johnston, "Thinking About Strategic Culture," *International Security* 19, no. 4 (Spring 1995): 45.

13. See Amitav Acharya, "Regional Security Arrangements in a Multipolar World: The EU's Contribution," in *Strategic Views on the European Union,* Chaillot Paper No. 72, November 2004, 94; Stanley Crossick, Fraser Cameron, and Axel Berkofsky, "EU-China Relations: Towards a Strategic Partnership," European Policy Centre Working Paper, July 2005; David Shambaugh, "China and Europe: The Emerging Axis," *Current History,* September 2004, 243–48; and Xu Jian, "Facing the Challenge of Unconventional Security: The Chinese Perspective," in *Overcoming Vulnerability: Managing New Security Challenges in Asia and Europe,* ed. Betrand Fort (Singapore: Marshall Cavendish Academic, 2005), 30–31.

14. The analogy to the "Concert of Europe" refers to the mid–nineteenth century arrangement involving Britain, Austria, Russia, Prussia, and France. See Amitav Acharya, "East Asia's Arrested Multilateralism," unpublished paper, June 2006; Aaron L. Friedberg, "Ripe for Rivalry: Prospects for Peace in Multipolar Asia," *International Security* 18, no. 3 (Winter 1993–94): 5–33; and Nicholas Khoo and Michael L. R. Smith, "A 'Concert of Asia'?" *Policy Review,* August 2001.

15. See Eric Ringmar, *The Mechanics of Modernity in Europe and East Asia: The Institutional Origins of Social Change and Stagnation* (London: Routledge, 2004), 2.

16. As the economic historian Angus Maddison has demonstrated, Asia comprised 60 percent of the world economy in 1500, and China represented a third of the world economy in the early nineteenth century, on the eve of Europe's industrial revolution. Asia's economic rise alongside the United

States and the EU is not the appearance of something new but rather a return after a prolonged hiatus. See Maddison, *The World Economy: A Millennial Perspective* (Paris: OECD Development Centre, 2001).

17. See Coral Bell, "The Twilight of the Unipolar World," *The American Interest,* Winter 2005, 20. See also David Gress, *From Plato to NATO: The Idea of the West and Its Opponents* (New York: Free Press, 1998). Toynbee too saw this psychological blind spot, writing, "The fact that our adversary [Communism] threatens us by showing up our defects, rather than by forcibly suppressing our virtues, is proof that the challenge he presents comes ultimately not from him, but from ourselves. . . . The speeding-up of the transfer of material power from the older powers . . . to the younger powers of the outer ring . . . in Asia . . . is awkward for the Americans. . . . As a unified world gradually works its way toward an equilibrium between its diverse component cultures, the Western component will gradually be relegated to the modest place which is all that it can expect to retain in virtue of its intrinsic worth by comparison with those of other cultures—surviving and extinct—which the Western society, through its modern expansion, has brought into association with itself and with one another." Toynbee, *Civilization on Trial,* 23, 129, 158.

18. Bracken, *Fire in the East,* 88.

19. Samuel Huntington, *Clash of Civilizations.* 69. Huntington further argues on p. 310 that "Western belief in the universality of Western culture suffers three problems: it is false; it is immoral; and it is wrong."

20. Some argue that Asian growth stems from resource mobilization (in other words, inputs: throwing people and resources at a problem), not greater efficiency of outputs, thus necessitating a slowing of growth as returns diminish. See Paul Krugman, "The Myth of Asia's Miracle," *Foreign Affairs,* November–December 1994.

21. For a discussion on East Asia's responses to the globalization challenge, see Samuel Kim, ed., *East Asia and Globalization* (Lanham, Md.: Rowman and Littlefield, 2000).

22. While Japan is currently the world's second-largest economy and China the fourth-largest (although the EU collectively is larger than all others), by 2020 China is projected to account for 20 percent of the world's economy and population, ranking right behind the EU and the United States. In PPP terms, China's economy has been larger than Japan's since 1992, and it already approaches two-thirds the value of the U.S. economy. See Ted C. Fishman, *China, Inc.* (New York: Scribner, 2005), 10.

23. Kenichi Ohmae, *The End of the Nation State: The Rise of Regional Economies* (New York: Simon and Schuster, 1996).

24. Ian Buruma and Avishai Margalit, *Occidentalism: The West in the Eyes of Its Enemies* (New York: Penguin, 2004), 95.

25. Bell, *East Meets West*, 111.

26. See Fareed Zakaria, *The Future of Freedom: Illiberal Democracy at Home and Abroad* (New York: W. W. Norton, 2003). Zakaria focuses on the phenomenon of illiberal democracy, in which the style of democracy (elections, parties, and so on) exists without the substance of liberalism (entrenched constitutional protections, separation of powers).

27. See Daniel A. Bell, *Beyond Liberal Democracy: Political Thinking for an East Asian Context* (Princeton, N.J.: Princeton University Press, 2006), 10–18.

28. Bell, *East Meets West*, 96, 155.

29. Chalongphob Sussangkarn, "East Asian Financial Cooperation and Integration," Thailand Development Research Institute, 2005.

28. CHINA'S FIRST-WORLD SEDUCTION

1. See Phillip C. Saunders, "China's Global Activism: Strategy, Drivers, and Tools," Occasional Paper no. 4, National Defense University, October 2006.

2. Japan's Meiji-era ascendance and post–World War II miracle involved strong ties to first the United Kingdom and then the United States; as with the United Kingdom, its security rests in being a naval power to protect its insular status from the unrelated continental mainland. During Japan's early twentieth-century modernization, "Leave Asia to join Europe" was a popular slogan. Many in Asia perceive Japan as acting more like a G-8 and OECD power than an Asian one. Some argue that the mere fact of China's growing might necessitates a stronger U.S.-Japan alliance. See Michael Green and Nicholas Szechenyi, "Common Values: A New Agenda for U.S.-Japan Relations," *Georgetown Journal of International Affairs*, Summer–Fall 2006, 47–55.

3. Howard W. French and Norimitsu Onichi, "Economic Ties Binding Japan to Rival China," *New York Times*, October 31, 2005.

4. See Mike M. Mochizuki, "China-Japan Relations," in *Power Shift*, ed. Shambaugh, 135–50; and Mixin Pei and Michael Swaine, "Simmering Fire in Asia: Averting Sino-Japanese Strategic Conflict," Carnegie Endowment Policy Brief no. 44, November 2005.

5. See Mikkal E. Herberg, "The Emergence of China Throughout Asia: Security and Economic Consequences for the U.S.," testimony before the U.S. Senate Committee on Foreign Relations, June 7, 2005; and Niklas Swanstrom, "An Asian Oil and Gas Union: Problems and Prospects," *China-Eurasia Forum Quarterly* 3, no. 3 (November 2005).

6. Byung-Kook Kim, "To Have a Cake and Eat It Too: The Crisis of Pax

Americana in Korea," in *Between Compliance and Conflict,* ed. Dominguez and Kim.

7. Sheila A. Smith, "Shifting Terrain: The Domestic Politics of the U.S. Military Presence in Asia," East-West Center Special Report no. 8, March 2006.

8. See Robert Paalberg, "A New Pax Americana? The U.S. Exercise of Hard Power in East Asia and Latin America," in *Between Compliance and Conflict,* ed. Dominguez and Kim.

9. See Jae Ho Chung, "China's Ascendancy and the Korean Peninsula," in *Power Shift,* ed. Shambaugh, 151–69.

10. See Robert D. Kaplan, "When North Korea Falls," *Atlantic Monthly,* October 2006, 64–73; and Jim Yardley, "Sanctions Don't Dent China–North Korea Trade," *New York Times,* October 27, 2006.

11. A 2005 poll by Australia's Lowy Institute showed that 69 percent of Australians had positive feelings about China, compared to only 58 percent for the United States.

12. See Paul Kelly, "Australian for Alliance," *The National Interest,* Spring 2003, 90.

13. The sale of uranium to China evokes little controversy because China already has enough fissile material for its nuclear program and is a signatory to the Nuclear Non-Proliferation Treaty.

14. See Robert D. Kaplan, "How We Would Fight China," *Atlantic Monthly,* June 2005.

15. Lee Kuan Yew, *The Singapore Story: Memoirs of Lee Kuan Yew* (New York: Prentice Hall, 1999), 23.

16. Ibid., 87.

17. Bell, *East Meets West,* 185. As Larry Diamond argues, "Democracy becomes truly stable only when people come to value it widely not solely for its economic and social performance but for its political attributes."

18. These criteria are adapted from Bell, *East Meets West,* 186.

19. Toynbee, *East to West,* 58–59.

20. Sugata Bose, *A Hundred Horizons: The Indian Ocean in the Age of Global Empire* (Cambridge, Mass.: Harvard University Press, 2006), 1.

21. Quotation from C. Raja Mohan, "India and the Balance of Power," *Foreign Affairs,* July–August 2006. America's Pacific Command (PACOM) already includes India in its orbit. See Amitav Acharya, "Will Asia's Past Be Its Future?" *International Security* 28, no. 3 (Winter 2003–04): 149–64.

22. The National Intelligence Council's *Trends 2020* report identifies China and India as "arriviste" powers that could either realign or reject the current international order permanently—or both.

23. Mark Minevich, Frank-Jürgen Richter, and Faisal Hoque, *Six Billion Minds: Managing Outsourcing in the Global Knowledge Economy* (Boston: Aspatore Books, 2006).

24. India's fabled IT sector employs a maximum of 2 million people, with perhaps up to 8 million enjoying indirect benefits. India's impressive economic growth is virtually jobless, as only 30 million of India's workforce of 420 million even register in the organized sector. As Amartya Sen has written, "Even a hundred Bangalores and Hyderabads will not, on their own, solve India's tenacious poverty and deep-seated inequality." Sen, *The Argumentative Indian: Writings on Indian History, Culture, and Identity* (New York: Farrar, Straus and Giroux, 2005), 197.

29. MALAYSIA AND INDONESIA: THE GREATER CHINESE CO-PROSPERITY SPHERE

1. Military rule came in different styles across the region: Burma and Thailand represented direct rule by a military class; North Korea's military formed the backbone of the Communist Party; in Indonesia and the Philippines, strongman rule gave the military a statutory role with the army acting as a praetorian guard for the leadership.

2. See Young Jong Choi, "The Rise of Regionalist Ideas in East Asia," in *Between Compliance and Conflict,* ed. Dominguez and Kim; Allan Collins, *Security in Southeast Asia: Domestic Regional and Global Issues* (Boulder, Colo.: Lynne Rienner, 2003), ch. 1; Donald K. Emmerson, "Goldilock's Problem: Rethinking Security and Sovereignty in Asia," in *The Many Faces of Asian Security,* ed. Sheldon W. Simon (Lanham, Md.: Rowman and Littlefield, 2001), 89–111; "Integration and Illusion: ASEAN in the New Century," *Georgetown Southeast Asia Survey 2002–3,* 34; *Perspectives from Asia on Military Intervention,* report of the conference on Regional Responses to Internal War, Fund for Peace, Washington, September 2002. For a skeptical perspective on ASEAN's future, see Nicholas Khoo, "Rhetoric versus Reality: ASEAN's Clouded Future," *Georgetown Journal of International Affairs,* Summer–Fall 2004, 49–56.

3. The United States has appointed a special ambassador to ASEAN and has begun to make larger contributions to its secretariat in Jakarta. The United States has also become more involved in the ASEAN Regional Forum (ARF), the broadest security platform for the region including countries from Europe and North America. Under the rubric of "cooperative security," the ARF's annual calendar features dozens of events about training peacekeepers and fostering cooperation among officials at all levels. ASEAN's move toward mutual interference could be a vehicle toward softening China's position on sovereignty. Given China's lack of military transparency, the ARF could be a

mechanism for Asians to compile more accurate data on military spending as a regional confidence-building measure. See "U.S. Security Relations with Southeast Asia: A Dual Challenge," Stanley Foundation Policy Bulletin, March 2004.

4. Samuel Huntington argued that if China was becoming dominant, the region would witness growing support for its territorial integrity, growing Chinese control over the South China Sea, acceptance of its military dominance and regional leadership, support for China on human rights and trade matters, lower barriers to Chinese migration, suppression of anti-Chinese activities, abstention from anti-China alliances, and promotion of the Mandarin language. All of these are more or less happening. See Huntington, *Clash of Civilizations*, 230–31. On China-ASEAN relations, see Dana Dillon and John J. Tkacik Jr., "China's Quest for Asia," *Policy Review*, December 2005; Michael A. Glosny, "Heading Toward a Win-Win Future? Recent Developments in China's Policy Toward Southeast Asia," *Asian Security* 2, no. 1 (2006): 24–57; Jane Perlez, "Asian Leaders Find China a More Cordial Neighbor," *New York Times*, October 18, 2003; Oded Shenkar, *The Chinese Century: The Rising Chinese Economy and Its Impact on the Global Economy, the Balance of Power, and Your Job* (Philadelphia: Wharton School Publishing, 2005); and Sutter, *China's Rise in Asia*, ch. 7.

5. Malaysia and Indonesia together lead a group called the "D-8," which also includes Bangladesh, Egypt, Iran, Nigeria, Pakistan, and Turkey, a mix of energy producers and consumers who have agreed to accelerate their internal trade relations. See Chairman's Report, International Conference of Islamic Scholars II, Jakarta, Indonesia, June 20–22, 2006; and Wayne Arnold, "Malaysia Works to Sell Islam on Trade Benefits," *International Herald Tribune*, June 23, 2005.

6. Bell, *East Meets West*, 144.

7. Naipaul, *Among the Believers: An Islamic Journey* (London: Penguin, 1982), 312, 442.

8. "Too High a Price: The Human Rights Cost of the Indonesian Military's Economic Activities," Human Rights Watch, June 2006.

9. Toynbee, *East to West*, 56.

10. Adam Schwarz, *A Nation in Waiting: Indonesia's Search for Stability* (Boulder, Colo.: Westview Press, 2000).

11. See Anthony Bubalo and Greg Fealy, "Between the Global and the Local: Islamism, the Middle East, and Indonesia," Saban Center Project on U.S. Policy Towards the Islamic World, Analysis Paper no. 9, October 2005; Greg Sheridan, "Jihad Archipelago," *The National Interest*, Winter 2004–05, 73–80; and *Terrorism in Southeast Asia: The Threat and Response*, Report of an International Conference Organised by the Institute of Defence and Strategic

Studies and Office of the Coordinator for Counterterrorism of the U.S. Department of State, Singapore, April 12–13, 2006.

12. Adam Schwarz, "Indonesia After Suharto," *Foreign Affairs*, July–August 1997.

13. The Chinese in Indonesia thus constitute what Amy Chua calls a "market-dominant minority." Chua, *World on Fire: How Exporting Free Market Democracy Breeds Ethnic Hatred and Global Instability* (New York: Doubleday, 2003), 43.

14. More than fifty thousand vessels pass through the Straits of Malacca each year, as well as eleven million barrels of oil per day.

15. Because China has become the fastest-growing consumer of timber, even EU certification standards for logging may have little impact on the rapid deforestation.

30. MYANMAR, THAILAND, AND VIETNAM: THE INNER TRIANGLE

1. In 2007, the World Bank, the Asian Development Bank, and Western donors offered Cambodia a combined $600 million, constituting most of the national budget. China then immediately offered an equal amount of untied aid.

2. Toynbee, *East to West*, 92.

3. Sterling Seagrave, *Lords of the Rim: The Invisible Empire of Overseas Chinese* (New York: Putnam, 1995), 304.

4. As Amy Chua writes, "In Burma, globalization has a Chinese face." Chua, *World on Fire*, 36.

5. Jane Perlez, "In Life on the Mekong, China's Dams Dominate," *New York Times*, March 19, 2005.

6. Toynbee, *East to West*, 86.

7. Panitan Wattanayagorn, "Thailand: The Elite's Shifting Conceptions of Security," in *Asian Security Practice*, ed. Alagappa.

8. Chulacheeb Chinwanno, "Thailand-China Relations: From Strategic to Economic Partnership," IUJ Research Institute Working Paper, Asia-Pacific Series no. 6.

9. Present estimates suggest the Kra Isthmus canal project will require ten years, thirty thousand workers, and cost approximately $25 billion.

10. See Thomas Menkhoff and Gerke Solvay, eds., *Chinese Entrepreneurship and Asian Business Networks* (London: Routledge Curzon, 2002).

11. Sterling Seagrave refers to this operative style as the "deliberately opaque empire of conglomerates." Seagrave, *Lords of the Rim*, 2.

12. See William A. Callahan, "Beyond Cosmopolitanism and Nationalism: Diasporic Chinese and Neo-Nationalism in China and Thailand," *International*

Organization 57 (Summer 2003): 481–517; and Busakorn Chantasasawat, "Bourgeoning Sino-Thai Cooperation: Heightening Cooperation, Sustaining Economic Security," *China: An International Journal* 4, no. 1 (March 2006): 86–112.

13. Quoted in "The Bold Coast," *Newsweek,* January 12, 2004.

14. Keith Bradsher, "Vietnam's Roaring Economy Is Set for World Stage," *New York Times,* October 25, 2006.

15. For a discussion of regional views of China's military and naval buildup, see Richard Sokolsky, Angel Rabasa, and C. R. Neu, *The Role of Southeast Asia in U.S. Strategy Toward China* (Santa Monica, Calif.: RAND Corporation, 2000); and Michael D. Swaine, "China's Regional Military Posture," in *Power Shift,* ed. Shambaugh, 266–85.

16. John Henderson and Benjamin Reilly, "Dragon in Paradise: China's Rising Star in Oceania," *The National Interest,* Summer 2003, 94–104.

31. SIZE MATTERS: THE FOUR CHINAS

1. Ross Terrill argues that China is in many ways still a "third world economy married to a superpower ego." Terrill, *New Chinese Empire,* 265.

2. See Kennan, *American Diplomacy,* 21. For a more skeptical account of America's intentions with the Open Door policy, see Williams, *Tragedy of American Diplomacy,* 144.

3. Wu Xinbo, "China: Security Practice of a Modernizing and Ascending Power," in *Asian Security Practice,* ed. Alagappa.

4. Lucian Pye, China (New York: Harper Collins, 1990), 58.

5. Bates Gill and Yanzhong Huang, "Sources and Limits of Chinese 'Soft Power,'" *Survival* 48, no. 2 (Summer 2006): 17–36.

6. Frank Viviano, "China's Great Armada," *National Geographic,* July 2005.

7. Geoff Wade, "The Zheng He Voyages: A Reassessment," *Journal of the Malaysian Branch of the Royal Asiatic Society* 78, no. 1 (June 2005): 37–58. See also Alastair Ian Johnston, *Cultural Realism: Strategic Culture and Grand Strategy in Chinese History* (Princeton, N.J.: Princeton University Press, 1995).

8. Joshua Cooper Ramo, "The Beijing Consensus," Foreign Policy Centre, May 2004. Mark Leonard argues that there is not yet a consensus on the "Beijing Consensus" since the country's economy and society are evolving so quickly. Leonard, "The Road Obscured," *Financial Times Magazine,* July 9–10, 2005.

9. Peter van Ness, "China's Response to the Bush Doctrine," *World Policy Journal,* Winter 2004–05, 40.

10. For a discussion of how China views global governance theory and practice, see Cai Tuo, "Global Governance: The Chinese Angle of View and Practice," *Social Sciences in China,* Summer 2004, 57–68.

11. See Peter Gries, *China's New Nationalism: Pride, Politics, and Diplomacy* (Berkeley: University of California Press, 2004); and Suisheng Zhao, *A Nation-State by Construction: Dynamics of Modern Chinese Nationalism* (Stanford, Calif.: Stanford University Press, 2004).

12. James Lilley, *China Hands: Nine Decades of Adventure, Espionage, and Diplomacy in Asia* (New York: Public Affairs, 2004).

13. As influential scholar Wang Jisi has written, "China and the United States cannot hope to establish truly friendly relations." Jisi, "China's Search for Stability with America," *Foreign Affairs,* September–October 2005. For a history of modern Sino-U.S. relations, see David Lampton, *Same Bed, Different Dreams: Managing U.S.-China Relations, 1989–2000* (Berkeley: University of California Press, 2001). For a discussion of various theoretical perspectives on the future of U.S.-China relations, see Aaron L. Friedberg, "The Future of U.S.-China Relations: Is Conflict Inevitable?" *International Security* 30, no. 2 (Fall 2005). As Henry Kissinger wrote, "As a new century begins, the relations between China and the United States may well determine whether our children will live in turmoil . . . or will witness a new world order compatible with . . . peace and progress." *Washington Post,* June 13, 2005.

14. As Li Shaojun argues, "China will not threaten any other state and will not put up with threats from other states." Shaojun, "Explaining Elements in China's Foreign Strategy," unpublished paper, 2006.

15. William S. Murray III and Robert Antonellis, "China's Space Program: The Dragon Eyes the Moon (and Us)," *Orbis,* Fall 2003, 645–52. For various aspects of the debate of the purposes and advancement of China's space programs, see the special issue of *China Security* on "China's Space Ambitions," issue no. 2, 2006.

16. However, China is already a nuclear power, one that is rapidly updating its nuclear arsenal and missile force, including long-range ICBMs, as well as acquiring submarines and destroyers to give it sea-denial capability and blue-water reach. Though it lacks global power-projection capability, the potential ends for which it seeks a more efficient and stealthy military—such as occupying small islands, sinking American or Japanese naval vessels, or fighting for control of the Taiwanese mainland or waters—do not require globally dispersed means. See Brad Roberts, Robert A. Manning, and Ronald N. Montaperto, "China: The Forgotten Nuclear Power," *Foreign Affairs,* July–August 2000, 53–63; and Edward Cody, "China Builds a Smaller, Stronger Military," *Washington Post,* April 12, 2005.

17. For observations and anecdotes on the relevance of the Chinese language for understanding its world-view and culture, see Tim Clissold, *Mr. China* (New York: HarperCollins, 2004).

18. Terrill, *New Chinese Empire,* 26.

19. See Gerald Segal, "East Asia and the 'Constrainment' of China," *International Security* 20, no. 4 (Spring 1996): 107–35; and Zalmay Khalilzad, "Congage China," RAND Issue Paper no. 187, 1999.

20. See Evan S. Medeiros and M. Taylor Fravel, "China's New Diplomacy," *Foreign Affairs,* November–December 2003.

21. Stanley Crossick, "The Rise of China and Its Implications for the EU," lecture at the National University of Singapore, May 26, 2006.

22. A mix of U.S. programs in the 1990s under the rubric of the "China Rule of Law Initiative" attempted to link most-favored-nation trade status to improvement in the arena of human rights, but economic liberalization proved not to be a Trojan horse for political reform in China, which easily set up firewalls to prevent reform in the commercial sphere from spreading to the political or judicial. See Matthew C. Stephenson, "A Trojan Horse Behind Chinese Walls? Problems and Prospects of U.S.-Sponsored 'Rule of Law' Reform Projects in the People's Republic of China," Working Paper no. 47, Center for International Development, Harvard University, May 2000. China does not look at civil society as an autonomous third sector alongside the state and private sector, but rather simply as a collection of "popular organizations" that are often government supported and monitored. China confidently dictates which foreign NGOs get to operate, where, and on what terms. They are at best a necessary interference, and best used as consultants toward the state's own ends, not to undermine it. Using a nonstop series of legal maneuvers, China for years blocked the International Committee of the Red Cross (ICRC) from opening an office there.

23. See Gordon Chang, *The Coming Collapse of China* (New York: Random House, 2001); George J. Gilboy, "The Myth Behind China's Miracle," *Foreign Affairs,* July–August 2004, 34; and Mixin Pei, *China's Trapped Transition: The Limits of Developmental Autocracy* (Cambridge, Mass.: Harvard University Press, 2006).

24. See Fishman, *China, Inc.,* 167; David Hale and Lyric Hughes Hale, "China Takes Off," *Foreign Affairs,* November–December 2003, 44; and Seth G. Jones and F. Stephen Larrabee, "Arming Europe," *The National Interest,* Winter 2005–06, 68.

25. Ian Bremmer and Fareed Zakaria, "Hedging Political Risk in China," *Harvard Business Review,* November 2006.

26. Jehangir S. Pocha, "One Sun in the Sky: Labor Unions in the People's

Republic of China," *Georgetown Journal of International Affairs*, Winter–Spring 2007, 11.

27. See Anne Stevenson-Yang and Ken DeWoskin, "China Destroys the IP Paradigm," *Far Eastern Economic Review* 168, no. 3 (March 2005); and Richard P. Suttmeier, "Assessing China's Technology Potential," *Georgetown Journal of International Affairs*, Summer–Fall 2004, 97–105.

28. See "Red, Inc.," *Harper's*, February 2006.

29. But Western firms can profit when Chinese companies enter the marketplace rather than merely dumping products on it. For example, Lenovo's purchase of an IBM division required it to *legally* install Windows operating software, transforming Microsoft from victim to winner in China in spite of all the pirated software circulating in the country.

30. This notion is both implied and supported by the doctrine of "small state, big society."

31. According to the Chinese Academy of Social Sciences (CASS), China has twelve distinct social strata, not the usual three, which is appropriate for a country of its size.

32. Most of China's poverty eradication happened in the 1980s, when FDI was much lower, as a result of nascent private-sector lending and rural investment, which gave a boost to high-employment sectors like food processing. Though 60 percent of China's population is still rural, agriculture now accounts for less than 15 percent of GDP. See Emile Kok-Kheng Yeoh, "Development Policy, Demographic Diversity, and Interregional Disparities in China," paper presented at the inaugural international *ChinaWorld* workshop, March 10–11, 2006, Asia Research Centre, Copenhagen Business School. See Shang-Jin Wei, "Is Globalization Good for the Poor in China?" *Finance and Development*, September 2002. China's Gini coefficient, a measure of income equality, has risen to .45 since the beginning of reforms as the rich get richer—but this is no worse than the United States. And its urban Gini coefficient is only .32, which is near the global average.

33. Hu Jintao's prioritization of rural development in fact sharpened the ideological debate over the merits of capitalism in light of the widening gap between urban and rural incomes.

34. Petrochemical factories have caused significant pollution in a third of rural rivers and 90 percent of urban rivers, most notably the Songhua River of Harbin, where in 2005 a chemical spill threatened the entire water supply of an already chronically water-short region. One-third of China's territories are already threatened by desertification, and thousands of villages have been abandoned due to the weakening flows of the Yellow River into the drying lakes of Qinhai province.

35. Jim Yardley, "China's Next Big Boom Could Be the Foul Air," *New York Times,* October 30, 2005.

36. See Wenran Jiang, "Beijing's 'New Thinking' on Energy Security," Jamestown Foundation China Brief, April 12, 2006.

37. Yongjin Zhang, "China Goes Global," Foreign Policy Centre, 2005.

38. The Three Gorges Dam on the Yangtze (the world's third-longest river behind the Amazon and the Nile) will provide up to 10 percent of the country's power needs upon completion in 2010. In Tibet, a dam on the Tsangpo River (which becomes India and Bangladesh's Brahmaputra) will generate thirty-eight million kilowatts at a power station in Mendok, while diversion of the river will channel water to six hundred cities in the north of the country. A twelve-hundred-mile grand canal, the world's longest man-made waterway, will soon link six provinces (including Beijing) and four river systems to feed water inward from Jiansu province. Like the Persian Gulf states, resource governance is highly political. China's coal, oil, and gas ministries compete among themselves as well as with state oil companies that themselves have ministry-like status, preventing a national energy strategy from emerging. As Abu Dhabi's sheikhs have done, China may have to graft its separate "State Energy Leading Group" on top of these stagnant ministries in order for real energy reform to emerge.

39. Joanna I. Lewis, "Leading the Renewable Energy Revolution," *Georgetown Journal of International Affairs,* Summer–Fall 2006, 147–54.

40. Seagrave, *Lords of the Rim,* 61–63.

41. Norimitsu Onishi and Howard W. French, "Chinese Warships Remind Japan of Challenge on the Seas," *International Herald Tribune,* September 11, 2005.

42. See Barry C. Lynn, *End of the Line: The Rise and Coming Fall of the Global Corporation* (New York: Doubleday, 2005).

43. See Banning Garrett, Jonathan Adams, and Franklin Kramer, "Taiwan in Search of a Strategic Consensus," Atlantic Council Issue Brief, March 2006.

44. See Bell, *Beyond Liberal Democracy,* ch. 7.

45. Shenzhen's per capita GDP is $12,000, while Shanghai's is $8,000.

46. See Bruce Gilley, *China's Democratic Future: How It Will Happen and Where It Will Lead* (New York: Columbia University Press, 2004).

47. Lilley, *China Hands,* 341.

48. Daniel A. Bell, "Chinese Leaders Rediscover Confucianism," *International Herald Tribune,* November 14, 2006.

49. The Politburo and State Council have become more like club teams than a monolithic party black box, with substantive debates and power

switches among factions and caucuses. See Cheng Li, "The New Bipartisanship Within the Chinese Communist Party," *Orbis*, Summer 2005, 387–400.

50. As Mixin Pei argues, "If economic success does not end one-party rule in China, corruption probably will." Pei, "The Chinese Communist Party," *Foreign Policy*, September–October 2005, 46.

51. Albert Keidel, "China's Social Unrest: The Story Behind the Stories," Carnegie Endowment Policy Brief no. 48, September 2006.

52. For a historical narrative of previous land-reform efforts, see Yuan-Tsung Chen, *The Dragon's Village: An Autobiographical Novel of Revolutionary China* (New York: Penguin, 1981).

53. A Political Reform Office was created in the 1980s, including frequent consultations with business experts and foreign-trained lawyers. See Mixin Pei, "Political Reform in China: Leadership Differences and Convergence," paper presented at the conference on Chinese Leadership, Politics and Policy, Carnegie Endowment for International Peace, November 2, 2005.

54. Zheng Bijian, "China's 'Peaceful Rise' to Great-Power Status," *Foreign Affairs*, September–October 2005.

55. For a full discussion of what democracy with Chinese characteristics might look like, see the proposal put forth in Bell, *East Meets West*, ch. 5.

56. See *Speak No Evil: Mass Media Control in Contemporary China* (Washington, D.C.: Freedom House, February 2006); and Clive Thompson, "Google's China Problem (and China's Google Problem)," *New York Times Magazine*, April 23, 2006.

CONCLUSION: THE SEARCH FOR EQUILIBRIUM IN A NON-AMERICAN WORLD

1. As Alberto Alesina and Enrico Spolaore explain, each power is a "Leviathan" trying to determine its optimal configuration, balancing tradeoffs between size and resources versus heterogeneity and the requirements of providing payouts to heterogenous members. Alesina and Spolaore, *The Size of Nations* (Cambridge, Mass.: MIT Press, 2003), ch. 5.

2. As realist scholar John Mearsheimer argues, "This cycle of violence will continue far into the new millennium. Hopes for peace will probably not be realized, because the great powers that shape the international system fear each other and compete for power as a result." Mearsheimer, *The Tragedy of Great Power Politics* (New York: W. W. Norton, 2001), xi.

3. George Kennan knew that this was not the full story, arguing that it gives Americans "pleasure to view ourselves as high-minded patrons, benefactors, and teachers of a people seen as less fortunate, and less advanced, than ourselves. . . . A form of national narcissism—of collective self-admiration . . . which could only conceal deep subconscious feelings of insecurity—a need

for reassurance about ourselves—something that contrasted very sharply with our pretentious external behavior. . . . The offenses we have offered to our world environment since the establishment of our independence have been ones arising as a rule not from any desire on our own part to bring injury to others or to establish power over them, but from our attempts to strike noble postures and to impress ourselves." Kennan, *American Diplomacy*, 158, 169. America's mantle of supremacy cannot reliably be based on its riches when, as Nobel laureate Robert Solow writes, "The notion that God intended for Americans to be permanently wealthier than rest of world becomes less and less likely as time goes on." (*New York Times*, December 14, 2003.) Indeed, the more that American superiority is viewed in material terms, particularly military terms, the more that other systems can justify their ideologies in the name of achieving equal material and military heft. There is thus a tradeoff between America's military superiority and its ideological leadership. It is often forgotten that the Soviet Union too once had considerable soft power, which was also dramatically undermined by its brutal usage of its hard power. Ultimately, neither hard nor soft power saved it from collapse.

4. As Benjamin Barber wrote, "As a consequence of its lawless anarchy, the state of nature for Hobbes is above all a state of fear. . . . The remedy is not power, which men have in the state of nature, but law and contract, which they lack." Barber, *Fear's Empire: War, Terrorism and Democracy* (New York: W. W. Norton, 2003), 70.

5. See Hans J. Morgenthau, *Scientific Man vs. Power Politics*.

6. Echoing Toynbee's landmark theory of challenge and response, George Kennan feared the consequences of America's overreliance on its military, writing that, "force, like peace, is not an abstraction; it cannot be understood or dealt with as a concept outside of the given framework of purpose and method." He further warned that the Cold War evolution of vested interests in militarization combined with America's habit of looking for the main external enemy to create a dependency on the pernicious practice of needless armament: "There seems a curious American tendency to search, at all times, for a single external center of evil, to which all our troubles can be attributed, rather than to recognize that there might be multiple sources of resistance to our purposes and undertakings, and that these sources might be relatively independent of each other." See Kennan, *American Diplomacy*, 90, 164, 173. See also Andrew J. Bacevich, *The New American Militarism: How Americans Are Seduced by War* (New York: Oxford University Press, 2005); and Victor Davis Hanson, *A War Like No Other: How the Athenians and Spartans Fought the Peloponnesian War* (New York: Random House, 2005).

7. As Emmanuel Todd writes: "At the very moment when the world is discovering democracy and learning to get along politically without the United

States, the United States is beginning to lose its democratic characteristics and is discovering that it cannot get along without the rest of the world." See Todd, *After the Empire: The Breakdown of the American Order* (New York: Columbia University Press, 2002), 13, quotation 20.

8. Because Americans live in what Tocqueville called a state of "perpetual self-adoration," they suffer from great historical amnesia with respect to the realities of their actual role in history. Mark Hertsgaard has identified a number of characteristic foreign views of the United States overseas that contradict American self-perceptions: America is parochial and self-centered, hypocritical and domineering, naïve about the world, full of philistines, self-righteous about democracy, and only looks out for itself. Hertsgaard, *The Eagle's Shadow: Why America Fascinates and Infuriates the World* (New York: Farrar, Straus and Giroux, 2002), 21. See also Julia Sweig, *Friendly Fire: Losing Friends and Making Enemies in the Anti-American Century* (New York: Public Affairs, 2006).

9. Harold Nicolson, *Peacemaking 1919.*

10. For a discussion of the increasing costs to the United States of its alliances over the course of the twentieth century, see David A. Lake, *Entangling Relations: American Foreign Policy in Its Century* (Princeton, N.J.: Princeton University Press, 1999); see also Julianne Smith and Thomas Sanderson, "Evaluating Our Partners and Allies Five Years Later," *Washington Post,* September 11, 2006.

11. Christopher Layne, "The Unipolar Illusion Revisited: The Coming End of the United States' Unipolar Moment," *International Security* 31, no. 2 (Fall 2006): 7–41.

12. Andrew Kohut and Bruce Stokes, *America Against the World: How We Are Different and Why We Are Disliked* (New York: Times Books, 2006), 49.

13. Toynbee, *A Study of History*, vol. 11.

14. Leon Fuerth, "Strategic Myopia," *The National Interest,* Spring 2006.

15. David J. Kilcullen, "New Paradigms for 21st Century Conflict" (eJournal USA: An Electronic Journal of the U.S. Department of State, May 2007).

16. See Michael Barnett and Raymond Duvall, "Power in International Politics," *International Organization* 59 (Winter 2005): 39–75; and Daniel H. Nexon and Thomas Wright, "What's at Stake in the American Empire Debate," *American Political Science Review* 101, No. 2 (May 2007). A series of articles has addressed the debate over the forms of hard and soft balancing against the United States currently under way. See Robert A. Pape, "Soft Balancing Against the United States"; T. V. Paul, "Soft Balancing in the Age of U.S. Primacy"; and Stephen G. Brooks and William C. Wohlforth, "Hard Times for Soft Balancing"; all in *International Security* 30, no. 1 (Summer 2005).

17. See Bruce Bueno de Mesquita and George W. Downs, "Development and Democracy," *Foreign Affairs,* September–October 2005. Jeane Kirkpatrick,

American ambassador to the UN during the 1980s, justified supporting autocrats because such regimes did not seek to reinvent society (as totalitarian
systems do). See Kirkpatrick, "Dictatorships and Double-Standards," *Com-
mentary*, November 1979.

18. Though control over the global money supply is a key vehicle of exporting influence, the paramount status of the U.S. dollar as a global reserve currency is not coterminous with American monetary dominance when currencies
are denationalized as they are today. See Benjamin J. Cohen, "The Geopolitics
of Currencies and the Future of the International System," University of California, Santa Barbara, Global and International Studies Program, Paper no. 10,
2003. For background on the relationship between money and territory, see
Cohen, *The Geography of Money* (Ithaca, N.Y.: Cornell University Press), 18.

19. Joseph Stiglitz, "The Roaring Nineties," *Atlantic Monthly*, October
2002.

20. Erik Erikson, *Childhood and Society*.

21. Ajay Kapur, Niall Macleod, and Narendra Singh, "Plutonomy: Buying
Luxury, Explaining Global Imbalances," Citigroup Industry Note, October 16,
2005.

22. See Robert B. Reich, *The Future of Success* (New York: Alfred A.
Knopf, 2001). The minimum wage in 2006 in real terms is 37 percent below
what it was in 1968.

23. The United States has spent less than 2 percent of GDP on infrastructure since 1980.

24. Steven A. Camarota, "Immigration from Mexico: Assessing the Impact on the United States," Center for Immigration Studies, 2001.

25. David Rieff, *Los Angeles: Capital of the Third World* (New York:
Touchstone Books, 1992).

26. Samuel P. Huntington, *Who Are We? The Challenges to America's National Identity* (New York: Simon and Schuster, 2004).

27. Alberto F. Alesina, Edward L. Glaeser, and Bruce Sacerdote, "Why
Doesn't the U.S. Have a European-Style Welfare State?" Harvard Institute of
Economic Research, Discussion Paper no. 1933, October 2001.

28. Michael Ignatieff, "The Broken Contract," *New York Times Magazine*,
September 24, 2005, 16.

29. Richard G. Wilkinson, *The Impact of Inequality: How to Make Sick
Societies Healthier* (London: Routledge, 2005).

30. As Christopher Lasch has written, "The mounting evidence of widespread inefficiency and corruption, the decline of American productivity, the
pursuit of speculative profits at the expense of manufacturing, the deterioration of our country's material infrastructure, the squalid conditions in our
crime-ridden cities, the alarming and disgraceful growth of poverty, and the

widening disparity between poverty and wealth, which is morally obscene and politically explosive as well—these developments, the ominous import of which can no longer be ignored or concealed, have reopened the historic debate about democracy. At the moment of its dazzling triumph over communism, democracy is coming under heavy fire at home, and criticism is bound to increase if things continue to fall apart at the present rate. Formally democratic institutions do not guarantee a workable social order, as we know from the example of India and Latin America. As conditions in American cities begin to approach those of the Third World, democracy will have to prove itself all over again." Lasch, *The Revolt of the Elites and the Betrayal of Democracy* (New York: W. W. Norton, 1996).

31. See Michael Lind, *Made in Texas: George W. Bush and the Southern Takeover of American Politics* (New York: Basic Books, 2003).

32. As Alan Wolfe observes, "The ideal political system should consist of a conservative party modeled on the British Tories under Benjamin Disraeli and a liberal one based on the social democratic idea brought to fruition in postwar Europe. The reason America has retreated from greatness is because its political system currently contains neither." Wolfe, *Return to Greatness: How America Lost Its Sense of Purpose and What It Needs to Do to Recover It* (Princeton, N.J.: Princeton University Press, 2005), 169.

33. John Kenneth Galbraith, *The Economics of Innocent Fraud: Truth for Our Time* (New York: Penguin, 2004).

34. See Gilpin, *War and Change in World Politics*, ch. 4. Amitai Etzioni argues that democracy decays when leadership ignores public needs. See Etzioni, "How Liberty Is Lost," *Society* 40, no. 5 (July–August 2003): 44–51.

35. Realism does not dictate the absence of rules or norms, nor does it necessitate conflict. It simply explains dynamics under the condition of anarchy, a world with no overarching authority. Though realism stems from the basic human drives for security, wealth, and dignity, it is not to be confused with pure, muscular aggression. Rather, it encourages a prudent calculation of means and ends, a mix of moral vision and shrewdness. While it is a common Machiavellian refrain that the ends justify the means, realism and pragmatism additionally dictate a consideration of costs. While Morgenthau argued that "power, however limited and qualified, is the value which international politics recognizes as supreme," the realism he prescribed—which has been adopted by those who best understand realism today—decries imperial ventures that lead to nasty entrapments, concentrating more on mitigating anarchy and maintaining relative power advantages. Hence Morgenthau opposed the Vietnam War, and George Kennan the 2003 war in Iraq. Realism is intensely psychological, and thus does not do away with morality, but lives in a state of uneasy awareness with it. As Robert Jackson

writes, "The ethics of statecraft is, above all else, a situational ethics the core of which is the norm of prudence." See Jackson, *The Global Covenant: Human Conduct in a World of States* (London: Oxford University Press, 2005), 21; and Anatol Lieven and John Hulsman, *Ethical Realism: A Vision for America's Role in the World* (New York: Pantheon, 2006); and Reinhold Niebuhr, *The Structure of Nations and Empires* (1959).

36. For a discussion of the implications of the rise of evangelical influence on American foreign policy, see Walter Russell Mead, "God's Country?" *Foreign Affairs*, September–October 2006, 24–43. Stephen Walt comments that "the combination of a universalist political philosophy and a strong evangelical streak is bound to be alarming to other countries, including some of our fellow democracies." Walt, *Taming American Power: The Global Response to U.S. Primacy* (New York: W. W. Norton, 2005).

37. Kevin Phillips, *American Theocracy: The Peril and Politics of Radical Religion, Oil, and Borrowed Money in the Twenty-first Century* (New York: Viking, 2006).

38. Toynbee, *Civilization on Trial.*

39. *American Public Opinion and Foreign Policy,* Chicago Council on Foreign Relations, 2002.

40. America persists in a false debate about public versus private investment in national infrastructure, since public investment has been shown to inspire higher levels of private investment. *Realizing America's Economic Potential: A Growth Agenda for the New Abundant Economy* (Washington, D.C.: New America Foundation, 2006).

41. Joel Kotkin and Delore Zimmerman, *Rebuilding America's Productive Economy: A Heartland Development Strategy* (Washington, D.C.: New America Foundation, 06).

42. America's trade deficit in manufacturing more than tripled between 1997 and 2005, to $662.5 billion.

43. Nicholas Kulish, "Things Fall Apart: Fixing America's Crumbling Infrastructure," *New York Times,* August 23, 2006.

44. Barry C. Lynn, "War, Trade, and Utopia," *The National Interest,* Winter 2005–2006.

45. Clyde V. Prestowitz, *Three Billion New Capitalists: The Great Shift of Wealth and Power to the East* (New York: Basic Books, 2005).

46. The competition for influence in the world's periphery, rather than elevating it, is likely to perpetuate its third world–ness. It seems logical that the combination of debt relief by the United States and the EU and rising investment and trade with China would help spark third-world development, but naughty imperial practices suggest otherwise. For example, Western agricultural subsidies remain a major barrier to free trade opportunities for third-

world countries in Latin America and Africa, and despite Western debt forgiveness, China has begun to emulate the classic Western practice of giving huge loans that lead to default and deep indebtedness—this time to China. Furthermore, since Chinese loans and aid are free of political conditions, they inspire no virtuous circle of transparency, democracy, or rising wages. And while the consumer boom of the world's three economic poles (plus India and Brazil) has boosted economic growth in some third-world countries, fueling that boom also requires the continued plunder of third-world natural resources, eroding their ecological base and causing environmental fallout. By relying on wasteful industries and environmentally exploitative tourism, third-world countries do not help themselves much either, yet they have little choice as they are wholly reliant on first-world investment and technology. Multipolarity may therefore appear a blessing for the third world, but its mercantilism may be a curse. The third world's great hope actually lies within itself, through globalized south-south trade and investment, which currently amounts to $50 billion annually and is growing rapidly.

47. Michael Mandelbaum, *The Case for Goliath: How America Acts as the World's Government in the Twenty-first Century* (New York: Public Affairs, 2005).

48. Huntington, *Clash of Civilizations,* 21.

49. Robert D. Kaplan, *Warrior Politics: Why Leadership Demands a Pagan Ethos* (New York: Random House, 2002), 139. See also Buzan, *United States and the Great Powers,* ch. 9. Such a clash of principles is inherently dangerous, for as Kennan warned, "A war fought in the name of high moral principle finds no early end short of some form of total domination." Kennan, *American Diplomacy,* 101.

50. It is not likely that many people around the world today would blindly subscribe to Woodrow Wilson's 1917 claim: "These are American principles, American policies. . . . And they are the also the principles and policies of forward-looking men and women everywhere, of every modern nation, of every enlightened community. They are the principles of mankind and must prevail." President Clinton echoed Wilson in declaring, "America's interests require the United States to lead an effort to build a world order shaped by U.S. values." It is not much of overstatement to say that all Americans, red state or blue, liberal or conservative, religious or secular, profess a belief in American exceptionalism. The philosopher Richard Hofstadter once remarked that America's fate is not to have ideology but to be one. Sixty percent of Americans believe their culture is superior to others. Yet an even greater percentage of the rest of the world begs to differ. America is viewed unfavorably around the world not only for the unpopularity of particular foreign policies, but is also disrespected on the basis of weaknesses within its own system. America

is tolerable only insofar as some other power is not preferred by the world. See Kohut and Stokes, *America Against the World*.

51. Woodrow Wilson believed that "the balance of power is the great game now forever discredited. It's the old and evil order that prevailed before this war." He told the U.S. Senate in 1917 that America would lead "not a balance of power, but a community of power; not organized rivalries, but an organized common peace." The League of Nations he designed (but which the United States never joined) proved unable to prevent the aggression of the Axis Powers in the 1930s. As E. H. Carr sardonically observed, "the metaphysicians of Geneva found it difficult to believe that an accumulation of ingenious texts prohibiting war was not a barrier against war itself." Carr, *The Twenty Years' Crisis, 1919–1939: An Introduction to the Study of International Relations* (New York: Harper Perennial, 1964 [1939]), 30. At Yalta in 1945, President Franklin D. Roosevelt declared an end to "unilateral action, exclusive alliances, spheres of influence, the balance of power, and all the other expedients that have been tried for centuries—and have always failed." He proposed the United Nations instead, which President Eisenhower later praised as the best hope to "substitute the conference table for the battlefield." In 1991, President George Bush proclaimed a "new world order" in which the United Nations, "freed from Cold War stalemate, is poised to fulfill the historic vision of its founders." Paul Kennedy, *The Parliament of Man: The Past, Present, and Future of the United Nations* (New York: Random House, 2006).

52. Toynbee, *Civilization on Trial*, 127.

53. Garton Ash, *Free World*, 3.

54. David A. Lake, "Hierarchy in International Relations: Authority, Sovereignty, and the New Structure of World Politics," unpublished working paper, University of California at San Diego, 2005.

55. See Alpo Rusi, *Dangerous Peace: New Rivalry in World Politics* (Boulder, Colo.: Westview Press, 1998), introduction and ch. 5. These pan-regions already constitute the lion's share of the world's economy. As natural gas becomes the fuel of choice, pan-regional energy markets are emerging as well: United States/Canada/South America, EU/Russia/North Africa, and China/Russia/Indonesia/Australia.

56. War is not an event apart from rise-and-fall dynamics, but a principal agent of them. Like previous world orders, the American era has moved in phases from institutionalization to delegitimization—which is followed by war. An unresolved disequilibrium leads to systemic conflict, which gives way in its aftermath to a new order based on the postwar power configuration. See Gilpin, *War and Change in World Politics*, ch. 5.

57. America was never viewed by Europe as "the next best thing" to its

own global hegemony but rather the least among various evils. There is no prior diplomatic analog, however, to match the scale of accommodating China into the existing world order while avoiding major systemic conflict. It makes little sense to speak of a "community of democracies" when one of the most significant powers in the world is not a democracy. And while it is true that democracies tend not to fight one another, they are quite aggressive against nondemocracies, choosing to fight enemies they know they can defeat (begging the question as to why they then fight at all). Global war might be most likely precisely because China may eventually democratize, in which case nationalism may become unrestrained just as its power comes to match that of the United States. See Michael C. Desch, "Democracy and Victory: Fair Fights or Food Fights?" *International Security* 28, no. 1 (2003): 180–94; Edward D. Mansfield and Jack Snyder, *Electing to Fight: Why Emerging Democracies Go to War* (Cambridge, Mass.: MIT Press, 2005); and Dan Reiter and Allan C. Stan, *Democracies at War* (Princeton, N.J.: Princeton University Press, 2002).

58. These scenarios are the focus of the geopolitical branch known as power transition theory, based on the writings of A. F. K. Organski, especially *World Politics* (New York: Alfred A. Knopf, 1958). Geopolitical power transitions are like phase transitions in physics: highly unstable periods during which magnetic filings cluster or repulse in unpredictable directions as the temperature rises; entropy without order. Churchill likened great powers to planetary bodies that elicit "profound magnetic reactions" when they come too close. As Charles Kupchan warns, the international system "is fickle and fragile," coming apart with remarkable speed. Kupchan, *The End of the American Era: U.S. Foreign Policy and the Geopolitics of the Twenty-first Century* (New York: Alfred A. Knopf, 2002), xv. As Robert Gilpin explains, power transitions begin when rising powers recalculate their willingness to conform to the existing order. Gilpin, *War and Change in World Politics*, chs. 2, 4. Fareed Zakaria adds, "Great powers are like divas, they enter and exit the stage with great tumult." Zakaria, "Is Realism Finished?" *The National Interest*, Winter 1992–93.

59. David Hume, *A Treatise on Human Nature* (1739).

60. See Michael Howard, *The Invention of Peace* (New Haven, Conn.: Yale University Press, 2000), ch. 5. As Robert Cooper writes, "Not all misunderstandings lead to wars, and not all wars are caused by misunderstandings. . . . Nothing is inevitable and great historical events still depend on the decisions and sometimes on the mistakes of individual men and women." Cooper, *The Breaking of Nations: Order and Chaos in the Twenty-First Century* (New York: Atlantic Monthly Press, 2003), 101.

61. Raymond Aron, *Peace and War: A Theory of International Relations* (Garden City, N.Y.: Doubleday, 1966).

62. As Kissinger wrote of Castlereagh and Metternich's creation of the post-Napoleonic concert of powers, "Their goal was stability, not perfection, and the balance of power is the classic expression of the lesson of history that no order is safe without physical safeguards against aggression. Thus the new international order came to be created with a sufficient awareness of the connection between power and morality; between security and legitimacy." Kissinger, *A World Restored: Metternich, Castlereagh, and the Problems of Peace, 1812–1822* (Boston: Houghton Mifflin, 1973), 317–18.

63. See Immanuel Kant, *Idea for a Universal History with Cosmopolitan Purpose* (1784); Lars-Erik Cederman, "Back to Kant: Reinterpreting the Democratic Peace as a Macro-Historical Learning Process," *American Political Science Review* 95 (March 2001). To learn from what Jose Ortega y Gasset called the "treasure of our mistakes" requires constantly augmenting this institutional memory. At the end of Ray Bradbury's *Fahrenheit 451*, Granger, leader of the itinerant book-protecting fugitives, tells their newest recruit, Fisher, "We know all the damn silly things we've done for a thousand years and as long as we know that and always have it around where we can see it, someday we'll stop making the goddamn funeral pyres and jumping in the middle of them. We pick up a few more people that remember every generation." Bradbury, *Fahrenheit 451* (New York: Ballantine, 1950).

64. As Brian Eno, the producer of the rock music band U2, has written, "Isn't civilization what happens when people stop behaving as if they're trapped in a ruthless Darwinian struggle and start thinking about communities and shared futures? . . . Perhaps it's asking a lot to expect America to act differently from all the other empires in history, but wasn't that the original idea?" Eno, "The U.S. Needs to Open Up to the World," *TIME International*, January 12, 2003.

65. Rasler and Thompson, *Great Powers and Global Struggle*, 191.

66. Robert Skidelsky describes a "fundamental contradiction at the heart of empires," namely that "they promise peace but beget war" through "continuous conflict on frontiers." Skidelsky, "Hot, Cold, and Imperial," *New York Review of Books,* July 13, 2006. Konrad Adenauer warned that "history is the sum total of things that could have been avoided," making the task of statesmanship today to fend off what David Lloyd George called the "hammer of destiny," to avoid crossing the line where "military logic supersedes diplomatic calculation." See Niall Ferguson, *1914: Why the World Went to War* (New York: Penguin, 1998), 27.

67. As Kissinger wrote with respect to the Napoleonic era, if there is no

"acceptance of the framework of international order," the system moves from legitimate to revolutionary. Furthermore, "states tend to be forgetful. It is not often that states learn from the past, even rarer that they draw the correct conclusions from it. For the lessons of historical experience, as of personal experience, are contingent. They teach the consequences of certain actions, but they cannot force recognition of comparable situations. . . . A people may be aware of the probable consequences of a revolutionary situation. But its knowledge will be empty if it cannot *recognize* a revolutionary situation. There is this difference between physical and historical knowledge, however: each generation is permitted only one effort of abstraction; it can attempt only one interpretation and a single experiment, for it is its own subject. This is the challenge of history and its tragedy; it is the shape 'destiny' assumes on the earth. And its solution, even its recognition, is perhaps the most difficulat task of statesmanship." Kissinger, *World Restored*, 1–3, 331–32.

68. Kant and Rousseau theorized an international federation of states to achieve a republican peace: Kant emphasized transparency and the rising costs of war, while Rousseau argued that a "General Will" would prevent states from coming into conflict out of self-interest alone. Today there are numerous equivalent statements on the pacifying effect of globalization, each echoing Norman Angell's Great Illusion claim of the "complete economic futility of conquest." Francis Fukuyama argues for the end of ideological struggle; John Mueller observes that the prospect of total, annihilating war makes it "subrationally unthinkable"; Jonathan Schell and Peter Singer see the emergence of global consciousness as the "moral equivalent of war" or a "weapon of civilization"; Robert Wright demonstrates that the accumulation of positive outcomes disincentivizes conflict; and Anatol Lieven and John Hulsman argue for a "Great Capitalist Peace." See Fukuyama, *The End of History and the Last Man* (New York: Avon Books, 1992); Mueller, *Retreat from Doomsday: The Obsolescence of Major War* (New York: Basic Books, 1989); Schell, *The Unconquerable World: Power, Nonviolence, and the Will of the People* (New York: Metropolitan Books, 2003); Singer, *One World: The Ethics of Globalization* (New Haven, Conn.: Yale University Press, 2003); Wright, *Non-Zero: The Logic of Human Destiny* (New York: Vintage, 2000); and Lieven and Hulsman, *Ethical Realism*.

69. Scholars perennially debate whether bipolarity or multipolarity is more stable, whether having more potential conflict dyads creates uncertainty or enables constant balancing and stability against the dominance by a single hegemon. Believing that there is no "once and for all time" solution to the "problem of power," Morgenthau wrote that "since the balance of power is the essence and the stabilizing factor of international relations, the distribution of power is here never permanently settled but always precarious and subject to

continuous fluctuations." In the quasi-homeostasis of tripolarity, each acts in its own interest, but others take countermeasures through automatic feedback, resulting in a continuation of the status quo. Jervis discusses the Lijphart effect, whereby the foreknowledge of danger or instability inspires policies that overcompensate toward moderation and compromise. Jervis, *System Effects*, 107–12, 275–79. See also Mearsheimer, *The Tragedy of Great Power Politics*, 338–44; and Waltz, *Theory of International Politics*.

70. B. H. Liddell Hart argued a half century ago that grand strategy must temper the geopolitical system's competitive instincts. As Charles Kupchan argues, "The central challenge of the future will be the same as in the past—managing relations among contending centers of power." Kupchan, *End of the American Era*, xviii.

71. As A. J. P. Taylor wrote, "Men have not always acquiesced in the perpetual quadrille of the Balance of Power. They have often wished that the music would stop and that they could sit out a dance without maintaining the ceaseless watch on each other." Taylor, *The Struggle for Mastery in Europe, 1848–1918* (Oxford, U.K.: Clarendon Press, 1954), xix. Hedley Bull further argued that "justice is only reliable in the context of order." Bull, *The Anarchical Society: A Study of Order in World Politics* (New York, Columbia University Press, 1977), 83.

72. If superpowers acted as a directorate, it would matter less which undertook what action than that the action was taken on behalf of shared principles. Charles Kupchan argues that if regional powers are "sufficiently benign in their exercise of power, the result could be a stable and cooperative system with a more decentralized leadership structure." Charles A. Kupchan, "After Pax Americana: Benign Power, Regional Integration, and the Sources of a Stable Multipolarity," *International Security* 23, no. 2 (Fall 1998): 40–79. Elsewhere he expands on the idea: "An ultimate vision for the future is the construction of a concert-like directorate of the major powers in North America, Europe and East Asia. These major powers would together manage developments and regulate relations both within and among their respective regions. Such regional centers also hold promise for the gradual incorporation of developing nations into global flows of trade, information and values. Strong and vibrant regional centers, for reasons of both proximity and culture, often have the strongest incentives to promote prosperity and stability in their immediate peripheries. North America might therefore focus on Latin America; Europe on Russia, the Middle East and Africa; and East Asia on South Asia and Southeast Asia. . . . Power will remain an inescapable determinant of international life. The aim should not be to negate it, but to channel it toward peaceful ends. It is far wiser and safer to get ahead of the curve and shape structural change by design than to find unipolarity giving way to chaotic mul-

tipolarity by default." Kupchan, "Empires and Geopolitical Competition: Gone for Good?" in *Turbulent Peace,* ed. Chester Crocker (Washington, D.C.: United States Institute of Peace, 2001).

73. Toynbee, *Civilization on Trial.*

74. See Fred Charles Iklé, *Every War Must End,* rev. ed. (Columbia Classics, 2005). As Charles Kupchan writes, "The child who rebels against overbearing parents is usually much more trouble than the one who is weaned off dependence and develops a mature responsibility and self-reliance." Kupchan, *End of the American Era,* 264.

75. As E. H. Carr wrote, "To internationalize government requires internationalizing power. . . . There must be a clear recognition of that play of political forces which is antecedent to all law. Only when these forces are in stable equilibrium can the law perform its social function without becoming a tool in the hands of the defenders of the status quo. The achievement of this equilibrium is not a legal, but a political task." Carr, *Twenty Years' Crisis,* 107, 192. Henry Kissinger echoes this: "The logic of war is power, and power has no inherent limit. The logic of peace is proportion, and proportion implies limitation. The success of war is victory; the success of peace is stability. The condition of victory are commitment, the condition of stability is self-restraint." Kissinger, *World Restored,* 138. On the concept of an "international constitution," see G. John Ikenberry, *After Victory: Institutions, Strategic Restraint, and the Rebuilding of Order After Major Wars* (Princeton, N.J.: Princeton University Press, 2000).

76. Banning Garrett, "A New Strategic Triangle? Relations Among China, Europe, and the United States in a Global Context," paper presented at the International Conference on China, Europe, and the United States in a Changing International System, Beijing, November 2–3, 2006. Globalization itself requires multilateral management, for at least half of globalization is a magnification of malevolent and destabilizing forces: supply chain disruptions from terrorism; illicit trafficking of arms, drugs, money, and people; environmental fallout from overexploitation of resources; the spread of deadly weapons and pathogens; and financial contagion all cause economic crises. These nefarious transnational forces have already made most of the world semisecuritized, with every country deploying greater numbers of military and police within its own borders to prevent globalization's vices from permeating too deeply. See Moisés Naím, *Illicit: How Smugglers, Traffickers, and Copycats Are Hijacking the Global Economy* (New York: Doubleday, 2005); and "The Five Wars of Globalization," *Foreign Policy,* September–October 2003, 28–37.

77. Morgenthau caricatured the idealism of Francis Bacon, in which the "empire of man over nature replaces the empire of man over man." Today's hopefulness that globalization can cure social problems reminded him of sim-

ilar nineteenth-century rhetoric about the peaceful possibilities created by
the advent of railroads and mass communication. Similarly, he derided the
"Liberals from Cobden to Hull [who] have been looking to free trade and sub-
stitutes for it as the solution for international political problems." Morgenthau, *Scientific Man vs. Power Politics,* 43, 87, 125.

78. As Edward Luttwak wrote, "Madness is rare only among individuals.
It is quite common in entire nations." Luttwak, "Worst Case Scenario," *Time,*
April 8, 2002, 30.

79. Examples include Zbigniew Brzezinski's "Trans-Eurasian Security
System" (TESS), Graham Allison's "Global Alliance for Security" (GAS), and
Amitai Etzioni's "Global Authorities." See Brzezinski, *The Grand Chessboard;*
Graham Allison, Karl Kaiser, and Sergei Karaganov, "The World Needs a
Global Alliance for Security," *International Herald Tribune,* November 21,
2001; and Etzioni, *From Empire to Community.*

80. Freud argued that "so long as there are nations and empires . . . all
alike must be equipped for war." In his masterful rebuttal of Karl von Clause-
witz's famous dictum that "war is the continuation of politics by other means,"
historian John Keegan argues that war is natural and cultural—nature, not
nurture—preceding even the creation of polities, states, and armies. From
cannibalism to conflicts among nations, strife is part of the human condition.
Keegan, *A History of Warfare* (New York: Vintage, 1993).

81. Harold Nicolson, *Diplomacy,* 13.

INDEX

Page numbers in *italics* refer to maps.

ABOUT THE AUTHOR

Parag Khanna is a senior research fellow and director of the Global Governance Initiative in the American Strategy Program of the New America Foundation. He has been a fellow at the Brookings Institution, and has worked for the World Economic Forum in Geneva and the Council on Foreign Relations. During 2007 he was a senior geopolitical adviser to U.S. Special Operations Forces in Iraq and Afghanistan. Born in India, Khanna was raised in the UAE, New York, and Germany. He holds undergraduate and graduate degrees from the School of Foreign Service at Georgetown University, and is completing his PhD at the London School of Economics. He has written for major global publications such as *The New York Times* and *Financial Times*, and has appeared on CNN, Al Jazeera, and other television media around the world. Khanna has traveled in close to one hundred countries and is a member of the Explorers Club.

www.paragkhanna.com

ABOUT THE TYPE

This book was set in Fairfield, the first typeface from the hand of the distinguished American artist and engraver Rudolph Ruzicka (1883–1978). Ruzicka was born in Bohemia and came to America in 1894. He set up his own shop, devoted to wood engraving and printing, in New York in 1913 after a varied career working as a wood engraver, in photoengraving and banknote printing plants, and as an art director and freelance artist. He designed and illustrated many books and was the creator of a considerable list of individual prints—wood engravings, line engravings on copper, and aquatints.